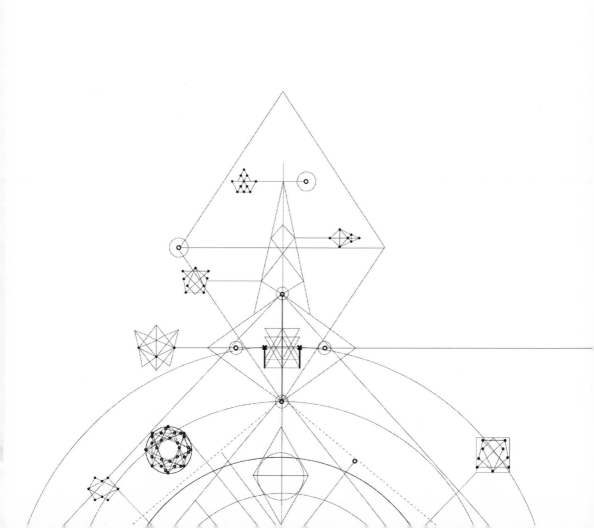

SHERMIN VOSHMGIR

TOKEN ECONOMY

How the Web3 reinvents the Internet

Token Economy: How the Web3 reinvents the Internet
Second edition, first amended printing, November 2020

The first edition was published in June 2019 under the title
"Token Economy: How Blockchain & Smart Contracts revolutionize the Economy"
by BlockchainHub Berlin and had two amended editions.

Author: Shermin Voshmgir

Publisher: Token Kitchen
Alte Schönhauserstrasse 9, 10119 Berlin
https://token.kitchen

Design: Justyna Zubrycka
Production: Caroline Helbing
Copy edit: Paisley Prophet
Cover & layout: Carmen Fuchs

Printed by Amazon Media EU S.à r.l.,
Luxembourg

Paperback ISBN: 978-3-9821038-1-5
A hardcover edition is available as ISBN: 978-3-9821038-4-6
An eBook is available as ISBN: 978-3-9821038-3-9

Table of Contents

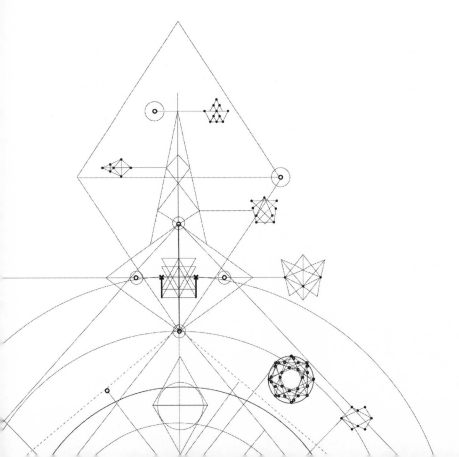

PART 1

Web3 Basics

PART 4
Token Use Cases

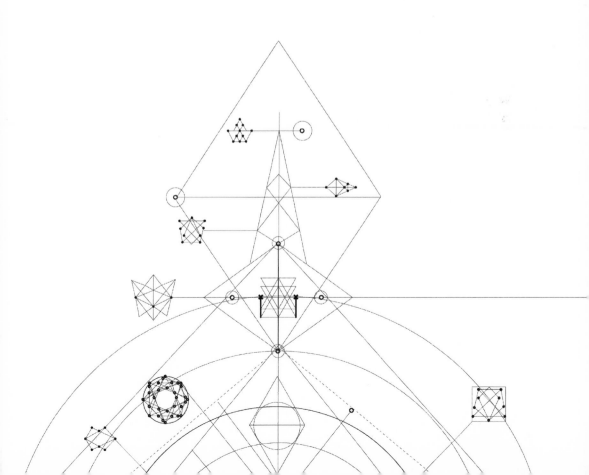

About the Author

Shermin Voshmgir is the founder of Token Kitchen and BlockchainHub Berlin. In the past she was the director of the Research Institute for Cryptoeconomics in Vienna which she also co-founded. She was also a curator of TheDAO (Decentralized Investment Fund), and an advisor to Jolocom (Web3 Identity), Wunder (Tokenized Art) or the Estonian E-residency program. Shermin studied Information Systems Management at the Vienna University of Economics and film-making in Madrid. She is Austrian, with Iranian roots, and works on the intersection of technology, art & social science.

About the Book

This book is an attempt to summarize existing knowledge about blockchain networks and other distributed ledgers as the backbone of the Web3, and contextualize the socio-economic implications of the Web3 applications, from smart contracts, tokens, DAOs to the concepts of money, economics, governance and decentralized finance (DeFi). It builds on the educational work that we started at BlockchainHub, an Info:Hub and Thinking:Hub based in Berlin, with the aim to make the Web3 accessible to a general audience.

Blockchainhub.net was the first website to systematically compile and disseminate blockchain and Web3 knowledge to a general audience and has been operational since 2015, first with a series of blog posts, which were later compiled and contextualized in the Blockchain Handbook, available for free.

Token Economy builds on the legacy of the past activities and goes one step beyond: The focus is now on tokens as the atomic unit of the Web3. The basic structure of the second edition of this book is the same as the first edition, with slightly updated content of existing chapters, minor corrections, revised terminology and four additional chapters: "User-Centric Identities," "Privacy Tokens," "Lending Tokens," and "How to Design a Token System."

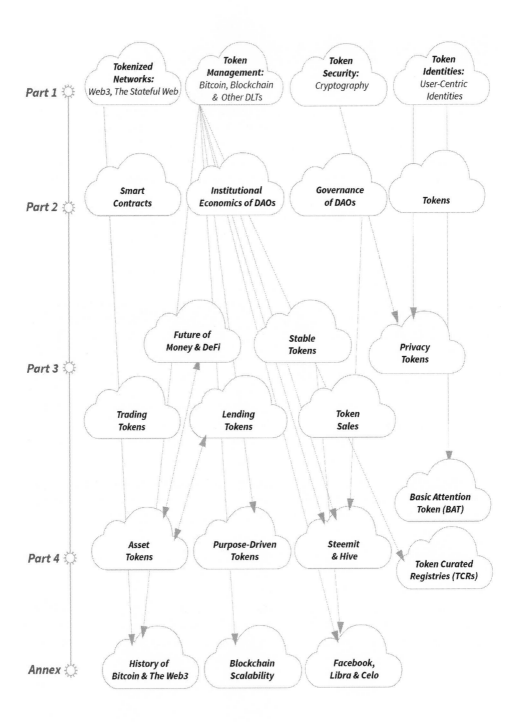

Part 1

Tokenized Networks: Web3, The Stateful Web

Token Management: Bitcoin, Blockchain & Other DLTs

Token Security: Cryptography

Token Identities: User-Centric Identities

Part 2

Smart Contracts

Institutional Economics of DAOs

Governance of DAOs

Tokens

Part 3

Future of Money & DeFi

Stable Tokens

Privacy Tokens

Trading Tokens

Lending Tokens

Token Sales

Part 4

Asset Tokens

Purpose-Driven Tokens

Steemit & Hive

Basic Attention Token (BAT)

Token Curated Registries (TCRs)

Annex

History of Bitcoin & The Web3

Blockchain Scalability

Facebook, Libra & Celo

How to Read This Book

While some readers might have a good understanding of blockchain networks and similar distributed ledgers, it is assumed that many readers still need an introduction to the topic. Without an understanding of the fundamental building blocks of blockchains, smart contracts, and the Web3, it will be hard for readers to assess how, when, and why token use cases might be a game changer. This book provides a general overview of the underlying technology and resulting socio-economic implications thereof, before deep-diving into the topic of tokens.

Chronological reading is recommended, especially for readers who are new to the topic. However, the book also works in a modular way, allowing for cross-reading between chapters. Certain sub-chapters of the first part might be considered to have too much detail for some readers and can easily be skipped. Some basic information on the cryptoeconomic mechanisms behind blockchain networks, and Bitcoin in particular, might be repeated over several chapters. Assuming that many readers will cross-read and might skip some chapters, this minimal repetition is intentional, as a basic understanding of the consensus mechanism behind public distributed ledgers is essential to the understanding of many of the other chapters.

In some cases, complementary technologies or the names of start-ups will be briefly mentioned to make the technology and its use cases more tangible, without describing them in detail. Certain topics can only be briefly explained on a high level, as a more thorough explanation would be beyond the scope of this book. In such cases, the references at the end of each chapter can help to deep-dive into the respective sections of interest.

Given the broad range and multidisciplinary nature of the topics discussed, it might be hard to please the needs of all readers, since not all specialist terms can be explained. It is assumed that the reader will conduct an independent Internet search in such cases.

The graphics in this book intend to visualize the core message of the topics discussed. They sometimes use metaphors or apply an intentional level of abstraction to allow for better understanding, especially for those who are new to the topic. Due to the emerging nature of token applications and their underlying Web3 networks, some details of the projects mentioned in this book might have become obsolete by the time of reading the book. The overall content of this book, however, is structured in a way that the general information will remain relevant.

Introduction

Tokens are to the Web3 what websites were to the Web1. With the emergence of the WWW in 1991, Tim Berner Lee introduced a new standard that allowed us to create visually appealing web pages with just a few lines of code, and surf the Internet following links, instead of using command-line interfaces. Back in the early 1990s, most people did not know how to code HTML, or how to create appealing, meaningful, user-friendly websites. It took us almost a decade to figure out how to use webpages beyond the scope of online directories and online billboards, and when we did, the Web2 emerged. Compared to those early days of the Web, we are at a very similar stage when it comes to understanding what we can potentially do with cryptographic tokens. While it has become easy to create a token with a few lines of code, the understanding of how to apply these tokens is still vague. Even though there are already more than 5400 publicly traded tokens listed on "Coinmarketcap" at the time of writing this book, most of these tokens still lack proper design; many of these might, therefore, soon fail simply because of that.

The technology is still in its early stages, rapidly evolving, with the potential to uproot many industries, in particular money and finance, including government and other organizations. However, we currently lack best practices, while simultaneously dealing with a myriad of technological and legal challenges. We also lack substantial education around the mechanisms, potentials, threats, and state of the technology, including its socio-economic implications.

Buzzwords like "smart contracts," "cryptocurrencies," and "tokens" add to the confusion of what is what. Partial and one-sided knowledge seem to be on the rise, but the big picture of why and how Web3 networks could prove to be one of the biggest game-changing innovations in the years to come is still vague. The media keeps referring to cryptocurrencies, even when talking of non-currency tokens, while reducing the underlying blockchain networks to objects of speculation, instead of focusing on the fact that they provide - first and foremost - a promising governance infrastructure that could resolve many problems of the Internet we use today, such as: (a) the fact that we have no control over what happens with our private data, (b) the lack of transparency along the supply chain of goods, services, and financial payments, or (c) the fact that the Internet lacks an inherent payment settlement layer, forcing us to rely on trusted Internet platforms like Amazon, Airbnb, and Uber, just to name a few.

The industry keeps referring to "Blockchain" as different from "Bitcoin," creating an artificial divide that is often misleading. There seems to be too little understanding about the fact that Bitcoin is a blockchain network, which is (a) globally managed by people who mostly do not know each other, and (b) enabled by the consensus protocol that (c) incentivizes all network actors for their contributions with a native token. The governance rules are tied to the minting of a native network token. The Bitcoin token can, therefore, be seen as the currency of a distributed Internet tribe, called the Bitcoin network, where network actors are rewarded with Bitcoins, just as the Ether is the currency of the distributed Internet tribe Ethereum network, or Sia is the native currency of the Sia network. The Bitcoin network and other distributed ledgers all represent a collectively maintained public infrastructure and are the backbone of the next generation Internet, what the crypto community refers to as the Web3.

While early tokens were first only minted as part of the incentive scheme of the underlying blockchain protocols, with the advent of the Ethereum network, tokens have moved up the technology stack. Ethereum made it cheap and easy to issue a token with just a few lines of code, with a simple smart contract, and without the need to build your own blockchain infrastructure. The challenge, however, is that most people still don't know what to do with these tokens, or how to properly design them. Other challenges are: technological challenges, sustainable mechanism design for purpose-driven tokens, unclear and balkanized legislation, and the lack of education about the potentials and threats of this emerging "token economy."

The goal of this book is, therefore, to first give an overview of the fundamental building blocks of the Web3 (Part 1) and introduce the most important Web applications such as smart contracts, DAOs and Token with focus on their socio-economic implications (Part 2). Part 3 will deep dive into the implications on money, finance and the economy and explain how Web3 based decentralized financial applications - colloquially referred to as DeFi - lead to the merging of the concept of money, finance and the real economy. Part 4 will analyze selected use cases and conclude with a hands on guide to "how to design your own token system."

I would like to express my gratitude to a few people who have inspired or supported me from the very beginning of the crypto journey, or who have contributed with input and feedback to this book: Peter Kaas, Valentin Kalinov, Alfred Taudes, Michael Zargham, Justyna Zubrycka, Caroline Helbing, Jakob Hackel, Kris Paruch, Susanne Guth, Guido Schäfer, Sofie Schock, Tom Fürstner, Robert Krimmer and all the advisors and collaborators of BlockchainHub, including my dear friends from Lunar Ventures in Berlin. I am also grateful for all the people who supported the creation of the Cryptoeconomics Research Lab at the Vienna University of Economics, and who believed in the necessity of dedicated interdisciplinary research on this topic.

I am especially grateful for the hospitality and open environment of the Ethereum Office in Berlin, who offered us shelter in their co-working space when setting up the BlockchainHub, and the open mind of all the people involved in post-"TheDAO hack" activities, working 24/7 to find a solution to recover depleted funds, which taught me a great deal about open-source software development and bug fixing in decentralized networks.

Shermin Voshmgir
May 2020

Web3 Basics

Part 1 will explain the fundamental building blocks of the Web3. It will give an introduction to the basic principles of the Web3: Bitcoin and other blockchain networks including alternative distributed ledger systems, the role of cryptography and user-centric digital identities, but without going into all the details, as that would be far beyond the scope of this book. Any reader who is interested in learning more is advised to follow up on the sources cited at the end of each chapter.

Tokenized Networks: Web3, the Stateful Web

If we assume that the WWW revolutionized information, and that the Web2 revolutionized interactions, the Web3 has the potential to revolutionize agreements and value exchange. The Web3 changes the data structures in the backend of the Internet, introducing a universal state layer, often by incentivizing network actors with a token. The backbone of this Web3 is represented by a series of blockchain networks or similar distributed ledgers.

The Internet we have today is broken. We do not control our data, nor do we have a native value settlement layer. Thirty years into mass adoption of the Internet, our data architectures are still based on the concept of the stand-alone computer, where data is centrally stored and managed on a server, and sent or retrieved by a client. Every time we interact over the Internet, copies of our data get sent to the server of a service provider, and every time that happens, we lose control over our data. As a result, and even though we live in an increasingly connected world, our data is mostly centrally stored: on local or remote servers, on our personal computers, mobile devices, flash drives, and increasingly also on our watches, cars, TVs, or fridges. This raises issues of trust. Can I trust those people and institutions that store and manage my data against any form of corruption—internally or externally, on purpose or by accident? Centralized data structures not only raise issues of security, privacy and control of personal data, but also produce many inefficiencies along the supply chain of goods and services.

There are historic roots to these issues since the computer preceded the Internet. In the early days of personal computers one could not send files from one computer to the other. You needed to save a file on a floppy disc, walk over to the person who needed the file, and copy the file onto their computer so they could use it. If that person was in another country, you would need to go to the post office and mail the floppy disc to them. The emergence of the Internet Protocol (IP) put an end to this, connecting all those stand-alone computers with a data transmission protocol that made the transfer of data faster, and slashed the transaction costs of information exchange. However, the Internet we use today is still predominantly built on the idea of the stand-alone computer, where most data is centrally stored and managed on the servers of trusted institutions. The data on these servers is protected by firewalls, and system administrators are needed to manage the security of the data stored on the servers.

The emergence of the WWW in the early 1990s increased the usability of the Internet with visually appealing and easy-to-navigate websites. Ten years later, the Internet became more mature, and programmable. We saw the rise of the so-called Web2, which brought us social media, e-commerce and knowledge platforms. The Web2 revolutionized social interactions, bringing producers and consumers of information, goods, and services closer together. The Web2 allowed us to enjoy peer-to-peer (P2P) interactions on a global scale, but always with a middleman: a platform acting as a trusted intermediary between two people who do not know or trust each other. While these Internet platforms have done a fantastic job of creating a P2P economy, they also dictate all the rules and they control the data of their users.

In this context, blockchain networks seem to be a driving force of the next-generation Internet, what some refer to as the Web3. They reinvent the way that data is stored and managed over the Internet, providing a unique set of data—a universal state layer—that is collectively managed by all nodes in the network. This unique state layer, for the first time, provides a native value settlement layer for the Internet in the absence of intermediaries. It enables true P2P transactions, and it all started with the emergence of Bitcoin.

While the Web2 was a front-end revolution, the Web3 is a backend revolution. The Web3 reinvents how the Internet is wired in the backend, combining the system functions of the Internet with the system functions of computers. However, nothing much will change on the front-end of the Internet for the average user. The Web3 represents a set of protocols, with distributed ledgers as their backbone. Data is collaboratively managed by a P2P network of computers. The management rules are formalized in the protocol and secured by majority consensus of all network participants, who are incentivized with a network token for their activities. The protocol formalizes the governance rules of the network and ensures that people who do not know or trust each other reach and settle agreements over the Web. While trying to manipulate data on a server resembles breaking into a house, where security is provided by a fence and an alarm system, the Web3 is designed in a way that you would need to break into multiple houses around the globe simultaneously, which each have their own fence and alarm system. This is possible but prohibitively expensive.

Blockchain: A Stateful Protocol

The Internet we use today is "stateless." It doesn't have a native mechanism to transfer what computer science refers to as "state." State refers to information, or the status of "Who is who?"; "Who owns what?"; and "Who has the right to do what?" in a network. The ability to transfer value easily and P2P is essential for efficient markets, and "state" is a key property for managing and transfering values. In the Web3, values are represented by cryptographically secured tokens.

If you can't hold state in the Internet, you cannot transfer value without centralized institutions acting as clearing entities. While today's Internet has accelerated information transfer by orders of magnitude of what was possible before, we still need trusted institutions such as Internet platform providers to broker our actions as a workaround for this lack of state. Stateless protocols like the current Web only manage the transfer of information, where the sender or receiver of that information is unaware of the state of the other. This lack of state is based on the simplicity of the protocols that the Web is built on, such TCP/IP, SMTP, or HTTP. This family of protocols regulates the transmission of data, not how data is stored. Data could be stored centrally, or decentrally. For many reasons, centralized data storage became the mainstream form of data storage and management.

The introduction of session cookies and centralized service providers offered workarounds to this stateless Web. Session cookies were invented so web-based applications could preserve state on local devices. Before session cookies—in the early days of the WWW—we had no browsing history, no favorite sites saved, and no auto-complete, which meant that we had to resubmit our user information every time we were using a website. While session cookies provide better usability, these cookies are created and controlled by a service provider, such as Google, Amazon, Facebook, your bank, your university, etc., whose role is to provide and manage the state of their user.

Web2 platforms have introduced many beneficial services and created considerable social and economic value over the years. However, wealth was mostly accumulated by the companies offering the services, and less by the general public contributing content and value to those services. Instead of decentralizing the world, Web2 platforms contributed to a re-centralization of economic decision making, R&D decision making, and subsequently, to an enormous concentration of power around these platform providers. Furthermore, since the early Internet was created around the idea of free information, customers were often not willing to pay for online content with a recurring subscription fee, and micropayments are still not feasible, in most cases. Therefore, many of these Web2 platforms needed to find alternative ways to profit from the free services they provided, and this alter-

History of the Web

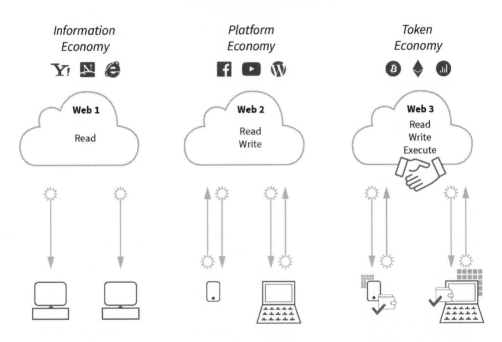

Information Economy	*Platform Economy*	*Token Economy*
Web 1 — Read	**Web 2** — Read Write	**Web 3** — Read Write Execute

Hello World

Tim Berners Lee introduced a new standard that allowed for creating visually appealing web pages with just a few lines of code, and surfing the Internet following links, instead of using command-line interfaces. The Internet became more usuable. Anyone could now use the Internet and was referred to as "Information Data Highway."

Apps: Web browsers, search engines.

Frontend Revolution

The Internet became more mature. Apps could be used to read and write simultaneously. This revolutionized social & economic interactions, bringing producers and consumers of information, goods, and services closer together. But always with a middleman: a platform acting as a trusted intermediary between two people who do not know or trust each other.

Apps: Wikipedia, social media, and e-commerce.

Backend Revolution

Frontend remains the same, but the data structures in the backend change. Anyone can participate in verifying transactions and be compensated for their contribution with a network token. Agreements are executed on the fly and P2P with smart contracts. Web3 applications need a connection to a dirstributed ledger, which is managed by a special application called "wallet."

App: Tokens

Client-Server Internet

Server   Clients

Data Monopoly vs. Data Sovereignty

Server

P2P Networks

Centralized vs. Distributed

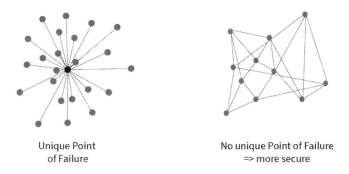

Unique Point
of Failure

No unique Point of Failure
=> more secure

native was advertising. What followed was targeted advertizing based on user behavior and the commodification of private data. Business models have, therefore, developed around targeted advertising that builds on the data sets collected, which provide "state" for these platforms. As a result of this, users are paying for services with their private data.

The Bitcoin protocol introduced a mechanism for each node in a network to send and receive tokens, and record the state of tokens, in a digitally native format. The consensus protocol of the Bitcoin network is designed in a way that the network can collectively remember preceding events or user interactions, resolving the "double-spending" problem by providing a single source of reference for who received what and when. The Bitcoin protocol can, therefore, be seen as a game changer, paving the way to a more decentralized Web. The Bitcoin white paper of 2008 initiated a new form of public infrastructure where the state of all Bitcoin tokens are collectively maintained.

Blockchain networks, such as the Bitcoin network, are only the backbone, and the starting point, but not the only building block in this new decentralized Web. The Web3 architecture leverages the collectively maintained universal state for decentralized computing. Decentralized applications can manage some or all of their content and logic by a blockchain network or other distributed ledger. But other protocols are also needed. Many developers have started to build alternative blockchain networks, as well as complementary protocols for the Web3.

Other Web3 Protocols

Blockchain is not the only technology needed to decentralize the Web. A multitude of other protocols are required to create a decentralized application. However, the term "blockchain" seems to be used as a synonym for many Web3[1] protocols or the Web3 itself, at least by some journalists and the general public. Apart from computation we need file storage, messaging, identities, external data (oracles) and many other decentralized services. A blockchain network is simply the processor for decentralized applications that operate on top of the Web3. It serves as a distributed accounting machine recording all token transactions and performing computation.

Blockchain networks are not at all ideal for storing data, for two main reasons: (i) public blockchain networks are too slow and too expensive to store large data sets; and (ii) storing plain-text data blockchain networks doesn't allow for "privacy by design."[2] To create a decentralized YouTube, for example, decentralized file storage is needed to manage the video files. A range of different decentralized storage network solutions have been emerging, such as "IPFS," "Filecoin," "Swarm,"

"Storj," or "Sia." Decentralized storage networks incentivize network nodes to share storage space with a native token, and turn cloud storage into algorithmic markets. They differ in their levels of decentralization, privacy and in their choice of incentive mechanisms. Some might not even have an incentive layer, like IPFS, for example. Protocols like "Golem," on the other hand, provide decentralize rendering power by rewarding contributions in the network with their native protocol token.

The Web3 developer community has been evolving over the last years. Different teams are working on various components of this emergent Web; however, many of these protocols are still in development. Web3 applications typically communicate with peers that are unknown in the beginning, and have varying quality in terms of speed and reliability. New libraries and APIs are needed to navigate such complexities. It is unclear when they will achieve critical mass to possibly replace the current Web applications on a larger scale, or which standards will ultimately prevail. The transition from "client-server Web" to the "decentralized Web" will, therefore, be gradual rather than radical. It seems to be shifting from centralized to partially decentralized to fully decentralized.

One of the most pressing applied research questions when developing complementary technologies for the Web3 is the question of how to reward network participants with a token, so that the network stays attack resistant. Examples thereof would be incentive mechanisms for decentralized file storage solutions, decentralized computation, data analysis, or reputation. Many different consensus mechanisms are currently being experimented with, such as: "Proof-of-Retrievability," "Proof-of-Storage," and "Proof-of-Spacetime." Fully decentralized solutions, such as IPFS and Swarm, are not functionally implemented yet.

While decentralized architectures are more resilient than their centralized Web2 predecessors, they are also slower. Speed, performance, and usability are bottlenecks in the Web3 that will very likely be resolved over time, once the core components of the Web3 are up and running (read more: Annex - Scalability). It is likely that the future of the Internet will be more decentralized, however, this does not mean that we will get rid of centralized systems altogether. Centralized systems have advantages and will likely prevail, at least for specific use cases.

---

[1] *Please note that similar terms, like Web 3.0, are used by other domains. They often refer to a more intelligent Web or semantic Web, including machine learning and AI, focusing on the convergence of several key emerging technologies. In the context of blockchain, the term is used by many in the scene to refer to a more decentralized Internet, and it is generally referred to as Web3 (not Web 3.0).*
[2] *"Privacy by Design" refers to "data protection through technology design." (https://gdpr-info.eu/issues/privacy-by-design)*

Decentralized Applications in the Web3

As opposed to centralized applications that run on a single computer, decentralized applications run on a P2P network of computers. They have existed since the advent of P2P networks and don't necessarily need to run on top of a blockchain network. "Tor," "BitTorrent," "Popcorn Time," and "BitMessage," are all examples of decentralized applications that run on a P2P network, but not on a blockchain network, which is a specific kind of P2P network (read more: Annex - Origins of Bitcoin and Web3).

Traditional applications use HTML, CSS, or javascript to render a webpage or a mobile app. The front-end of a webpage or a mobile application interacts with one or more centralized databases. When you use a service like Twitter, Facebook, Amazon, or Airbnb, for example, the webpage will call an API to process your personal data and other necessary information stored on their servers, to display them on the front-end. User ID and passwords are used for identification and authentication, with low levels of security, since personalized data is stored on the server of the service provider.

Decentralized applications do not look any different from current websites or mobile apps. The front-end represents what you see, and the backend of a decentralized application represents the entire business logic. A decentralized application is a blockchain client - often also referred to as the "wallet." It uses the same technologies to render a webpage or a mobile app (like HTML, CSS, Javascript) but communicates with a blockchain network instead of a server and, in the case of smart contract networks, also the smart contracts (read more: Part 2 - Smart Contracts). The wallet also manages the public-private key-pair and the blockchain address, to provide a unique identity for network nodes so they can securely interact with the network (read more: Part 1 - Token Security & User-Centric Identities). The smart contracts represent the core business logic of the decentralized application and processes data feeds from inside and outside the network to manage the state of all network actors (read more: Part 1 - Smart Contracts). If the blockchain-client is a full-node, it will also manage the full state of the ledger (read more: Part 1 - Bitcoin, Blockchain & other Distributed Ledgers). In this case, the blockchain-client performs the functions of an HTTP client and a server, as all data is stored client-side. The front-end data, including audio or video files and other documents, could be collectively stored on and managed by decentralized storage networks like "Swarm" or "IPFS." At the time of writing this book such data is still, for the most part, stored on and managed by servers.

For the average user, decentralized applications need to look and feel the same as existing applications, which means that they need to be as easy and intui-

Web2 Applications vs. Web3 Applications

Web 2 Application (client)
communicates
with servers.

Web 3 Application (client)
also referred to as "wallet"
communicates with a blockchain network.

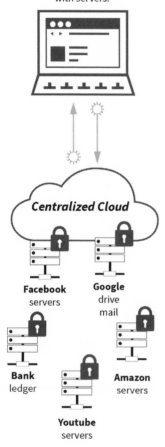

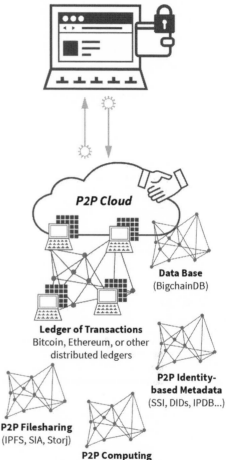

Web2 applications run on a combination of servers owned by different organizations performing various backend operations. Security is provided by system administrator working for those companies which act as trusted intermediary. They manage all identities (user ID & password combination) and related personal data.

Web3 applications run on a combination of public and/or private networks, performing various backend operations. The distributed ledger serves as the backbone for other the Web3 networks that are all collectively managed and are often incentivized by a token. Security is provided by a P2P network validating transactions by majority consensus.

tive to use if they are to be adopted on a larger scale. Currently, wallet software and key management are difficult, which might be a bottleneck to the mass adoption of Web3 applications. Furthermore, wide-scale adoption can only happen if distrust of centralized solutions is high enough to warrant current trade-offs in usability.

Chapter Summary

- *The Internet we have today is broken. We do not control our data, nor do we have a native value settlement layer. Every time we interact over the Internet, copies of our data get sent to the server of a service provider, and every time that happens, we lose control over our data. This raises issues of trust.*

- *The Internet we use today stores and manages data on the servers of trusted institutions. In the Web3, data is stored in multiple copies of a P2P network, and the management rules are formalized in the protocol, and secured by majority consensus of all network participants, often (but not always) incentivized with a network token for their activities.*

- *While the Web2 was a front-end revolution, the Web3 is a backend revolution, introducing a universal state layer. It is a set of protocols led by a blockchain network or similar distributed ledger, which intends to reinvent how the Internet is wired in the backend. The Web3 combines the system functions of the Internet with the system functions of computers.*

- *As opposed to centralized applications that run on a single computer, decentralized applications run on a P2P network of computers. They have existed since the advent of P2P networks. Decentralized applications don't necessarily need to run on top of a blockchain network.*

- *A decentralized application is a blockchain client called "wallet." It uses the same technologies to render a webpage or a mobile app (like HTML, CSS, Javascript) but communicates with a blockchain network instead of a server and, in the case of smart contract networks, also the smart contracts. The wallet also manages the public-private key-pair and the blockchain address, to provide a unique identity for network nodes and allow them to interact with the network.*

Chapter References & Further Reading

- Benet, Juan: "IPFS - Content Addressed, Versioned, P2P File System (DRAFT 3)," retrieved, Sept 10, 2018: https://ipfs.io/ipfs/QmR7GSQM93Cx5eAg6a6yRzNde1FQv7uL6X1o4k7zrJa3LX/ipfs.draft3.pdf
- Ehrsam, Fred; "The dApp Developer Stack: The Blockchain Industry Barometer", Apr 30, 2017, retrieved from: https://medium.com/@FEhrsam/the-dapp-developer-stack-the-blockchain-industry-barometer-8d55ec1c7d4

- Gaúcho Pereira Felipe Gaúcho: "The Web3 Video Stack Charting the infrastructure for a decentralized mediaverse!"Aug 16, 2018, retrieved from: https://tokeneconomy.co/web3videostack-c423481c32a5
- Gillies, James; Cailliau, Robert: "How the Web was Born: The Story of the World Wide Web", Oxford University Press, 2000, retrieved from https://books.google.de/books?id=pIH-Ji-jUNS0C&lpg=PA25&ots=MKZj0F7pJN&pg=PA25&redir_esc=y#v=onepage&q&f=false
- Koblitz, N.: "Elliptic curve cryptosystems". Mathematics of Computation. 48 (177): 203–209, 1987
- Laplante, Philip A.: "Dictionary of Computer Science, Engineering and Technology", 2000, CRC Press. p. 466.
- McConaghy, Trent: "Blockchain Infrastructure Landscape: A First Principles Framing Manifesting Storage, Computation, and Communications", Jul 15, 2017, retrieved from: https://medium.com/@trentmc0/blockchain-infrastructure-landscape-a-first-principles-framing-92cc5549bafe
- Miller, V.; "Use of elliptic curves in cryptography". CRYPTO. Lecture Notes in Computer Science. 85. pp. 417–426, 1985
- Misra, Jayadev: "A Discipline of Multiprogramming: Programming Theory for Distributed Applications" Springer, 2001.
- Monegro, Joel: "Fat Protocols", Aug 8, 2016, retrieved from: https://www.usv.com/blog/fat-protocols
- Nakamoto, Satoshi: „Bitcoin: A Peer-to-Peer Electronic Cash System," Bitcoin.org, 2008, Archived from the original on 20 March 2014, retrieved from: https://bitcoin.org/bitcoin.pdf
- N.N.: "Web3 Foundation - Website," retrieved from: https://web3.foundation/
- N.N.: "Comprehensive wiki of generalised Web3 stack," retrieved, Sept 10, 2018: https://github.com/w3f/Web3-wiki/wiki
- Pon, Bruce: "Blockchain will usher in the era of decentralised computing", Apr 15, 2016, retrieved from: https://blog.bigchaindb.com/blockchain-will-usher-in-the-era-of-decentralised-computing-7f35e94af0b6
- Samani, Kyle: "The Web3 Stack", July 10, 2018, retrieved from: https://multicoin.capital/2018/07/10/the-web3-stack/
- Stallings, W.: "Computer Networking with Internet Protocols and Technology", Pearson Education, 2004.
- Tekisalp, Emre: "Understanding Web 3 — A User Controlled Internet. Coinbase breaks down the motivation and technology behind the development of Web 3", Coinbase, Aug 29, 2018, retrieved from: https://blog.coinbase.com/understanding-web-3-a-user-controlled-internet-a39c21cf83f3
- Thomas, John; Mantri, Pam: „Complex Adaptive Blockchain Governance", MATEC Web of Conferences 223, 01010 (2018) https://doi.org/10.1051/matecconf/201822301010 ICAD 2018, retrieved from: https://www.matec-conferences.org/articles/matecconf/pdf/2018/82/matecconf_icad2018_01010.pdf
- Tual, Stephan: "Web 3.0 Revisited — Part One: "Across Chains and Across Protocols", May 26, 2017: https://blog.stephantual.com/web-3-0-revisited-part-one-across-chains-and-across-protocols-4282b01054c5
- Vinton G. Cerf; Robert E. Kahn (May 1974). „A Protocol for Packet Network Intercommunication". IEEE Transactions on Communications. 22 (5): 637–648. doi:10.1109/tcom.1974.
- Wolpert, John: "Bring on the Stateful Internet", Aug 2, 2018, retrieved from: https://media.consensys.net/bring-on-the-stateful-internet-d589adc7bb65
- Wood, Gavin: "ĐApps: What Web 3.0 Looks Like", April 17. 2014, retrieved from: http://gavwood.com/dappsweb3.html
- Filecoin: https://filecoin.io/
- Golem: https://golem.network/
- IPFS: https://ipfs.io/
- SIA: https://sia.tech/
- Storj: https://storj.io
- Swarm: https://swarm-guide.readthedocs.io/en/latest/

Keeping Track of the Tokens: Bitcoin, Blockchain, & Other Distributed Ledgers

Blockchain networks build on the idea of P2P networks, providing a universal data set that every actor can trust, even though they might not know or trust each other. Immutable copies of that data are stored and managed on every node in the network. Economic incentives in the form of native network tokens are applied to make the network fault tolerant, attack resistant, and collusion resistant.

The concept of a "chain-of-blocks" was introduced in the Bitcoin white paper in October 2008, with the aim to create "P2P money without banks." The paper, published under the pseudonym Satoshi Nakamoto, proposed a system where all computers in the network hold an identical copy of a ledger of transactions, which acts as a single point of reference for everyone in the network. All network nodes collectively update and manage this ledger, which represents a universal data set that every actor can trust, even though they might not know or trust each other. People and institutions who do not know or trust each other, reside in different countries, are subject to different jurisdictions, and who have no legally binding agreements with each other can now interact over the Internet without the need for trusted third parties like banks, Internet platforms, or other types of clearing institutions.

Double-Spending Problem: This new form of distributed data management resolved the double-spending problem over the Internet. The way the Internet is designed today, one can spend the same value—issued as a digital file—multiple times, because digital information can be copied, and copies of that same digital file can be sent from one computer to multiple other computers at the same time. Before the emergence of Bitcoin, ideas around cryptographically secured P2P networks had been discussed in different evolutionary stages, mostly in theoretical papers, since the 1980s (read more: Annex - Origins of Bitcoin). However, there had never been a practical implementation of a P2P network that managed to avoid the double-spending problem, without the need for trusted intermediaries guaranteeing value exchange. The Bitcoin protocol introduced a mechanism of making it expensive to copy digital values.

Chain of Blocks: In a blockchain network, token transactions are recorded in batches of data called "blocks" that are "hashed." This cryptographic hash creates a digital fingerprint of the block (read more: Part 1 - Token Security: Cryptography.) Each block includes the hash of the prior block, thereby linking one block with another into a chain of blocks. This process guarantees the historic integrity of all the blocks back to the first block, also referred to as the genesis block. If data in one block is altered, the hash value of the block and all subsequent blocks will change, and every node in the network will know that the data has been tampered with. This growing list of chained blocks is also referred to as the ledger.

The ledger is a file that maintains a growing list of transaction records, chained in blocks that are cryptographically secured from tampering and revision. If manipulation attempts were made, the hash value of the manipulated ledger would not coincide with the hash value recorded on the copies of the ledger on all other nodes. The hash value of a block therefore serves as a counterfeit protection that can be used to check the authenticity of a transaction on a ledger.

Distributed Ledger: A copy of the ledger is stored on multiple nodes of a cryptographically secured P2P network. In order to change the ledger data on all copies of the ledger throughout the whole network, the network nodes need to reach a mutual agreement about such a change. A distributed ledger is a shared, trusted, public ledger of transactions that everyone can inspect, but which no single user controls. Each independent node has the latest version of the ledger, which contains all transactions that have ever been made, and can verify transactions. This process is referred to as "consensus." This is particularly useful in inter-organizational setups where no institution wants to trust another institution with the management of their data.

Tokens: The term "token" is simply a metaphor. Contrary to what the metaphor might suggest, a token does not represent a digital file that is sent from one device to the other. Instead, it manifests as an entry in the ledger that belongs to a blockchain address. Only the person who has the private key for that address can access the respective tokens, using a wallet software, which acts as a blockchain client (read more: Part 1 - Token Security: Cryptography, Wallets.)

Unlike distributed databases, where data is distributed but managed and controlled by one single entity, blockchain networks allow for distributed control.

Different people and institutions that do not trust each other share information without requiring a central administrator.

Like a spreadsheet in the cloud: The ledger could also be described as a spreadsheet in the cloud. Think of cloud applications like "Google Sheets," where everyone can access and edit a file simultaneously. But, as opposed to Google Sheets, where that file is centrally stored on the Google servers, the ledger of a blockchain network is a document that is not centrally stored. Instead, each node of the network keeps an identical copy of the same file at all times (with temporary exceptions every time a new block is created).

Universal State: Every computer in the network manages its own identical copy of the ledger, which acts as a universal data set across the whole network, guaranteeing that each token is transferred only once. The ledger therefore represents the universal state of the network, that all nodes in the network agree upon. It serves as a digital notary and a publicly verifiable timestamp.

Bitcoin Transactions: When using the Bitcoin network, instead of a bank validating financial transactions, all computers in the network check their copies of the ledger for validity of the transaction, and collectively confirm transactions by majority consensus. No user is trusted more than any other. Instead of a single trusted third party validating transactions through their servers with authority (single vote), a P2P network of computers running the blockchain protocol validates transactions by consensus (majority vote).

The Protocol is a set of rules and processes that define how all the (anonymous) nodes in the network can reach an agreement on the true state of the network. The protocol defines how the participants in the network interact with each other: (i) under which conditions sending tokens from A to B is valid; (ii) the economic rewards for validating transactions with a cryptographic token; (iii) how to reference identities and sign transactions; and (iv) who decides over network upgrades.

Cryptoeconomics: Cryptography secures the network and provides full transparency for all participants, while maintaining the privacy of each individual actor. It also makes sure that past transactions are true. Game theory is applied to make sure that future transactions will be conducted in a truthful manner by majority consensus of all network actors, assuming that all network actors could potentially be corrupt. The consensus mechanism is designed to make it difficult to manipulate the ledger.

Consensus: Proof-of-Work is the "consensus mechanism" used by the Bitcoin network that steers collective action of an unknown set of anonymous network actors. It builds on cryptoeconomic principles. Reverse game theory is used to reward

How Blocks of Transactions are Chained

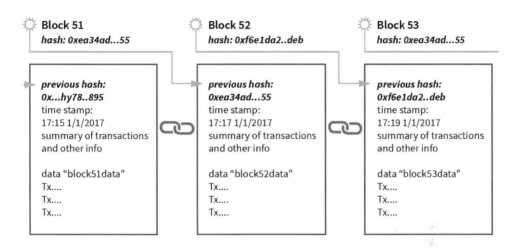

Block 51
hash: 0xea34ad...55

previous hash:
0x...hy78..895
time stamp:
17:15 1/1/2017
summary of transactions
and other info

data "block51data"
Tx....
Tx....
Tx....

Block 52
hash: 0xf6e1da2..deb

previous hash:
0xea34ad...55
time stamp:
17:17 1/1/2017
summary of transactions
and other info

data "block52data"
Tx....
Tx....
Tx....

Block 53
hash: 0xea34ad...55

previous hash:
0xf6e1da2..deb
time stamp:
17:19 1/1/2017
summary of transactions
and other info

data "block53data"
Tx....
Tx....
Tx....

Why is the Ledger Tamper Resistant?

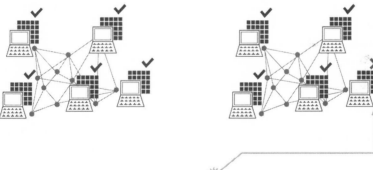

Each network participant manages an identical copy of the entire ledger - the file where all past transactions are recorded. New transactions are collectively verified by consensus of the nodes in the network. In the Bitcoin network, transactions are validated by network miners who are incentivized to verify transactions through PoW (Proof-of-Work) function with Bitcoin tokens.

If a malicious node makes unauthorized changes to their copy of the ledger, <u>other nodes in the network will refuse the transaction</u>, since that malicious version of the blockchain data will differ from the versions held by other network nodes.

network actors with a native network token. In the case of the Bitcoin network, this would be the Bitcoin token. This reward mechanism is designed to make it economically infeasible to cheat the network, due to the prohibitively large amount of computing power that would be required to do so, and taking into account extreme attack scenarios. The consensus rules are designed in a way that make the network attack resistant, in spite of the lack of centralized parties to govern the truthfulness of network activities.

Identities: A blockchain address, which is derived from the private key, represents a pseudonymous digital identity of the token owner. Tokens are noted to belong to a certain address in the public ledger. Only the owner of that address can request to send these tokens somewhere else. In order to prove their ownership to other participants of the network, token holders need to sign transactions with their private key. This form of identity management is purely based on mathematical functions, allowing other computers in the network to confirm the validity of a transaction without needing to know the actual person or his secret private key (read more: Part 1 - Cryptography & User-Centric Identities).

Accounting & Governance Machine: Blockchain networks can also be described as distributed accounting machines, or supranational governance machines that are public and transparent. They provide a governance layer for the Internet. All network participants have equal access to the same data in (almost) real time. Transactions are collectively managed. They are transparent to all actors and can be traced back to their origin.

Decentralized & Autonomous Organization (DAO): The ledger is collectively managed by autonomous network nodes, which is why it is also heralded a new form of organizational infrastructure often referred to as Decentralized Autonomous Organization (read more: Part 2 - Institutional Economics & Governance of DAO; Part 4: Purpose-Driven Tokens.)

Block-explorer: Due to the public nature of the blockchain networks, everyone can run big data on the ledger, like tracking all token transactions, total network hash rate, token supply, and transaction growth, etc. However, while all the data on the ledger is public, few people have the skills to run advanced data analytics on the blockchain. Block-explorers are third-party applications that allow anyone to publicly explore all transactions of a particular network, like Bitcoin and other public blockchain networks. Block-explorers are like a dedicated search engine for blockchain-related data. However, this level of transparency also raises privacy-related issues. These privacy-related issues are being addressed with newer blockchain protocols that use more privacy-preserving cryptographic methods (read more: Part 3 - Privacy Tokens.)

Like a Spreadsheet in the Cloud

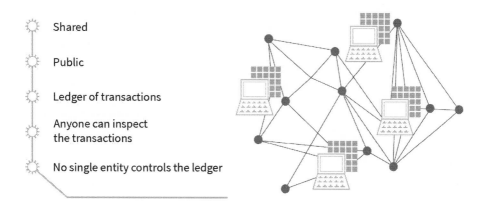

- Shared

- Public

- Ledger of transactions

- Anyone can inspect the transactions

- No single entity controls the ledger

Behind the Blockchain Protocol

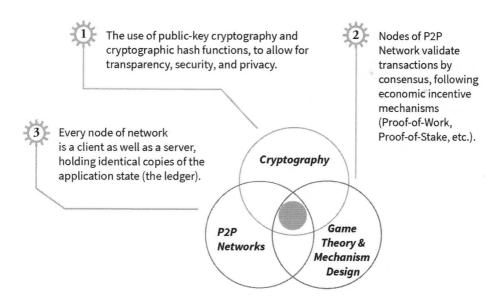

1 The use of public-key cryptography and cryptographic hash functions, to allow for transparency, security, and privacy.

2 Nodes of P2P Network validate transactions by consensus, following economic incentive mechanisms (Proof-of-Work, Proof-of-Stake, etc.).

3 Every node of network is a client as well as a server, holding identical copies of the application state (the ledger).

Cryptography

P2P Networks

Game Theory & Mechanism Design

Cryptoeconomics, Consensus & Proof-of-Work

The underlying challenge of a P2P network with a set of anonymous network nodes is how to deal with malicious network nodes in the absence of centralized parties securing the system. One must always assume that there will be bad actors trying to disrupt any open and public network. How can such a distributed network reach consensus about which data is correct or which is not correct, or which process is true or false in such an untrusted setup? This is referred to as the "Byzantine Generals Problem." A malicious node, also called a byzantine node, can intentionally send wrong information to all other nodes involved in the consensus process. Byzantine failures are considered the most difficult class of failures in distributed networks. Reliable consensus mechanisms must be resilient against DDoS (Distributed Denial of Service) attacks, sybil attacks[3], and other cyber attacks. Before the emergence of Bitcoin, it was believed to be impossible to achieve fault-tolerant and attack-resistant consensus among untrusted nodes in a P2P network.

For the first time in the history of distributed computing, the Bitcoin protocol introduced a mathematical solution to this problem with the introduction of "Proof-of-Work," which made the economic cost of attacking the system disproportionate to the benefit of doing so. It sparked a new field of science around economic coordination games using cryptographic tools, also referred to as "Cryptoeconomics." Cryptoeconomics can be defined as the study of economic interaction in untrusted environments, where every actor could potentially be corrupt. It is interdisciplinary, and requires a deep understanding of cryptography, economics, and P2P networks, and what motivates network actors. Public-private key infrastructure guarantees attack-resistant access control of one's tokens. Hashing functions allow nodes to verify transactions that are done over the network. Both hashing functions and public-private key cryptography are also required for the economic coordination game called Proof-of-Work to reward miners for adding truthful transaction blocks to the ledger. Cryptoeconomic mechanisms can provide a security equilibrium to make the network fault tolerant, and attack and collusion resistant. This allows anonymous network nodes to reach consensus about the state of all network interactions. The Bitcoin network is the first practical instance of cryptoeconomics. It produces "trust by math" rather than "trust by legal contract."

However, security depends on the resilience of the assumptions made on how network actors will react to economic incentives. How people react to incen-

---

[3] *In an anonymous network, a so-called sybil attack is an attack where a single user could generate multiple entities (under pseudonyms) to influence the consensus process.*

tives has long been a field of study in economics. Cryptoeconomics therefore has much in common with mechanism design, a field of economics related to game theory. Game theory analyzes strategic interactions, which are referred to as games. It tries to understand the best strategies for each player if both players maximize the best outcome for themselves. Mechanism design defines desirable outcomes and works backward to create a game that incentivizes players toward that desired outcome. While cryptoeconomics is interdisciplinary, it is a discipline that was predominantly developed in the computer science community. It seems that there is still much room to incorporate methods from various economic disciplines, and other disciplines (more in the next chapter and in Part 4 - Purpose-Driven Tokens).

"Proof-of-Work" (PoW) is the consensus mechanism used in the Bitcoin network and similar blockchain networks to guarantee that a token transaction sent over the network is valid. The mechanism builds on the assumption that all network nodes could potentially be corrupt, and that the least common denominator is money. Proof-of-Work is designed in a way that (i) if you spend money and play by the rules, you can earn network tokens; (ii) it doesn't pay to cheat because mining requires special-purpose computer hardware and consumes large amounts of power.

When tokens are sent over the network, each node in the network can propose new entries to be added to the ledger. These nodes validate transactions and compete with each other to solve a complex computational puzzle. In this process, they have to collect all recent network transactions, including some additional metadata, verify the transactions, guess a pseudo-random number ("nonce"), and run all the data through a cryptographic algorithm (SHA-256) to find the hash of the new block. This means that they have to perform computational work, which is the reason why this process is referred to as "Proof-of-Work."

If a node is the first one in the network to find that hash value, it can add the block to its ledger and broadcast the hash value of the new block, including all block data, to the rest of the network. The other nodes can now verify the validity of the hash. If they accept this newly added block of transactions as valid, they add the new block to their copy of the ledger. Proof-of-Work is designed in a way that the hash is difficult to find, whereas the solutions can be easily verified as true. By participating in this race of finding the hash value, mining nodes collectively make sure that all transactions included in a block are valid. The winning node is rewarded with the "block reward" in the form of newly minted network tokens (plus potential transaction fees). This is why the process is referred to as "mining." The hash of a validated block therefore represents the work done by the miner. At the time of publishing this book, the reward for successful block creation in the Bitcoin network is 6.25 BTC per block. The block reward gets reduced by 50 percent every 210,000 blocks, around every four years. The next "halving" of block rewards is in 2024.

Finding the correct hash value requires some work, in the form of the processing time of a computer, which is also referred to as "CPU cost function." If a cheating miner were the fastest computer to find the hash, the rest of the network would not accept their block of transactions. The cheating miner would, therefore, not get the block reward, even though they invested computational power and energy. This is an economic measure to deter network attacks. A rational economic actor would, therefore, refrain from cheating the system, as this would result in sunk costs of energy and infrastructure investment. Through the backdoor of infrastructure and electricity costs, network attacks are made prohibitively expensive. A successful attack would require a lot of computational power, energy consumption, and time. Because of its computational intensity, the Bitcoin network is also very energy consuming.

The "difficulty" of finding that hash value, and therefore creating a block, adjusts over time in order to keep the interblock-time of 10 minutes[4] relatively constant. It is adjusted periodically as a function of how much hashing power has been deployed by the network of miners. If blocks are created in less time than 10 minutes, difficulty increases. Likewise, if blocks take longer than 10 minutes to be created, difficulty decreases. Difficulty also increases with the level of competition—the number of other computers competing to validate a block.

Network Nodes

The Bitcoin network is (i) open source, (ii) public, and (iii) permissionless. The open-source nature refers to the fact that anyone with adequate skills can contribute to the protocol in a public manner. Furthermore, anyone can take the code, modify it, and create their own version of a P2P payment network. "Public" refers to the fact that anyone can use the network as a payment system (user), and that anyone can download the protocol and the ledger and verify transactions (full nodes). "Permissionless" refers to the fact that anyone can download the protocol and the ledger and write transactions to the ledger (miners). In the Bitcoin Network, there are four types of nodes: full nodes, mining nodes, mining pools, and light nodes.

Full nodes manage the entire history of the Bitcoin network (the ledger) and validate new transactions as they are being added to the ledger. Anyone running such a full node can send and receive Bitcoin tokens, and verify the integrity of the transactions, without having to rely on any third party. Verifying transactions is a complementary function to Bitcoin mining. While Bitcoin mining is done almost

---

[4] *The Bitcoin network, as a worldwide network of computers, has network latencies (delays in the processing of network data). To account for latencies, the Bitcoin protocol specifies that a block should be created every 10 minutes on average.*

Why is it called Blockchain?

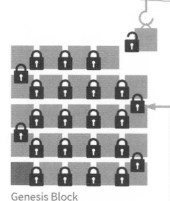

Genesis Block

The network stores all the information in cryptographically secured data pieces called blocks. The first block is called the <u>Genesis Block</u>. Each block has limited storage size.

Blocks store the hash value of the previous blocks, thus they are "<u>chained</u>" <u>together</u> <u>with cryptography</u>.

③ *Cryptography*

② *Game Theory*

Each new block of transaction is added to the blockchain network by consensus of network nodes at even time intervals. Nodes are rewarded with a native token for validating transactions according to the rules, with a fault-tolerant and attack-resistant incentive mechanism.

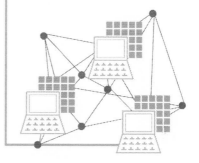

① *P2P Network*

<u>Each full node</u> in the network manages a copy of the entire transaction history (the ledger) represented by a chain of blocks.

exclusively on special-purpose hardware, a full node that only validates transactions can run on a regular home PC with standard processing hardware. In the early days of the Bitcoin network, everyone had to download the full ledger in order to be able to send transactions. Today, wallet software developers also offer the option of light nodes (see below).

Mining nodes (miners) compete for the right to create new blocks and add transactions to the ledger. They can "solo mine" or "pool mine." If they mine alone, they need to maintain their own full copy of the ledger. The winning miners are rewarded with Bitcoin tokens for creating new blocks (block reward). The exact reward mechanism is specified in the protocol. In addition to the block reward, miners can also earn transaction costs. However, these transaction costs are not mandated by the protocol but can be demanded by a miner on the free market. Transaction fees usually increase when network traffic is high and the network becomes congested.

Mining Pools: Over the years, individual miners have begun to collaborate and form cartels of mining nodes. In a mining pool scenario, individual miners collaborate with other miners to write to the ledger and receive the block reward. The mining pool operator maintains a full node and the individual miners contribute their CPU (also referred to as hash-power). Using the cumulative hash-power of all individual miners, they can boost their chances to be the fastest computer to solve the puzzle and write a block of transactions to the ledger. However, the original Bitcoin white paper did not account for this form of collaboration amongst miners. The economic assumptions build on "simple game theory," not "collaborative game theory." As a result, the Bitcoin network has become a much more centralized system than originally intended. Some people therefore argue that the reality of Bitcoin's consensus mechanism can be described as a "delegated Proof-of-Work," and has become an oligopoly of a handful of mining pools, which might not reflect the original intentions of Bitcoin's creator, Satoshi Nakamoto.

Light nodes were created for simplified payment verification (SPV) of smartphone wallet applications. This is why they are also referred to as SPV-nodes or SPV-clients. As opposed to full nodes, they do not maintain the whole ledger, and only store copies of all the headers of all the transaction blocks. They cannot verify transactions autonomously, as they don't have access to all information stored on the ledger. Light nodes rely on the information given out by other peers in the network who have access to all ledger data.

As opposed to mining nodes, full nodes don't have a direct economic incentive to validate transactions. However, there are indirect incentives to run a full node instead of a light node. In the possible event of a protocol upgrade, running a full node is the only way to vote on how the network should upgrade. Another reason to run a full node is the higher degree of privacy since full nodes maintain the full ledger and all transaction data on their own device. This is quite different from how light nodes work. Light nodes rely on third-party servers to broadcast transactions to the network, which means that the servers of those third-party services know the transaction history of the light node.

Why is it expensive to manipulate a network transaction?

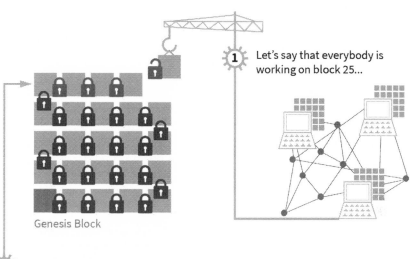

1 Let's say that everybody is working on block 25...

Genesis Block

2 ...but one mining node wants to manipulate a transaction in block 21. The miner would have to make his/her own changes and redo all the transactions for blocks 21-24 and compute block 25. That's 4 blocks of expensive computing. What's worse, the miner would have to do this before everybody else in the network finished just the one block, in this case block 25, that everyone is working on.

Network Attacks

All entries on the ledger are read-only. Once a block of transactions is accepted by the network, it cannot be easily changed or removed. All blocks would have to be recomputed for that to happen, which would require the majority of the network participants to agree over such changes. An attacker would need to redo the computational work of all successor blocks, on the majority of the network nodes. This would require control over, or bribing of, the majority of the network nodes. Even if it would be possible to perform these computations within the block-creation period, the cost would be much higher than the rewards for attacking the network. While manipulation is possible, the mechanism is designed to make it infeasible.

These websites provide real-time information about how much it currently costs to attack different blockchain networks in a so-called "51% attack." A Proof-of-Work network is safe as long as more than 50 percent of the work is being put in by miners who are honest. A "51% attack" happens when a single person or institution is able to control the majority of the hash rate or computing power to manipulate the network. In the ten-year history of Bitcoin, no manipulation by outside attackers has been successful.

- *Online tool to check what it would cost to attack the Bitcoin network:* https://gobitcoin.io/tools/cost-51-attack/
- *Online tool to check what it would cost to attack different blockchain networks:* https://www.crypto51.app/

A successful 51 percent attack could have the following impact: It would allow you to (i) change blocks by adding or removing transactions, which requires additional PoW (the older a transaction is, the harder an attack gets); (ii) censor participants and therefore transactions of these participants; (iii) send transactions and then reverse them; and (iv) change protocol rules.

What a 51 percent attack cannot do is change existing transactions or fake transactions, like: (i) changing the amount sent in an existing transaction; (ii) changing the recipient of an existing transaction; or (iii) sending someone's tokens without their approval. This is because all transactions need to be signed with the private key of the token owner, which cannot be revealed by majority agreement of the network. Changing a detail in an existing transaction would render the ledger "illegitimate," as a transaction without a valid signature would be in it. These types of manipulations can only be achieved by brute-forcing the private-keys of a network actor. Alternatively, one could also break the cryptographic algorithm (SHA) to attack the network, which is why it is essential to use cryptographic algorithms that have been properly stress-tested (read more: Part 1 - Token Security: Cryptography).

Protocol Forks & Network Splits

In software engineering, "software forks" refer to the fact that any free and open-source software may be copied and modified without prior permission of the original development team and without violating copyright law. The term sometimes also refers to a split in the developer community of an existing project, rather than only the code. This way, one can either (i) create a new network from scratch by simply copying the existing codebase and modifying it to build a new network ("Zcash" and "Litecoin," for example, are based on Bitcoin codebase), or (ii) fork an existing network, including the existing ledger and the community, into a different continuation for the sake of a protocol update. These protocol updates can cause a split of the network as a result of protocol upgrade disputes (as was the case with "Bitcoin Cash" and "Ethereum Classic") or deliberate secession for economic reasons, which are often designed to extract economic value above any philosophical protocol discussions (as was the case with "Bitcoin Gold," "Bitcoin Diamond," and "Bitcoin Platinum"). The types and rules of software forks depend on the formal and informal protocols of each network. The Bitcoin network and similar networks distinguish between "hard forks" and "soft forks."

- A "hard fork" is a type of protocol change that is not backward-compatible. Nodes that don't update to the new version of the protocol won't be able to process transactions. All nodes that validate transactions according to the old protocol will treat the blocks produced according to the new protocol as invalid. Nodes that want to adopt the new protocol will therefore need to upgrade their software.

- A "soft fork" is a type of protocol change that is backward-compatible. Nodes that didn't update the protocol are still able to process transactions if they don't break the new protocol rules. Blocks produced by miners running the upgraded protocol are accepted by all nodes in the network. Blocks produced by miners running the old version are rejected by the nodes running the new version of the protocol. If old-version miners get their blocks rejected by part of the network, they might be inclined to upgrade too. Soft forks are, therefore, a bit more gradual in their voting process than hard forks and take several weeks. If a majority of miners upgrade to the new protocol, it is referred to as a miner-activated soft forks (MASF). If full nodes coordinate, without support from the miners, it is referred to as a user-activated soft fork (UASF).

A split can occur when some nodes in the network continue to use the old protocol while all others use the new protocol. Technical protocol updates happen quite frequently, and don't usually create too much controversy, especially when they involve minor technical upgrades. The shorter chain dies and the token has no market value. However, the short history of blockchain networks has shown that more politicized decisions on protocol upgrades can lead to a split in the network, where the minority chain has enough followers or political narrative to maintain an economy of its own. A key aspect of this is a split in brainpower of the developers that support one network or the other. As the community splits, developers often have to take a stance for one network or the other, which can result in a lack of necessary developer power. Miners also have to choose which network they continue supporting (read more: Part 2 - Institutional Economics & Governance of DAOs.).

In the case of a hard fork, anyone who owned tokens in the old network will also own an equivalent amount of tokens in the new minority network, which they can then sell or hold on to. This, however, requires at least one token exchange to list the new token of the minority network; otherwise, there is no market for the token of that network, and as a result, the network fades into oblivion. A politicized hard fork is a black swan event and could have a serious effect on the value of one's tokens, depending on which network will gain traction in the long run. Examples of politicised hard forks that split the network are "Ethereum Classic" (ETC)[5] and "Bitcoin Cash" (BCH)[6]. As a result of these prominent forks of the Bitcoin network and Ethereum network, the question of governance has sparked an ongoing debate in the community, and seems to be one of the more prominent research questions for the years to come (read more: Part 2 - Institutional Economics of DAOs & On-Chain vs. Off-Chain Governance).

Furthermore, temporal splits in the network can happen accidentally, due to network latencies. If two miners find different solutions for the same block at the same time, which are both valid, it is possible for the network to temporarily split. When this happens, the nodes in the network have two alternative versions of the ledger on different parts of the network. This creates two parallel blockchain networks. The Bitcoin protocol has a provision to resolve these temporal splits so that only one branch of the network survives. In a Proof-of-Work network like Bitcoin, the network with the most „cumulative Proof-of-Work," also referred to as "hashing power" or "network power," is always considered the valid one by the network nodes. In this process, the winning ledger version gets determined by a majority "vote" of the network. Nodes vote for a version by upgrading the protocol (or not). The "length of the blockchain" refers to the network branch with the most cumulative Proof-of-Work, not the one with the most blocks.

---

[5] *The Ethereum hard fork resulted from "TheDAO" incident, where around 50 million USD was drained as a result of a vulnerability in the code. The hard fork, which retroactively censored the transaction that led to the drain, was highly politicized. Opponents of the hard fork insisted on the immutability of the ledger. As a result, the token of the minority network opposing the hard fork - Ethereum Classic - made history for being the first minority network token to be listed on an exchange.*

[6] *Increasing transaction fees on the Bitcoin network due to network congestion was the motivation for a proposal by some developers in the community to increase the block size in a protocol update that required a hard fork. The proposal faced considerable opposition by other network developers. After a two-year debate, the controversial hard fork was conducted in July 2017, and led to the formation of a new community with a different proposal, called Bitcoin Cash. On 1 August 2017, Bitcoin Cash began trading at about 240 USD, while Bitcoin traded at about 2700 USD.*

Alternative Distributed Ledger Systems

The above mentioned forks are a result of protocol upgrades of an existing blockchain network, which all led to a split of the existing network nodes into two groups. Such a split can influence the market price of the network token, as both networks are smaller than the original network. Another form of fork would be a simple software fork typical for open-source projects. As Bitcoin's codebase is open source, anyone can use this codebase as a template and create an alternative block-chain network by adapting some variables, parameters, or functions.

Over the years, the Bitcoin protocol has been modified hundreds of times to create alternative versions of Bitcoin that are either faster or more anonymous, such as "Litecoin" or "Zcash." At some point, it became clear that a blockchain protocol provides an operating system that allows a group of people who do not know or trust each other to organize themselves around specific objectives, not only "money without banks." Many projects, therefore, tried to modify the Bitcoin codebase to facilitate other types of P2P value transfers, like decentralized file storage without Amazon Web Services, as in the case of "Sia," or social networks without Facebook, Twitter, and the like, as in the case of "Steemit." The idea emerged to move away from single-purpose networks that only have one smart contract[7], and instead create a protocol where you can perform any type of P2P value transaction over the same network. Some of the most interesting early projects were "Colored Coins" and "Mastercoin." They used the Bitcoin token as a piggyback vehicle for any kind of value transfer or legal contract. Vitalik Buterin, who was involved in those projects for a short while, realized that these adaptations of the Bitcoin protocol were possible but not efficient or flexible enough. Subsequently, he introduced the idea of decoupling the smart contract functionalities from the processing functionalities of the network and started the Ethereum project. This allowed for a more flexible development environment than the Bitcoin network and other special-purpose blockchain networks. The Ethereum network, for the first time, introduced a decentralized network that allowed for the processing of any type of value transfer using smart contracts. These smart contracts can be easily created with a few lines of code, and are processed by the Ethereum network, without the necessity of creating your own special-purpose blockchain infrastructure. Unlike the Bitcoin network, which is designed for a single smart contract that settles P2P remittances, the Ethereum network is designed as a decentralized computer network on which any kind of smart contract can be processed using the Ethereum Virtual Machine

---

[7] *Smart contracts are computer programs that regulate, audit, and execute arbitrary rules of token transfer that have been written in the code. These rules are self-enforced by consensus of all computers in the network, the blockchain network (read more: Part 2 - Smart Contracts).*

(EVM) and any type of tokenized value can be transferred (read more: Part 2 - Smart Contracts, Part 3 - Tokens).

The emergence of Ethereum inspired many newer blockchain projects to develop similar smart contract networks. Examples of such projects include: "Cardano," "Neo," "EOS," "Hyperledger Fabric," "Ontology," and many more. There are various factors that will be relevant for the assessment of their feasibility, such as technical, economic, and legal factors. It is still unclear which alternative solutions to the Ethereum network could become popular, and whether there will be a "winner takes all" scenario or a co-existence of multiple networks. For now, the Ethereum community seems to have the biggest traction, and the first-mover advantage with many developers, but this can change.

Furthermore, alternative distributed ledger systems have emerged with completely different types of consensus mechanisms, such as directed acyclic graphs (DAGs) that do not require the creation of a chain of blocks anymore, and instead use alternative cryptoeconomic mechanisms to reach consensus. Examples of networks that use DAGs as a consensus mechanism are "IOTA," "Byteball," or "Nano."

On the other hand, private institutions like banks, insurance companies, and many supplychain-heavy industries realized that the concept of collective data management by a distributed ledger system could be a useful industry collaboration tool. As opposed to public and permissionless blockchain networks, the industry started to design "permissioned ledgers," where all validators are members of an industry consortium, or at least separate legal entities of the same organization. However, the term "blockchain" in the context of permissioned and private networks is highly controversial and disputed. Critics question whether a permissioned ledger, where you have "trust by authority," can be considered a blockchain network at all. Proponents of permissioned ledgers argue that the term "blockchain" applies to any distributed data structure where transactions are hashed as linked blocks, and therefore also to permission networks that batch transactions to a chain of blocks.

Public networks use cryptoeconomic mechanisms (trust by math) to keep the network safe with a consensus mechanism that incentivizes individual behavior (computation efforts) to achieve a collective goal. The incentive mechanism is tied to the network token. It is essential to make this network of untrusted actors safe from attacks and manipulation. Permissioned networks, on the other hand, are collectively managed by a set of network actors who know and trust each other and don't need computationally intense consensus mechanisms like Proof-of-Work, and don't need a token. Trust relies on the legal system and the reputation of known network actors (trust by legal contract). The least common denominator of these networks is the existence of a distributed ledger. This is why the term "distributed ledger" has emerged as a more general term to describe technologies that

Blockchain Concept
Ethereum and similar networks

Smart Contracts
Automated policy enforcement (App)

Automated agreements on application level that define the
business logic and behavioral rulesets of all participants.

Application

Record of Transactions (Ledger)
Assets

File (ledger) containing all information, tracking all assets since
genesis block, which is stored on every (full) node of the network.

Consensus Rules
Automated policy enforcement (Infratructure)

Encoded rulesets of all rights and obligations of all nodes in the
network: conditions under which transactions are created, sent,
and verified by the network, including economic incentive (token)
& the creation/referencing of identities & addresses.

Nodes in the Network
Network

A network of all devices running the blockchain
protocol and keeping records of transactions (ledger).

Distributed Ledger

Data Routing
Transport

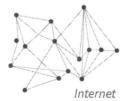

Torrent, Tor, Telehash, etc. (Overlay Networks)
TPC/IP or UDP (Base-Layer Communication)

Internet

have derived from the Bitcoin network. They might be permissioned or permissionless, bundle transactions in chains of blocks or, as in the case of IOTA, not use a chain of blocks at all.

Blockchain protocols and similar distributed ledgers operate on top of the Internet and can be conceptualized in several components: (i) physical network: represented by a P2P network of computers that run the same protocol; (ii) protocol: defines the network rules and enforces them by consensus[8] of all network nodes. This includes economic incentives tied to the native token; (iii) ledger: managing all assets in the form of a shared and public ledger of all transactions from the genesis block until today; (iv) identification & addressing: Assets belong to identities which need to be addressed so we can transfer values from one to another. These identities can be more or less anonymous, depending on the types of cryptographic algorithms used; in the case of the smart contract networks like Ethereum the (v) smart contracts manage the relationships of the involved actors, and represent the business or governance logic.

Alternative Consensus Mechanisms to PoW

Bitcoin's Proof-of-Work is groundbreaking, but it comes at a cost. While it guarantees security in an untrusted network, it is slow, energy intense, and favors those who have more economic resources to spend. This is why many researchers and developers started to explore alternative consensus mechanisms to try to tackle some of Bitcoin's major challenges. The research questions that need to be resolved are:

- How do we reach consensus on one version of history that the majority accepts as true?

- How can one align scarce natural resources (like electricity and CPU) with network resources to prevent malicious actors from spamming the system with bad behavior?

- What are security risks and attack vectors?

Even though many different consensus algorithms are being experimented with, Proof-of-Work and Proof-of-Stake (PoS) are currently the most widely spread. However, it is important to note that blockchain networks using the same general

---

[8] *Smart contracts are computer programs that regulate, audit, and execute arbitrary rules of token transfer that have been written in the code. These rules are self-enforced by consensus of all computers in the network, the blockchain network (read more: Part 2 - Smart Contracts).*

consensus mechanism might have different specifications.[9] The Bitcoin and Ethereum networks use different variations of Proof-of-Work.

The same is true for Proof-of-Stake, a consensus mechanism where only network actors who have a financial stake in the network can add the blocks to the ledger. As opposed to Proof-of-Work, validators don't compete with each other to create a block of transactions. Instead of sacrificing energy to validate a block, users must prove they own a certain amount of the network tokens to generate a block. The tokens in your wallet represent your stake. There are many variations of Proof-of-Stake implementations.

Early Proof-of-Stake proposals assumed that those who have more stake in the system have a natural incentive to act in a truthful manner when validating transactions and writing blocks. It was assumed that token holders would have a natural interest in the long-term success of the network; otherwise, their stake in the system would devalue if they were to contribute in an untruthful manner. It was furthermore assumed that the more tokens one owns, the more one has at stake if the network is attacked. Voting rights were therefore designed proportional to the amount of network tokens held. However, there is a problem in the original Proof-of-Stake mechanism: as opposed to Proof-of-Work, where mining is costly, and it is therefore not smart to waste your energy on a fork that won't earn you any money, Proof-of-Stake does not require computationally intensive work to create a block. It is assumed that the validator has nothing to lose but a lot to win.

The "Peercoin" network was the first project to introduce Proof-of-Stake. Other networks followed with their own variations of Proof-of-Stake, such as "Tendermint" ("Cosmos"), "Ouroboros" ("Cardano"), "Tezos," "Dfinity," "Nxt," "BlackCoin," "NuShares/NuBits," and "Qora," each of which have different properties. Some, like "Decred," combine elements of both Proof-of-Work and Proof-of-Stake. The Ethereum project is planning to transition from Proof-of-Work to Proof-of-Stake with a hard fork (Casper). Ethereum developers have developed different proposals of how this should be done.

Delegated Proof-of-Stake (DPoS) is a variation of Proof-of-Stake, first implemented by "BitShares". It is a more radical variation, a kind of representative democracy where token owners can transfer their vote to delegates to validate on their behalf. There are generally between 21 and 101 elected delegates that might be shuffled periodically or given an order to deliver their blocks in. These delegates can create blocks and prevent non-trusted parties from creating blocks. They can-

---

[9] *Proof-of-Work in Bitcoin and Ethereum differ. Examples of such differences are: varying in type of hashing algorithms (SHA-256 vs. Ethash), varying average block time target (10 minutes vs. ~15 seconds), and varying payout schemes (only actual block producer vs. some non-accepted blocks are rewarded, e.g. Uncles).*

not change transactions, but they can veto specific transactions from being included in the next network block. Different networks have adopted their own variation of DPoS, examples of which are "Steemit," "EOS," and "Lisk." Instead of competing on validating blocks, each delegate has a time slot to publish their block. Token holders can withdraw their vote for a delegate, if delegates continually miss their blocks or publish invalid transactions. This partial centralization of block creation results in better transaction throughput (also referred to as "scalability") than most other consensus mechanisms.

There are even more variations of Proof-of-Stake, most of which are only conceptual or have been implemented by one network only: "Leased Proof-of-Stake," "Transactions as Proof-of-Stake," "Proof-of-Importance," "Proof-of-Capacity," "Proof-of-Weight," "Proof-of-Authority," and "Proof-of-Elapsed-Time."

Another group of consensus mechanisms are variations of Byzantine Fault Tolerance (BFT) like Federated Byzantine Agreements (FBA) as implemented by "Ripple" or "Stellar", Practical Byzantine Fault Tolerance (pBFT) as implemented by "Hyperledger Fabric", and Delegated Byzantine Fault Tolerance (dBFT) as used in "NEO." Yet another group of protocols uses a combination of mechanisms, such as "Hashgraph" that combines asynchronous Byzantine Fault Tolerance with "gossip protocols" and "virtual voting" mechanisms.

Furthermore, there is a whole series of protocols that use Directed Acyclic Graphs, such as "IoT Chain," "Byteball," "Nano" (Block Lattice), and IOTA (Tangle). The consensus mechanism of DAGs is fundamentally different from blockchains. Instead of bundling data together into blocks that are then confirmed one after another, Directed Acyclic Graphs require newly added data to reference and validate past data. Usually, each new transaction would have to reference and validate two transactions that came before. In doing so, the network comes to form a graph of converging and confirmed transactions. If a node incorrectly validates a past transaction, that node's transaction would fail to be confirmed by other participants.

Explaining each of the consensus mechanisms listed above in detail is beyond the scope of this book and would require one or several dedicated publications. Literature on these protocols in the context of distributed ledgers is still scarce but growing. However, many of these protocols are still in a conceptual stage, without proper documentation. In many cases they are implemented by one project only, sometimes without being properly researched, or without having undergone the academic peer-review process.

Public Ledgers vs. Private Ledgers

	Public Permissionless	Private Invite Only
Access	Read & write is public to anyone.	Read & write is upon invitation only.
Network Actors	Don't know each other.	Know each other.
Native Token	Yes	Not necessary
Security	Economic Incentives Proof-of-Work Proof-of-Stake Proof-of-Space Proof-of-Burn etc.	Legal Contracts Proof-of-Authority
Speed	Slower	Faster
Examples	Bitcoin Ethereum Monero Zcash Steemit Dash Litecoin Stellar, etc.	R3 (Banks) EWF (Energy) B3i (Insurance) Corda
Effects	Lower infrastructure cost: no need to maintain servers or system admins. Decentralized applications run on a public & permissionless infrastructure at a fraction costs. P2P processes can radically change market dynamics and generate completely new business & governance models.	Reduces transaction costs and data redundancies, replacing legacy systems with an industry solution. Not likely to change market dynamics Similar to SAP in the 1990s: Reduces costs, but not disruptive for business models.

With or without a Token?

With the advent of derived technologies using modified governance rules to the original Bitcoin protocol, it seems necessary to classify different distributed ledger systems. The main distinction is designed around the question of who is allowed to (i) validate transactions, (ii) write transactions to the ledger, and (iii) read transactions, and (iv) use the network. Depending on the type of ledger, the answer will vary. To keep things simple, we can say that in public networks, anyone can read, write, and validate transactions and use the network. Whereas in private networks, only invited members can read, write, and validate transactions and use the network. Hybrid variations are also possible. An example would be that validating and writing transactions is invite only, but reading (certain) transactions is public.

In public and permissionless networks, all nodes participating in the consensus protocol are untrusted, as they are not known beforehand. Without the permission of a centralized entity, anyone can download the protocol and the current version of the ledger to:

- Run a full node on their local device, validating transactions in the network.

- Mine a block of transactions, adding data to the ledger, thus participating in the consensus process (Proof-of-Work) and earning network tokens in the process.

- Send tokens through the network and expect to see them included in the ledger if the transaction is valid.

- Use public block-explorer software to real all transactions-related data in the network, or conduct chain analysis (big data) on all blockchain-related data stored on a full node.

The consensus mechanism for such a setup has to account for maliciousness. The token is an essential component to make this network of untrusted actors attack resistant. While tokenized incentives make the untrusted networks safe, they also make them very slow. Public and permissionless networks can only handle a few transactions per second, which makes them unfeasible for large-scale applications with high transaction volumes. However, various technological solutions are currently being proposed and implemented to resolve these scalability issues (read more: Annex - Scalability Solutions).

Private and permissioned ledgers, on the other hand, have a federated setup with bilateral contractual agreements. It's an invite-only members club. The network is not accessible to arbitrary participants. Members trust each other because they have bilateral contractual agreements with each other, and if anything goes wrong, they know who to sue. Permissioned ledgers, therefore, do not need a token to incentivize coordinated action, whereas it is integral to permissionless networks. The fact that the identities of all participating nodes are known beforehand provides a natural protection against "sybil attacks." Private and permissioned ledgers can therefore settle many more transactions per second, as they don't have to deal with an unknown amount of anonymous nodes. They also provide more privacy than current state-of-the-art public blockchain networks, since the ledger data is not publicly accessible. Permissioned ledgers are mostly being developed by industry consortia. Transaction verification is conducted by a pre-selected set of participants, for example, sixty financial institutions, each of which operates a node, and where forty must sign each block in order for the block to be valid. Depending on the industry and use case, the right to read data of the ledger may be public, partially public, or restricted to the participants.

While most blockchain literature makes a binary distinction between permissioned and permissionless ledgers, I would like to argue that there is no such thing as "100 percent permissionless." Every consensus mechanism requires a minimum threshold of investment that one needs to make in order to be able to validate transactions or write to the ledger. However, most of the world population does not have the economic means to purchase a specialized hardware powerful enough to mine Bitcoin tokens. Even for a full node that only validates transactions in a public blockchain network, and does not require the same level of hardware investment as a mining node, one would need to invest in a regular PC. At the time of writing this book, buying a PC means that one would have to spend at least a few hundred EUR[10] to validate transactions. While 500 EUR is not much money for an average European household, it surpasses the monthly income of a considerable part of the world's population. Not to mention the costs needed for a mining computer.

Also, while for example a "Proof-of-Stake"–based consensus is public, it is not entirely permissionless. The consensus mechanism requires you to own a minimum amount of network tokens to be eligible to validate transactions. "Permissionless" is therefore a relative term that we cannot use in a binary way but rather as a gradient, ranging from "less permissioned" to "fully permissioned." In such an early stage of distributed ledger systems, permissioned solutions can be useful in highly regulated industries that want to build on a distributed ledger but are subject to government regulation. Industry advocates claim that federated solutions can provide higher levels of efficiency and security and lessen fraud problems of

---

[10] It is possible to run a full node on a Raspberry PI (an affordable mini computer) and an SD card, which would be less than 100 EUR. However, you still need a regular PC to download the full blockchain (at least BTC and ETH). Once the full ledger is downloaded, one can run a full node on a Raspberry PI.

traditional financial institutions. It is not very likely that private blockchains will revolutionize the financial system, but they can replace legacy systems, making the industry more efficient. Permissioned ledgers might also be one step toward a wider adoption of public and permissionless networks, once the underlying technology becomes more scalable and mature, and better understood by regulators.

It is unclear how the technology will pan out in the medium-to-long run. Some predict that permissioned ledgers might suffer the same fate as "Intranets" in the early 1990s, when private companies built their own private networks, because they were afraid to connect with the public Internet. Over time, this fear disappeared. Today, Intranets are used in very limited cases where high levels of security are required.

Use Cases & Applications

Blockchain networks and derived distributed ledger systems provide an infrastructure for rights management. Every process, task, and payment would have a digital record and signature that could be identified, validated, stored, and shared. Many tasks of intermediaries like lawyers, brokers, bankers, and public administrators might be replaced by distributed ledger systems. Individuals, organizations, machines, and algorithms can now interact with one another with little friction and a fraction of current transaction costs. This new infrastructure allows for many new applications, the most important of which are:

- Transparency & control: Blockchain networks and other distributed ledgers allow more transparency and control along the supply chain of goods and services, including financial services that have been tokenized, which would resolve many questions around supply chain transparency, reduction of corruption, and more control over what happens to our private data.

- Reduction of bureaucracy: Smart contracts and similar rights management solutions have the potential to reduce bureaucracy and the coordination costs of business transactions (read more: Part 2 - Smart Contracts).

- Resolve principal-agent dilemma of organizations: Distributed ledgers also provide a global coordination tool for new types of decentralized and sometimes also autonomous organizations (read more: Part 2 - Institutional Economics & Governance of DAOs).

- Tokens as the killer-app: Cryptographic tokens as an application of blockchain networks and derived ledgers might be as revolutionary as the emergence of the WWW, which allowed the creation of visually appealing web pages with just a few lines of code, and surfing the Internet by following links instead of using command-line interfaces. It has become just as easy to create a token with a few lines of smart contract code (read more: Part 3 & Part 4).

One of the biggest use cases of distributed ledgers is transparency and provenance along the supply chain of goods and services. Supply chains represent a complex network of geographically distant and legally independent entities that exchange goods, payments, and documents across a dynamic network. Their architecture is quite similar to blockchain networks, but as opposed to blockchain networks, all documents are managed in data silos. As a result, document handling systems along these supply-chain networks are often inefficient, have complex interfaces, and are cost intense. Sustainable behavior of companies and individuals alike is hard to track and not well rewarded. Buyers and sellers have little or no information about the provenance of the products they buy, including potential fraud, pollution, or human rights abuses.

Distributed ledgers allow a disparate group of network actors along a supply chain to exchange data seamlessly. Documents and transactions can be processed in almost real time, since auditing and enforcement can be automated, mitigating challenges such as multiple document copies and data inconsistencies. Tracking the provenance of goods and services along global supply chains can become much more feasible than today. Web3-based solutions can provide (i) more transparency of environmental impacts and (ii) origins, production type, and ingredients of the food we eat, and conditions under which the plants are grown or how animals are treated. Many companies and industry initiatives, such as "Provenance," "Ambrosus," "Modum," "OriginTrail," "Vechain," "Wabi," or "Wantonchain," have started to implement Web3-based infrastructures to optimize their value chains, improve inefficiencies, free up working capital, and make goods and services more accessible. Such solutions, however, always need a combination of a set of technologies, including machine learning algorithms and data from the physical Web, the Internet of Things (read more: Part 2 - Smart Contract Oracles). Distributed ledger applications can also provide better accountability regarding human rights, such as general working conditions, child labor, or fair wages. Projects working on such solutions: "bext360," "fairfood," and "Namahe." They can further be used to provide more control over our private data (read more: Part 1 - User-Centric Identities - Data Protection) and create P2P data markets (Ocean Protocol). While in theory this level of transparency of what happened to one's private data could also be provided with current solutions, we would have to trust a centralized institution.

Chapter Summary

- *Blockchain networks are public infrastructures that collectively maintain a shared and distributed ledger, where immutable and encrypted copies of the information are stored on every computer in the network.*

- *The ledger contains all transactions ever made. Transactions are stored in a tamper-proof fashion: alteration in a block will change the subsequent blocks. The ledger, stored on all the computers of the network, guarantees that each token is transferred only once. It acts as a digital notary, and a publicly verifiable timestamp.*

- *All network participants have equal access to the same data in real time. Transactions processed by the network are transparent to all actors and can be traced back to their origin.*

- *Unlike distributed databases, blockchains allow for distributed control, where different parties that do not trust each other can share information without requiring a central administrator. Algorithmic administration of business logic and governance rules, with consensus protocols and smart contracts provide for the next level of automation of our socio-economic activities*

- *Blockchain builds on the idea of P2P networks and provides a universal data set that every actor can trust, even though they might not know or trust each other. People and institutions who do not know or trust each other and reside in different countries, being subject to different jurisdictions, and who have no legally binding agreements with each other can now interact over the Internet without the need for trusted third parties like banks, Internet platforms, or other types of clearing institutions.*

- *Ideas around cryptographically secured P2P networks have been discussed in the academic environment in different evolutionary stages since the 1980s. However, before the emergence of Bitcoin, there had never been a practical implementation of a P2P network that managed to avoid the double-spending problem, without the need for trusted intermediaries guaranteeing value exchange.*

- *The "double-spending problem" refers to the fact that in the current Internet, digital money, in the form of a file, can be copied, and copies of that same digital file can be sent from one computer to multiple other computers at the same time.*

- *Consensus mechanisms, such as Proof-of-Work, allow for distributed control. They are based on the combination of economic incentives and cryptography. Applied game theory is used to reward network actors with a native network token. This reward mechanism is designed in a way that it is economically infeasible to cheat the network. It makes it exceedingly difficult to falsify the blockchain, due to the immense amount of computing power that would be required to do so.*

- As opposed to public and permissionless networks, permissioned networks are invite only, which means that all validators are members of a consortium.

- "Distributed ledger" has emerged as an umbrella term used to describe technologies which distribute records or information among all those using it, whether permissioned or permissionless, and independent of their consensus mechanisms or data structures.

Chapter References & Further Reading

- Agreda, Victor: "Taxonomy of Blockchain Consensus",
  https://strategiccoin.com/taxonomy-of-blockchains-consensus-2018/

- Antonopoulos, Andreas; „Bitcoin security model: trust by computation". Radar. O'Reilly, 2014,
  Archived from the original on 31 October 2018:
  http://radar.oreilly.com/2014/02/bitcoin-security-model-trust-by-computation.html

- Antonopoulos, Andreas M.; "Mastering Bitcoin. Unlocking Digital Cryptocurrencies", Sebastopol, CA: O'Reilly Media, 2014

- Back, Adam; „A partial hash collision based postage scheme", October 2014
  http://www.hashcash.org/papers/announce.txt

- Ballandies, Mark C.; Dapp, Marcus M.; Pournaras, Evangelos: "Decrypting Distributed Ledger Design - Taxonomy, Classification and Blockchain Community Evaluation", 2018: https://arxiv.org/pdf/1811.03419.pdf

- Bitcoin.Wiki contributors: "Softfork", Bitcoin Wiki: https://en.bitcoin.it/wiki/Softfork (accessed Nov 30, 2018).

- Buterin, Vitalik: "The Meaning of Decentralization", Feb 6, 2017:
  https://medium.com/@VitalikButerin/the-meaning-of-decentralization-a0c92b76a274

- Buterin, Vitalik: "On Public and Private Blockchains", Aug 6, 2015:
  https://blog.ethereum.org/2015/08/07/on-public-and-private-blockchains/

- Catalini, Christian; Gans, Joshua S.; „Some Simple Economics of the Blockchain".
  SSRN Electronic Journal, 2016

- Ethereum White Paper: https://github.com/ethereum/wiki/wiki/White-Paper

- Ethereum Yellow Paper: https://ethereum.github.io/yellowpaper/paper.pdf

- Gervais, Arthur; Karame, Ghassan O.; Capkun, Vedran; Capkun, Srdjan. „Is Bitcoin a Decentralized
  Currency?", InfoQ & IEEE computer society, Archived from the original on 10 Nov 2018:
  https://www.researchgate.net/publication/270802537_Is_Bitcoin_a_Decentralized_Currency

- Golden, Sara; Price, Allison: "Sustainable Supply Chains. Better Global Outcomes with Blockchain."
  Jan 2018, retrieved from: https://www.newamerica.org/documents/2067/BTA_Supply_Chain_Report_r2.pdf

- Jackson, Matthew O.: "Mechanism Theory", Humanities and Social Sciences 228-77, California Institute
  of Technology Pasadena, California 91125, U.S.A. October 12, 2000, revised December 8, 2003

- Kravchenko, Pavel: "Ok, I need a blockchain, but which one?", Sep 26, 2016:
  https://medium.com/@pavelkravchenko/ok-i-need-a-blockchain-but-which-one-ca75c1e2100

- Nakamoto, Satoshi: "Bitcoin: A Peer-to-Peer Electronic Cash System", 2008: https://bitcoin.org/bitcoin.pdf

- N.N. "A Crash Course in Mechanism Design for Cryptoeconomic Applications - Understanding the
  Basic Fundamentals of "Cryptoeconomics", BlockChannel, Oct 17, 2017: https://medium.com/block-
  channel/a-crash-course-in-mechanism-design-for-cryptoeconomic-applications-a9f06ab6a976

- N.N.: „Blockchains: The great chain of being sure about things", The Economist, 31 October 2015:
  https://www.economist.com/briefing/2015/10/31/the-great-chain-of-being-sure-about-things

- Poelstra, Andrew: "Mimblewimble", 2016-10-06 (commit e9f45ec)
  diyhpl.us/~bryan/papers2/bitcoin/mimblewimble-andytoshi-draft-2016-10-20.pdf

- Satyawan, Tarar *"A Crash Course on Consensus Protocols"*, May 9, 2018: https://medium.com/@satyawan.tarar1985/a-crash-course-on-consensus-protocols-29264c393097
- Tasca, Paolo; Tessone, Claudio J.: *"A Taxonomy of Blockchain Technologies: Principles of Identification and Classification"*, Ledger, Vol 4, 2019: http://ledger.pitt.edu/ojs/index.php/ledger/issue/view/5
- Stark, Josh: *"Making Sense of Cryptoeconomics"*, Aug 19, 2017 https://www.coindesk.com/making-sense-cryptoeconomics
- Tomaino, Nick, *"Cryptoeconomics 10"*, Jun 4, 2017, https://thecontrol.co/cryptoeconomics-101-e5c883e9a8ff
- Wang, Wenbo; Dinh Thai Hoang, Hu, Peizhao; Xiong, Zehui; Niyato, Dusit; Wang, Ping; Wen, Yonggang; In Kim, Dong: *"A Survey on Consensus Mechanisms and Mining Strategy Management in Blockchain Networks"*: https://arxiv.org/pdf/1805.02707.pdf
- Wei, Bai: *"Mechanism Design in Cryptoeconomics"*, May 31, 2018: https://medium.com/secbit-media/mechanism-design-in-cryptoeconomics-6630673b79af
- Voshmgir, Shermin: *"Blockchain & Sustainability,"* Crypto3conomics blog, Medium, Aug 11, 2018, retrieved from: https://medium.com/crypto3conomics/blockchain-sustainability-7d1dd90e9db6
- Wikipedia contributors: „Blockchain," Wikipedia, The Free Encyclopedia, https://en.wikipedia.org/wiki/Blockchain (accessed Nov 11, 2018).
- Witherspoon, Zane :*"A Hitchhiker's Guide to Consensus Algorithms,"* November 28th 2017: https://hackernoon.com/a-hitchhikers-guide-to-consensus-algorithms-d81aae3eb0e3
- Bitcoin 51% Attack Calculator: https://gobitcoin.io/tools/cost-51-attack/
- 51% Attack Calculator: https://crypto51.app/
- Ambrosus: https://ambrosus.com/
- Bitcoin Gold: https://bitcoingold.org/
- Bitcoin Diamond: https://www.bitcoindiamond.org/
- Bitcoin Cash: https://www.bitcoincash.org/
- Bitcoin Platinum: https://bitcoinplatinum.github.io/
- BitShares: https://bitshares.org/
- Block Lattice: https://docs.nano.org/integration-guides/the-basics/#block-lattice-design
- BlackCoin: http://blackcoin.co/
- Bitcoin Cash: https:bitcoincash.org/
- Byteball: https://byteball.org/
- Cardano: https://cardano.org/en/home/
- Colored Coins: http://coloredcoins.org/
- Cosmos: https://cosmos.com/
- Decred: https://decred.org/
- Dfinity: https://dfinity.org/
- fairfood: http://fairfood.nl/
- Ethereum Classic: https://ethereumclassic.org/
- EOS: https://eos.io/
- Hyperledger Fabric: https://hyperledger.org/projects/fabric
- Litecoin: https://litecoin.org/
- Lisk: https://lisk.io/
- IOTA: https://iota.org/
- IoT Chain: https://iotchain.io/
- Mastercoin: https://en.wikipedia.org/wiki/Mastercoin

- *Modum: https://modum.io/*
- *Nano: https://nano.org/*
- *Neo: https://neo.org/*
- *Nxt: https://nxt.org/*
- *NuShares/NuBits: https://nubits.com/nushares*
- *Ocean: https://oceanprotocol.com/*
- *OriginTrail: https://origintrail.io/*
- *Provenance: https://provenance.org/*
- *Qora: http://www.qora.org/*
- *Ontology: https://ont.io/*
- *Ripple: https://ripple.com/*
- *Stellar: https://stellar.org/*
- *Steemit: https://steemit.com/*
- *Tezos: https://tezos.com/*
- *Vechain: https://www.vechain.org/*
- *Wabi: https://wacoin.io/*
- *Wantonchain: https://www.waltonchain.org/*

Token Security: Cryptography

Cryptography is an important tool for the secure management of tokens in a network of anonymous and untrusted actors. It allows for transparency of interactions while maintaining the privacy of all network actors. Cryptography is used to trustfully identify all network actors and is also an integral part of the consensus protocol in a blockchain network.

Cryptography is the practice and study of secure communication in the presence of third parties. The aim is to create information systems that are resilient against eavesdropping, manipulation, and other forms of attack. While the history of cryptology dates back to the advent of handwritten texts, it has evolved significantly in the computer age. Cryptography represents a subfield of cryptology and mainly refers to the process of encryption, where a piece of information (plaintext) is converted into unintelligible text (ciphertext). A ciphertext is unreadable without the corresponding cipher to decrypt it.

Ciphers were one of the first encryption techniques developed to encrypt plain text with either substitution ciphers (where units of plaintext are replaced with single letters, pairs of letters, or triplets of letters) or transposition ciphers (where units of the plaintext are rearranged in a different and usually quite complex order). Decryption is the process of converting the unreadable ciphertext back to the original plaintext. A cipher is, therefore, a pair of algorithms that creates the encryption as well as the reversing decryption: It is designed in a way that makes it easy to encrypt a message, but very hard to reverse it if you don't know the code.

Historically, cryptography has been used in various forms, such as a carved ciphertext on a stone in Egypt. Other forms of ciphers date back to Sassanid Persia, Ancient Greece, The Roman Empire, India, etc. Since the development of the enigma machine (a rotor cipher machine) in World War I, and the emergence of computers in World War II, cryptographic applications and methods have radically evolved. Classical ciphers became redundant because they were very easy to guess with simple "brute-force attacks," where a computer algorithm runs all possible combinations until it guesses the right code. Computers not only enhanced the possibilities of cryptanalysis, which refers to the process of breaking encryption, they also made more complex ciphers possible. Modern cryptographic algorithms are designed to be infeasible to break them in terms of time and money applying brute-force. However, such "computational hardness assumptions" have to consider the continuous increase in processing power of computers.

Computers, furthermore, introduced new forms of encryption of any kind of digital information, not only pieces of text. With the advent of quantum computers, many researchers are studying the relationship between cryptographic problems and quantum physics. Post-quantum cryptography is being developed by some researchers and engineers who have already started factoring in potential effects of quantum computing when designing new algorithms. In the information age, the use of cryptography also raises many legal questions. Some governments limit or prohibit the use of cryptography, and in some cases, even classify it as a weapon. Certain jurisdictions might permit government authorities to mandate the disclosure of encryption keys for documents that could be relevant to an investigation. Additionally, cryptography can be an interesting factor when discussing human rights in a digital era. The question of how to guarantee privacy in the machine age is slowly becoming a discussion led by a wider general public, and will probably become more dominant in the years to come. The crucial question, in this context, is whether and how the constitutional right to privacy of communication, or the sanctity of one's home, could correspond to the right to encrypted communication or encrypted data trails (read more: Part 3 - Privacy Tokens).

While early attempts to encrypt electronic communication focused on providing secrecy and preserving technologies for the communications of government institutions, the field has expanded. Over the past decades, encryption technologies have been applied in various other domains, such as electronic commerce, digital payments, digital rights management, password management, message integrity checking, authentication of identity, digital signatures, interactive proofs, and secure computation. In the context of blockchain networks and other distributed ledgers, cryptography is used for identification, verification, and security purposes on the core protocol level. Three relevant cryptographic building blocks are used in the context of public blockchain networks and other Web3 technologies: (i) hash functions, (ii) symmetric cryptography, and (iii) asymmetric cryptography (public-key cryptography).

Hash Functions are mathematical algorithms that convert any type of data of an arbitrary size (message) into data of a fixed size (hash value or hash). The only way to recreate the original data (message) from the hash is to attempt to try all possible variations to see if they produce a match. While this is possible, it is time consuming and therefore expensive, which is why it is referred to as a one-way function. Hash functions can be used for assuring the integrity of transmitted data and privacy. Selected applications are digital signatures, authentication services, fingerprinting, detection of duplicates, unique identification of files, or the creation of checksums to detect data corruption. In order to be considered resilient, cryptographic hash functions need to fulfill certain properties: They need to be designed in a way that they are (i) easy to compute; (ii) deterministic, meaning that the same message always results in the same hash; (iii) time consuming and expensive to generate a message from its hash value with sheer brute force; (iv) small changes to the original input value should change the hash value. It should furthermore be (v) infeasible to find two different messages (input) with the same hash value (output).

Symmetric Systems: Before the emergence of public-key cryptography, two parties relied on one encryption key that they exchanged over a non-cryptographic method, through secret meetings, sealed envelopes, or trusted couriers. If you wanted to communicate privately with somebody, you would need to physically meet and agree on a secret key. In the world of modern communications, where one needs to coordinate over a network of many untrusted actors (the Internet), such methods would not be feasible. This is why symmetric encryption is not used for communication in public networks. It is, however, faster and more efficient than asymmetric encryption, and therefore used for encrypting large amounts of data, certain payment applications, or random number generation.

Asymmetric Systems, also referred to as public-key cryptography, resolved the coordination problem by introducing two keys, a public key and a private key. The private key is only known to the owner and needs to be kept private, while the public key may be given to anyone. The public key can be broadcasted to the network, which allows anyone in the network to use the public keys to send an encrypted message to the "owner" of the public-key. This encrypted message can only be decrypted with the receiver's private key. Senders can combine a message with their private key to create a digital signature on the message. Now, anyone can verify with the corresponding public key whether the signature is valid. How the keys are generated depends on the cryptographic algorithms used. Examples of asymmetric systems include RSA (Rivest-Shamir-Adleman) and ECC (Elliptic-Curve Cryptography), which is also used in Bitcoin. Use of asymmetric cryptography enhanced the security of communication in untrusted networks, like the Internet, in a scalable way.[11] The following chapters will focus on how cryptography is used in the Bitcoin network and similar blockchain networks.

---

[11] *While elliptic-curve cryptography provides the same level of security as RSA, it needs less computation and smaller key size, thus reducing storage and transmission requirements. It therefore allows for reduced storage and transmission requirements.*

Symmetric Key Cryptography

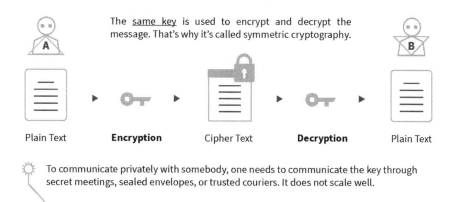

The <u>same key</u> is used to encrypt and decrypt the message. That's why it's called symmetric cryptography.

Plain Text   **Encryption**   Cipher Text   **Decryption**   Plain Text

To communicate privately with somebody, one needs to communicate the key through secret meetings, sealed envelopes, or trusted couriers. It does not scale well.

Asymmetric Key Cryptography

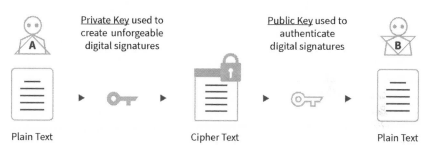

<u>Private Key</u> used to create unforgeable digital signatures

<u>Public Key</u> used to authenticate digital signatures

Plain Text   Cipher Text   Plain Text

Resolved the coordination problem by introducing two keys, a public key and a private key. The private key is only known to the owner and needs to be kept private, but the public key may be given to anyone. Senders can combine a message with their private key to create a digital signature on the message. Anyone with the corresponding public key can now verify whether the signature is valid.

The Bitcoin network mainly uses hashes in combination with digital signatures to protect the integrity of the data flowing through the network using public-key cryptography. Hashes are furthermore used in the context of the consensus protocol "Proof-of-Work." Bitcoin uses public-key cryptography, and more specifically, elliptic-curve cryptography. Please note that alternative blockchain networks and other distributed ledger systems might use alternative cryptographic tools to the ones described below. Some blockchain networks, for example, use more privacy-preserving cryptography, such as "Zcash" (zero-knowledge proofs)[12] and "Monero" (ring signatures)[13]. The Bitcoin community itself is currently looking into alternative cryptographic signature schemes that are more privacy preserving and more scalable, for example, with "Mimblewimble" (read more: Part 3 - Privacy Tokens).

Public-Key Cryptography

The Bitcoin network uses public-key cryptography to create a secure digital reference about the identity of a user with a set of cryptographic keys: a private key and a public key. Secure digital references about who is who, and who owns what, are the basis for P2P transactions. In combination with a transaction, these keys can create a digital signature that proves ownership of one's tokens and allows control of the tokens with a wallet software. Similar to how a check is signed by hand, and passwords are used to authenticate in Internet banking, public-key cryptography is used to authenticate and sign Bitcoin transactions.

The public key is mathematically generated from the private key. While it is very easy to compute the public key from the private key, the reverse is only possible with sheer brute force; guessing the key is possible but prohibitively expensive. It would take the world's most powerful supercomputer trillions of years to crack, making it practically impossible. This means that, even though one's public key is known to everybody, nobody can derive one's private key from it. A message that is encrypted with the public key can now travel securely to the owner of the private key, and only the owner of this private key is able to decrypt the message. This method also works the other way around. Any message with a private key can be verified with the corresponding public key.

An analog example for a public key would be the example of a padlock. If Bob wants to send a message to Alice, but is scared that somebody might intercept and read it, he will ask Alice to send her padlock (unlocked) over to him, and to keep her key to that padlock. Bob can now put his letter in a small box and lock it with the padlock that Alice sent him, closing it with a simple push. The letter can now be sent around the world without being intercepted by an unauthorized per-

---

[12] *Zero-knowledge proofs cryptography allows for the validation of information without revealing that information with the verifier of that information.*

[13] *Ring signatures can be used to obfuscate the identity of token owners, combining a group of partial digital signatures from various transactions sent by different users, to form a unique signature that is used to sign a transaction.*

son. Only Alice, who has the key to her padlock, can open the letter. Of course, someone could try and break the box with sheer brute force, instead of using the key. While it is possible, the difficulty would depend on the resilience of the box, and the strength of the lock. The same basic principles apply to modern cryptography.

Secure Algorithms

The crucial question in public-key cryptography revolves around computational hardness assumptions: How one can widen the computational effort between deriving the private key from the public key, compared to deriving the public key from the private key? How hard is it to break the encryption by guessing the result, how long would it take to guess the private key, and how expensive would it be? The private key is represented by a number, which means that the larger the number, the harder it is to guess that (random) number by someone who does not know the number. If it takes a couple of decades to guess a random number, the number is considered secure. However, every cryptographic algorithm is vulnerable to brute-force attack, which refers to guessing one's private key by trying all possible combinations until a solution fits. As computers are becoming faster and more efficient, one must come up with more sophisticated algorithms, either by using bigger numbers or by inventing more resilient algorithms.

To make sure that it is hard to guess the number, a resilient private key has minimum requirements: It needs to be a (i) randomly generated number. It needs to be a (ii) very large number. It has to use a (iii) secure algorithm for the generation of the keys. Randomness is important, as we don't want any other person or machine to use the same key, and humans are bad at coming up with randomness. Large key sizes allow for further distribution of randomness, and are much harder to crack with brute force, but also slower to compute. Due to their complexity, secure algorithms need to be scientifically proven and stress tested against security breaches. One should avoid inventing one's own algorithm. This issue became obvious when the team developing the IOTA network decided to implement their own hash function, called Curl. IOTA is an alternative distributed ledger solution to blockchain, which claims to resolve Bitcoin's scalability problem with an alternative consensus mechanism and alternative cryptography. Their self-made Curl function, however, was later found to be "non-collision resistant."[14] Since the emergence of

---

[14] *Hashing functions take an arbitrary-length input and return a seemingly random but fixed-length output. When more than one input resolves to the same output, serious problems can result from such a collision. A team of MIT and Boston University researchers found exactly such flaws in the IOTA Curl function. While the IOTA team fixed said vulnerabilities, they claimed that these flaws were introduced on purpose, which was highly criticized by the open-source community.*

Bitcoin, cryptographic algorithms used in the Bitcoin network have withstood all attempts of data-tampering.

Without cryptography, there could be no distributed consensus in a network of actors who do not know or trust each other. As computers get more powerful and can guess numbers faster, the algorithms used will need to withstand time and rapidly evolving technological standards to maintain the current level of security. Many researchers and developers argue that supercomputers, in particular quantum computers, will soon be able to crack most conventional encryption algorithms through brute force. This is not entirely true and depends on the cryptographic algorithm. While quantum computers are not significantly better at cracking hashes, they are much more powerful when it comes to elliptic curves and prime factorization. The answers are complex and not fully resolved yet. Quantum-computer-resistant cryptographic algorithms are, therefore, a mission-critical research area. For more details on this topic, see references at the end of this chapter.

Hashing

Hashing is a method for transforming large amounts of data into short numbers that are difficult to guess. One can convert a text or a picture, which represents a variable-length bit sequence, to produce a fixed-length bit sequence in the form of a hash. These functions ensure data integrity. The Bitcoin network uses Secure Hash Algorithms (SHA), such as SHA-256. An important property of hashes is that if one single bit of input data is changed, the output changes significantly, which makes it easy to detect small changes in large text files, for example. As you can see from the example below,[15] an entirely different hash gets generated when we change only one symbol. This is based on the "avalanche effect," and it is useful for easily providing data integrity. An entirely different string results from hashing the hash.

- *Hash of the sentence **"How to buy Bitcoin?"**:*
  156aedcfab1d49f73abddd89faf78d9930e4b523ab804026310c973bfa707d37

- *Hash of the sentence **"How to buy Bitcoin"**:*
  4314d903f04e90e4a5057685243c903fbcfa4f8ec75ec797e1780ed5c891b1bf

- ***Hashing the hash** produces:*
  4c9622e1148ff0b855de50e62999d194039eb2faa9e715cc9d9ef604015aa1fe

The avalanche effect describes the behavior of a mathematical function where even a slight change in an input string should cause the resulting hash value to

---

[15] *Calculate hash values here: https://www.browserling.com/tools/all-hashes*

change drastically. This means that if one adds only one word, or even a comma, to a document of several hundred pages, the hash of that document will change. A document's hash value can, therefore, serve as a cryptographic twin of the document, which is why it is often referred to as a "digital fingerprint." As a result of this, one does not need to encrypt the entire document with a sender's private key, as this consumes time, bandwidth and money. Instead one can compute the document's hash value.

Hashing in the Bitcoin network is part of the following processes: (i) encoding wallet addresses; (ii) encoding transactions between wallets; (iii) verifying and validating the account balances of wallets; and for the consensus mechanism (iv) Proof-of-Work.

Wallets & Digital Signatures

A blockchain wallet is a piece of software that stores your private key, public key, and blockchain address, and communicates with the blockchain network. This wallet software can run on a computer or a mobile phone (like "Bitcoin Core," "Electrum") or a dedicated hardware device (like "Trezor," "Ledger"). The wallet software allows for user-authentication and the management of tokens. With a wallet software one can send tokens and inspect the receipts of tokens that were sent to you. Every time you send Bitcoin tokens, you need to use a wallet to sign the transaction with your private key. Subsequently, your personal balance of tokens is adjusted on all copies of the ledger, which is distributed across the P2P network of computers.

When launched for the first time, a Bitcoin wallet generates a key pair consisting of a private key and a public key. In a first step, the private key is a randomly generated 256-bit integer. The public key is then mathematically derived, using elliptic-key cryptography, from the private key. In a second step, the blockchain address is derived from the public key, using a different type of cryptographic function from the one that was used to derive the public key, adding metadata like checksums and prefixes. Using a different type of cryptographic function to derive the address adds an extra level of security: if the first layer of security, elliptic-key cryptography, is broken, then someone who has the public key would be able to crack the private key. This is important, as elliptic-key cryptography is especially vulnerable to being broken if quantum computers become a reality, while the hashing, which is used in a second layer to derive the address, is not as vulnerable to quantum computer brute-force attacks. This means that if someone has the blockchain address, and has cracked the elliptic-key cryptography, that person would still have to get through the second layer of security that was used to derive the address from the public key. This is similar to why locking your bicycle twice, with two different locks that have different security mechanisms (key or number lock), gives you an added layer of security when locking your bike on the street. As a result of this, the address acts as a digital fingerprint of the public key but does not give any information about the person's public key (unless they send the first transaction). Blockchain addresses have a similar function to a bank account number in the context of traditional financial transactions, or an email address when people want to send you an electronic mail.

Digital signatures in the Bitcoin network and similar blockchain networks are performed using a wallet software. Similar to a handwritten signature, a digital signature is used to verify that you are who you say you are. Properly implemented, they are more difficult to forge than handwritten signatures. Digital signatures have been in use for decades, mostly in the context of financial transactions, software licenses, or contract management software. In blockchain networks, digital signatures are used for the authentication (proof that the sender of tokens is, in fact, the sender) and integrity of the transaction (i.e. the amount of tokens sent). The private key is used for signing token transactions. The public key is used by the validating nodes in the network to verify the signature. This way, a wallet cannot pretend to be another wallet. This is also referred to as "non-repudiation." Practically speaking, this means that another person cannot pretend to control your wallet, unless they have your private key.

Types of Wallets & Key Management

Your private key must always be kept secret and should not be shared with other people unless you want to give them deliberate access to your tokens. Because of the two-step process of deriving the public key from the private key and the address from the public key, one only needs to back up the private key; everything else can be derived from the private key with the cryptographic algorithm used in the network. If you lose access to your wallet, without having a backup of your seed phrase[16] or your private key, you will lose access to your tokens. While your tokens will still exist in the network you won't be able to access them.

Contrary to popular belief, a blockchain wallet does not store any tokens. It only stores the public-private key pair associated with your blockchain address. It also keeps a record of all transactions where the wallet's public keys are involved,

---

[16] *A seed phrase, also called a "mnemonic seed," is a method to tie the private keys with an easy-to-remember combination of words, which can be provided and managed by your wallet software. "Mnemonics" is a mapping technique that helps to reproduce something that is hard to remember, with random words that are easy to remember.*

Generation of Keys and Addresses

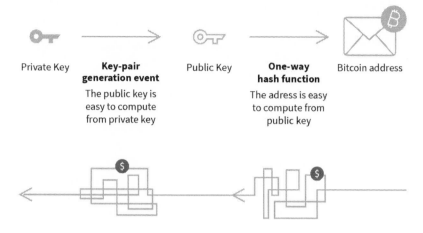

Private Key	**Key-pair generation event**	Public Key	**One-way hash function**	Bitcoin address
	The public key is easy to compute from private key		The adress is easy to compute from public key	

the reverse is very hard/<u>expensive</u> to compute

Public Key not same as Bitcoin Adress

Public Key   Bitcoin address

The public key is derived from the private key, and the address is derived from the public key. A one-way function is easy to compute, but hard to invert given the image of a random input. This means that guessing the private key if you know the adress or the public key, using reverse mathematics, would take the world's most powerful supercomputer many years to crack. It is possible, but expensive.

along with some other data. Therefore, the term "wallet" is misleading. The word "keychain" would be more appropriate, as it acts as a secure key storage, and as a communication tool with the blockchain network. A blockchain wallet has more similarities to a keychain containing your home keys. If you lose the keys to your apartment, the apartment is still yours, but you cannot access your apartment as long as you don't recover the key; maybe you have a backup key that you left with a neighbor, friend, or family member, or find a locksmith to help you break into your own house. Breaking your lock would translate to a brute-force attack to guess your private key. There are two different types of wallets, custodial and non-custodial wallets:

- "User-controlled wallets" offer personal control over one's tokens. Private keys are in the sole custody and responsibility of the users and transactions are signed directly from the users' devices. With user-controlled wallets, however, the user becomes a unique point of failure in the case of loss or theft of their keys.

- "Hosted wallets" are custodial services, offered by online exchange services, where the service provider manages one's wallet on their servers. In most cases, the private keys related to one's wallet are also managed by those intermediaries. The wallet software replicates the user's private key in such a way that a third party can submit transactions on the user's behalf. Many people, therefore, prefer to host their tokens on online exchanges and delegate key-management responsibilities to those trusted institutions. Similar to banks today, these token-exchange services act as custodians of one's funds (read more: Part 3 - Token Exchanges).

A more autonomous solution to the problem of losing your private keys could be so-called "social key recovery solutions," where you can appoint a set of trusted friends, family members, or institutions to confirm your identity and allow key recovery in a multi-signature process. In such a setup, you could, for example, appoint five trusted people who could be contacted in case of loss of your private key. Three out of five could be defined to sign with their private keys to recover your private key. This way, you fine-tune who you trust, without making yourself a unique point of failure. However, if these people know each other, they could collude or be bribed to collude against you. In order to enable a true P2P token economy, where people can send and receive tokens wallet to wallet, without the need for trusted third parties, we will need better wallet management solutions, where the individual is the sovereign of their tokens, maintaining high levels of security and usability. A less sophisticated solution for key recovery would be to automatically create a backup on a cloud service such as Google Drive. While this is not at all advisable, for convenience reasons, it seems to have become a trend with some token exchanges, such as "Coinbase."

Digital Signature

Similar to your signature, a digital signature is used to verify that you are who you saye you are:

 +  =

Transaction   Private Key   Digital Signature

 + =

Transaction   Public Key   Verification of
Valid Signature

Blockchain Wallet

Bitcoin Wallet   ≠

Bitcoin Wallet   =

 A blockchain wallet simply acts as secure key storage, and a communication tool with the blockchain. It does not contain any tokens. The tokens are managed collectively on the ledger.

At the time of writing this book, most wallets only allow the management of one type of token, and in some cases, a limited number of tokens. This is due to the fact that different distributed ledger systems are, for the most part, not interoperable. Most token systems have different technical specifications, which depend on the type of distributed ledger they are issued on, and therefore require individualized wallet development. Wallets that are multi-ledger compatible are time consuming and expensive to develop. Multi-ledger compatibility also bloats the wallet software. Another aspect of wallet design is whether a wallet (in combination with the underlying distributed ledger) enables co-signing of transactions. Many blockchain networks, such as Ethereum, do not enable native multi-signature transactions. In the case of Ethereum, you need to resolve this via a smart contract, which has been subject to security issues.

Ring signatures, collective signatures, and "Shamir's Secret Sharing" are all examples of alternative cryptographic algorithms that need to be enabled by the blockchain networks and supported by the wallet software to allow for co-signing of transactions. Co-signatures are an important feature that allow transferring custodianship over your tokens to someone else (a bank or an exchange manages your tokens), collective management of assets (in cases of collective ownership of the same asset or collective management as in the case of a DAO, Decentralized Autonomous Organization), or social key recovery. Chapters 3 and 4 of this book will deep-dive into the aspects of token management and token use cases, where the role of wallets will become more tangible.

Sending Tokens

If Alice wants to send Bitcoin tokens to Bob, she will use a wallet software to authenticate herself, specify the amount she wants to send, and indicate Bob's address. Her wallet software broadcasts the transaction to all computers in the network. Every computer in the network can now check if the transaction is valid, according to the network rules. The steps are as follows:

- *Alice uses a wallet software that manages her private key. By performing standard mathematical operations, the wallet software can always derive her public key and her address from the private key.*

- *If Alice wants to send tokens to Bob, she uses her wallet software to create a transaction that includes all the necessary details: her public key. Alice needs to specify Bob's address, and the number of tokens she wants to send.*

- *Alice then creates a digital signature of this transaction, a hash (performed by her wallet software).*

- *In order to prove to the rest of the network that she is the owner of the address, and thus the tokens, Alice signs the hash with her private key (automatically performed by her wallet software).*

- *Alice now broadcasts this transaction to any computer in the network: she sends out both the plaintext transaction and the signed hash (automatically performed by her wallet software).*

- *Any computer in the network receiving the transaction can now verify the validity of the transaction. They can use Alice's public key to mathematically verify whether the signed hash was really signed by her. They can use the hashing operations on her readable transaction and will receive the same hash value.*

- *After confirming all of these details, by consensus of all network actors, validated transactions are stored into a block and hashed. This block becomes part of the updated ledger if other computers in the network validate that the hash number on the block is valid. This process of creating new blocks of transactions is subject to the consensus mechanism Proof-of-Work (read more about Proof-of-Work in the next chapter).*

- *All network nodes will amend their ledger accordingly upon creation of the next block, so that Bob now owns the funds that Alice sent him. This transaction becomes part of the universal state of the Bitcoin network and is tamper resistant. The information on the ledger can be altered, but at prohibitively high costs (read more about how much it costs in the next chapter).*

Chapter Summary

- *Cryptography is the practice and study of secure communication in the presence of third parties. The aim is to create information systems that are resilient against eavesdropping, manipulation, and other forms of attack.*

- *Cryptography in blockchain networks allows for transparency of interactions while maintaining the privacy of all network actors.*

- *Public-key cryptography is used to prove one's identity with a set of cryptographic keys: a private key and a public key, which in combination with a transaction creates our digital signature. This digital signature proves ownership of our tokens and allows us to control them through a piece of software called a "wallet."*

- *Similar to a handwritten signature, a digital signature is used to verify that you are who you say you are. In Bitcoin and other blockchains, digital signatures are mathematical functions that reference a specific wallet address that manages your tokens on a blockchain.*

- *A hash function is a mathematical algorithm that can take any type of input, such as a string, a text file, or a picture file, and digest it to a fixed-size output string called a hash. It is a one-way function, which means that the only way to recreate the original input data (message) from the hash is to attempt to try all possible variations to see if they produce a match. While this is possible, it is time consuming and therefore expensive.*

Chapter References & Further Reading

- Alonso, Kurt M.: "Zero to Monero: First Edition a technical guide to a private digital currency; for beginners, amateurs, and experts", June 26, 2018 (v1.0.0): https://www.getmonero.org/library/Zero-to-Monero-1-0-0.pdf
- Antonopoulos, Andreas M.: "Mastering Bitcoin: Programming the Open Blockchain", O'Reilly, 2017
- Becket, B.: "Introduction to Cryptology", Blackwell Scientific Publications, 1988
- Ben-Sasson, Eli;Chiesa, Alessandro; Garman, Christina; Green, Matthew; Miers, Ian; Tromer, Eran; Virza, Madars: „Zerocash: Decentralized Anonymous Payments from Bitcoin" May 18, 2014 (extended version): http://zerocash-project.org/media/pdf/zerocash-extended-20140518.pdf
- Ben-Sasson, Eli; Chiesa, Alessandro; Tromer, Eran; Virza, Madars: "Succinct Non-Interactive Zero Knowledge for a von Neumann Architecture", February 5, 2019 (updated version): https://eprint.iacr.org/2013/879.pdf
- Boyle, David: "The Little Money Book", Alastair Sawday Publishing, 2003
- Buterin, Vitalik: "Bitcoin Is Not Quantum-Safe, And How We Can Fix It When Needed": https://bitcoinmagazine.com/articles/bitcoin-is-not-quantum-safe-and-how-we-can-fix-1375242150/
- Buterin, Vitalik: "Privacy on the Blockchain", January 2016: https://blog.ethereum.org/2016/01/15/privacy-on-the-blockchain/
- Castryck, Wouter: "ELLIPTIC CURVES ARE QUANTUM DEAD, LONG LIVE ELLIPTIC CURVES", n COSIC Cryptography Blog, 31/05/2017: https://www.esat.kuleuven.be/cosic/elliptic-curves-are-quantum-dead-long-live-elliptic-curves/
- Esslinger, Bernhard: "The CrypTool Script: Cryptography, Mathematics, and More", 10th edition, distributed with CrypTool version 1.4.30: https://web.archive.org/web/20110722183013/ http://www.cryptool.org/download/CrypToolScript-en.pdf
- Flannery, Sarah; Flannery, David: "In Code: A Mathematical Journey", Workman Publishing Company, 2001
- Goldreich, Oded: "Foundations of Cryptography" Cambridge University Press, 2001
- Ito, Joi: "Our response to „A Cryptocurrency Without a Blockchain Has Been Built to Outperform Bitcoin", Dec. 20, 2017: https://www.media.mit.edu/posts/iota-response/
- Katz, Jonathan; Lindell, Yehuda: "Introduction to Modern Cryptography", Chapman & Hall/CRC, Cryptography and Network Security Series, 2nd Edition, 2014
- Nakamoto, Satoshi: "Bitcoin: A Peer-to-Peer Electronic Cash System", 2008: https://bitcoin.org/bitcoin.pdf
- Narula, Neha: "Cryptographic vulnerabilities in IOTA", September 7, 2017 https://medium.com/@neha/cryptographic-vulnerabilities-in-iota-9a6a9ddc4367
- Narula, Neha:"IOTA Vulnerability Report: Cryptanalysis of the Curl Hash Function Enabling Practical Signature Forgery Attacks on the IOTA Cryptocurrency", 7 September, 2017: https://github.com/mit-dci/tangled-curl/blob/master/vuln-iota.md
- N.N.: "Bitcoin", Github repository: https://github.com/bitcoin
- N.N.: "Bitcoin Core", Github repository, https://github.com/bitcoin/bitcoin

- N.N.: "Bitcoin Core Integration", Staging tree: https://bitcoincore.org/en/download
- N.N.: "Mimblewimble Protocol", Github Archives: https://github.com/mimblewimble/grin/blob/master/doc/intro.md
- N.N.: Monero Research Lab, Technical Resources: https://ww.getmonero.org/resources/research-lab/
- N.N.: "Post-Quantum Cryptography" Information Technology Laboratory, COMPUTER SECURITY RESOURCE CENTER: https://csrc.nist.gov/projects/post-quantum-cryptography/round-1-submissions
- Prasanna: "Litecoin To Implement Mimblewimble", Altcoin News, February 8, 2019: https://cryptoticker.io/en/litecoin-implement-mimblewimble/
- Rogaway, Phillip; Bellare, Mihir: "Introduction to Modern Cryptography", May 11, 2005: http://web.cs.ucdavis.edu/~rogaway/classes/227/spring05/book/main.pdf
- Schär, Fabian; Berentsen, Aleksander: "Bitcoin, Blockchain und Kryptoassets: Eine umfassende Einführung", Books on Demand, 2017
- Schor, Lukas: "On Zero-Knowledge Proofs in Blockchains", Argon Group, March 2018: https://medium.com/@argongroup/on-zero-knowledge-proofs-in-blockchains-14c48cfd1dd1
- Stallings, William: "Cryptography and Network Security: Principles and Practice", Prentice Hall, 6th ed., 2013
- Stolbikova, Veronika: „Can Elliptic Curve Cryptography be Trusted? A Brief Analysis of the Security of a Popular Cryptosystem", ISACA Journal Volume 3, 2016 https://www.isaca.org/Journal/archives/2016/volume-3/Pages/can-elliptic-curve-cryptoraphy-be-trusted.aspx
- Tibco, Nelson Petracek: "What zero-knowledge proofs will do for blockchain", Venturebeat, Dec 16, 2017: https://venturebeat.com/2017/12/16/what-zero-knowledge-proofs-will-do-for-blockchain/
- Wetzel, Tyler: "Understanding the Jargon of the Blockchain and Cryptocurrency World" Medium, Aug 23, 2018: https://medium.com/@twwetzel76/understanding-the-jargon-of-the-blockchain-and-cryptocurrency-world-64b5f431bcd5
- Wikipedia contributors, „Cryptography," Wikipedia, The Free Encyclopedia, https://en.wikipedia.org/wiki/Cryptography (accessed Jun 10, 2017).
- Wikipedia contributors, „Digital signature," Wikipedia, The Free Encyclopedia, https://en.wikipedia.org/wiki/Digital_signature (accessed Jun 10, 2017).
- Wikipedia contributors, „Cryptographic hash function," Wikipedia, The Free Encyclopedia, https://en.wikipedia.org/wiki/Cryptographic_hash_function (accessed Jun 10, 2017).
- Young, Joseph: "Anonymous Cryptocurrencies: Why Edward Snowden Supports Zero-Knowledge Proofs", January 2018: https://journal.binarydistrict.com/anonymous-cryptocurrencies-why-edward-snowden-supports-zero-knowledge-proofs/
- Bitcoin Core: https://bitcoin.org/de/download
- Electrum: https://electrum.org/
- Ledger: https://www.ledger.com/
- Monero: https://getmonero.org/
- Mimblewimble: https://github.com/mimblewimble/grin/blob/master/doc/intro.md
- Trezor: https://trezor.io/
- Zcash: https://z.cash/

Who Controls The Tokens?
User-Centric Identities

Blockchain networks and similar distributed ledgers use public-key cryptography for the identification of all network actors. These identity-systems, however, are insufficient for the array of possible Web3-applications. Decentralized Identifiers (DIDs) in combination with distributed ledgers can provide "user-centric" identity solutions that are suitable for the Web3, allowing for more privacy and control over one's digital assets and digital footprint than "server-centric" solutions used in the Web2.

Disclaimer: The intention of this chapter is to give a general overview, and shed a light on the urgency and importance of adequate digital identity solutions as a pivotal building block for the Web3. However, the topic of digital identities is much more complex than outlined in this chapter and cannot be discussed in detail, as that would be beyond the scope of this book.

Identity management refers to the process by which organizations, individuals, and objects can be trustfully identified, authenticated, and certified. Trusted identity services are the basis for access rights management over the Internet and a necessary prerequisite for many socio-economic activities in general—offline or online. Identity-related use cases can be found in government (birth certificates, national ID cards, passports, or driver's licenses), education (certifications and licenses), healthcare (personal health-related data records), e-commerce, banking or finance (client, B2B and employees' data). In the Internet-of-Things, an increasing number of objects that are connected to the Internet also need proper identification systems (such as serial numbers). From a computer science perspective, the term "identity" can be reduced to the data elements related to the identity management process: "identifier," "authentication," and "credentials."

- Identifiers are needed to uniquely identify a person, institution, or object. A phone number or an email address is unique in nature and would qualify as an identifier. The name of a person is not necessarily unique, and does not always qualify as an identifier. On the other hand, while the residential address and phone number of a person are unique in nature, they can change over time. Ideally, an identifier needs to be unique and persistent over time. A social security number, passport number, or driver's license number could be a unique identifier for a person, if it does not change over time. Whether or not such identifiers persist over time depends on the country in question and whether document numbers expire or not. Unique identifiers also exist for objects and companies: A serial number is a unique identifier for an object. A company registration number is a unique identifier for a for profit organization, so public authorities know how to identify companies for collecting taxes or granting subsidies.

- Authentication is the process with which a person, institution, or object can prove that they are who they claim they are. A person can authenticate themselves by proving ownership of an object (ID card, hardware wallet, software wallet), knowledge (password or PIN), or by a personal property (biometric data, signature). Often, a combination of these systems is used. At least one strong and reliable method must exist to authenticate a person, institution, or object. Biometrics are the strongest forms for proving authentication for people. An ID card is an analogue form of authentication, as the picture and handwritten signature on the ID card are authentication methods. Passwords are the digital equivalent to a handwritten signature in the current Internet. However, usernames and passwords and all other personal data are controlled by mostly private institutions such as your bank, your university, or Facebook, Twitter, and Google. Blockchain networks and other distributed ledgers have popularized more user-centric identity-systems, applying public-key cryptography as a method of authentication.

- Claims & Credentials: An identity is useless without linking relevant information to a person (personal data), institution (institutional data), or object (object-related data) to the identifier. Personal data, for example, involves claims made by the person themselves (claim) or by other people or institutions (credential). Such claims can include information about who I am, where I live, where I was born, or which degrees I have successfully completed and need to be attested by trusted authorities. Personal data can also include additional data, such as personal browsing histories, social media activities, or geo-locations, which are automatically authenticated by machines and also tied to the personal identifier.

Historically, identity processes, such as passports, driver's licenses, social security cards, or serial numbers for goods, have been issued by centralized institutions such as local and national governments and other trusted institutions. The emergence of the Internet created the need for digital identification systems. However, the current Internet does not provide a native identity layer for people, institutions, or objects other than the operating nodes in a network of computers. Problems such as "Can I trust my customer to pay their bills?" or "Can I trust the service provider to deliver my goods?" could not be resolved by the Internet Protocol. Companies and public institutions started to implement workaround solutions on the application layer of the Internet—often using internal databases and username-password combinations—the type of identification systems that had been in use since the time of mainframe computers and before the emergence of the Internet.

Server-Centric Identities

The Internet Protocol has no native format for managing the identities of people, organizations, and objects. Workaround solutions have been built on the application layer using internal databases (private infrastructure) to manage all the data involved with digital identity management processes. Due to the client-server structure of the Internet, any Web-based service—from university websites to online banking, social media, and e-commerce sites—provide their own identity-management-service, which means that all user-related data is managed by the service provider, on their private computer infrastructure. All elements related to the identity management process—such as issuing an identifier, providing an authentication method, providing the credentials, and managing user-related data—are centralized. The result is a series of incompatible data silos with proprietary—and often incompatible—identity-management-service which have created considerable costs and trade-offs, both for companies and users alike such as:

Password chaos: Over the decades, as the number of Internet services grew, password management became a chaotic task. Users have to manage hundreds of usernames and passwords for each application or new online service they register for. Fragments of their personal data are scattered all over the Web. In the early days of the Internet, every online service required users to register with a username and password with their services, including more data if needed. Today, users can use "single sign-on solutions" provided by companies such as Google, Facebook, or Twitter, with the downside that these identities can be observed and revoked unilaterally by that service provider at any time, which can have cascading lockout effects from all other services one uses with this login.

<u>Protection against bad actors</u>: In an e-commerce setup, companies need to identify bad actors that might order goods they never pay for in order to prevent potential business losses. Due to the fragmented nature of current digital identity systems, the process of identifying bad actors for fraud protection is a cost-intensive business overhead. "82% of businesses struggle with fake users and on average 10% of a web-facing organisation's user base will be fake. The average retailer cost for each stolen record containing sensitive and confidential information is $165. $15 billion in losses from 13.1 million consumers in 2015 is the US alone."[18]

<u>Data protection & custodial costs</u>: Users have to trust the service providers to maintain the integrity and privacy of their data. A growing number of personal data is in the custody of often private institutions who manage a growing amount of customer data on their private servers, which results in what many privacy activists have been referring to as "Surveillance Capitalism."[19] Username-password combinations are often compromised by internal or external data breaches. Workarounds such as multi-factor authentication methods have been introduced to mitigate this problem. But security management of identity-related data against theft or loss still remains an expensive and patchy task. With the emergence of a growing body of data protection laws, and in light of potential lawsuits and government fines, collecting sensitive information about their users and storing that data on their servers has become an increasing business risk for companies.

<u>Data portability</u>: In Business-to-Business applications, portability is especially relevant along the supply chain of goods and services to process the provenance of goods and services and reduce document-handling costs. In Business-to-Consumer applications, new legislation such as Article 20 of the European Union General Data Protection Regulation grants users the right to have their personal data ported from one company to another, and mandates companies to provide for such data portability. In a client-server setup, however, such data portability with other institutions comes at high operational costs.

<u>Lack of Control & Sovereignty</u>: Users have no direct control over what happens with their data, and don't know whether and to whom it has been passed on. Depending on the regulation of a country, users of Internet-based services can be locked out from using the services (and their data) at any time. Data protection depends on the applied business ethics of the company providing the identity

---

[18] *https://sovrin.org/wp-content/uploads/2017/07/The-Inevitable-Rise-of-Self-Sovereign-Identity.pdf*
[19] *Such as Zuboff, Shoshana in "The Age of Surveillance Capitalism: The Fight for a Human Future at the New Frontier of Power." New York: PublicAffairs, 2019. Zuboff describes the commodification of personal information. She describes the tendency of accumulation of data, criticizing that many companies and institutions harvest and capitalize personal data without mechanisms of consent. She compares "industrial capitalism" and "surveillance capitalism," explaining "industrial capitalism" as exploitation of nature, and "surveillance capitalism" as exploitation of human nature.*

services, and is also subject to the jurisdiction of the country under which the company falls.

Re-centralization of the Internet: Network effects have the tendency to lock in customers and business partners to use one service provider only. Take the example of Amazon or eBay. Once users have undergone an authentication process with Amazon or eBay, they tend to stay on Amazon or Ebay, rather than buying products with others online. Buying a product on the website of a neighborhood store would require a separate authentication process on the website of that store and create a new identity (username and password) including payment information, which many people tend to avoid due to the time-consuming nature of this process. On the other hand, the more users Amazon and eBay have, the more these services become attractive to sellers, and vice versa. As a result of such network effects, power started to accumulate around these networks. This led to a re-centralization of the Internet around Internet platform providers, who not only manage the identities of their users, but also control all other user-related data. The "digital footprint" of all users is often stored in plain text (not encrypted) on the servers of the companies and used for data mining that creates recommendation algorithms, advertising algorithms, and other forms of user profiling that generate more income for these Internet platforms.

History of Digital Identity Management

Over the decades, several initiatives tried to find alternative solutions to centralized identity management. In 1999, "Microsoft Passport" launched an initiative to provide a "federated identity solution" that people could use across various Internet services. The main idea was to provide an online identity service that mitigated the password chaos for the users. However, this solution put Microsoft at the center of the federation. Sun Microsoft initiated the "Liberty Alliance" in 2001 as a more distributed solution, where control over digital identities was now divided among several institutions, but personal data still remained under the authority of each individual site. In 2001, the "Identity Commons" began to consolidate all works on digital identity with a focus on decentralization, which ultimately led to the creation of the "Internet Identity Workshop" in 2005. The open-source developer community started to work on alternative concepts, such as "OpenID," that countered the "server-centric model" with a "user-centric model" where individuals could control their identity using their own personal domain name, and fill their own data store with personal data that could be provided to other organizations with the permission of the individual. However, these solutions were not very user friendly and required some technical know-how.

In the meantime, companies such as Facebook adopted the idea of "Open-ID" but provided better usability, which was one of the reasons why, "Facebook Connect" became more successful than "OpenID" around 2008. Anyone could use their Facebook identity to sign up for other Internet services, which could now use a Facebook API instead of managing their own identities. This was very useful to smaller Internet startups that could save costs on identity management, and to users who could save time and headaches on password management. Soon Google, Amazon, Apple, and Twitter followed in providing similar "server-centric" identity solutions—all of which control the majority of the online identity market today. This also includes the personal browsing history, social media behavior, and geo-locations of their users.

Meanwhile, a growing set of initiatives continued to work on the idea of more "user-centric" identity solutions, such as the Web-of-Trust initiative, which had its roots in the Pretty Good Privacy (PGP) movement. They proposed the use of asymmetric cryptography where anyone could be a validator of identities. Unfortunately, both initiatives focused on email addresses as identifiers, which meant that they still depended on institutions such as ICANN[20] to issue the domain names on which these email addresses are based. For a variety of reasons, PGP never became broadly adopted.

Years later, individuals such as Christopher Allen and initiatives such as Re-booting-the-Web-of-Trust picked up on these efforts, especially as blockchain networks emerged and allowed the use of public-key cryptography for pseudo-anonymous identification without linking identities to an email address. The emergence of blockchain networks and other distributed ledgers provided a natural continuation of previous decentralization efforts. Christopher Allen and other individuals elevated the discussion of identity management to a political level and proposed the concept of "Self-Sovereign Identity," a type of user-centric identity management system that needs to meet a series of guiding principles:

- Access & Control: Direct control of one's personal identity data, where users are the ultimate authority and have control over the level of anonymity of their data.

- Transparency & Interoperability: Algorithms governing identity-related data should be transparent, open source, and independent from any particular infrastructure. Identity-related data must be long-lived and should preferably last forever, or at least for as long as the user wishes.

---

[20] *ICANN (Internet Corporation for Assigned Names and Numbers) is a nonprofit organization that coordinates the maintenance and procedures of several databases related to the namespaces and numerical spaces of the Internet, ensuring the network's stable and secure operation. It is a multi-stakeholder group based in the United States.*

- Portability: Identity-related data must be portable to other services, otherwise they are subject to censorship or control. Portable identities ensure that users remain in control of their identities independent of the services they use.

- Consent & Minimization: Users must, at all times, agree to the access of third parties to their personal data. Furthermore, when personal data is disclosed, that disclosure should involve only the minimum amount of data necessary.

In his manifesto Allen outlined the delicate balance between the right to privacy and the need to disclose certain information for the security of the whole network of people. He warned that these principles can be a double-edged sword, usable for both beneficial and malevolent purposes, and concluded that an identity system must balance transparency, fairness, and support of the common interests of a group while at the same time guaranteeing protection for the individual. However, such discussions are not new and have been subject to political science, as well as centuries of debates that have been resolved to varying degrees depending on the political regime and governing laws of the nation state in question. The balance between individual privacy versus public interest has been—and still is—a topic of constitutional law in many democratic countries, subject to regulation around the "secrecy of correspondence" or "sanctity of the home" (read more: Part 3 - Privacy Tokens).

The above mentioned principles have been incorporated into a series of user-centric identity initiatives and working groups over the years, such as "Social Linked Data," "Rebooting the Web of Trust," "WebIDs," and most recently the "W3C Working Group on Decentralized Identifiers (DIDs)." The aim of all these initiatives has been to provide international open standards that decouples the process of issuing a credential and marking a claim from verifying those claims over a set of actors, which removes many of the issues that server-centric solution face.

User-Centric Identities using DIDs

Blockchain networks currently only offer a minimum set of identity attributes that are not sufficient for many socio-economic interactions over the Web. However, if set up correctly, the ledger can offer critical components for a user-centric and privacy-preserving identity management system, providing less friction and lower costs for everyone involved. Decentralized Identifiers (DIDs) in combination with distributed ledgers allow for a more sophisticated identity-management-systems.

History of Identities

Diclaimer: This table is a simplification for the sake of overview.

	Analogue Identities	Web2 Identities	Web3 Identities
Identifier	i.e.: Social Security Number	i.e.: Email Address	Depending on setup, ledger address or DID
Authentication	ID card including picture & signature.	Email & Password combination.	Private key, managed with Wallet-Software
Credential	Credentials directly recorded on the ID card, and also stored in physical documents and/or on the servers of the Issuing Institution.	Credentials manages on the servers of the Web-service provider.	Credentials are managed by a P2P network: Attetation of credentials, making claims, and verifying those claims can be managed by each participant (issuer, owner, verifyer) using their wallet.
User Autonomy	Server-centric	Server-centric	User-centric
Security	Security mechanisms built into physical ID Card	Centralized Key-Management & Assymetric Cryptography	Decentralized Key-Management & Assymetric Cryptography
Substrate	Analogue object	Server (private infrastructure)	Ledger & other P2P networks such as KERI (public infrastructure)
Check & Balances *Who controls the process of issuance, management, & verification of identity-related data?*	One institution has full control over issuance and management of credentials and other identity-related data.	One institution has full control over issuance and management of credentials and other identity-related data.	In a DID setup, control over issuance, management & verification of identity related data is divided between several institutions: issuer, identity owner, verifier, nodes in a distributed ledger or other P2P network.

A Decentralized Identifier (DID) is a public and pseudo-anonymous unique digital identifier for a person, company, or object that grants personal control over one's digital identity without the need for centralized institutions managing those identifiers. To guarantee independence of centralized registries, DIDs need to have certain properties. They need to be permanent so they cannot be reassigned to other entities by whomever is in control. They need to be resolvable so everyone understands how to interact with the subject identified by the DID, and they need to be cryptographically verifiable.

Public-key infrastructure, inherent to distributed ledgers, allows for the registration of DIDs of all actors involved in a publicly verifiable way. Any user can create and register a DID when activating a new blockchain wallet, which creates a pair of private and public keys. Any DID can be linked to credentials that are issued by other people and institutions attesting specific characteristics for an identity owner (claims they make about themselves), such as name, address, email, age, existing diplomas, or other certifications such as a driver's license.

The wallet is the digital equivalent to a physical wallet, which—in addition to storing one's cash—also acts as a container for ID cards, such as driver's license, bank card, gym membership, national ID card, social security card, or loyalty cards. A Web3 wallet can be used to manage all your cryptographically secured digital credentials that others have issued about you, tokenized credentials that represent the digital version of your driver's license, bank card, gym membership, national ID card, social security card, loyalty cards, etc. Just as you open your wallet to reveal your ID card, you need to activate your Web3 wallet to reveal your digital credentials to third parties (using a password). No one can see the contents of your Web3 wallet without your consent. The content of the wallet remains concealed until you choose to reveal something. The players in such a setup are:

- Identity: trusted institutions such as local governments, universities, and other public and private institutions, and in some cases, even private individuals. These identity issuers can provide credentials for an identity owner (such as name, age, and date of birth) and attest to the validity of the personal data.

- Identity owners: manage the credentials that have been issued by third parties mentioned above, in their Web3-wallet, and can use them at any point in time to prove statements about their identity to another third party.

- Identity verifiers are third parties that provide services upon verification of certain identity-related attributes. For example, if there is an age limit on buying alcohol, or watching a movie, the identity verifier (the shop or movie theater) can validate the signature of the government that issued and attested to this credential.

92

User-Centric Identities with DIDs

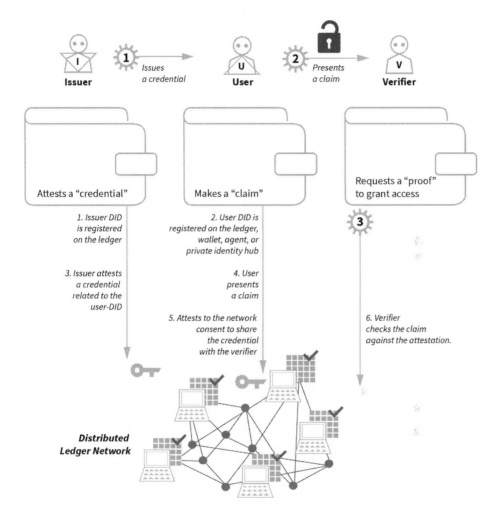

Issuer — 1 Issues a credential — User — 2 Presents a claim — Verifier

Attests a "credential"

Makes a "claim"

Requests a "proof" to grant access

1. Issuer DID is registered on the ledger

2. User DID is registered on the ledger, wallet, agent, or private identity hub

3. Issuer attests a credential related to the user-DID

4. User presents a claim

5. Attests to the network consent to share the credential with the verifier

6. Verifier checks the claim against the attestation.

Distributed Ledger Network

Identity-related data itself should never be stored in plain text on the ledger!
Personal data and credentials are usually maaged directly by the user's device or by private identity stores, or "identity hubs." Less sensitive data can be collectively managed using distributed file storage systems such as the "InterPlanetary File System" (IPFS) or "OrbitDB."

The credentials are signed by their issuers using public-key cryptography. Once signed by an issuer, credentials can be managed by the identity owner to make claims, simply by using their wallet. Identity owners use their wallet to disclose which data they want to share with the outside world. They get to decide and control not only with whom they want to share their data, but also when to share that data. To do that, they need to attest to the network their consent to share selected data with authorized institutions.

Both identity issuers and identity owners need to be registered on a public ledger with their DIDs. In such a setup, distributed ledgers can be used to attest the authenticity of the data and attestations, only registering indirect "pointers" for the purpose of verification. Distributed ledgers can be used as a public infrastructure to facilitate the verification of identity-related data. Anyone in a blockchain network can now verify whether a claim made by an identity owner is valid and which institutions attested to the validity of the claim, without having to reveal the data itself.

Pairing the private key with a DID allows the identity owner to create a QR code, for example, that represents that verified identifier. Scanning the QR code, a service provider can now run the data through a blockchain network or similar distributed ledger and verify if an attestation is associated with that person's DID. The public key is used to attest to the authenticity of the issuing authority's signature associated with a credential. If attestation and DID match, access is granted, and a person can qualify to buy alcohol, rent a car, etc. In addition to such attestations, any other data can also be associated to a DID and directly controlled by the identity owner through the wallet software. Examples of such "non-attested" data are personal browsing histories or social media posts. In such a setup, one would not rely on third-party digital identity providers such as Google or Facebook anymore. The "Brave browser" is a practical example for how a Web3 wallet allows direct control of your digital footprint (read more: Part 4 - Basic Attention Token).

Revocation registries give identity issuers the possibility to revoke a claim since certain identity-related data can change over time. Personal data such as address, marital status, and number of children can change over time and therefore need to be updated.

Separating the process of (i) issuing a credential, (ii) making a claim, and (iii) validating those claims against credentials is crucial to a user-centric setup. It can be seen as a system of checks and balances in a data-driven economy that guarantees the level of autonomy and privacy over one's digital footprint, and is very contrary to how the Internet is set up today.

KERI (Key Event Receipt Infrastructure) is a novel technology—a type of consensus network—that allows to move certain functions of decentralized identity-management systems off-chain to a different layer, and minimize the role of the distributed ledger. The aim is to provide a simple, scalable, more modular, identity-management system that is more interoperable across different blockchain networks and other distributed ledgers. It is currently being adopted by many players in the user-centric identity space and shows a lot of potential to act as a catalyst for user-centric identities.

Outlook

User-centric identity solutions based on distributed ledgers and DIDs can disintermediate the identity industry. They can increase operational efficiency with on-the-fly auditing and real-time direct data access, while reducing costs. If set up correctly, they provide higher data security and protection from identity imposters, and provide more efficient regulatory compliance, granting more control to the data owners. User-centric identity solutions can provide for data portability, where individuals and institutions can easily reuse credentials to re-verify themselves for new services. For companies, this can reduce the costs and time involved with customer-onboarding and drop-out rates, as well as overall opportunity costs related to a full Know-Your-Customer identification process.

For the storage of personal data, user-centric identity solutions can use either personal data stores or distributed file storage networks. Credentials can be stored directly on the user's device or securely in a private identity store, or identity hub, such as "TrustGraph" or "3Box." Less privacy-sensitive data can be collectively managed by distributed file storage networks such as the "InterPlanetary File System" (IPFS) or "OrbitDB" to reduce data redundancies and disintermediate the identity management process. In both setups, data is designed around the user, and thus more interoperable across multiple service providers that can use the same set of information for different purposes. User data is not locked into one platform.

While some forms of zero-knowledge proof cryptography are already in use in user-centric identity solutions, there is more room to improve even stronger privacy-preserving cryptographic tools. A set of Web3 networks is already working to incorporate more privacy-preserving cryptographic mechanisms into distributed ledgers, such as "Zero-Knowledge Proofs" as implemented by "Zcash," or "Ring Signatures" as implemented by "Monero," or to perform computation on encrypted information using "Secure-Multi-Party-Computation" (read more: Part 3 - Privacy Tokens). KERI might also be a game changer in that aspect.

One of the most interesting future use cases will be the digital identification of objects. Currently, most Internet-of-Things (IoT) devices have no secure digital identity and access management capabilities. A DID-powered serial number can make any object in the Web3 addressable. Once we start tagging objects with mini computers (crypto accelerators) that come with a DID-powered serial number and communicate with a distributed ledger network, any object along the supply chain can prove ownership and credentials to others in the network using cryptographic proofs. Objects that have their own unique Web3 identity and Web3 wallet can become autonomous and trustable economic entities. Such a "cyber-physical link" between objects and DID allows for effective product tracking and data sharing on the provenance of goods and services between producers and consumers.

Selected Web3-based identity solutions are: "Ageify," "Civic," "Edge," "Hu-manity.co," "Jolocom," "Keyp," "Madana," "Metadium," "NewBanking Identity,""Object-Tech," "THEKEY," "Trusti," "PeerMountain," "REMME," "Riddle & Code," "Spherity," "uPort,""UniquID," "ValidatedID," and "WoTT."

Chapter Summary

- *Historically, identity processes, such as passports, driver's licenses, social security cards, or serial numbers for goods, have been issued by centralized institutions such as local and national governments and other trusted institutions. The emergence of the Internet created the need for digital identification systems.*

- *From a computer science perspective, the term "identity" can be reduced to the data elements related to the identity management process: "identifier," "authentication," and "credentials."*

- *Identifiers are needed to uniquely identify a person, institution, or object. An identifier needs to be unique and persistent over time.*

- *Authentication is the process with which a person, institution, or object can prove that they are who they claim they are. A person can authenticate themselves by proving ownership of an object (ID card, hardware wallet, software wallet), knowledge (password or PIN), or by a personal property (biometric data, signature). Often, a combination of these systems is used.*

- *An identity is useless without linking data related to a person (personal data), institution (institutional data), or object (object-related data) to the identifier.*

- *The current Internet was built around connecting machines, not people. The Internet does not provide a native identity layer for people, institutions, or objects other than the operating nodes in a network of computers. Workaround solutions have been built on the application layer using internal databases (private infrastructure) to manage all the data involved with digital identity management processes. All user-related data is managed by the service provider, on their private server infrastructure, and that all elements related to the identity management process are centralized.*

- *These data silos and proprietary identity solutions have created considerable costs and trade-offs, both for companies and users alike such as (i) password chaos, (ii) protection against bad actors, (iii) data protection & custodial costs, (iv) data portability, (v) lack of control & sovereignty over data, and the (vi) re-centralization of the Internet.*

- *Blockchain networks and similar distributed ledgers use public-key cryptography for the identification of all network actors, but they are insufficient for a thriving tokenized economy. However, combined with DIDs, they can offer critical components for more "user-centric" identity solutions that are suitable for the Web3, and provide more privacy and control than "server-centric" solutions used in the Web2.*

- *The user-centric identity process requires three actors: (i) identity issuers, (ii) identity owners, and (iii) identity verifiers. If set up correctly, anyone in a blockchain network can verify whether a piece of data (credential) is valid and which institutions attested to the validity of the data without revealing the data itself.*

- *While plain text data should never be stored on a public ledger, a privacy-preserving identity management system can use distributed ledgers to allow a person to prove that their personal identity-related data fulfills certain requirements without revealing the actual data. In such a setup, distributed ledgers can be used to attest the authenticity of the data and attestations, only registering indirect "pointers" for the purpose of verification.*

- *A user can create and register a DID when activating a blockchain wallet, which creates a pair of private and public keys. Public-key cryptography is used for authentication and encryption. Only the private key can prove one's identity. The private key acts as your personal lock on the wallet.*

- *Any DID can be linked to attestations (verifiable credentials) that are issued by other people and institutions attesting specific characteristics for an identity owner, such as name, address, email, age, existing diplomas, or other certifications such as a driver's license. The credentials are signed by their issuers using public-key cryptography. Once signed by an issuer, credentials can be managed using the wallet of the identity owner directly.*

- *The separation of the "identifier," "authentication," and "data" is crucial to a user-centric setup. It can be seen as a system of checks and balances in a data-driven economy that guarantees the level of autonomy and privacy over one's digital footprint, and is very contrary to how the Internet is set up today. Using a public infrastructure such as a collectively maintained ledger as a unique source of truth, while splitting the roles in the identification management process, makes user-centric identity management systems "decentralized."*

- *The wallet acts as a personal container that allows you to control your digital identities. The wallet is the digital equivalent to a physical wallet, which usually acts as a container for all your ID cards, such as driver's license, bank card, gym membership, national ID card, social security card, or loyalty cards, in addition to your money. While it is initially empty, over time, one can fill it with credentials that represent the digital version of your driver's license, bank card, gym membership, national ID card, social security card, loyalty cards, etc.*

- *Just as you open your wallet to reveal your ID card, you need to activate your Web3 wallet to reveal your digital credentials to third parties (using a password). No one can see the contents of your Web3 wallet without your consent. You choose who to share these credentials with. The content of the wallet remains concealed until you choose to reveal something. The digital wallet is portable, as a dedicated hardware device, or an app in your mobile phone or your notebook.*

Chapter References & Further Reading

- Allan, Christoper: "The Path to Self-Sovereign Identity," March 1 2017, https://github.com/ChristopherA/self-sovereign-identity/blob/master/ThePathToSelf-SovereignIdentity.md
- Ellison, Carl: "Establishing Identity without Certification Authority," 1996, https://irl.cs.ucla.edu/index.html
- Feisthammel, Patrick: "Pretty good Privacy, PGP, Web of Trust," Oct 7 2004, https://www.rubin.ch/pgp/weboftrust.en.html
- Jordan, Ken; Hauser, Jan; Foster, Steven: "The Augmented Social Network," White paper, 2000, https://firstmonday.org/ojs/index.php/fm/article/view/1068/988
- Kameron, Kim: "The Laws of Identity," March 2007, https://docs.microsoft.com/en-us/previous-versions/dotnet/articles/ms996456(v=msdn.10)?redirectedfrom=MSDN
- Kütt, Andres: „MyData Webinar #5: Identity in the Digital Era," Mydata Global, Youtube Video, retrieved from: https://www.youtube.com/watch?v=XjzJeys7PvM&fbclid=IwAR0qMDGYuZVk0c6a-DHOX46AdFQMGdsI24SSZ6-lMfj7XZY-TrbkbT5LFlqk
- Many authors: "Rebooting the Web of Trust," Papers and Specs, http://www.weboftrust.info/papers.html
- Many authors: "Charta for Digital Human Rights," Version: 01.12.2016 Unofficial English translation of the German original text, published by ZEIT-Stiftung Ebelin und Gerd Bucerius https://digitalcharta.eu/wp-content/uploads/2016/12/Digital-Charta-EN.pdf
- Many authors: "Self-sovereign Identity A position paper on blockchain enabled identity and the road ahead," October 23 2018, Identity Working Group of the German Blockchain Association, https://www.bundesblock.de/wp-content/uploads/2019/01/ssi-paper.pdf
- Many authors: "The Respect Trust Framework," Version 2.1, Feb 2016, https://oixnet.org/wp-content/uploads/2016/02/respect-trust-framework-v2-1.pdf
- Marlinspike, Moxie: "Sovereign Source Authority," Moxytongue, Feb 2012, https://www.moxytongue.com/2012/02/what-is-sovereign-source-authority.html
- Miller, Ron: „The Promise of managing identities on the blockchain," Sep 10, 2017, https://techcrunch.com/2017/09/10/the-promise-of-managing-identity-on-the-blockchain/?lipi=urn%3Ali%3Apage%3Ad_flagship3_profile_view_base_recent_activity_details_all%3BknkLT7NkR5Cex9bx3zogKg%3D%3D&guccounter=1
- Mire, Sam: "Blockchain Research Technologies Blockchain For Identity Management: 7 Possible Use Cases" Dec 5 2018, https://www.disruptordaily.com/blockchain-use-cases-identity-management/
- N.N.: "Enterprise Ethereum Blockchain in Digital Identity," Consensys website, https://consensys.net/blockchain-use-cases/digital-identity/#usecases
- N.N.: "Identity Management with Blockchain: The Definitive Guide (2020 Update)," TYKN website: https://tykn.tech/identity-management-blockchain/
- Preukschat, Alex; Reed , Drummond: „Self-Sovereign Identity Decentralized Digital Identity and Verifiable Credentials" MEAP began December 2019 Publication in January 2021 (estimated) ISBN 9781617296598 300 pages (estimated), electronically retrieved from:https://www.manning.com/books/self-sovereign-identity
- Reed, Drummond; Tobin, Andrew: "Sovereign White Paper," Sept 29 2016, https://sovrin.org/wp-content/uploads/2017/07/The-Inevitable-Rise-of-Self-Sovereign-Identity.pdf
- Reed, Drummond; Sabadello, Markus: „Chapter 8 Decentralized identifiers" in Self Sovereign Identity, retrieved from on October 27, 2020: in https://livebook.manning.com/book/self-sovereign-identity/chapter-8
- Ruff, Timothy: „When Explaining SSI, Start with the Wallet," Apr 21 2020, https://medium.com/@rufftimo/when-explaining-ssi-start-with-the-wallet-bee5d2af6696
- Sabadello, Markus: "Human Rights in the Information Society," 2011, https://danubetech.com/download/Human-Rights-in-the-Information-Society.pdf

- Shea, Michael;Smith, Samuel M.; Stöcker,Carsten, Caballero, Juan; Condon, Matt G.: "Decentralized Identity as a Meta-platform: How Cooperation Beats Aggregation a white paper from Rebooting the Web of Trust IX, https://nbviewer.jupyter.org/github/WebOfTrustInfo/rwot9-prague/blob/master/final-documents/ CooperationBeatsAggregation.pdf
- Spike, Marlin: "Self Sovereign Identity, how the term has evolved," Feb 2016, https://www.moxytongue.com/2016/02/self-sovereign-identity.html
- Smith, Samuel M.: "Key Event Receipt Infrastructure (KERI)", Cornell University, retrieved from: https://arxiv.org/abs/1907.02143
- Smolenski, Natalie: "The EU General Data Protection Regulation and the Blockchain," Aug 2 2017, https://medium.com/learning-machine-blog/the-eu-general-data-protection-regulation-and-the-blockchain-1f1d20d24951
- Stöcker, Carsten: "The Economic Value of Decentralized Identity — Part 2 Reimagining the economics of trust and reputation," Mar 11 2020, https://medium.com/spherity/the-economic-value-of-decentralized-identity-part-2-733aa977eaf8
- Stöcker, Carsten: "Spherity's Identity Tech Predictions for the decade of the 2020's — Part 1," Jan 16 2020 https://medium.com/spherity/spheritys-identity-tech-predictions-for-the-decade-of-the-2020-s-part-1-410bc9b48be4
- Stöcker, Carsten: "Spherity's Identity Tech Predictions for the decade of the 2020's — Part 2," Feb 13 2020 https://medium.com/spherity/spheritys-identity-tech-predictions-for-the-decade-of-the-2020-s-part-2-6e480d2a57ea
- Stöcker, Carsten: "SSI201: Upgrading products with intelligent serial numbers and DIDs How smart can an object's identifier be? How can it enable cradle-to-grave traceability and other innovative capabilities?" Nov 26, 2019 ·, https://medium.com/spherity/ssi201-upgrading-products-with-intelligent-serial-numbers-and-dids-78da623b91dd
- Stöcker, Karsten: „KERI: A more Performant Ledger for Trusted Identities Securing the control of decentralized identifiers at the root with ambient verifiability", Medium, Sperity Blog, July 2 2020, https://medium.com/@cstoecker
- Voshmgir, Shermin: "Identity as a Bottleneck for Blockchain," Oct 17, 2017, https://stories.jolocom.com/identity-blockchain-the-road-to-self-sovereign-identity-f9f4439c52cb
- Voshmgir, Shermin: "Self Sovereign — Identity vs Data?" Feb 27 2018, https://stories.jolocom.com/self-sovereign-identity-vs-data-5abe5947a62
- Wikipedia contributors: „Pretty Good Privacy," Wikipedia, The Free Encyclopedia, https://en.wikipedia.org/w/index.php?title=Pretty_Good_Privacy&oldid=959437666 (accessed May 31, 2020).
- Zuboff, Shoshana: " The Age of Surveillance Capitalism: The Fight for a Human Future at the New Frontier of Power." New York: PublicAffairs, 2019.
- Ageif: https://age-ify.com/
- Civic: https://www.civic.com/wallet/
- Edge: https://edge.app/
- General Data Protection Regulation (GDPR): https://gdpr-info.eu/
- Hu-manity.co: https://hu-manity.co/
- Jolocom: https://jolocom.io/
- Keyp: https://keyp.io/
- List of Blockchain & Identity Solutions: https://github.com/peacekeeper/blockchain-identity
- Madana: https://www.madana.io/
- Metadium: https://www.metadium.com/
- NewBanking Identity: https://newbanking.com/#/
- ObjectTech: https://www.objectivetgg.com/

- THEKEY: *https://www.thekey.vip/#/homePage*
- Trusti: *https://trusti.com/*
- PeerMountain: *https://www.peermountain.com/*
- PGP WOT: *https://www.linux.com/training-tutorials/pgp-web-trust-core-concepts-behind-trusted-communication/*
- Rebooting the Web of Trust:*http://www.weboftrust.info/papers.html*
- REMME: *https://remme.io/*
- Riddle & Code: *https://www.riddleandcode.com/*
- Spherity: *https://spherity.com/*
- SPKI/SDSI project: *http://world.std.com/~cme/html/spki.html*
- SoLid (Social Linked Data: *https://github.com/solid/solid-spec*
- uPort: *https://www.uport.me/*
- UniquID: *https://uniquid.com/*
- ValidatedID: *https://www.validatedid.com*
- WebIDs: *https://www.w3.org/2005/Incubator/webid/spec/tls/*
- WoTT: *https://wott.io/*
- W3C working group on verifiable claims: *https://www.w3.org/2017/vc/WG/*
- W3C Verifiable Claims Task Force FAQ: *https://w3c.github.io/webpayments-ig/VCTF/charter/faq.html*
- W3C initiative of Decentralized Identifiers (DIDs): *https://w3c.github.io/did-core*

PART 2

Web3 Applications

The first chapter explains how smart contracts can encode and algorithmically enforce the business logic or governance rules of simple or complex agreements. The following two chapters will shed light on the institutional economics and governance aspects of Decentralized Autonomous Organizations, the most complex form of a smart contract that are steered by purpose-driven tokens. The last chapter will introduce tokens as the atomic unit of the Web3 and dive into the history, definition, and properties of different types of tokens.

Smart Contracts

A smart contract is a piece of software that is processed by a distributed ledger. It is a rights management tool that can formalize and execute agreements between untrusted participants over the Internet, and comes with inbuilt compliance and controlling. Smart contracts can reduce the costs of formalization and enforcement of a simple agreement between two parties, the bylaws of an organization, or to create different types of tokens.

Would you enter into a contract with someone whom you've never met, and therefore don't know and don't trust? Would you become an investor in a small company in a foreign country? Would you agree to lend money to a stranger, like a farmer in Guatemala, a teacher in China, or a cashier in the UK? Or would you set up a legally binding contract for a 1 EUR purchase over the Internet, like buying a song from an artist? The answer in all of the above mentioned cases is probably no, as the cost of setting up the necessary legal contract to secure your transaction is too high. Alternatively, you could use trusted intermediaries to settle such contracts, paying them settlement fees for their services. The business models of many Web2 tech giants like Amazon, eBay, Airbnb, and Uber result from the lack of a trustful native value-settlement layer and user centric-identity systems. Smart contracts in combination with user-centric identity systems can provide a solution to both problems. They can formalize the relationships between people and institutions and the assets they own, entirely P2P, without the need for trusted intermediaries.

Although the concept of smart contracts is not new, blockchain networks seem to be the catalyst for smart contract implementation. A more primitive form of a smart contract is a vending machine. The rules of a transaction are programmed into a machine. You select a product by pressing a number related to the product you want and insert money. If you insert enough money, the machine is programmed to eject the product. If not, you would not receive the product, or if the machine ran out of the product, you would get your money back. Automatic vending machines made certain street sellers obsolete, but they also expanded service, offering 24/7 availability instead of the limited opening hours of a human-operated vendor.

Self-Enforcing Agreements

A smart contract is a self-enforcing agreement, formalized as a software. The code contains a set of rules under which the parties of that smart contract agree to interact with each other. If and when the predefined rules are met, the agreement is automatically enforced by majority consensus of the blockchain network. Smart contracts provide mechanisms for efficiently managing tokenized assets and access rights between two or more parties. One can think of it like a cryptographic box that unlocks value or access, if and when specific predefined conditions are met. Smart contracts therefore provide a public and verifiable way to embed governance rules and business logic in a few lines of code, which can be audited and enforced by the majority consensus of a P2P network.

A smart contract can be invoked from entities within (other smart contracts) and outside (external data sources) a blockchain network. External data feeds, so-called "oracles," inject data that is relevant to the smart contract from the off-chain world into the smart contract. They can track performance of the agreement in real time and can therefore save costs, as compliance and controlling happen on the fly. Smart contracts reduce the transaction costs of agreements. Specifically, they reduce the costs of (i) reaching an agreement, (ii) formalization, and (iii) enforcement. If implemented correctly, smart contracts could provide transaction security superior to traditional contract law, thereby reducing coordination costs of auditing and enforcement of such agreements. Smart contracts also bypass the principal-agent dilemma[21] of organizations, providing more transparency and accountability, and reducing bureaucracy (read more: Part 2 - Institutional Economics of DAOs).

The term "smart contract" itself is a bit unfortunate, since smart contracts are neither particularly smart nor do they reflect legal contracts: (i) A smart contract can only be as smart as the people coding it, taking into account all available information at the time of coding; (ii) While smart contracts might have the potential to enforce legal contracts if certain conditions are met, we first need to resolve many techno-legal questions, which will require time and interdisciplinary discourse between lawyers and software developers.

---

[21] *Principal-agent dilemma occurs when someone (the agent) has the power to make decisions impacting another person or institution (the principal), but fails to do so in their best interest, such as the relationship between politicians and voters, or managers and shareholders.*

Smart Contracts

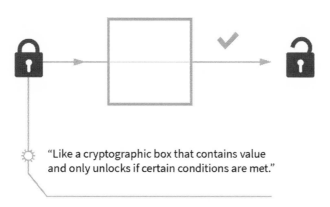

"Like a cryptographic box that contains value and only unlocks if certain conditions are met."

Furthermore, smart contract security is still an issue that needs to be resolved on a technical level. More sophisticated contractual clauses need to be implemented to make smart contracts compliant with legal contracts, including decentralized dispute settlement mechanisms. While such developments might take more time to mature, some interesting dispute-resolution solutions are already under development, examples of which are "Kleros," "Openlaw," or "Jur." We will probably see a fusion of legal contracts and smart contracts emerge over the next few years. At the time of writing this book, best practices are still rare and will require a collective learning process. The technology is still nascent, and legal standards need to be adopted.

Industry Use Cases

Smart contract use cases range from simple to complex. They can be used for simple economic transactions like sending money from A to B. Smart contracts can also be used for registering any kind of ownership and property rights, like land registries and intellectual property, or managing smart access control for the sharing economy. Use cases can be found in banking, insurance, energy, e-government, telecommunications, music and film industry, fine art, mobility, education, and many more. Each agreement, process, task, or payment can be collectively managed. Many traditional intermediaries, like lawyers, brokers, and bankers, or public administrators, and Internet platforms might no longer be necessary, or at least some of their services might become obsolete: Cars could use smart contracts to pay their own bills upon fueling up at the gas station, or charging up at an electric charging pole. Invoices could be settled upon arrival of a product shipment. Smart share certificates in the form of tokenized securities could be programmed to conduct automated payout of dividends (read more: Part 4 - Asset Tokens & Fractional Ownership).

Smart contracts can provide a native settlement layer for the sharing economy, currently brokered and processed by Internet platform operators. The P2P nature of payments enabled by smart contracts reduces the transaction costs, which means that micropayments could become economically more feasible than they are today.[22] Smart access controls between two peers who do not trust each other could provide a practical solution for the sharing economy without centralized platform providers, who currently own a disproportionate part of our data, and therefore also the economic value created. This could lead to a sharing economy on steroids: apartments, cars, washing machines, bicycles, lawn mowers—once all those devices are tagged with their own blockchain address (or DID) they could be managed by a smart contract that acts as a digital lock.

A more complex example of a smart contract is the use case of a self-managing forest, as in the case of "Terra0," where a smart contract on the Ethereum blockchain manages the logging and selling of trees from a forest in Germany. Drones and satellites monitor the growth of the forest and trigger events in the smart contract, like subcontracting agreements to log the forest and sell off the wood.

Furthermore, smart contracts can be used for much more complex agreements between a multitude of actors, along the supply chain of goods or services, or for governing a group of people that share the same interests and goals without the need of traditional centralized institutions. Decentralized autonomous organizations (DAOs) are such an example and probably represent the most common form of complex smart contracts. The smart contract hereby formalizes the governance rules of an organization—like the bylaws, governing statutes, rules of procedure—and replaces day-to-day operational management with self-enforcing code.

Smart contracts and DAOs could also disrupt social media as we know it. Web2-based social media networks extract rent in the form of data from the users that they monetize. In the Web3, smart contracts can enable purpose-driven ecosystems, in which users can benefit from their network activities by getting rewarded with network tokens. An example thereof would be "Steemit," a decentralized social network that is organized as a DAO and incentivizes user contributions with network tokens (read more: Part 4 - Steemit).

---

[22] *The challenge with micropayments today is that the fee charged by third-party payment providers is higher than the micropayment itself.*

Aspects of Smart Contracts

Technical Aspects	*Legal Aspects*	*Economic Aspects*
Self-verifying (Auditing on the fly.)	Smart contracts can map legal obligations into an automated process. If implemented correctly, they can provide a greater degree of contractual security at lower costs than current legal systems.	Higher transparency
Self-executing (Enforcement on the fly.)		Fewer intermediaries
Tamper resistant (No cheating.)		Lower transaction costs

Smart contracts and distributed ledgers could also be a catalyst for machine-to-machine settlement in an "Internet of Things." This, however, requires that all objects in such an Internet of Things have a blockchain identity, and can thus be uniquely addressed. Addressability of each single machine or other physical object needs to be tamper proof. This can be achieved by tagging or chipping objects with a so-called "crypto accelerator," which is also referred to as a "digital twin." A crypto accelerator is a small micro-controller optimized to run the most important cryptographic algorithms. It can have the size of a sticker on a piece of fruit and therefore serve as a basis for use cases like supply chain transparency. With a digital twin, any physical object can send unique digital signatures, or send and receive tokens. Projecting the current rate of development of this technology into the future, and taking into account convergence with other emerging technologies like IoT, Big Data, and AI, we can now envision a world where individuals, organizations, and machines can freely interact with one another with little friction and at a fraction of current costs.

Smart contracts can furthermore be used to create and manage cryptographic tokens that can represent any asset or access rights, and even incentivize behavior. Tokens might emerge to be one of the most important applications of smart contracts, potentially revolutionizing asset management as we know it. This is why the last two parts of this book are dedicated entirely to the topic of tokens.

Buying a Car in the Web2

1 B

Bob wants to sell a car. Bob uses the Internet to find a website where he can post his used car and define the terms of sale. There, he will create a listing where he defines the terms and conditions of selling his used car.

Contract

3

Alice agrees to pay $20,000 for the car. Once Bob gets the deposit, he will transfer the car ownership to Alice by handing over the car documents and keys.

A <u>trusted third party</u> is required for verification. In order to officially transfer the ownership of the car, the terms of the contract have to be met. The process differs from country to country but always involves one or more trusted-third-parties: motor vehicle registration authority, in combination with notary and/or insurance company. It's a complicated and lengthy process. Middlemen fees apply.

Alice wants to buy a car. Alice will also use the Internet to find a service like eBay to buy a used car. Once she finds the car she wants to buy (Bob's car), both will coordinate by messenger, phone, and in person to resolve final questions, define the terms of sale, and sign the contract to finalize it.

2 A

Buying a Car in the Web3

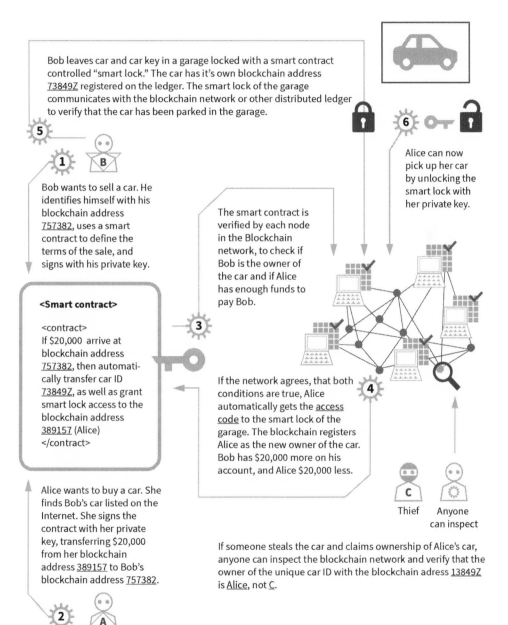

Bob leaves car and car key in a garage locked with a smart contract controlled "smart lock." The car has it's own blockchain address 73849Z registered on the ledger. The smart lock of the garage communicates with the blockchain network or other distributed ledger to verify that the car has been parked in the garage.

5

1 **B**

Bob wants to sell a car. He identifies himself with his blockchain address 757382, uses a smart contract to define the terms of the sale, and signs with his private key.

<Smart contract>

<contract>
If $20,000 arrive at blockchain address 757382, then automatically transfer car ID 73849Z, as well as grant smart lock access to the blockchain address 389157 (Alice)
</contract>

3

The smart contract is verified by each node in the Blockchain network, to check if Bob is the owner of the car and if Alice has enough funds to pay Bob.

6

Alice can now pick up her car by unlocking the smart lock with her private key.

4

If the network agrees, that both conditions are true, Alice automatically gets the access code to the smart lock of the garage. The blockchain registers Alice as the new owner of the car. Bob has $20,000 more on his account, and Alice $20,000 less.

Alice wants to buy a car. She finds Bob's car listed on the Internet. She signs the contract with her private key, transferring $20,000 from her blockchain address 389157 to Bob's blockchain address 757382.

2 **A**

C Thief

Anyone can inspect

If someone steals the car and claims ownership of Alice's car, anyone can inspect the blockchain network and verify that the owner of the unique car ID with the blockchain adress 13849Z is Alice, not C.

Oracles

Blockchain networks and smart contracts cannot access data from outside of their network. In order to know what to do, a smart contract often needs access to information from the outside world that is relevant to the contractual agreement, in the form of data feeds, also referred to as "oracles." These oracles are services that feed the smart contract with external information that can trigger predefined actions of the smart contract, which in turn induce state changes to the ledger. This external data stems either from software (Big Data application) or hardware (Internet of Things).

- <u>Software Oracles</u>: handle information data that originates from online sources, such as temperature, prices of stocks or commodities, flight or train arrival times, etc.

- <u>Hardware Oracles</u>: Some smart contracts need information directly from the physical world, for example, a car crossing a barrier where movement sensors must detect the vehicle and send the data to a smart contract, or RFID sensors in the supply chain industry.

- <u>Inbound Oracles</u>: provide data from the external world.

- <u>Outbound Oracles</u>: provide smart contracts with the ability to send data to the outside world.

- <u>Consensus-based oracles</u>: get their data from human consensus and prediction markets like "Augur" or "Gnosis." However, using only one source of information could be unreliable, as markets can be manipulated; rating systems for oracles might be needed. A combination of different oracle services might further increase data reliability if, for example, three out of five oracles could determine the outcome of an event.

The main challenge with oracles is that people need to trust these outside sources of information, whether they come from a website or a sensor. Since oracles are third-party services that are not part of the blockchain consensus mechanism, they are not subject to the underlying security mechanisms that this public infrastructure provides. One could replicate "man-in-the-middle attacks"[23] standing between contracts and oracles. The robustness assurance of this "second layer" is of utmost importance. Different trusted cryptographic tools and computing techniques can be used as a way of solving these issues. If oracle security is not

---

[23] *In computer security, "man-in-the-middle attacks" refer to incidents where an attacker relays and possibly alters the communication between two parties who believe they are directly or secretly communicating with each other.*

adequately provided, it will be a show stopper for widespread smart contract implementation.

It is important to note that a smart contract does not wait for the data from an outside source to flow into the system. The contract has to be invoked, which means that one has to spend network resources for calling data from the outside world. This induces network transaction costs. In the case of Ethereum, this would be the cost of "Gas."

Use Case of Buying a Second-Hand Car

If two people, let's say Alice and Bob, don't know and don't trust each other, they usually need a trusted third party to serve as an intermediary to verify transactions and enforce them. With smart contracts and blockchain networks, you no longer need those trusted intermediaries for the clearing or settlement of your transactions. Take the example of buying and selling a car: If Alice wants to purchase a car from Bob today, a series of trusted third parties are required to verify and authenticate the deal. The process differs from country to country but always involves at least one, but usually more, trusted third parties: motor vehicle registration authority, in combination with a notary and/or insurance company. It can be a complicated and lengthy process, including resulting fees. If and when all involved authorities and companies use distributed ledgers, a smart contract could be used to formalize all the rules of a valid car sale, including the settlement for add-on services like buying a car insurance policy. If Alice wanted to buy the car from Bob using smart contracts, the potential process could look like this:

1. Bob will use the Internet to find a service where he can post his used car and define the terms of sale, using a smart contract—on some decentralized version of eBay, for example. This step is no different from today, but smart contract–based services need to be Web3 compatible, to communicate with a blockchain network. This smart contract service might also provide a smart garage that also communicates with a blockchain network. Bob will therefore need to download a software that is Web3 with an inbuilt wallet, which will provide him with a unique blockchain identity—a blockchain address with a related public-private key pair (read more: Part 1 - Cryptography).

2. Alice will also use the Internet, just as she does today. She will search the Web to find the decentralized version of eBay, where Bob posted his car. Alice will also need to download a Web3-compatible browser.

3. If Alice finds a car that she likes and wants to buy—let's say Bob's car—she will click on "buy," and the smart contract-based service will use a blockchain

network to check whether Bob is the owner of the car, and whether Alice has enough funds available. The information about both states—the ownership titles of the car Bob claims to sell, and the amount of tokens Alice has—is recorded on the ledger. Upon clicking the "buy" button, the smart contract service might also give her the option to select an insurance plan, with selected insurance companies that are also registered on the ledger and connected with the smart contract service providing this insurance (in such a future scenario, the insurance plan could probably be calculated on the fly, where rates would be based on the car's data and Alice's driving history).

4. If the network agrees that both states are true—that Alice has enough funds, and that Bob is really the owner of the car—the blockchain network registers Alice as the new owner of the car, and their funds balances are automatically updated: Bob now has 20,000 more tokens on his account, while Alice has 20,000 less tokens in her wallet. Alice then receives an access code to the smart lock for the garage. Furthermore, Alice is now also registered with the car insurance company of her choice, which she selected upon buying the car, triggering another smart contract.

   • Bob can now park his car in the garage. His car, which also has a unique identity on the blockchain, will now be registered as being parked in the garage, and Alice will receive a notification about where to pick up the car with her access code.

   • Alice can now pick up the car in the specified garage, protected by a smart lock connected to the blockchain and managed by the smart contract that both Bob and Alice use. She can unlock the garage with her private key, which identifies her as the rightful owner of the car. The car is hers, it is registered to her name, and it has insurance.

Using smart contracts, we can now avoid manual interference of certain institutions like motor vehicle authorities, insurance companies, and in some countries, also notaries, if and when the regulatory environments permit it. Every computer running the blockchain protocol will be able to check whether someone is the rightful owner of a car or not. Stealing cars won't be as easy as it is today, once cars are equipped with digital keys using smart contracts for access control. Certain automated processes will also require the convergence of smart contracts with data feeds from external software and hardware, as would be the case of pictures taken in the garage to monitor the state of the car. As the owner of the car, you could furthermore use smart contracts to authorize other people to drive your car, registering their blockchain identity with the smart contract of your car.

Smart contract security is an important issue for widespread adoption of use cases: (i) Oracle security: making sure that data coming from off-chain sources can be trusted; (ii) Secure coding and formal verification: computer-aided checking and testing of code with respect to behavioral specifications; (iii) Procedural security and dispute settlement: additional on-chain and off-chain mechanisms to resolve complaints or unforeseen situations arising from the runtime usage of smart contracts. Alternative smart contract programming languages to the ones that are in use today might be an interesting aspect to tackle, both from a security point of view and from a market adoption point of view. The merging of smart contracts and legal contracts is another important question that will require cross-disciplinary research and development. Furthermore, smart contracts should be designed in a way where personalized data is only revealed to those actors involved in the process who need to know explicit information. Smart contracts will need to be compliant with privacy-preserving regulations (privacy by design).

As indicated above, many smart contract use cases will only be possible interplaying with other technologies like big cata applications and the "Internet of Things." Such an interplay of technologies can pave the way for completely new products, services, and asset classes over the decades to come. However, many socio-political questions might also arise. Once all objects have been tagged with a unique blockchain address (identity), and can therefore be uniquely referenced in a blockchain network, and if they are controlled by more or less intelligence software, these devices could become autonomous economic agents in a man-machine economy. However, the questions of (i) whether and how we will transfer the mandate from humans to machines, (ii) what socio-political implications such developments could have, and (iii) how we want to shape such phenomena as a society, need to be publicly discussed before designing such systems.

History of Smart Contracts

While the term "smart contract" has become more mainstream since the advent of first Bitcoin and then Ethereum, it was first coined by Nick Szabo in 1996, and thus precedes the development of blockchain networks. It was in the early days of the Web when Szabo pointed out that the digital revolution would not only create new institutions but could also formalize economic and social relations. That was twenty years before Ethereum saw the light of day, and created a renaissance of this term. Szabo justified the term "smart" with the functionality that comes with digital contracts to be automatically verified and executed: a digital transaction log that automatically executes the terms of an agreement with the aim of fulfilling the agreed contractual terms. Automatic management of relationships and obligations of all parties involved, purely with computer code.

As opposed to traditional contracts, which guarantee contractual security with reactive procedures using instruments of the existing legal system, smart contracts—according to Szabo—could proactively prevent this reactive "after the fact" security through automated mechanisms, by making a potential breach of contract possible but expensive. Szabo pointed out that the reactive procedures of existing legal systems could be minimized but never fully eliminated. To provide for such a level of proactive security, smart contracts should be automatic and (a) observable, (b) verifiable, and (c) enforceable. In any case, Szabo warned that (d) the privacy of the data must be guaranteed by only revealing necessary data, and only to contracting parties that are entitled to view it.

Szabo was very specific in his descriptions of how to technically formalize these relationships, and listed a variety of cryptographic methods that could be used, such as public-key cryptography and digital signatures, and in particular, blind signatures[24] and zero-knowledge proof cryptography.[25] Some of these cryptographic methods described by Szabo can be found in the implementation of Bitcoin. However, Szabo was much more far-sighted in his thought processes than Satoshi and many other early developers of Bitcoin and alternative blockchain networks, such as Ethereum. While he was referring to more privacy-preserving methods like blind signatures and zero-knowledge proofs back in 1996, these methods are only slowly finding their way into the blockchain world. Such privacy-preserving techniques also have the potential to meet the requirements of "Privacy by Design," specified in the General Data Protection Regulation (GDPR) of the European Union, much better than the cryptographic methods that are currently used in most state-of-the-art blockchain networks (read more: Part 1 - Cryptography).

Szabo said that for smart contracts to "be embedded in the real world in the form of self-enforcing code," they must be designed to be trustworthy and attack resistant, both against intentional attacks and against unintentional vandalism. However, at that time, Szabo had no idea how to fully decentralize trust and make such a system sybil attack resistant, and therefore described the necessity of a trusted intermediary. He described the economic utility function of a potential attacker and referred to concepts of theoretical computer science and information security when outlining solutions. In 1998, he went on to develop his ideas around smart contracts into real life implementation of P2P value transfer. He came up with an idea for electronic cash that would be as inflation resistant as gold, which he called "Bit Gold." Bit Gold was never implemented because Szabo didn't find a way to replace the trusted intermediary with a sybil attack-resistant system. Ten years later,

---

[24] *Blind signatures are digital signatures that disguise the content of a message before it is signed. They can be verified against the original message just like a regular digital signature.*

[25] *Zero-knowledge proof cryptography allows the validation of information without revealing that information to the verifier of that information.*

Bitcoin's major breakthrough was addressing exactly this issue with the introduction of "Proof-of-Work."

Szabo envisioned an entanglement of different scientific fields in order to formalize smart contracts, such as law, economics, and cryptography, but criticized that these disciplines hardly communicated with each other. However, he was not the first to think about contractual automation. Two years earlier, Ian Grigg described his thoughts on Ricardian Contracts, specifying how to make real-world contracts machine readable and machine enforceable. He wanted to create a system that would allow maintaining human readability of contract intentions as well as resulting actions, before an agreement is executed, while optimizing machine authentication and processing through encryption techniques, such as hash functions and digital signatures. His aim was to guarantee the linking and processing of legal documents and related matters to provide more transparency and security than traditional legal procedures. The first hybrid solutions of smart contracts and Ricardian Contracts exist. Openbazaar is a P2P e-commerce platform that is already working with Ricardian Contracts.

Since the advent of the Ethereum project, the term "smart contract" has experienced a renaissance. Ethereum decoupled the concept of programming smart contracts from the underlying blockchain network processing the agreements. As opposed to Bitcoin, the Ethereum protocol aims to provide a cost-saving infrastructure where one can create any type of smart contract with just a few lines of code. Ethereum inspired many more projects to work on similar smart contract blockchain networks, such as EOS, Cardano, or Waves, all of which have varying degrees of technical maturity, scalability, network security, and often use different smart contracting languages.

Chapter Summary

- *A smart contract is a piece of software that is processed by a distributed ledger. It is a rights management tool that can formalize and execute agreements between untrusted participants over the Internet, and comes with inbuilt compliance and controlling.*

- *Smart contracts can reduce the costs of formalization and enforcement of a simple agreement between two parties, the bylaws of an organization, or to create different types of tokens.*

- *The term "smart contract" was first coined by Nick Szabo in 1996 and precedes the development of blockchain networks. It was still the early days of the Web when Szabo pointed out that the digital revolution would not only create new institutions but could also formalize economic and social relations.*

- *Smart contract use cases range from simple to complex. The most complex form of a smart contract is a decentralized autonomous organization. Smart contracts can also be used to create tokens.*

- *Smart contracts have the potential to disrupt many industries. Use cases can be found in banking, insurance, energy, e-government, telecommunication, music & film industry, fine art, mobility, education, and many more.*

- *Oracles provide the external data necessary for the smart contract and trigger smart contract executions when predefined conditions are met. Oracles are services that find and verify real world occurrences and submit this information to a smart contract, automatically triggering state changes on the blockchain. The primary task of oracles is to provide these values to the smart contract in a secure and trusted manner. These data flows stem either from software (Big Data application) or hardware (Internet of Things).*

Chapter References & Further Reading

- *Blocher, Walter; "The next big thing: Blockchain – Bitcoin –Smart Contracts", AnwBl 2016, S. 615; 2016*
- *Buterin, Vitalik: "SchellingCoin: A Minimal-Trust Universal Data Feed", March 28, 2014, https://blog.ethereum.org/2014/03/28/schellingcoin-a-minimal-trust-universal-data-feed/*
- *Glatz, Florian: "What are Smart Contracts? In search of a consensus", Dec 12, 2014: https://medium.com/@heckerhut/whats-a-smart-contract-in-search-of-a-consensus-c268c830a8ad*
- *Greenspan, Gideon: "Why Many Smart Contract Use Cases Are Simply Impossible", Apr 17, 2016: https://www.coindesk.com/three-smart-contract-misconceptions*
- *Grigg, Ian; "The Ricardian Contract", In Proceedings of the First IEEE International Workshop on Electronic Contracting, pages 25-31. IEEE, 2004: http://iang.org/papers/ricardian_contract.html*
- *Internet of Agreements: http://internetofagreements.com/*
- *Nisan, Noam; Ronen, Amir; „Algorithmic mechanism design", Proceedings of the 31st ACM Symposium on Theory of Computing (STOC ,99), pp. 129–140, 1999*
- *N.N.: "Hardware Pythias: bridging the Real World to the Blockchain", Ledger Blog, 31 Aug 08 2016: https://blog.ledger.co/2016/08/31/hardware-pythias-bridging-the-real-world-to-the-blockchain/#.2zeggzh6f*
- *N.N.: "Understanding oracles" Oraclize Blog, Feb 18, 2016: https://blog.oraclize.it/understanding-oracles-99055c9c9f7b*
- *N.N.: „1,749,693 blocks later" Provable Things, Sep 16, 2016: https://medium.com/provable/1-749-693-blocks-later-4225f55c68f1*
- *N.N.: „A Visit to the Oracle Smart contracts are poised to revolutionize the ways that humans, machines, and organizations create and enforce contractual relationships" ConsenSys, Jun 1, 2016: https://media.consensys.net/a-visit-to-the-oracle-de9097d38b2f#.97rovs1ho*
- *N.N.: „Hardware Oracles: bridging the Real World to the Blockchain," Ledger Blog. Retrieved Nov 2, 2016: https://blog.ledger.co/hardware-oracles-bridging-the-real-world-to-the-blockchain-ca97c2fc3e6c#.2zeggzh6f*
- *Szabo, Nick: "Smart Contracts: Building Blocks for Digital Markets", 1996: http://www.fon.hum.uva.nl/rob/Courses/InformationInSpeech/CDROM/Literature/LOTwinterschool2006/szabo.best.vwh.net/smart_contracts_2.html*
- *Szabo, Nick: "Formalizing and Securing Relationships on Public Networks" First Monday, Volume 2,*

Number 9 - 1 September 1997d: http://journals.uic.edu/ojs/index.php/fm/article/view/548/469

- *Voshmgir, Shermin: "Blockchain, Smart Contracts und das Dezentrale Web", Technologiestiftung Berlin, 2017: https://www.technologiestiftung-berlin.de/de/blockchain/*

- *Voshmgir, Shermin: "Smart Contracts, Blockchains und automatisch ausführbare Protokolle", in: Braegelmann/Kaulartz (Hg.): Rechtshandbuch Smart Contracts, CH Beck Verlag, p. 13-27.*

- *Zhang, F., Cecchetti, E., Croman, K., Juels, A., Shi, E.: "Town Crier: An Authenticated Data Feed for Smart Contracts", Published by ACM 2016, Published in: Proceeding CCS ,16 Proceedings of the 2016, ACM SIGSAC Conference on Computer and Communications Security Pages 270-282: https://eprint.iacr.org/2016/168.pdf*

- *Cardano: https://www.cardano.org/en/home/*

- *Bernstein: https://www.bernstein.io/*

- *EOS: https://eos.io/*

- *Kleros: https://kleros.io/*

- *Open Bazaar: https://openbazaar.org/*

- *OpenLaw: https://media.consensys.net/introducing-openlaw-7a2ea410138*

- *Jur: https://jur.io/*

- *Terra0: https://terra0.org/*

- *Waves: https://wavesplatform.com/*

Institutional Economics of Web3 Networks & other DAOs [26]

Institutional economics studies the role of formal or informal institutions-such as procedure, convention, arrangement, traditions and customs-in a socio-economic context. Since the emergence of the Internet many distributed Internet tribes have formed, like social media platforms, e-commerce platforms or knowledge platforms. Web3 networks introduce a new type of Internet-based institutional infrastructure that enables distributed Internet tribes to self organize and coordinate in a more autonomous way, steered by purpose-driven tokens, and executed with machine-enforceable protocols. They are commonly referred to as Decentralized Autonomous Organizations (DAOs).

Blockchain networks and similar distributed ledgers can disrupt traditional governance[27] structures and challenge the current forms of how society organizes itself. They can (i) reduce the principal-agent dilemma of organizations by providing transparency; (ii) incentivize network actors with a native token, thereby disintermediating and reducing management costs, and (iii) replace the reactive procedural security of the current legal system, with proactive and automated mechanisms that make a potential breach of contract expensive, and therefore infea-

---

[26] *The following two chapters are partially based on a journal article which was published by the author in 2017: Voshmgir, Shermin: "Disrupting governance with blockchains and smart contracts,", Journal for Strategic Change. A prior version was published on blockchainhub: https://blockchainhub.net/blog/blog/ disrupting-organisations-with-blockchain/ and Voshmgir, S.; Zargham, M.: "Foundations of Cryptoeconomic Systems," Cryptoeconomic Systems Journal, March 2020, retreived from: https://assets.pubpub.org/ sy02t720/31581340240758.pdf*

[27] *„Governance" is a political science term that refers to the rules, norms, and actions of how people interact within a community or organization - whether formal or informal.*

sible. Web3 networks generally provide for a more decentralized and spontaneous coordination over the Internet between people and institutions who might not even know or trust each other. The coordination structures are referred to as Decentralized Autonomous Organizations (DAOs).

DAOs tackle an age-old problem of governance that political scientists and economists refer to as the "principal-agent dilemma," which occurs when the agent of an organization has the power to make decisions on behalf of, or impacting, the principal—another person or entity in the organization. Examples thereof could be managers that act on behalf of shareholders or politicians that act on behalf of citizens. In such setups, moral hazard occurs when one person takes more risks than they normally would, because others bear the cost of those risks. More generally, it occurs when the agent acts in his own interest rather than the interest of the principal, because the principal cannot fully control the agent's actions. This dilemma usually increases when there is underlying information asymmetry at play.

The Bitcoin network can be considered to be the first true decentralized and autonomous organization, coordinated by the Bitcoin protocol, and which anybody is free to adopt. The Bitcoin network provides an operating system for money without banks and bank managers, and has stayed attack resistant and fault tolerant since the first block was created in 2009. No central entity controls the network, which means that as long as people keep participating in the network, only a worldwide power outage could shut down Bitcoin. The governance rules are tied to the network token, with the aim to steer the behavior of network nodes with an incentive mechanism that has proven to be an effective motivator for performing network services (read more: Part 1 - Blockchain & Other Distributed Ledgers, Part 4 - Purpose-Driven Tokens).

With the emergence of the Ethereum network, the concept of DAOs moved up the technology stack from blockchain protocol to the smart contract. Whereas before one needed a blockchain network with an attack-resistant consensus protocol to create a DAO, smart contracts made the creation of DAOs easily programmable, often with just a few lines of code, and without the need of setting up your own blockchain infrastructure. DAO use cases range from simple to complex. The complexity depends on the number of stakeholders, as well as the number and complexity of processes within that organization governed by the smart contract. The token governance rules incentivize and steer a network of actors, replacing the need for top-down organizations with self-enforcing code. Depending on the purpose and governance rules of a DAO, and the level of autonomy of the DAO stakeholders, the use cases can resemble a company or nation state. Organizations that use smart contracts as their operating infrastructure can use the legal system for some protection of physical property, but such usage is secondary to the preemptive security mechanisms that smart contracts can offer.

"TheDAO" in 2016 was a very early example for such a complex smart contract on the Ethereum network. The purpose of TheDAO was to provide an autonomous vehicle for fund management without traditional fund managers. During a four-week token sale, TheDAO issued DAO tokens against ETH, collecting an equivalent of 150 million USD, resulting in the biggest token sale at its time. The idea was that every DAO token holder would be a co-owner of this decentralized investment fund, proportional to the number of tokens held, and could participate in investment decisions with proportional voting rights. Specialized services to TheDAO could be conducted by subcontractors hired by TheDAO token holders by majority consensus. However, due to a programming error in the software, this vision of TheDAO never became reality, as the project was drained of roughly a third of its funds before it became operational. This led to a controversial hard fork of the Ethereum network. One of the major shortcomings was that the governance rules of TheDAO did not account for decision-making processes in the case of unforeseen events (read more in the next chapter: On-Chain vs. Off-Chain Governance).

This early use case of a smart contract-based DAO showed that what the Bitcoin network resolved with a complex consensus protocol, building on decades of applied and theoretical research, cannot be simply replicated with a few lines of code. The purpose of TheDAO was different from the Bitcoin network, and therefore required a new type of attack-resistant steering mechanism, but the governance rules of TheDAO were developed in only a few months, mostly by engineers with no governance expertise at all. TheDAOs token governance rules were based on oversimplified assumptions of how token holders would behave: They did not sufficiently account for psychological phenomena such as "free-rider problem"[28] or "bounded rationality"[29] which are subject to the field of Behavioral Economics (read more: Part 4 - Purpose-Driven Tokens). Instead, they based their token governance design on the assumption that small token holders would mimic the behaviour of big token holders, who were assumed to take the time for sensible decision-making as they had more "skin in the game." In reality, most small token holders did not participate in any voting processes at all, probably hoping that other token holders would make the right decision on their behalf. Furthermore, the voting process involved personal intervention, with bad wallet usability, excluding many smaller and technically less adept token holders from participating in voting processes. The whole incident showed that "decentralization" is also a question of human behavior, and thus also subject to behavioral economics, and never only a

---

[28] *The "free-rider" problem refers to members of a group taking advantage of being able to use a common resource, or collective good, without contributing to it.*

[29] *Behavioral economics assumes that the rationality of individuals and institutions is "bounded" and that 90 percent of their decisions are based on mental shortcuts or "rules of thumb." Especially under pressure and in situations of high uncertainty people tend to rely on anecdotal evidence and stereotypes to help them understand and respond to events more quickly.*

mathematical or technical question.

We are seeing many more DAOs, with a wide range of purposes, emerge on top of the Web3. Newer Web3 applications have focused on providing a plug-and-play end-to-end framework to build DAOs. The tool-set provided include elements such as constitutional frameworks, dispute-resolution frameworks, and many more, so that new DAO projects don't have to build all organizational and institutional elements necessary from scratch. They reduce the technical costs of setting up a decentralized organization, so you can focus on what you want to build (the purpose of your network) and how you want to build it (the governance rules of your network.) Many of the projects build on top of the Ethereum network and offer a modular smart contract framework, with an easy to use user interface, that allows people without technical knowledge to create their own decentralized organization. The level of decentralization of such organizations can vary according to the needs. Examples of such projects are "Aragon," "Bitnation," "Colony," "Commonstack," "DAOStack," or "MolochDAO," each of which differ in their focus, ideology, or levels of progression and success.

DAOs vs. Traditional Organizations

Large parts of our society are organized in top-down command and control structures. The role of the legal system is to secure and enforce all contractual agreements of all institutions that regulate our socio-economic interactions. The example of such legal frameworks are (i) the constitution of a country, (ii) employment contracts between employee and organization, (iii) supply agreements, purchase agreements, or sales contracts between the organizations, or (iv) bilateral or multilateral agreements between governments of different nations. The organizational structures of our economic institutions have evolved over time and are a subject of research in institutional economics, management science and cybernetics. Political Institutions governing the members of a geographical area, also referred to as citizens, have also evolved over time and are subject to the study of political science, economics, in particular institutional economics, sociology and cybernetics.

Evolution of Companies and the "Theory of the Firm": In his book "The Theory of the Firm," economist Ronald Coase argued that firms arise if they can produce what they need internally more efficiently than through outsourcing—taking into account all costs, such as search, information acquisition, bargaining, and policing of business partnerships or engaging in bilateral trading in the marketplace. His theories explain the concentration of economic production, through vertical integration of production, and the subsequent rise of multinational corporations, from the Industrial Revolution until the late 20th century. In recent decades, these highly structured, centralized, and bureaucratic organizations of the 20th century have given way to looser, flatter organizational forms, such as "Holacracy," which is an example for a more autonomous organizational structure steered by self-reliant units. The Internet, as an information-sharing technology, has facilitated much of this organizational innovation, and started an outsourcing revolution, and reduced the size of companies (in number of employees). Furthermore, the emergence of the Web2 has facilitated global market-making mechanisms at lower transaction costs, enabling new forms of organizing around, for example, the prosumer. However, there remains one powerful intermediary, a trusted third party—like Amazon, eBay, Zalando, Uber, Airbnb, or similar companies—providing a trusted platform for two people interacting over the Internet. While products and services around those platforms have become more and more unbundled, bringing producers and consumers closer to each other, the terms of service are always dictated by those platform providers, mostly privately held companies which also control all user data. Smart contracts have the power to disintermediate these platforms, introducing new ways of coordinating activities, such as task allocation, coordination, and supervision of a group of people who share common economic interests but are geographically distributed.

The Governance of Nation States and Representative Democracy: Democracy is a system of governance where people who share a geographical area and are affected by collective decisions of the group agree to participate in said decision-making process equally. The question of how individuals should participate is and has been the source of many debates and conflicts, and has also greatly evolved over time. Direct democracy is a form of democracy in which people decide upon all policy initiatives directly. However, the bigger the group, the harder it is for members of that group to participate in each and every decision-making process for various reasons, such as the large cost of coordination, and mental transaction costs for each individual involved. Centralized institutions and bureaucratic organizational structures have, as a result, emerged around modern representative democracies. In such a representative setup, elected representatives govern on behalf of all eligible members of a state, the sovereign. Both systems have merits and deficiencies, depending on the size and type of group governed. Recent political history suggests high levels of disenchantment in the general public toward established political governance systems, which political scientists refer to as "Post Democracy." It is characterized by an increasingly remote governing elite, coupled with increased clamor from the citizenry to reclaim their place in decision making. Globalization effects, such as free trade, cheaper and faster transport, and the Internet, have further undermined the power of a nation state to regulate the life of its citizens. One suggested solution to this disenchantment is "Liquid Democracy," a type of democratic governance whereby an electorate delegates voting power in a

Traditional Top-Down Organisation

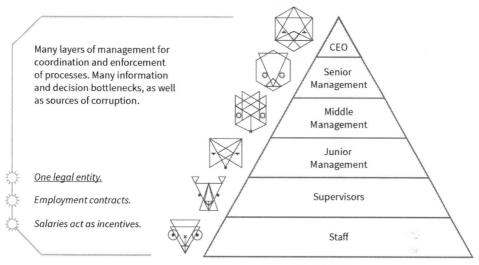

Many layers of management for coordination and enforcement of processes. Many information and decision bottlenecks, as well as sources of corruption.

One legal entity.

Employment contracts.

Salaries act as incentives.

CEO

Senior Management

Middle Management

Junior Management

Supervisors

Staff

Top-Down Management

Decentralized Autonomous Organization

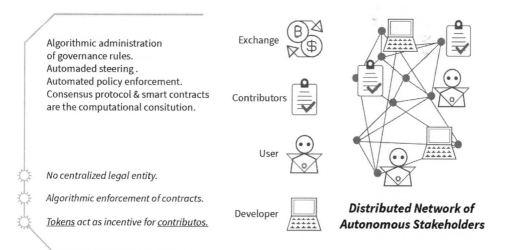

Algorithmic administration of governance rules.
Automaded steering .
Automated policy enforcement.
Consensus protocol & smart contracts are the computational consitution.

No centralized legal entity.

Algorithmic enforcement of contracts.

Tokens act as incentive for _contributos._

Exchange

Contributors

User

Developer

Distributed Network of Autonomous Stakeholders

more flexible manner, allowing for differentiation in the powers delegated and the timeframe of the delegation. It is a way of collaborative decision making that does not depend on elected representatives but rather on the partial or temporal delegation of votes. While "Liquid Democracy" may offer a solution to some of the problems of established democratic systems, it is an unfeasible way to govern given our current structures, which are predominantly based on (i) national legal silos that are a relict of a pre-Internet and pre-Globalization era, and (ii) the predominance of paper-based voting systems.

Decentralized Autonomous Organizations involve a set of people interacting with each other according to a self-enforcing, open-source software protocol in the absence of bilateral agreements. The blockchain protocol and/or the smart contract code formalize the governance rules of a DAO, regulating the behavior of all network participants. DAOs offer the possibility to establish more fluid decentralized organizations over the Internet and around a specific economic, political, or social purpose. They provide an operating system for people and institutions that do not know nor trust each other, who might live in different geographical areas, speak different languages, and be subject to different jurisdictions. Elements of Liquid Democracy can be applied on a protocol level (delegated Proof-of-Stake, or Proof-of-Work mining pools) and on a smart contract level with lower operational costs than in the "off-chain" world we live in today. Performing network tasks can be rewarded with a network token. Tokens can also be used for exercising voting rights. Once deployed, a fully decentralized autonomous organization is independent of its creator and cannot be controlled by one single entity, only by majority consensus of the organization's participants.[30] The exact majority rules are defined in the consensus protocol or the smart contract coded, and vary from use case to use case. DAOs have the potential to resolve global coordination problems such as the intransparency along international supply chains and lack of enforceability of global policy making. This is probably one of the reasons why many organizations of the United Nations are already looking into smart contract applications, such as the World Food Program, UNICEF, UNOPS, and UNDP.

DAOs are open source, thus transparent, and if well designed, incorruptible. All transactions of the organization are recorded and maintained by a blockchain network. Code upgrade proposals can be made by anyone in the network, and are voted for by majority consensus of involved network actors. As such, DAOs can be

---

[30] *However, in some countries, like Austria, there are trends in legal literature to see DAOs as a civil law partnership, a "Gesellschaften bürgerlichen Rechts (GesBR)" pursuant to §§ 1175 ABGB. A civil law partnership is an association of individuals or enterprises who unite to achieve a joint purpose. While a written partnership agreement is recommended, it is not mandatory. All partners are jointly liable with their private assets for debts incurred by the joint enterprise. Even if one would classify DAOs as GesBRs, many unsolved problems (for example, the solidary liability) persist.*

Complex Socio-Economic Systems

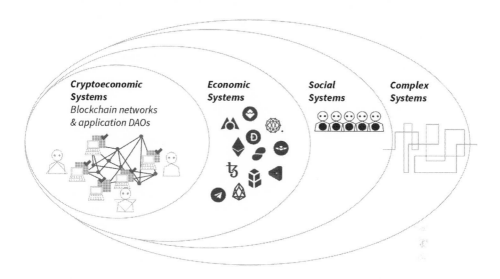

Amanded version of a graphic that was published in Voshmgir, S.; Zargham, M.: "Foundations of Cryptoeconomic Systems"

seen as distributed organisms, or distributed Internet tribes, that live on the Internet and exist autonomously, but also heavily rely on specialist individuals or smaller organizations to perform certain tasks that cannot be replaced with automation. However, I would like to argue that there is no such thing as a fully decentralized and autonomous organization. Depending on the governance rules, there are different levels of decentralization. Furthermore, while the network might be geographically decentralized, with many independent but equal network actors, the governance rules written in the smart contract or blockchain protocol will always be a point of centralization and loss of direct autonomy. DAOs can be architecturally decentralized (independent actors run different nodes), and are geographically decentralized (subject to different jurisdictions), but they are logically centralized around the protocol. The question of how to upgrade the protocol, when and if necessary, is very often delegated to a set of experts who understand the techno-legal intricacies of the code, and therefore represent a point of centralization (read more: Part 2 - On-Chain vs. Off-Chain Governance).

Web3 networks and smart contract based DAOs are complex systems that are composed of three interdependent networks: (i) a network of computers, (ii) a network of people, (iii) a network of flow of tokens. They are adaptive socio-economic networks that are dynamic in time and space. Dynamic refers to the continued state changes of the network as a result of the actions set by their human agents (sending tokens or consuming other network services, contributing with code, or forking into another network.) Adaptive means that DAO participants constantly adapt to the network they are part of because of the feedback-loops between the individual actors and the whole network. Individual actions affect the system and as a result, the system as a whole evolves over time. Complex systems differ from other (less complex) systems, in that the system level behaviour cannot be easily concluded or predicted from the local state changes induced by individual network actors.

System theory is one of many tools associated with "cybernetics," an interdisciplinary field of science that studies self-governing systems of living organisms, machines, and organizations. The term "cybernetics" has its roots in the Greek language and can be translated with „to steer, navigate or govern the ship." Steering refers to establishing goals, not telling the system what to do. These goals can be individual (individual wants and needs) and communal (social consensus about collective policies). Self-steering and co-steering systems, in political science, are often referred to as democracy. The Economist Friedrich von Hayek referred to cybernetics as a discipline that could also help economists understand markets as „self-organizing or self-generating systems complex phenomena" using the cybernetic feedback mechanism for economic pattern predictions. He explained Adam Smith's idea of the "invisible hand" as anticipation of the operation of the feedback mechanism in cybernetics.

Institutional Economics of DAOs

Institutional economics is a subset of economics that intersects with political science, sociology, or history and studies the role of formal or informal institutions in a socio-economic context. "Institutions" represent a set of rules or contracts that enable social interaction such as procedure, convention, arrangement, traditions, or customs. They are often embedded into a setup of different interdependent layers: natural, cultural, and legal rulesets. Institutions can also reflect the entities that channel and incentivize actions of individuals in a group. The institutional economist Gustav von Schmoller said: "The study of the organ and the institution is, for the knowledge of the social body, what anatomy is for the physical body."

Different schools of Institutional Economics apply different definitions of what they consider an institution. Early social bodies were communities, such as the tribe, the Sippe, the family. As technological and social evolution made the governance of increasing amounts of people and over larger geographic areas feasible, new social organs emerged, most prominently the nation state and companies.

Since the emergence of the Internet many distributed Internet tribes have formed, such as social media platforms and other platforms. In this historic context, blockchain networks introduce a new type of internet-based institutional infrastructure governed by machine-enforceable protocols. Decentralized autonomous organizations can, therefore, be seen as a new social organism for the Web3. They represent socio-economic networks that come with real-time data on all network activities, but as opposed to the Web2, that data is public to all and not controlled by one single entity. The Web3 allows us to document and analyze the emergence of new institutions in almost real time and in a publicly verifiable way. Given the advances in data science, this allows for new data-driven coordination mechanisms, and enables new supranational governance forms with almost real-time feedback loops. The coming years will unveil the implications of machine-enforced economic mechanisms, and the implications of smart contracts on the evolution of legal contracts and collective socio-economic steering mechanisms.

In their institutional structure, Web3 networks resemble nation states much more than they resemble companies. The blockchain protocol is comparable to the constitution and the governing laws of a nation state. The autonomous actors in the network are the sovereigns of the network, and are therefore subject to the network constitution, the blockchain protocol or smart contract code. The monetary policy of a Proof-of-Work network, for example, is defined in the protocol, and regulates the circumstances under which a network token is minted. The fiscal policy is also defined in the protocol, and regulates the transaction fees. Stakeholders can opt in and opt out at any time, decide to become active members of the community and participate in the development of the code, or decide over code changes when there is a code upgrade.

Nation states are comparable to permissioned networks, rather than permissionless networks. In most countries, only citizens of said nation states have the privilege to be part of the network, or in other words, to live and work in that country. Non-citizens may receive temporary permission to enter the country or work in the country. While you can opt in and opt out, by way of immigration or emigration, this option usually comes at high personal and economic cost, and takes time. Nation states steer the actions of their citizens mostly by disincentive: when you break the law, you have to pay a fine or go to jail. Taxes can be considered as network transaction costs that citizens pay to receive government services. In some cases, national governments institute tax breaks and subsidies that act as positive incentives to "nudge" their citizens into a specific behavior. Tax policy is part of the fiscal policy of a country that, together with the policies of the central bank, decides over monetary policies, which intend to steer the network actors into certain economic behavior.

Institutional Economics of DAOs

Disclaimer: This table is an attempt to map institutional similarities of fully decentralized autonomous organizations, like Bitcoin, with current social organisms like nation states and companies. Please note that the word "similarity" does not imply equivalence. Furthermore, the table does not cover less autonomous forms of decentralized organizations, as often reflected by smart contract applications.

	Nation States	*DAOs*	*Companies*
Examples	China, Australia, Iran, Spain, USA, Canada, Uganda, ...	Bitcoin, Ethereum, Steem, Zcash, ...	Privately held companies Publicly held companies
Token	USD, EUR, AUD, GPP, YEN, ...	BTC, ETH, LTC, ADA, ...	Rewards & loyalty programs
Governance Models	Autocracy: Civilian or military dictatorship Oligarchy: Aristocracy, Plutocracy Kraterocracy Stratocracy, Meritocracy, Technocracy, ... Democracy: Direct, Representative, Liquid, Liberal, Social, ...	"Algorithmic administration of governance" allows for automated policy enforcement: PoW, PoS, DPoS, LPoS, TPos, BFT, FBA, pBFT, dBFT, DAGs, gossip protocols, etc. in combination with "Social Governance," the process of finding a collective position on future policies.	Types of legal entities in UK - Limited company (Ltd) - Public limited company - Limited partnership - Unlimited partnership - Chartered company - Statutory company - Holding company - Subsidiary company - One-man company
Agents	- Citizens - Temporary immigrants - Tourists - For-profit organizations - Non-profit organizations	- Token holders - Full nodes - Miners - Developers - Exchanges	- Shareholders - Board of Directors - Advisory Board - Employees - Freelancers
Governing Law	Constitution: In most representative democracies, constitutional amendments require a super-majority consensus of usually ⅔ of all votes, often of more than one governing body.	Consensus protocol /smart contracts are "computational consitution." Changes via protocol upgrade (hard-fork) or smart contract code upgrade. Rights of network nodes and stakeholders are regulated in the consensus protocol or smart contract code.	Statutes of company: Statutes can usually only be changed by shareholders. Depending on the type of legal entity, the company, their shareholders and statutes need to be registered with publicly accessible registry.
Simple laws	Simple laws build on the constitution and mostly require a simple majority.	Soft-fork (if blockchain profocol) Not an exact analogy, but probably the best in the context of this table. Who gets to vote depends on type of consensus protocol & differs often from hard-fork rules.	Whatever operational procedures the board of directors decides, which will trickle down to lower levels of management and execution.
Secession	- Revolution - War	Contentious hard-fork	- Part of the company breaks - M&A

	Nation States	**DAOs**	**Companies**
Legislation	Any member of parliament can make proposals for new legislation or change of current legislation. Usually a min. amount of members need to sign proposal before it qualifies for a vote, on national and/or federal level.	Any developer, even anonymous developers, can make improvement proposals. Chances of acceptance higher when dev is known or code improvement proposals holds true to standard forms and show technical expertise.	Board of directors and shareholders.
Execution	Government and related administrative bodies transform new legislation into operationally feasible procedures, and manage oversight of compliance with rules through institutions like tax bodies, police, military, etc.	Collective algorithmic administration of governance. Automated policy enforcement by all computers in the network executing the consensus protocol or smart contract code.	Board of directors and management.
Dispute Settlement	Judiciary: interprets law, dispute resolution - Small cause courts - District & session courts - High court - Supreme court - International courts	(a) Decentralized arbitration services (b) Retroactively changing ledger with hard fork or on-chain governance	Internal dispute settlement Mediation, Court of law (Judiciary), etc.
Identification	- Birth certificate - National ID card - Residence registration - Passport - Driver's licence - Company registry number	- Token holder's address - Validator address - Miner's address - IP addresses of the server all in combination with public-prvate keypairs.	- National ID card - Or working permit - Social security number - Bank account number - Employee ID number/card
Separation of Powers	Yes with democracies, no with autocracies.	Depends on the type of DAO, in the case of Bitcoin: full nodes validate, miners write, developers code.	Departments: HR, Controlling, Quality Management, Management, Legal Department.
Legal Tender	National currency: monetary policy defined by fiscal policy in coordination with central bank activities.	Native blockchain token. Monetary policy defined in protocol ,which can be amended in a protocol update.	No internal currency, therefore no monetary policy. But policy on how much is spent, saved, distributed as dividend (fiscal policy?)
Incentive Mechanism	- Taxation incl. nudging - Penalty systems - Implicit incentive through government spending and nudging: studying, having children, retirement insurance, social security	- Block reward - Transaction fees - Token price - Slashing	- Fixed salary, variable salary (KPI driven), bonus payments, extra holidays, possibilities of further studies. - Return on investment - Return on share

Monetary & Fiscal Policy of DAOs

Monetary policy refers to the governance of the money supply of a national currency, such as inducing interest rates that are strategized and implemented by central banks, currency boards, and other relevant regulatory authorities with the aim to achieve macroeconomic objectives such as inflation, consumption, economic growth, and liquidity. The primary objective of most central banks is to manage inflation while reducing unemployment. In those cases, the goal is usually to achieve economic growth, or at least stability, which is measured in terms of the GDP (gross domestic product), to maintain a low unemployment rate and a stable foreign exchange rate. Most central banks use a combination of following tools to regulate the monetary policy of a country: (i) open-market operations,[31] (ii) reserve requirements,[32] (iii) exchange rate intervention, and (iv) short-term interest rates.

The token supply policy of a blockchain network can be regarded as the "monetary policy" of a blockchain network. This token supply policy is defined in the protocol and establishes the supply and availability of the native network token. Just as the monetary policies of nations might vary from country to country, token supply policies of blockchain networks and other DAOs can differ greatly, introducing a new area of applied research and development. Token supply could be fixed from the beginning, as is the case with the Bitcoin network, or undefined, as in the case of the Ethereum network.

Bitcoin's token supply, for example, is regulated in the protocol and was defined before the protocol was implemented and deployed. Each time a miner discovers a new block, new BTC are created. The first BTC were created in the genesis block in 2009. The number of BTC generated per block decreases by 50 percent every 210,000 blocks, or approximately every four years. The number of Bitcoin tokens is therefore limited to slightly under 21 million BTC. The last BTC is estimated to be mined in 2140, when the block reward would drop below 1 Satoshi, which represents the smallest denomination of BTC. Miners would still be incentivized to maintain the network, in spite of decreasing block rewards, since they could collect fees for securing transactions. Changing the monetary policy of the Bitcoin network would require a majority consensus of network actors, which is possible, but unlikely. Token inflation is determined by the number of newly minted tokens each year, minus the amount of tokens burnt. If a protocol comes with a fixed token

---

[31] *Open-market operations define how and when central banks buy or sell securities from and to private banks to regulate the amount of credit private banks can issue to customers and businesses.*

[32] *The reserve requirement refers to the money banks must keep in their vaults or with the central bank overnight. A low reserve requirement allows banks to lend more of their deposits, increasing credit volume. A high reserve requirement decreases credit volume.*

supply, this will potentially lead to deflationary price development of the native token, when demand surpasses the supply of new tokens, taking into account sunk tokens.[33]

Ethereum's token supply was not predefined but collectively governed by the stakeholders of the network: (i) developers, (ii) full nodes, (iii) miners, and other network participants. Initial contributors to the Ethereum token sale were allocated 60 million ETH in the genesis block. An additional 12 million ETH were distributed to early contributors and the Ethereum Foundation. Block rewards have decreased over time due to changes in the consensus protocol. An event that impacted the issuance rate was the "Homestead fork" in 2016. Block times were reduced, which temporarily led to an increase in the issuance rate. In 2017, a mechanism was activated that increased the difficulty of mining a block, which slowed down blocks and decreased the issuance of newly minted tokens. It is referred to as the "Difficulty Bomb,"[34] or the "Ethereum Ice Age." Later that same year, the "Byzantium fork" was released, reducing block rewards from 5 to 3 ETH. The most recent drop was from 3 to 2 ETH in 2019.

Depending on the type of governance rules, token holders with a big stake in the system could influence market demand or affect the price of a token and therefore the exchange rate of that token, acting as a "quasi" central bank. In a network where token holders do not know or trust each other, coordinated action might be hard to implement, as it would require collusion of major token holders to coordinate over buying or selling tokens to manipulate the market and steer the internal token economy. If a large stake in the network token is held by one single token holder, or a limited number of token holders that are known to each other, it will be easier to steer through coordinated action. In the wake of many early token sales, this has been a big issue (read more: Part 2 - Token Sales).

Fiscal policy refers to the use of government spending and tax policies to influence macroeconomic conditions. Taxation is an important fiscal policy tool to steer economic activity while funding government spending, another fiscal policy tool. The government can spend money on subsidies, transfer payments including welfare programs, public works projects, and government salaries. While

---

[33] *There is an estimate that roughly 3.7 million BTC issued to date have been lost forever, as a result of people losing access to their private keys.*

[34] *The Difficulty Bomb is a mechanism of "Ethereum's Ice Age," during which the Ethereum protocol will transition from Proof-of-Work, which allows miners to earn ETH by competing against each other to find a hash value, to Proof-of-Stake, where rewards depend on the amount of tokens you own, or tokens you have staked. The Difficulty Bomb is a piece of code that raises the difficulty level of mining a block on the Ethereum blockchain exponentially over time to act as a disincentive for miners, and to facilitate the transition to PoS. As the difficulty level rises, miners will find it more difficult to earn ETH; otherwise, they would possibly fork the Ethereum network to keep earning mining rewards.*

higher taxes reduce the autonomy of individual actors, government spending can incentivize beneficiaries to spend the funds and can be used for directed economic growth.

In public and permissionless blockchain networks, fiscal policy could be reflected by the level of "transaction costs" that one has to pay for network transactions. This might be comparable with value-added taxes that national governments collect, only that the tax collectors, in the case of a public blockchain, are autonomous nodes validating transactions and getting rewarded for their network services. In a Proof-of-Stake setup, "fiscal policy" mechanisms are reflected in protocol variables such as (i) staking, (ii) vesting periods, and (i) reserve pools that fill or deplete based on bonding curve mechanisms.[35]

Chapter Summary

- *Since the emergence of the Internet, a vast array of distributed Internet tribes have formed, culminating in the social media platforms of today. DAOs represent dynamic networks governed by machine-enforceable protocols. They promise more decentralized and spontaneous coordination over the Internet between users who do not know or trust each other.*

- *Web3 networks provide a public governance infrastructure that can minimize the existing principal-agent dilemma of organizations and subsequent moral hazards. Their native tokens provide a new form of incentives to automatically align interests in the absence of third parties. The Bitcoin network can be seen as the first decentralized autonomous organization of this kind.*

- *Principal-agent dilemmas occur when the agent of an organization has the power to make decisions on behalf of or impacting the principal, another person or entity in the organization. Examples thereof could be managers that act on behalf of shareholders or politicians that act on behalf of citizens. Moral hazard occurs when one person takes more risks than they normally would, because someone else bears the cost of those risks.*

- *A DAO can be formalized by a smart contract. Use cases range from simple to complex. The complexity depends on the number of stakeholders, as well as the number and complexity of processes within that organization. Depending on the purpose and governance rules, a DAO organization could resemble either companies or nation states.*

---

[35] *A bonding curve is a smart contract that defines a relationship between price and token supply via a mathematical curve. Bonding curve contracts issue their own tokens through buy-and-sell functions. They are an emerging cryptoeconomic primitive that can enable price discovery and autonomous markets. In their simplest form, they act as an automated market maker. The contract can accept collateral and issues its native token in return and vice versa. They have debt and equity qualities, and can incentivize collective contribution to projects.*

- *Web3 protocols are comparable to the constitution and the governing laws of nation states. Similar to a blockchain network, nation states also have a code, the constitution, which is public, and open-source, but the laws cannot be self enforced.*

- *In their institutional structure, public and permissionless blockchain networks resemble nation states much more than they resemble companies. The autonomous actors in the network are the sovereigns of the network, and are therefore subject to the network constitution, the blockchain protocol or smart contract code. The monetary policy of that network is defined in the protocol, and regulates the circumstances under which a network token is minted. The fiscal policy is also defined in the protocol, and regulates the transaction fees.*

- *The monetary policy of a network token establishes the supply and availability of these tokens. These monetary policies, or "token supply," can differ greatly from network to network.*

Chapter References & Further Reading

- *Bevir, Mark: "Governance: A very short introduction", Oxford University Press, 2013*
- *Buterin, Vitalik: "DAOs, DACs, DAs and More: An Incomplete Terminology Guide", May 6, 2014: https://blog.ethereum.org/2014/05/06/daos-dacs-das-and-more-an-incomplete-terminology-guide/*
- *Caplan, Bryan: "From Friedman to Wittman: The Transformation of Chicago Political Economy", Econ Journal Watch, Issue 2(1) Pages 1-21. 2005*
- *Chavance, Bernard: "Institutional Economics," Routledge Frontiers of Political Economy, 2009, http://ipaa.ir/files/site1/pages/0415449111%20-%20Institutional%20Economics.pdf*
- *Chappelow, Jim: „Monetary Policy", Investopedia: https://www.investopedia.com/terms/m/monetarypolicy.asp (accessed Nov 12, 2018).*
- *Coase, Ronald: "The Nature of the Firm", Economica. Blackwell Publishing, 386–405, 1937*
- *Crouch, C.: "Coping with Post-democracy", Fabian Society, 2000*
- *Dahlman Carl J.: "The Problem of Externality", Journal of Law and Economics. 22 (1): 141–162, 1979*
- *Downs Anthony: "An Economic Theory of Political Action in a Democracy", Journal of Political Economy, The University of Chicago Press. 65 (2): 135–150, 2014*
- *Eisenhardt, K.M.; Graebner, M.E; "Theory building from cases: opportunities and challenges", Academy of Management Journal, 50, 25-32, 2007*
- *Eisenhardt, Kathleen: "Agency Theory: An Assessment and Review. The Academy of Management Review, 14(1), 57–74, 1989*
- *Empson, L.: "My affair with the "other:" Identity journeys across the research–practice divide," Journal of Management Inquiry, 22, 229-248.*
- *EthHub Contributors: „Monetary Policy", Ethhub: http://ethhub.eth.link/ethereum-basics/monetary-policy/ (retrieved Feb 2 2019)*
- *Fierlbeck, Katherine: "Globalizing Democracy: Power, Legitimacy and the Interpretation of democratic ideas," Manchester University Press. 1998*
- *Ford Brian: "Delegative Democracy," 2002, retrieved from: http://www.brynosaurus.com/deleg/deleg.pdf*
- *Ford Bryan: "Delegative Democracy Revisited," Nov 16 2014, retrieved from: http://bford.github.io/2014/11/16/deleg.html*

- Friedman, Milton: "A Monetary and Fiscal Framework for Economic Stability" *American Economic Review*. 38 (3): 245–264. 1948
- Friedman, Milton: "A Program for Monetary Stability. *Fordham University Press*. 1960
- George, G., Haas, M.R. & Pentland, A.: "Big Data and Management," *Academy of Management Journal*, 57, 321-326. 2014
- Giddens, A.: "The Constitution of Society," *Berkeley, CA, University of California Press*. 1984
- Hayek, Friedrich: "Law, Legislation and Liberty: Volume 1: Rules and Order. *London: Routledge*. p. 37. 1998
- Hayek, Friedrich: Studies in Philosophy, Politics and Economics. *London: Routledge*. p. 26. 1967
- Hayek, Friedrich: „Competition as a discovery procedure". *The Quarterly Journal of Austrian Economics*. 5: 12. 2002
- Hayek, Friedrich: "Law, Legislation and Liberty: Volume 3: the Political Order of a Free People. *London: Routledge*. p. 158. 1998
- Jensen, Michael & Meckling William: "Theory of the Firm: Managerial Behavior, Agency Costs and Ownership Structure", *Journal of Financial Economics*. 3(4): 305–360, 1976
- Kim, Christine: "Ethereum's Blockchain Is Once Again Feeling the 'Difficulty Bomb' Effect", Feb 14, 2019: *https://www.coindesk.com/ethereum-blockchain-feeling-the-difficulty-bomb-effect*
- Hamilton, W.: "The institutional approach to economic theory', *American Economic Review*, 9(1), March: 309–18, 1919
- Hamilton, W.: "Institution", in E. Seligman and A. Johnson (eds), *Encyclopaedia of the Social Sciences*, vol. 8, New York, Macmillan (repr. in *Journal of Institutional Economics*, 1(2), December, 1932
- Hamilton, David: "Why is Institutional economics not institutional?" *The American Journal of Economics and Sociology*. Vol. 21. no. 3. July 1962. pp. 309–17.
- Heckscher, C.; Donnellon, A. (Editors): "The Post-Bureaucratic Organization: New Perspectives on Organizational Change," *Sage Publications*. 1994
- Hurwicz, Leonid; Reiter, Stanley: "Designing Economic Mechanisms", *Cambridge University*, 2006
- Jacobides., M. G.: "The inherent limits of organizational structure and the unfulfilled role of hierarchy: Lessons from a near-war", *Organization Science*, 18, 3, 455-477, 2007
- Matsusaka, J.G.: "Direct democracy works," *The Journal of Economic Perspectives*, 19, 185-206. 2005
- Nelson, Edward: "Milton Friedman and U.S. Monetary History: 1961–2006," *Federal Reserve Bank of St. Louis Review* (89 (3)): 171. 2007
- O'Donnell Guillermo: "Why the rule of law matters," in Larry Diamond & Leonardo Morlino, *Assessing the quality of democracy*, Baltimore: Johns Hopkins University Press. 2005
- Olpinski Maciej, 2016, May 5, Why I no longer explain Ethereum as a 'World Computer', *Medium Blog Post. https://medium.com/@maciejolpinski/why-i-no-longer-explain-ether-eum-as-a-world-computer-5adf7220b3eb#.smx6d7vm2*
- Olpinski, Maciej: "Explaining DAOs to a non-technical person in 10 points", Apr 13, 2016: *https://medium.com/@maciejolpinski/explaining-daos-to-a-non-technical-person-in-10-points-9a9618e718e8*
- Olpinski Maciej, 2016, Nov 2, Building 'Google For The Economic Web' on The Ethereum Blockchain, *Medium Blog Post. Blockchain.https://blog.userfeeds.io/building-google-for-the-economic-web-on-the-ethereum-blockchain-de27cb3d23b#.ski5jhoye*
- Paulin, A.: "Through liquid democracy to sustainable non-bureaucratic government," *Proceedings of the International Conference for E-Democracy and Open Government*, 205-217. 2014
- Roberts, Jeff John; Rapp, Nicholas: "Nearly 4 Million Bitcoins Lost Forever, New Study Says", November 25, 2017, retrieved from: *https://fortune.com/2017/11/25/lost-bitcoins/*
- Sharma, Rakesh: "What Is Ethereum's „Difficulty Bomb"?", Invesopedia, Aug 10, 2018: *https://www.investopedia.com/news/what-ethereums-difficulty-bomb/*

- *Toffler, A.: "The rise of the prosumer: The third wave," New York: Bantam Books. 1984*
- *Veblen, T.: "Why is Economics Not an Evolutionary Science," The Quarterly Journal of Economics, 12., 1898*
- *Virtanen, Akseli; Bryan, Dick; Lee, Benjamin; Wosnitzer, Robert: "Economics Back in Cryptoeconomics," Sep 11 2018, retrieved from: https://medium.com/econaut/economics-back-into-cryptoeconomics-20471f5ceeea*
- *Voshmgir, Shermin: "Disrupting governance with blockchains and smart contracts", Journal for Strategic Change, Special Issue: The Future of Money and Further Applications of the Blockchain, Volume 26, Issue 5, September 2017, Pages 499-509.*
- *Walch, Angela: "The Bitcoin Blockchain as Financial Market Infrastructure: A Consideration of Operational Risk." New York University Journal of Legislation and Public Policy, 18: 837. 2015*
- *Walch, Angela: "In Code (Rs) We Trust: Software Developers as Fiduciaries in Public Blockchains," 2019*
- *Werbach, Kevin. 2018. "Trust, but verify: Why the blockchain needs the law." Berkeley Tech. LJ, 33: 487*
- *Weber Max, 1948, Essays in Sociology, translated, edited and with an introduction by H. H. Gerth and C. W. Mills. London: Routledge and Kegan Paul.*
- *Weber Max, 1978/1922, Economy and Society, edited by Guenther Roth and Claus Wittich. Berkeley: University of California Press.*
- *Walton H. Hamilton (1919). „The Institutional Approach to Economic Theory," American Economic Review, 9(1), Supplement, pp. 309–18. Reprinted in R. Albelda, C. Gunn, and W. Waller (1987), Alternatives to Economic Orthodoxy: A Reader in Political Economy, pp. 204-12.*
- *Wiener, Norbert: "Cybernetics or Control and Communication in the Animal and the Machine," Vol. 25, MIT press,1965.*
- *Williamson, Oliver: "The Economics of Organization: The Transaction Cost Approach," The American Journal of Sociology, 87(3). 1981*
- *Wuisman, Iris; Mannan, Morshed; De Filippi, Primavera; Wray, Christopher; Rae-Looi, Vienna; Cubillos Vélez, Angela; Orgad, Liav: "Now the Code Runs Itself: On-Chain and Off-Chain Governance of Blockchain Technologies" Topoi, An International Review of Philosophy, ISSN 0167-7411. Topoi DOI 10.1007/s11245-018-9626-5, pp 1–11, 2018*
- *Zargham, Michael: "The age of networks and the rebirth of cybernetics," Web3 Summit 2019, Sep 13, 2019, https://www.youtube.com/watch?v=IyNvoYuSFII&t=369s*
- *Zargham, Michael; Shorish,Jamsheed; Paruch, Krzysztof: „From Curved Bonding to Configuration Spaces," Research Institute for Cryptoeconomics, working paper series, retrieved from: https://epub.wu.ac.at/7385/1/zargham_shorish_paruch.pdf*
- *Aragon: https://aragon.org/*
- *Bitnation: https://tse.bitnation.co/*
- *Colony: https://colony.io/*
- *Commonstack: https://commonsstack.org/*
- *DAOStack: https://daostack.io/*
- *MolochDAO: https://www.molochdao.com/*

Governance of Web3 Networks & Other DAOs

Governance is the term that is colloquially used by many to describe the social consensus process over protocol evolution. It is a decision-making process that can happen either "off-chain" or "on-chain." How-ever, the governance process of a public blockchain network consists of two parts. In addition to the "social governance" process, that defines the network's policies on a collective level, the "algorithmic administration of governance" automates the enforcement of those policies.

Governance is a political science term that refers to the formal or informal rules, norms, and processes of how people interact within a community or organization such as a government, market, family, tribe or a computer network. The governance rules of an organization or group of people regulates the process of decision making among all stakeholders involved. This is achieved through laws, norms, force, or language.

The governance of Web3 networks and their decentralized application consists of two parts: "social governance" and "algorithmic administration of governance." Algorithmic administration of governance refers to the protocol rules written in machine-readable code - a blockchain protocol or smart contract code - which are automatically enforced by the P2P network of computers. These protocol rules also define how protocol updates are to be conducted. In an autonomous setup, tokenized invectives are at the core of the economic coordination game forming the protocol. While Web3 and their applications allow us to automate certain bureaucratic functions of organization and formalize institutional rules with self-enforcing code, what we write in the code, or how we upgrade the code, is a result of public debate and collective action of all network agents.

Social governance refers to the human decision-making process over when and how to conduct potential protocol upgrades in a Web3 network or in the smart contract code of a DAO. It deals with the institutionalized decision-making process of how stakeholders in the network receive necessary information to make educated decisions about future protocol upgrades. Discussions over protocol upgrades happen on social media, like YouTube, Twitter, Reddit, or other open or closed online forums like Slack, Telegram, etc. Information is vital for node operators to decide over which protocol upgrade to accept. They need to be properly informed to make informed decisions. However, navigating in a sea of information, and evaluating the authenticity and credibility of that information and signaling is difficult.

DAOs are co-steered by the human agents acting as node operators who all have different preferences and goals. They have collective influence over the general network behaviour (system outcome) and will react to the system outcome. It is assumed that each stakeholder in the network has their own individual self-interest, and that these interests are not always fully aligned. Stakeholders in the network propose or vote for policy changes that will be formalized as protocol upgrades, reflecting their own self-interest. The human agents are part of the system and actively participate in the systems, either by using the services of a DAO (users), by contributing code to the network constitution (developers), or by contributing to maintain network services. In the case of the Bitcoin network, miners individually contribute to collective maintenance of a P2P payment network (read more: Part 1 - Bitcoin, Blockchain & Other Distributed Ledgers). In the case of Steemit, curators and content creators contribute to the collective maintenance of a social network (read more: Part 4 - Steemit & Hive). In the case of MakerDAO contributors are rewarded for the collective maintenance of the Stable Token DAI (read more. Part 3 - Stable Tokens). In the case of Aragon network actors are/were rewarded for the collective maintenance for a DAO platform. As a result, there are feedback-loops between the individual actors and the whole network. Since individual actions affect the system, who all have interdependencies with external events, the system as a whole evolves over time.

While the governance structures of nation states had centuries to evolve and mature, blockchain networks have only existed for ten years, and many governance questions around how to conduct protocol changes are still unresolved. What we can see from the brief history of blockchain networks is that, while blockchain protocols and smart contracts are a great tool to replace large-scale bureaucracy, in their current form, they are an insufficient tool when confronted with "unknown unknowns" in complex multi-stakeholder environments. Smart contracts can only be as smart as the people who developed and audited them, based on the information, coding practices, and toolchains available to these people at the time of coding. Algorithmic administration of business logic and governance rules can therefore only depict known knowns, and known unknowns, but not unknown unknowns that are a result of: (i) conditions that change over time; (ii) human error; or (iii) information asymmetries in complex multi-stakeholder environments.

Conditions that change over time are best understood through the events that unfolded in the Bitcoin network around the so-called "Block Size Debate," which took over two years and resulted in a subsequent hard fork that led to splitting the network.[36] As the blockchain networks are still nascent, there is continuous need to improve and adapt the protocol to new circumstances and needs. Most of the recent protocol changes in the Bitcoin network and similar blockchain networks deal with issues of scalability, privacy, and decentralization (for example, building ASIC resistance[37] into the protocols to avoid the centralization of mining). Public networks, therefore, need to be able to continuously adapt their protocols and make improvements. Such improvements, however, require a consensus of network actors on how to conduct these protocol updates, the dynamics of which are subject to political science, organizational science, and sociology. How the different stakeholders respond to changes in the code has become increasingly critical for the success of many blockchain projects and the design of smart contract based DAOs.

Unforeseen events that might trigger protocol upgrades can be best understood when analyzing the events around TheDAO, and the subsequent Ethereum hard fork in 2016. A vulnerability in one of the smart contract functions, designed to represent minority rights, was exploited and used to drain 3.6 million ETH (roughly 50 million USD at the time) from TheDAO smart contract. This incident exposed the lack of dispute settlement and governance mechanisms for "edge cases" induced by unforeseen events, both on a smart contract level (the token governance rules of TheDAO) and on the level of the Ethereum network itself. The incident displayed the limitations of pre-defining and pre-regulating all possible human interactions, including potential attack vectors of bad actors, with complex lines of code.

The reality of these complex socio-economic systems is that they are technology-enabled social organisms. They require an iterative social governance process of finding consensus about policy upgrades. This process can be conducted either "off-chain" or "on-chain." The topic of the governance of Web3 networks is gaining

---

[36] *As more people started to use the Bitcoin network, the capacities of the network became insufficient. Various proposals were made by different groups of developers, but consensus among the fractionalized community was hard to reach. One part of the community suggested allowing bigger blocks which would allow for more transactions to be included, but also lead to more centralization, as better hardware was required to compute such blocks. Another proposal suggested to preserve decentralization by finding off-chain solutions like the lightning network. As the discussion got more heated, a contentious hard fork resulted in a network split, giving birth to Bitcoin Cash in 2017.*

[37] *As mining hardware becomes more specialized, only computers running special computer chips can profitably mine Bitcoin. These chips are called ASIC (application-specific integrated circuit). While such higher efficiency results in higher security for the network, it also drives out solo or smaller miners that cannot afford ASICs. This further centralizes the mining power, both in the hands of those who own ASICs and maybe even more in the hands of those who are able to build such ASICs. Some communities are actively fighting against specialization of hardware to allow smaller miners to stay in the game, which results in better decentralization at the cost of security.*

Governance Feedback Loop

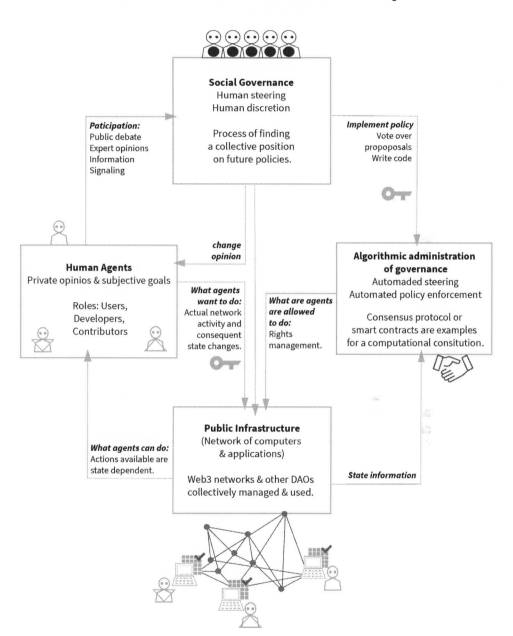

Social Governance
Human steering
Human discretion

Process of finding
a collective position
on future policies.

Paticipation:
Public debate
Expert opinions
Information
Signaling

Implement policy
Vote over
propoposals
Write code

change opinion

Human Agents
Private opinios & subjective goals

Roles: Users,
Developers,
Contributors

What agents want to do:
Actual network
activity and
consequent
state changes.

What are agents are allowed to do:
Rights
management.

Algorithmic administration of governance
Automaded steering
Automated policy enforcement

Consensus protocol or
smart contracts are examples
for a computational consitution.

What agents can do:
Actions available are
state dependent.

Public Infrastructure
(Network of computers
& applications)

Web3 networks & other DAOs
collectively managed & used.

State information

Amanded version of a graphic that was published in Voshmgir, S.; Zargham, M.: "Foundations of Cryptoeconomic Systems" more importance, especially in the light of the increasing number of disputed protocol updates of public and permissionless networks, like the above mentioned cases of the Bitcoin and Ethereum networks, the Aragon network, or in the case of the Steemit network and the subsequent hard fork into the Hive protocol (read more: Part 4 - Steemit & Hive) There seems to be a growing consensus that questions of governance of large multi-stakeholder environments are often complex, and conditions are unpredictable and emergent and cannot be fully engineered in advance. However, there is no common understanding on what an ideal system of governance could look like. The "human governance process" is a messy one, and this, after all, is what what cryptoanarchist movement behind the Bitcoin network wanted to avoid in the first place. However, governance problems are applied social problems, and often need to be resolved by human intervention, not only math.

Checks & Balances in the Network

As more diverse and alternative distributed ledger systems are entering the Web3 playing field, it is hard to generalize the stakeholders in such networks. To keep it simple, however, the main stakeholders of public blockchain networks can be summed up as (i) miners, (ii) developers, (iii) users running full nodes, (iv) users not running full nodes, and (v) the business ecosystem that might act as a market maker, including exchanges, merchants, etc.

Miners write transactions to the ledger and keep the network safe from attacks. Their network contributions are incentivized by block rewards and transaction fees, which means that they tend to prefer protocol upgrades that could secure or increase their future earnings. Miners generally have a better ability to coordinate, as they are a smaller and more concentrated group. This gives them disproportionate power compared to other stakeholders who are more scattered and usually with less means to coordinate their interests. In theory, wealthy miners could pay developers to pursue protocol updates that are in their best interest, thereby gaining more power in the network.

Developers create the protocol and maintain the network with regular protocol upgrades. Many public protocols like Bitcoin or Ethereum have no native mechanism to incentivize developers, which is one of the short-comings of the

---

[38] *In the Bitcoin network, where there was no token sale, it is up to the developer to decide if they mine or buy tokens, or none at all. Other blockchain projects, such as Zcash, rewarded their founding developers with tokens, which were distributed over the first four years of the project. In such a setup, developers are at risk of being bribed or "sponsored" by individuals and institutions with self interests. Overall, it seems safe to say that there needs to be a better system of developer incentives in place for long-term development of protocols, since the developers have the biggest direct influence on protocol evolution.*

decentralized governance of early blockchain networks.[38] Personal ideology and reputation very often seems to be a driving force to contribute with code. Indirect incentives could result from contributing to the network's resilience, which could potentially increase the value of their existing token holdings.

Token holders running full nodes: Depending on the type of network, and the type of software fork, users running full nodes have more or less say in the case of protocol upgrades. If full nodes have a right to contribute, they are likely to prefer upgrades that could improve the functionality of the network and/or increase future token prices.

Token holders running light nodes usually have no say in the network, since they use third-party services without running their own full node. In some cases, these token holders might be able to "coin-vote" with their tokens. They can also sell their tokens altogether, thereby influencing the market price and a potential mass exodus from the network.

There is a certain form of checks and balances in place, where miners and token holders who run full nodes can adopt proposed changes or not. The process is as follows: Developers submit so-called "pull requests," a code improvement proposal. Miners decide whether or not to actually adopt the laws in practice. Token holders who run full nodes of the network can veto by not running a version that aligns with what the miners are running. Any token holder, full node or not, can revolt by selling his tokens or by using different networks. Some argue that forking reflects a strong exit, while selling tokens reflects a weaker exit.

Experience has shown that community dynamics with protocol upgrades are quite similar to public discussion led by media, including social media, before national elections. We therefore need an institutionalized mechanism to coordinate stakeholders in the network while balancing the interests of everyone. If a certain group of stakeholders can coordinate better than others, this could result in information asymmetries and power imbalances.

While different stakeholders have some incentives in common, it is hard for any consensus protocol to fully align the interests of all stakeholders. Token holders running full nodes and developers might prefer upgrades that result in lower transaction fees. Miners will find such a proposal unattractive, since transaction fees are a source of income for them. They might favor protocol upgrades that would yield larger block rewards, which would increase the inflation rate and thus would probably not be in the long-term interest of any of the stakeholders involved. Since an absolute incentive alignment is not feasible, the question of how to institutionalize the social governance process of protocol upgrades is a delicate balancing act.

Off-Chain vs. On-Chain Governance

Early blockchain protocols like the Bitcoin and Ethereum protocols rely on a simplistic assumption of "code is law" and have a rather spontaneous and not well institutionalized social consensus process that happens "off-chain." Several newer blockchain projects, such as "Tezos," "Dfinity," and "Decred," have introduced alternative proposals of how to mitigate the shortcomings of the governance processes of the Bitcoin and Ethereum networks. They introduce various "on-chain governance" models where protocol governance is regulated and implemented, at least partially, on the protocol level.

"Off-chain governance" describes a protocol upgrade process where decision making first takes place on a social level, and is then encoded into the protocol by developers. It has to be accepted by miners and users. Both the Bitcoin network and Ethereum network rely on off-chain governance processes. Developers share their improvement proposals online. Any developer can submit the so-called "pull requests" of an improvement proposal to the community. This is similar to how representative democracy works: anyone can make a proposal to change a law, however, there are certain institutionalized procedures in place that might vary from country to country. The same is true for blockchain protocols.

The Bitcoin governance process: In the Bitcoin network, developers coordinate via a mailing list and a repository of improvement proposals, also referred to as BIP (Bitcoin Improvement Proposals), where anyone can contribute proposals for a protocol upgrade. Developers coordinate and discuss implementation proposals via Slack channels, Skype, IRC, etc. Users can contribute with opinions on discussion forums like "bitcoin-talk," on subreddits like "r/bitcoin" and "r/Crypto-Currency," or via Twitter. It is important to note, however, that there is no native reward mechanism in the Bitcoin protocol for developer contributions. Some developers are paid by companies, who have their own interest in the Bitcoin network, to contribute with code.[39] The Bitcoin Network has gone through several soft forks and hard forks in the past. More politicized protocol updates like the aforementioned "Bitcoin Block Size Debate" resulted in heated and prolonged discussions in the community, giving rise to several hard forks of the chain, like "Bitcoin Cash." Since hard forks require all miners to upgrade their clients to the new protocol, which can lead to splits in the network, many protocol upgrades were included as soft forks (read more on forks: Part 1 - Bitcoin, Blockchain, & Other Distributed Ledgers).

---

[39] *The biggest company sponsoring developers is Blockstream, but Bitmain and Circle have also sponsored developers in the past, as well as the MIT Media Lab.*

The Ethereum governance process: As opposed to the Bitcoin network, which is more decentralized, the development of the Ethereum network was funded and governed by the Ethereum Foundation in the first years of its creation, and was therefore less decentralized. The foundation raised funds in a public token sale that issued some amount of pre-mined Ether (ETH) to investors against Bitcoin, and allocated some additional pre-mined Ether to the foundation. Similar to Bitcoin, the Ethereum protocol is open source, and anyone can contribute with code and make improvement proposals, also referred to as EIPs. Developers, hired by the foundation, drive new ideas and try to be transparent about the development process, for example, by broadcasting their core developer discussions on YouTube. Similar to Bitcoin, developers who are not hired by the foundation have limited incentives to contribute to core development, except for bug-bounties and development grants. Past protocol upgrades have shown that coordination around challenging issues happens faster than in the Bitcoin network. This might be the result of a different network culture. After all, Ethereum was created as a reaction to Bitcoin's tendency toward a more conservative understanding of "code is law." Furthermore, as opposed to Bitcoin, where the creator Satoshi Nakamoto is anonymous, and stopped communicating over the Internet on his view of Bitcoin's state of development a few years back, Vitalik Buterin, the founder of Ethereum, is visible, outspoken, and trusted by the community. His opinions seem to matter to many when it comes to controversial decision making. The similarities to Bitcoin's improvement proposal process will change, however, if and when Ethereum switches to Proof-of-Stake. Current miners will lose power to token holders with a sufficient amount of ETH to run a so-called "virtual miner" (validator). Given the fact that solutions like "1protocol" allow even the smallest ETH holder to participate, the distinction between a miner and a user could also potentially democratize the validation process, which is currently concentrated around an oligopoly of mining pools.

The lack of incentives for developers is one of the greatest challenges in current protocol development, which leaves the maintenance of these networks under the control of a small group of core developers who are either paid by private companies (Bitcoin) or a foundation (Ethereum). In both cases, the development process of the public infrastructure is limited to a small group of people, which makes the whole network vulnerable to bribery and attack.

"On-chain governance" refers to mechanisms of some blockchain networks to allow developers to broadcast their improvement proposal on-chain, to be voted upon and deployed on the test network for a certain amount of time, after which the proposal will be voted upon again and deployed on the main network. This means that any decision that is being taken is automatically executed. In this process, developers get compensated with tokens on the fly when their improvement proposals are executed. Anyone with the necessary skills can submit a proposal and be rewarded with network tokens, providing a strong incentive for decentralizing maintenance of the network. Users can also coordinate on-chain, which could reduce the power of developers and miners compared to off-chain decision processes. On-chain governance protocols might also be designed in a way to roll back and edit ledger history, allowing a "self-amending ledger," as opposed to off-chain governance that requires a hard fork to erase a past transaction. It is possible that such retroactive amendments will require different voting thresholds, depending on the type of change.

The Tezos governance process: Tezos is a public and permissionless blockchain network similar to Ethereum, with built-in governance and more security mechanisms around smart contracts. While the project has faced serious managerial problems,[40] their governance model is quite interesting: token holders can approve protocol upgrades, which are automatically deployed on the network once approved. The proposed protocol upgrade comes with an attached invoice in the form of a smart contract, which pays out the developer upon approval and inclusion of their upgrade. Improvement proposals to the protocol can be conducted by any developer. Once approved, changes would go live on a test network, and upon further approval, be implemented on the main network. On final implementation of the improvement proposal on the mainnet, the developer would be paid in newly minted network tokens.

The Dfinity governance process: Dfinity is a tokenized and decentralized network for cloud computing. In addition to the Tezos proposal, they allow retroactive changes to the ledger in cases of consensus among the token holders. Amending the ledger is highly controversial, since "immutability" is considered by many as the core USP of the Bitcoin network and other public distributed ledgers. However, proponents of the self-amending ledger appreciate its ability to remove what some might consider "illegal activities by bad actors." However, the definition of "illegal" is subject to jurisdiction and also prone to censorship limiting freedom of speech; it is therefore considered a double-edged sword.

A challenge with current proposals for "on-chain governance" is that they are plutocratic, which means that protocol upgrades are decided proportional to one's token holdings. Token holders with more tokens would therefore have more voting power than smaller token holders. This is a considerable design question, given that token distribution is often disproportionately uneven. In the case of Bitcoin, at the time of writing this chapter, 3.06 percent of addresses hold 95.66 percent of the total supply. In May 2016, from a total of 11,000 investors, the top 100 holders

---

[40] *In July 2017 Tezos raised 230 Million USD in Ether and Bitcoin tokens during their ICO. They faced troubles with the SEC as a result of communication break-down and managerial problems between the founders and the Tezos Foundations president. Lawsuits by frustrated token buyers followed.*

held over 46 percent of all TheDAO tokens. In light of such plutocratic voting mechanisms, using the term "decentralization" could be perceived as contradictory.

Most on-chain governance solutions are proposals or have not been operational for a long time. It is, therefore, hard to foresee what the implications of such systems will be. Furthermore, while on-chain solutions can increase coordination and fairness, they are also risky, as they are harder to change once instituted, and might be exploited more easily. Off-chain governance, on the other hand, is relatively centralized and excludes many small token holders, especially those who lack the technical knowledge or financial power to assess network decisions adequately. However, despite potential centralization tendencies, token holders in a blockchain network can always easily exit by selling or hard-forking.

One can only assume that a certain amount of on-chain coordination makes global coordination easier, but it does not resolve the human factor. It is still unclear what the right balance between "on-chain" vs. "off-chain" coordination could look like. A meaningful combination of both approaches would most likely be best to resolve the decision-making process in large multi-stakeholder environments.

The Myth of Decentralization & Trustless Networks

Smart Contracts as a default state: The inability to foresee unknown future events, as in the case of TheDAO incident, showed that smart contracts can only be a default state, which might need to be overruled by supermajority consensus within the relevant community whenever deemed necessary. The absence of dispute settlement and governance mechanisms for edge cases divided the community on a smart contract level (TheDAO), as well as on the blockchain level (Ethereum). Furthermore, code does not write itself, and is therefore prone to human error. While so-called "formal verification" in software development can reduce human error, it cannot eradicate all errors, or short-sighted assumptions. Artificial Intelligence may have, in the future, some impact. For the time being, however, while code can simplify transactions, it remains susceptible to human bias. Code can therefore only be a default state, based on which social consensus happens, if and when necessary.

Inertia: Similarly, the Bitcoin scaling debate of 2016 and 2017 demonstrates how inertia can result from inadequate governance rules that account for large-scale decisions in a multi-stakeholder environment with unaligned interests at stake. In the absence of more flexible governance structures, the movers and shakers of the community inadvertently become the thought leaders and quasi agents of the principal (the token holder and other stakeholders). This might lead to inertia (case of Bitcoin) or the splitting of the network (case of Ethereum).

Immutability & Censorship Resistance: TheDAO incident and subsequent Ethereum hard fork also raise questions about censorship resistance and immutability. Advocates of the Ethereum hard fork were accused of censoring the ledger, by going back in time and invalidating the transaction of the attacker. Advocates of the hard fork claimed that in a decentralized community, like TheDAO or the Ethereum network, no single entity can make such a decision without the majority of the community agreeing. They argued that, if there is consensus about changing the ledger, it wouldn't count as censorship, but rather a community-driven natural evolution of the code or state of the ledger.

New Gatekeepers: While smart contracts can reduce bureaucracy, and resulting principal-agent problems, there will always be a need for experts. The community of network stakeholders who get to decide on protocol updates must trust the design judgement of those experts. While such experts are more distributed, none of whom have executive power to decide what to do, they do concentrate power around their expert knowledge, and become the new "quasi" agents in a distributed network where "code is law."

Yes, it's open source, but how many people can read it? Currently, only a handful of software developers and system architects understand the ins and outs of specific blockchain protocols to make educated decisions about protocol upgrades. Centralization is likely to coalesce around experts, developers, and system architects. Given the fact that coding skills are still not part of mainstream curricula in schools, educated decision making in a machine economy is a far illusion, from today's perspective. While anyone, in theory, can contribute to the code, the required engineering skills needed might be considered an entry barrier, creating new principal-agent problems around understanding not only simple code (smart contracts) but also complex blockchain protocols.

Information: The distributed nature of expertise, the multiple channels of communication, and the current lack of effective reputation systems make it hard for stakeholders to follow the online discussion process. While issues of communication and information dissemination are also concerns of contemporary (political) governance systems, Web3 communities are even more susceptible for such concerns. Where does reliable information come from, and what tools, such as visualizations and decision trees, are required to facilitate such processes? Experience from past protocol upgrades shows that if issues of information, moderation, transparency, aggregation, and reputation are not resolved, decentralization might become a meaningless word.

Chapter Summary

- Governance is the term that is colloquially used by many to describe the social consensus process over protocol evolution. It is a decision-making process that can happen either "off-chain" or "on-chain." However, the governance process of a public blockchain network really consists of two parts. In addition to the "social governance" process, that defines the network's policies on a collective level, the "algorithmic administration of governance" automates the enforcement of those policies.

- Algorithmic administration of governance refers to the protocol rules written in machine-readable code-a blockchain protocol or smart contract code-which are automatically enforced by the P2P network of computers. These protocol rules also define how protocol updates are to be conducted.

- While Web3 and their applications allow us to automate certain bureaucratic functions of organization and formalize institutional rules with self-enforcing code, what we write in the code, or how we upgrade the code, is a result of public debate and collective action of all network agents.

- Social governance refers to the human decision-making process over when and how to conduct potential protocol upgrades in a Web3 network or in the smart contract code of a DAO. It deals with the institutionalized decision-making process of how stakeholders in the network receive necessary information to make educated decisions about future protocol upgrades.

- DAOs are co-steered by the human agents acting as node operators who all have different preferences and goals. They have collective influence over the general network behaviour (system outcome) and will react to the system outcome.

- The human agents are part of the system and actively participate in the systems, either by using the services of a DAO (users), by contributing code to the network constitution (developers), or by contributing to maintain network services.

- It is assumed that each stakeholder in the network has their own individual self-interest, and that these interests are not always fully aligned. Stakeholders in the network propose or vote for policy changes that will be formalized as protocol upgrades, reflecting their own self-interest.

- Early blockchain protocols like Bitcoin and Ethereum rely on a simplistic assumption of "code is law" and have rather spontaneous and not well institutionalized social governance layers that happen "off-chain." Several newer blockchain projects have introduced various "on-chain governance" models, with more sophisticated provisions for upgrade processes baked into the protocol.

- Depending on the protocol, there are certain checks and balances in place, where miners and token holders who run full nodes can adopt proposed changes or not. The main stakeholders in a tokenized network can be summed up as (i) miners, (ii) developers, (iii) token holder running full nodes, (iv) token holders running light nodes, and (v) the business ecosystem that might act as a market maker, including exchanges, merchants, etc.

- Off-chain governance describes a protocol upgrade process where decision making first takes place on a social level, and is then encoded into the protocol by developers. It has to be accepted by miners and users. Both the Bitcoin network and Ethereum network rely on off-chain governance processes. Developers share their improvement proposals online. Any developer can submit the so-called "pull requests" of an improvement proposal to the community.

- On-chain governance allows developers to broadcast their improvement proposal on-chain, to be voted upon and deployed on the test network for a certain amount of time, after which the proposal will be voted upon again before it is deployed on the main network. This means that any decision that is being taken is automatically executed.

- On-chain governance protocols might also be designed in a way to roll back and edit ledger history, allowing a "self-amending ledger," as opposed to off-chain governance that requires a hard fork to erase a past transaction.

Chapter References & Further Reading

- Alex T.: "On Chain VS. Off Chain Governance: The Ins And Outs", April 25, 2018, retrieved from: https://coinjournal.net/on-chain-vs-off-chain-governance-the-ins-and-outs/
- Axelrod, Robert: "The Emergence of Cooperation among Egoists", The American Political Science Review, Vol. 75, No. 2, Published by: American Political Science Association, pp. 306-318, June 1981
- Balaji, Arjun: "Zcash & the founder incentive trilemma Reorganizing the firm presents new principal-agent problems", Jun 28, 2018, retrieved from: https://medium.com/@arjunblj/zcash-the-founder-incentive-trilemma-fe7689fc8293
- De Filippi, Primavera: "A $50M Hack Tests the Values of Communities Run by Code The ideal of a perfectly trustless technology is nothing more than an ideal", Jul 11 2016, retrieved from: https://vice.com/en_us/article/qkjz4x/thedao
- De Filippi, Primavera; Mcmullen, Greg: "Governance of blockchain systems: Governance of and by Distributed Infrastructure" Blockchain Research Institute and COALA, [Research Report]. 2018. Ffhal02046787: https://hal.archives-ouvertes.fr/hal-02046787/document
- Daian, Phil: "Analysis of TheDAO", June 18, 2016: https://hackingdistributed.com/2016/06/18/analysis-of-the-dao-exploit/
- Ehrsam, Fred: "Blockchain Governance: Programming Our Future", Nov 27, 2017: https://medium.com/@FEhrsam/blockchain-governance-programming-our-future-c3bfe30f2d74
- Hacker,Philip; Lianos, Ioannis; Dimitropoulos, Georgios; Eich Stefan, "Corporate Governance for Complex Cryptocurrencies? A Framework for Stability and Decision Making in Blockchain-Based Organizations", Regulating Blockchain. Techno-Social and Legal Challenges, Oxford University Press, 2019
- N.N.: „Difference Between On-Chain and Off-Chain Governance", BLMP Medium Blog, Jun 5, 2018: https://medium.com/@BLMPNetwork/difference-between-on-chain-and-off-chain-governance-c881cd3e6374

- N.N.: *"Revisiting the on-chain governance vs. off-chain governance discussion,"* Pool Of Stake, Medium Blog, May 22, 2018, retrieved from: https://medium.com/@poolofstake/revisiting-the-on-chain-governance-vs-off-chain-governance-discussion-f68d8c5c606

- Voshmgir, Shermin: *"Blockchain's Problem with Unknown Unknowns"*, Mar 12, 2017: https://medium.com/blockchain-hub/blockchains-problem-with-unknown-unknowns-6837e09ec495

- Van Wirdum, Aaron: *"Who Funds Bitcoin Core Development? How the Industry Supports Bitcoin's , Reference Client'"*, Apr 6, 2016: https://bitcoinmagazine.com/articles/who-funds-bitcoin-core-development-how-the-industry-supports-bitcoin-s-reference-client-1459967859/

- Voshmgir, Shermin: *„To Fork of Not to Fork?"*, Jul 4, 2016: https://medium.com/blockchain-hub/to-fork-of-not-to-fork-a9b077718fe3

- Voshmgir, Shermin: *"Disrupting governance with blockchains and smart contracts"*, Journal for Strategic Change, Special Issue: The Future of Money and Further Applications of the Blockchain, Volume26, Issue5, September 2017, Pages 499-509.

- Zamfir, Vlad: *"Against on-chain governance Refuting (and rebuking) Fred Ehrsam's governance blog"*, Dec 1, 2017: https://medium.com/@Vlad_Zamfir/against-on-chain-governance-a4ceacd040ca

- Bitcoin Cash: https://bitcoincash.org/

- Bitcoin Talk: https://bitcointalk.org/

- Bitcmain: https://www.bitmain.com/

- Blockstream: https://blockstream.com/

- Circle: https://www.circle.com/de/

- Dfinity: https://dfinity.org/

- Decred: https://decred.org/

- r/Bitcoin: https://www.reddit.com/r/Bitcoin/

- r/CryptoCurrency: https://www.reddit.com/r/CryptoCurrency/

- TheDAO: https://en.wikipedia.org/wiki/The_DAO_(organization)

- Tezos: https://tezos.com/

- zCash: https://z.cash/

Tokens

Tokens are the atomic unit of the Web3 and are collectively managed by a distributed ledger. They can be issued with just a few lines of code with a smart contract. Token contracts are rights management tools that can represent anything from a store of value to a set of permissions in the physical, digital, and legal world. They might affect the financial world similar to how the Internet affected the postal system.

While the existence of tokens in general and digital tokens in particular is not new, the speed with which these cryptographic tokens are being deployed and issued is an indicator that these tokens might be the killer application of blockchain networks. As of May 2020, an ecosystem of over 5400 publicly traded cryptographic tokens are listed on "Coinmarketcap," and a total of over 260,000 Ethereum token contracts were found on the Ethereum main network. These tokens are often issued with just a few lines of code in the form of a smart contract that is collectively managed by a blockchain network or similar distributed ledger. As such, they represent the atomic unit of the Web3, they represent "local" part of the entire state of the network. All nodes in the network have the same information about who owns which tokens, and the transfer of those tokens - the state change - is collectively managed.

A token contract is a special type of smart contract that defines a bundle of conditional rights assigned to the token holder. They are rights management tools that can represent any existing digital or physical asset, or access rights to assets someone else owns. Tokens can represent anything from a store of value to a set of permissions in the physical, digital, and legal world. They facilitate collaboration across markets and jurisdictions and allow more transparent, efficient, and fair interactions between market participants, at low costs. Tokens can also incentivize an autonomous group of people to individually contribute to a collective goal. These tokens are created upon proof of a certain behavior (read more: Chapter 4 - Purpose-Driven Tokens).

The ability to deploy tokens at a low cost relatively effortlessly on a public infrastructure is a game changer, because it makes it economically feasible to represent many types of assets and access rights in a digital way that might not have been feasible before. Examples could be fractional ownership of art or real estate. Such fractional tokenization might improve the liquidity and transparency of existing asset markets. Increasing tokenization of existing assets and access rights could fundamentally impact global economic dynamics, much more than might meet the eye at such an early stage of the Web3 (read more: Part 4 - Asset Tokens & Fractional Ownership).

Whereas state-of-the-art digital assets are controlled by centralized entities, they can now be issued with a few lines of code, and managed by a public and verifiable infrastructure like a blockchain network. They can be easily issued and securely traded on a public infrastructure without an intermediary or escrow service. Tokens can provide (i) more transparency along marketplaces than existing financial systems currently offer. This could significantly reduce fraud or corruption along the supply chain of goods, services, and financial transactions. Tokens also have the potential of (ii) reducing the transaction costs of developing, managing, and trading cryptographic assets along distributed ledgers, as opposed to managing assets along state-of-the-art systems. As a result, (iii) increased liquidity, lower costs of price discovery, and less fragmented markets could reduce market friction, enabling more efficient marketplaces for certain assets like art or real estate. Tokenization of the economy could also enable (iv) completely new use cases, business models, and asset types that were not economically feasible before, and potentially enable completely new value-creation models.

While more and more people are starting to create and invest into cryptographic tokens, the understanding of different token types out there is still limited. To add to the confusion, terms like "cryptocurrency," "crypto assets," and "tokens" are very often used synonymously. The media mostly tends to refer to these new assets as "cryptocurrencies," which is often used to describe a diverse range of "crypto assets" or "tokens" that could represent anything from a physical good, a digital good, a security, a collectible, a royalty, a reward, or a ticket to a concert. I would, therefore, like to argue that the term "cryptocurrency" is not ideal, since many of these new assets were never issued with the intention to represent money in the first place. "Cryptographic asset" would be a more generic term that one could use. The term "token" is becoming more widespread since it is more generic, encompassing all token types rather than only asset-backed tokens.

While a lack of clear, agreed-upon terminology and definitions is quite common in emerging domains, precision in language and terminology is a basis for informed decisions and general discourse on the subject matter. It is important to understand that we are still throwing around a set of overlapping terms to refer to more or less the same thing, which generates much confusion. This chapter will, therefore, try to give a brief overview of the history and different properties of cryptographic tokens, from a technical, legal, and business perspective, clarifying some terms along the way.

History of Tokens

Tokens are not a new thing and have existed long before the emergence of blockchain networks. Traditionally, tokens can represent any form of economic value or access right. Shells and beads were probably the earliest types of tokens used. Other types of tokens are, for example, casino chips, vouchers, gift cards, bonus points in a loyalty program, coat-check tokens, stock certificates, bonds, concert- or club-entry tokens represented by a stamp on your hand, dinner reservations, ID cards, club memberships, or train or airline tickets. Most tokens have some inbuilt anti-counterfeiting measures, which may be more or less secure, in order to prevent people from cheating the system. Paper money or coins are also tokens. Tokens are furthermore used in computing, where they can represent a right to perform an operation or manage access rights. A web browser, for example, sends tokens to websites when we surf the web, and our phone sends tokens to the phone system every time we use it. A more tangible form of computer tokens are tracking codes that you get to track your parcel with postal services, or QR codes that give you access to a train or plane. In psychology, tokens have been used as a positive reinforcement method of incentivizing desirable behavior in patients, especially in a hospital setting. Cognitive psychology uses reward tokens as a medium of exchange that can be exchanged for special privileges within the setting of a hospital stay. Another example of inventive tokens are customer loyalty programs that offer bonus points for using an airline that can be redeemed for other goods or services.

A recyclable bottle is an analogue example for a token. In some countries, bottles you buy in supermarkets are issued with their recycling value, of usually a few cents, printed on them. This recycling value is paid on top of the initial price of the product and has become a method for governments to encourage the recycling of materials and subsequent reduction of litter in public places. Upon return of the bottle, the recycling value will be reimbursed. Losing the bottle is, therefore, equivalent to losing money.

A garbage bag could also represent a token. In some parts of Switzerland, for example, you can't just throw out your trash using random bags. You have to buy special-purpose plastic bags that include a dumpster fee, issued by local authorities, and you can only use those bags to dispose of your trash. As opposed to most other countries, where you pay your garbage bill monthly, as part of your utilities bill tied to the rent of your apartment or house, this system requires you to purchase special-purpose plastic bags.

Tokens always need a substrate that ensures their validity, including some inbuilt anti-counterfeiting measure. Historically, tokens have been issued and managed by centralized entities, to ensure validity, and have had security mechanisms built into the substrate. Central banks issuing coins and bills need to make sure that their tokens, the coins and bills, are hard to copy. The same is true for a concert organizer issuing tickets to a concert. The validity and security of cryptographic tokens is managed by the smart contract that created them, together with the underlying distributed ledger by majority consensus of the network nodes.

Cryptographic Tokens

Cryptographic tokens managed by a distributed ledger can combine all above mentioned concepts. They can represent access rights to a property or service that can be either public (Bitcoin network) or private (an apartment that is rented out by a private person). They represent a set of rules, encoded in a special type of smart contract, also referred to as the token contract. In the context of blockchain networks, tokens don't manifest as digital files; instead, they are represented as an entry in the ledger and are mapped to a blockchain address which represents the blockchain identity of the token holder. Tokens are therefore only accessible with a dedicated wallet software that communicates with the blockchain network and manages the public-private key pair related to the blockchain address. Only the person who has the private key for that address can access the respective tokens. This person can, therefore, be regarded as the owner or custodian of that token.[41] If the token represents an asset, the owner can initiate transfer of the token by signing with their private key. If the token represents an access right to something somebody else owns, the owner of that token can also initiate access by signing with their private key. The same applies to tokens that represent voting rights (read more: Part 1 - Cryptography).

The first blockchain tokens were the native tokens of public and permissionless blockchain networks. These native tokens—also referred to as protocol tokens—are part of the incentive scheme of blockchain infrastructure. With the advent of Ethereum, however, tokens have moved up the technology stack and can now be issued on the application layer. Such application tokens can have simple

---

[41] *From a regulatory point of view, however, it is not definitively clear whether or how it is possible to acquire ownership or possession on such tokens. Therefore, concepts like custodianship would probably need legal modifications in many jurisdictions.*

or complex behaviors attached to them. Ethereum made it particularly easy to issue tokens with a few lines of code. Standardized smart contracts like the "ERC-20" standard define a common list of rules for Ethereum tokens, including how the tokens are transferred from one Ethereum address to another and how data within each token is accessed. These token contracts manage the logic and maintain a list of all issued tokens, and can represent any asset that has features of a fungible commodity. A vast majority of early tokens issued on the Ethereum network have been ERC-20 compliant fungible tokens. Fungibility refers to the fact that every token has an identical value with any other token of the same kind and can be easily traded.

Over the last year, however, more complex token standards have emerged that can represent any asset or access rights with special properties, including identities and voting rights. "ERC-721" introduced a free and open standard that describes how to issue so-called "non-fungible tokens" on the Ethereum network. This has introduced the era of building more complex features into the tokens. ERC-721 has made it easy to create a token that represents any type of collectible, art work, property, personalized access rights, or voting rights. These non-fungible tokens have special properties that make the token unique, or that are tied to the identity of a certain person, and therefore represent less fungible or non-fungible assets and access rights. ERC-721 enables the emergence of a much richer spectrum of smart contracts that exceed the possibilities of the fungible tokens, which have been dominating the narrative in the early years of the technology, paving the way for a diverse set of use cases.

Different ledger systems have varying standards that are often incompatible. At the time of writing this book tokens issued on one network are, for the most part, incompatible with other networks and cannot cross ledgers directly. The different standards make it currently infeasible for wallet developers to provide multi-token wallets, which means that very often we will need multiple wallets to manage different token systems directly. This is a usability bottleneck. However, token interoperability and standardization are issues that are being tackled by interoperability protocols like "Cosmos" and "Polkadot" and other standardization efforts worldwide. Interoperability and standardization will influence potential mass adoption of tokens and resulting network effects.

Properties of Tokens

While it is technically possible to represent any asset of the existing economy as a cryptographic token, we still lack adequate taxonomy, and adequate legal framework that understands the full scope and potential of this new substrate with

Token Properties

Technical	Protocol tokens	Application tokens
Rights	Property right	Access right
Fungibility	Identical	Non-identical
Transferability	Transferable	Non-transferable
Durability	Proven to withstand censorship/attack over time thus retain stable value.	Unclear if it can withstand censorship/attack over time thus retain stable value.
Regulation	Easy to classify and regulate	Hard to classify and regulate
Incentives	Minted upon proof-of-certain behaviour (value creation).	Represents existing assets or access rights.
Supply	Fixed supply	Unlimited supply
Token flow	Linear	Circular
Expiry date	Expiry date	No expiry date
Privacy	More privacy by design	Less privacy by design
Stability	Stability mechanism	No stability mechanism

which we can issue any type of asset and access right, including completely new asset classes. However, establishing a consistent and reliable taxonomy for token properties, as well as classification models, is the basis from which developers, policy makers, and investors can make more sense of how to design, apply, or regulate tokens.

We are still in the very early stages of exploring different roles and types of tokens. Many of the terminologies we use today will adapt to the realities of emerging use cases, and should be considered as temporary. With every new network and every new token application, we will collectively learn by trial and error about possible use cases of cryptographic tokens, and resulting classifications thereof. The taxonomy presented here intends to give a broad overview of the different properties and types of tokens, but it is far from complete. It is a big picture of the most important economic, technical, and regulatory questions tied to such taxonomy. Classifying the properties of a token is necessary for modeling tokens (development perspective) and evaluating tokens (investor perspective). A classification and taxonomy of the token itself would be legal, business, economics, and social sciences questions. A legal taxonomy is furthermore subject to a specific jurisdiction, and would be far beyond the scope of this book.

Identifying different properties of a token can be used as a first step to fine-tune a future classification framework and also for designing the properties of a token (read more: Part 4 - How to Design a Token System). This identification of properties is a result of a process called "morphological analysis." It is a framework for structuring the relevant questions as a first approach in a heuristic way, especially useful for exploring all the possible solutions to a multi-dimensional, non-quantified complex problem. I would, therefore, like to introduce the most important perspectives from which we can derive the properties of a token: (i) Technical perspective; (ii) Rights perspective; (iii) Fungibility perspective; (iv) Transferability perspective; (v) Durability perspective; (vi) Regulatory perspective; (vii) Incentive perspective; (viii) Supply perspective; and (ix) Token flow perspective.

Technical Perspective: From a technical perspective, tokens can be implemented on different layers of the technology, either as (i) protocol tokens, (ii) second-layer tokens, like application tokens or tokens created on a sidechain,[42] or as (iii) multi-asset ledger tokens. Protocol tokens, also referred to as intrinsic, native, or built-in tokens, have a very clear role in a public network: to keep the network safe from attack by acting as block validation incentives (miner rewards), and for transaction spam prevention. Native protocol tokens might furthermore be needed to pay for transaction fees in the network and can be regarded as the "currency" of the distributed Internet. Application tokens, on the other hand, can have any function or property. They can represent anything from a physical good, a digital good, or a right to perform an action in a network or in the real world. The Ethereum network has one protocol token (ETH) and a whole economy of application tokens running on top of the network (ERC-20 and other Ethereum token standards allow the creation of application tokens with a smart contract). Second-layer tokens can also be issued by a sidechain and are more dominant in the Bitcoin ecosystem. Side-

---

[42] *Sidechains are separate blockchains, compatible with the mainchain, and have been used to resolve scalability issues in Bitcoin (read more on Sidechains: Annex - Scalability Solutions)*

Technical Perpective
Where Tokens are Generated

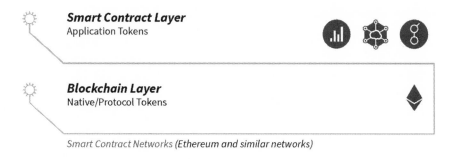

Smart Contract Layer
Application Tokens

Blockchain Layer
Native/Protocol Tokens

Smart Contract Networks (Ethereum and similar networks)

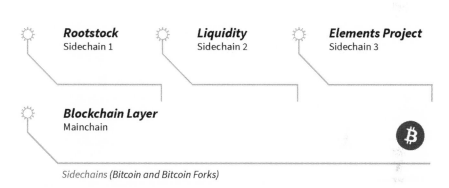

Rootstock
Sidechain 1

Liquidity
Sidechain 2

Elements Project
Sidechain 3

Blockchain Layer
Mainchain

Sidechains (Bitcoin and Bitcoin Forks)

Blockchain Layer
Apart from the native token any token can
be created directly on the blockchain layer

Multitoken Networks (i.e Stellar)

chains that allow the creation of second-layer tokens are, for example, "Elements," "Liquid," or "Rootstock." They interact with a blockchain to manage the state of the tokens. Due to network effects, the value of application tokens and other second-layer tokens is likely to be interdependent with the value of the underlying native blockchain token. An example thereof is the value of ETH (the native Ethereum token), which rose in the ICO bubble of 2016 to 2017 due to the large amount of ETH that was needed to buy app tokens issued through ICOs (read more: Part 3 - Token Sales). Multi-asset ledgers like "Ripple" and "Stellar" allow the creation of multiple tokens on the native level. Stellar allows anyone to create token contracts with all kinds of variables. On Ripple (XRP), everyone can issue any kind of token on the network, but they are issued as IOUs,[43] essentially debt. XRP is therefore considered as credit, which is why some call it the "credit network." To get to use these tokens, others must enable trust to one's wallet, which means that one transfers debt. Ripple and Stellar can therefore be regarded as a settlement bus for other assets. The tokens XRP and XLM are essentially protocol tokens, but in their networks, they are representations of other assets and those representations are used to track credits and debts in a multi-dimensional value space. One can think of them as nascent cryptographically enforced foreign-exchange networks.

Rights Perspective: Tokens can represent a right to some underlying economic value, whether digital or physical, long term or temporary. A token can represent (i) a right to an asset I own, or (ii) limited access rights to assets or services that others own or provide, or a (iii) voting right. The economic definition of an asset is a resource that has an economic value and is controlled by an individual or a legal entity or a country. The legal definition of an asset is anything which has monetary value attached to it. Ownership right is the legal right to possession of a thing, including all usage rights, both physical and intellectual. In some countries, ownership is only possible in connection with physical things. Rights of use, or access rights, are contractual rights to use something in possession of someone else. Therefore, a token could represent any asset or resource, representing one's ownership or the right to use said resource. These can be public or private assets, utilities, or services of any kind.

Asset tokens can represent a unit of account (fungible) or a unique good (non-fungible). Fungible tokens represent ownership of any fungible physical goods, like fiat money, silver, petrol, gold, diamonds, shares in a company, or any collateralized debt instrument. They can be compared to commodity money and are therefore sometimes referred to as crypto-commodities. Asset tokens can also be unique

---

[43] *Abbreviation for "I Owe You," a written promise that you will pay back some money that you borrowed. It is an informal document acknowledging debt. They usually specify the debtor, the amount owed, and sometimes the creditor. They differ from promissory notes in that they do not specify repayment terms, like the time of repayment.*

Rights Perspective

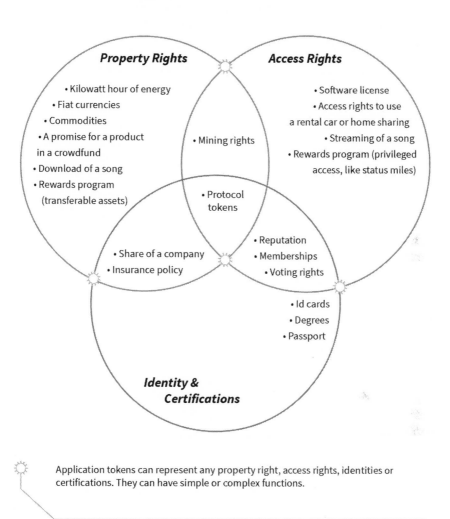

Property Rights
- Kilowatt hour of energy
- Fiat currencies
- Commodities
- A promise for a product in a crowdfund
- Download of a song
- Rewards program (transferable assets)

Access Rights
- Software license
- Access rights to use a rental car or home sharing
- Streaming of a song
- Rewards program (privileged access, like status miles)

- Mining rights

- Protocol tokens

- Share of a company
- Insurance policy

- Reputation
- Memberships
- Voting rights

- Id cards
- Degrees
- Passport

Identity & Certifications

Application tokens can represent any property right, access rights, identities or certifications. They can have simple or complex functions.

and therefore non-fungible. Some refer to them as crypto-goods. Examples would be real estate tokens, crypto-collectibles, or tokens that represent unique pieces of art. Representing such an asset with a token makes the asset more easily tradable and divisible, thus creating more liquidity for some assets that might not have been that easily tradable off-chain.

Examples of access right tokens that are limited in time or in scope of using an asset someone else owns or a service someone else provides are: an entry ticket to a concert, a public transport ticket, apartment sharing access, car sharing access, a time slot for a doctor's appointment, membership access to a club, or access to network services.

Credential tokens can be used to verify personal information that is a prerequisite of a specific access right, such as the verification of your age to allow you to rent a car, buy alcoholic beverages, board an airplane, or other personal details to allow you to enter your hotel room, vote, cross a border, collect a tax refund, or get a discount, just to name a few examples.

Hybrid tokens: This is not a binary classification, as many use cases might be more hybrid in nature, like mining rights on a piece of land, which are an access right but also represent a productive asset. A security token that represents a share in a company could also include voting rights. Native protocol tokens like Bitcoin (BTC) and Ether (ETH) can be seen as assets, but also represent access rights to the network, as they are needed to pay for network fees.

Fungibility Perspective: Fungibility refers to the interchangeability of a unit of an asset with other units of the same asset. Examples thereof could be any durable goods, such as precious metals or currencies. Fungible assets have two key properties: (i) Only quantity matters, which means that units of fungible assets of the same kind are indistinguishable. (ii) Any amount can be merged or divided into a larger or smaller amount of it, making it indistinguishable from the rest. If you were to lend 10 EUR to someone, for example, it would not matter if that person returns the exact same 10 EUR bill or another one, or various bills and coins that amount to the value of 10 EUR. The same applies to one barrel of crude oil. Flour is another example of a fungible asset, and is also one of the reasons why it was used as a commodity currency in the past. Fungibility is an important property of any currency or commodity to serve as a store of value, medium of exchange, and a unit of account (read more: Part 3 - The Future of Money?).

Equally, fungible cryptographic tokens can represent any physical or digital assets that are identical to each other and can therefore be easily replaced. They are not unique and are therefore exchangeable with other tokens of the same type. If two parties have the same amount, they can swap them without losing or gaining anything. Unique tokens, on the other hand, are non-fungible. Examples thereof are ID cards, or a token that represents the ownership of a house, a car, a piece of art, or a gym membership. Non-fungible tokens can be transferable or not, depending on the use case.

The more easily divisible a token is, the more fungible it is. Divisibility refers to the fact that you can send a fraction of the token to someone else. In the real

Fungibility Perspective

Fungible Tokens	Non-fungible Tokens
Identical	*Unique*
Tokens of the same type are identical to one another. They have identical attributes.	Each token is unique and differs from all other tokens of the same type. They have unique attributes.
Interchangeable	*Non-interchangeable*
A token can be interchanged for another with the same value. A 20 EUR bill can be replaced with a combination of other bills and coins that amount to the same value.	NFTs cannot be replaced with tokens of the same type as they represent unique values or access rights. A university degree or drivers license would be non-interchangeable.
Divisible	*Non-divisible*
Fungible assets are divisible into smaller amounts. It is irrelevant which and how many units one uses, as long as it adds up to the same value.	Tokens that are tied to one's identity, like certificates and degrees, are not divisible. It does not make sense to have a fraction of a degree or drivers's license.

world, many real assets cannot be divided, which makes them less easily tradeable. Cryptographic tokens can represent assets that were not easily divisible before, and can now be fractionalized at lower transaction costs than with established systems. Physical goods that are non-divisible can be first tokenized and then divided and sold off in different parts. Fractional tokenized ownership might allow a new array of asset classes, like real estate or art, and make those assets more liquid and fungible. However, there are practical limitations of redeeming a represented asset, for example, a piece of art (read more: Part 4 - Asset Tokens & Fractional Ownership). While in theory, there is no limit to making tokens divisible to 100 decimals, it is not economically feasible to do so. The overhead is huge when dealing with trillions of addresses that can and will hold leftover "dust." Dust in this context refers to very small amounts of unspent tokens that are often not worth it to transfer, as the transaction fees might be higher than the dust is worth. There is a point where the marginal utility of extra divisibility is outweighed by the extra computational effort (storage and bandwidth). Furthermore, dusting attacks, where minuscule amounts of tokens are sent to random addresses to make them easily traceable, will be more feasible.

Privacy Perspective: As opposed to common belief, the Bitcoin network does not provide full anonymity, hence privacy, but rather pseudonymity. This means that one can use the power of big data to correlate other data points, which might be publicly available or accessible to certain national security agencies, against the metadata connected to a certain BTC transaction and address. If someone behind a Bitcoin address becomes a person of interest, and the provenance of their tokens' history becomes tainted or blacklisted, this person might have problems trading their tokens. In such cases, authorities could correlate your Bitcoin address against other, more traditional data points that are subject to know-your-customer regulations (KYC), like banks and exchanges, or even e-commerce platforms like Amazon. If you were to pay for your purchase on Amazon with Bitcoin, for example, and your tokens have a history that is tainted, Amazon might decide not to accept it. The privacy, and as a result also the fungibility of Bitcoin and similar tokens, may therefore be up for debate. If a tokens' history can be tracked and that token is linked to illicit activity that would make the token "tainted," limiting its role as a medium of exchange. Newer blockchain networks like "Zcash" and "Monero" are working with alternative cryptographic tools that could make their tokens more private and thus more fungible (read more: Privacy Tokens).

Transferability Perspective: Tokens can be transferable or non-transferable, or have restricted transferability. Unique (non-fungible) tokens can be transferable or non-transferable depending on the use case. A plane ticket might be transferable or non-transferable depending on the type of ticket you bought. A piece of art or the registration paper of your car, for example, are unique but transferable. Identity-bound tokens like certificates or licenses are usually non-transferable. A token that allows you to pick up your kids from kindergarten is unique, but could have some limited or temporary transferability to allow you to arrange for someone else to pick up your kids by temporarily granting that person pickup rights. While fungible tokens tend to be transferable in most cases, there are also exceptions to the rule.

Durability Perspective: In economics, durability refers to the ability of a currency to withstand repeated use. This means that the substrate of that currency should not easily vanish, decay, or rot. Metals or durable foods like wheat have high durability, and were therefore often used as commodity money. The Bitcoin token

Transferability Perspective

	Transferable	Non-transferable
Identical	Fiat money, commodity money, poker chips, discount codes, coupons, gift cards, public transport tickets, commodity certificates, native blockchain tokens.	Non-transferable plane ticket (I can exchange the ticket for another flight, but I cannot transfer it to another person).
Unique	Lottery tickets, keys that open real estate or a car, land title deeds, registration documents of a car, piece of art.	Anything that is tied to the identity of a person: Club memberships, drivers license, university certificate, identity documents, voting rights (except for liquid democracy), drug prescriptions.

	Transferable	Non-transferable
Access Right	Event tickets, doctors appointments, public transport tickets.	Airline tickets, memberships, prescriptions, personalized government services.
Property Right	Securities, currencies, commodities, art, real estate.	An example might be: mining rights on a piece of land that represent a temporary asset which I can exploit for economic reasons.

	Transferable	Non-transferable
Fixed Supply	Event tickets, doctors appointments, shares in a company.	Airline tickets, entry tickets, government services.
Unlimited Supply	Currencies, Commodities.	Airlines miles, Award points.

and similar protocol tokens have so far proven to withstand time, being resilient against any type of censorship or network attack. A resilient network is expected to contribute to a "relatively" stable long-term value of the token. If one can correlate network resilience to the value of the network token, the token can be expected to be durable, as it will not cease to exist. As long as the network is robust and used, new tokens will be minted and demand for tokens will increase. Token prices might decrease due to price fluctuations, but the token as such will not vanish as long as the network is intact. A network with a weak consensus protocol, on the other hand, might be attacked and manipulated, in which case token holders could lose their tokens if the ledger is tampered with.

Regulatory Perspective: Regulation is a complex topic that could cover a book on its own, especially taking into account all 200+ jurisdictions in the world. To simplify matters, at this point, it is sufficient to say that regulators need a clear taxonomy of the different types of tokens to understand what they are potentially regulating. Regulatory authorities all over the world are catching up to understand the full potential and implications of the Web3 and it's tokenized applications. While some tokens might represent completely new asset classes, like native protocol tokens that very often have hybrid functions and are not easy to classify, other token types might represent assets of the existing economy that are understood and regulated. An example for assets that are easy to classify or regulate are tokenized securities and other assets (read more: Part 4 - Asset Tokens & Fractional Ownership). In more complex cases, entrepreneurs will be confronted with uncertainties of how the regulator might retroactively classify the token. To provide regulatory certainty to entrepreneurs, some jurisdictions have started to offer governmental sandboxes to guarantee innovation while allowing for a process of regulatory learning.

Incentive Perspectiv: As opposed to tokens that represent existing assets or access rights to an asset or services someone else owns, tokens can also be programmed to incentivize a new form of collective value creation. They can be used to incentivize individual behavior or contributions to a collective goal of a group of people, if and when one provides proof of contributing to a collective goal. Bitcoin and other protocol tokens are a good example for such purpose-driven tokens. Rewards programs or loyalty programs are another example for tokens that are designed to reward behavior. While incentivizing behavior is not a new concept, cryptographic tokens have spurred a lot of innovation around purpose-driven tokens that incentivize behaviors, like CO_2 tokens, time bank tokens, social media tokens, attention tokens, etc. (read more: Part 4 - Purpose-Driven Tokens).

Token Supply Perspective: Protocol tokens vary in their token supply strategies. Bitcoin's token supply is regulated in the protocol and limited to 21 million. The Ethereum network, on the other hand, did not predefine the token supply in the same way (read more: Part 2 - Institutional Economics of DAOs). For tokens that represent an access right, the number of tokens is usually limited to the maximum capacity and frequency of the access provider. The only limit is the capacity of a system, such as the capacity of a bus in a public transport network, which can always be extended if necessary, most often including a time lag. Many of the tokens listed on "Coinmarketcap," especially those that were used for early token sales to raise funds, have a limited token supply. This is especially true for tokens that represent equity in a network. Asset tokens are naturally limited by the amount of assets available to back them with. Any token with a limited supply could potentially serve as a de-facto store of value and medium of exchange, depending on the expected durability, short-term volatility, and fungibility.

Stability Perspective: Short-term stability of value is one of the most important functions of a medium of exchange, so that it can serve as a unit of account and is fundamental for economic planning. While Bitcoin introduced a groundbreaking consensus algorithm, it comes with a rudimentary monetary policy that simply regulates and limits the amount of tokens minted over time. The protocol does not provide an economic algorithm that guarantees price stability. Depending on the type of token designed, price stability might be desirable, especially in the case of payment tokens that are intended as a day to day medium of exchange. If price stability is needed, according mechanisms need to be built into the mechanism of the token.

Token Flow Perspective: Another dimension revolves around the question of the token flow. Tokens might be created for a single purpose and destroyed when the purpose has been fulfilled to complete the cycle. In this case, they flow in a straight line from source to sink. Examples thereof are casino chips that can be used within the realm of the casino and are issued against fiat currency. Once players leave the casino, they can convert the chips back to the local currency. Transportation tickets that pay for access to a system and expire after one-time use, or after a period of time, are another example. They are destroyed upon consumption or after a certain expiry date. Their supply is unlimited, or it is limited to the infrastructural capacities. On the other hand, tokens that can be exchanged back and forth indefinitely, without an artificial expiration condition, can be said to have a circular flow. Most asset tokens that are transferable and have no expiry date, like any currency or commodity token or tokenized art, have circular token flows. Tokens with a circular token flow will only sink when you lose your private keys, or if the physical underlying asset is accidentally destroyed.

Temporal Perspective: Another question when designing a token is whether the token has an expiration date. Any fungible token might be programmed in a way that it expires after a certain date, to prevent hoarding of the tokens. Practically speaking, the token would expire; technically speaking, the token would change state. Bonus points of loyalty programs usually come with an expiry date. In the past, some regional currencies, like the "Wörgl Schwundgeld" (Austria) in the 1930s, experimented with an inbuilt deflation of their currency to prevent hoarding and inflation. The currency was introduced as a parallel currency that could only be spent in the region of Wörgl. By losing 1 percent of its value each month, individual spending was encouraged while saving was disincentivized. This measure was introduced to combat a country-wide deflationary policy and helped with both unemployment numbers and infrastructure investment.

Non-Fungible Tokens

Non-fungible tokens (NFTs) are unique in nature, with varying properties that can be distinguished from each other. NFTs can represent digital, unique, and thus scarce assets, such as art and other collectibles or real estate. NFTs can also represent identities and certificates, such as licenses, degrees, keys, passes, identities, wills, voting rights, tickets, loyalty tokens, copyrights, warranties, software licenses, medical data, and certificates of any kind, such as supply chain or art certificates. Before the emergence of the Web3, identification and certification systems, as well as unique and scarce assets, were costly to manage, as they relied on the validation and security of the centralized issuing entities. Distributed ledgers, on the other hand, enable a decentralized and publicly verifiable infrastructure to issue and manage these assets at very low operational costs.

In 2013, "Colored Coins" was one of the first projects that attempted to attach unique properties to a token. The idea was to use Bitcoin tokens to represent real-world assets like stocks, bonds, commodities, or the deed for a house. "Counterparty" was another project that built on this idea, but went one step further. It enabled users to create their own virtual assets on top of the Bitcoin network. With the emergence of the Ethereum network, both projects struggled to gain wide adoption. NFTs started to attract a lot of attention when the ERC-721 token standard was introduced, especially following the success of "Crypto Kitties," a game on the Ethereum network where players can collect and breed digital cats, and where each cat's unique digital "genetic code" is stored on Ethereum's ledger.

The ERC-721 token standard allows for more detailed attributes that make a token special, beyond the attributes that can be found in ERC-20 tokens. It allows the inclusion of metadata about an asset and information about ownership. When validated, such additional information can add value, guaranteeing the provenance of art, collectibles, or along the supply chain of other goods and services. The success of ERC-721 probably also triggered other blockchain projects, such as the NEO network, to develop their own non-fungible token standards.

Crypto-collectibles & Crypto-games: Crypto-collectibles allow the tokenization of unique goods. NFTs can be used to represent any in-game asset, to be in control of the user instead of the game developer. Crypto Kitties spurred a lot of attention to this new asset class when it clogged the Ethereum Network. Major League Baseball in the US has launched "MLB Crypto"; now, "MLB Champions" is one of the few blockchain-based games on Google Play where unique digital items can be traded outside of the game itself on marketplaces such as "Opensea." Just to have an idea of how much is already in development, here is a selection of games, collectibles, and marketplaces that trade them: "Cryptofighters," "Decentraland," "Etherbots," "Ethermon," "Gods unchained," "Plasmabears," "0x universe," "Hyperdragons," "Loom," "Spells of Genesis," "Crafty," "Superrare," "FlowerToken," "Unico," "OpSkins," or "Rarebits."

Asset Tokens: Asset tokens allow unique investments tied to a physical object, like unique artwork, real estate, or any other real-world assets and securities. One could tokenize a building, where some tokens could grant simple ownership titles of a fraction of the real estate, while other tokens could grant special privileges like access rights. Non-fungible tokens can also be used to represent artworks. Such tokenization of existing assets in the real world can give investors a chance to expand their portfolio, and provide the market with more liquidity. NFTs can grant token holders different levels of control over their assets (read more: Part 4 - Asset Tokens & Fractional Ownership).

Credential Tokens, Certificates and Reputation: Anything that uniquely represents a person could be represented as a non-fungible token: any type of ID or certificate like school transcripts, university degrees, or software licenses that are tied to the existence of one single person. A diploma could be issued and collectively managed by a distributed ledger with no need to be translated, manually notarized, or verified. Wallet-like software could manage all personal data without the need for centralized institutions storing our data. The token would represent a container for identity information related to a specific person without giving information about what is identified. Certification claims can be associated with the token, which would be issued by the trusted entities that issue these certifications. If properly designed, reputation tokens could be attached to identities and resolve challenges like "fake news."

Access Tokens: NFT could be used to manage any type of access right that is tied to a special person, a special property, or a special event. Collectively managed distributed ledgers using public key cryptography can offer more secure and decentrally verified access-rights management than centrally managed digital access-rights management solutions and can replace physical keys, digital keys, and passwords.

<u>Transfer Tokens</u>: When someone passes away today, the will often needs to be split between multiple people, which can produce considerable bureaucratic overhead and coordination costs to split the value of these assets. This is especially true in the case of intangible assets that have a lengthy process to liquidate before the value can be split among the beneficiaries. While fractional ownership is possible today, transfer tokens managed by a distributed ledger would make the transfer of assets in the case of wills much more frictionless.

Chapter Summary

- *Tokens might affect the financial world similar to how the Internet affected the postal system. They can represent any assets or access rights, and are collectively managed by distributed ledgers. Tokens can be issued with just a few lines of code in the form of a smart contract.*

- *Tokens are accessible with a piece of software, a wallet that communicates with a blockchain network or similar distributed ledger and manages the public-private key pair related to the blockchain address. Only the person who has the private key for that address can access the respective token.*

- *Tokens can represent anything from a store of value to a set of permissions in the physical, digital, and legal world. They facilitate collaboration across markets and jurisdictions and allow for a more transparent, efficient, and fair interaction between market participants, at low costs. Tokens can also incentivize an autonomous group of people to individually contribute to a collective goal. These tokens are created upon proof of a certain behavior.*

- *Tokens are not a new thing and have existed since long before the emergence of blockchain networks. Traditionally, tokens can represent any form of economic value. Tokens are furthermore used in computing, where they can represent a right to perform some operation or manage access rights. A more tangible form of computer tokens are tracking codes that you get to track your parcel with postal services, or QR codes that give you access to a train or plane.*

- *Cryptographic tokens can represent property rights, access rights, or voting rights.*

- *The term "token" is simply a metaphor. Contrary to what the metaphor might suggest, a token does not represent a digital file that is sent from one device to another. Instead, it refers to an entry in a ledger that is collectively managed by a network of computers.*

- *The most important perspectives from which we can deduce the properties of a token: (i) Technical perspective; (ii) Rights perspective; (iii) Fungibility perspective; (iv) Transferability perspective; (v) Durability perspective; (vi) Regulatory perspective; (vii) Incentive perspective; (viii) Supply perspective; (ix) Token flow perspective; (x) Privacy perspective; and (xi) Stability perspective.*

- While fungible tokens are identical, non-fungible tokens are unique in nature, with varying properties that can be distinguished from each other. Non-fungible tokens are a more diverse asset class and can also represent identities and certificates, such as licenses, degrees, certificates, keys, passes, identities, wills, voting rights, tickets, loyalty tokens, copyrights, supply chain tracking, medical data, software licenses, warranties, and many more.

Chapter References & Further Reading

- Catalini, C., Gans, Joshua S.: "Some Simple Economics of the Blockchain", NBER Working Paper No. 22952, 2016
- Chen, Y., "Blockchain Tokens and the Potential Democratization of Entrepreneurship and Innovation". Business Horizons, Forthcoming; Stevens Institute of Technology School of Business Research Paper, 2017.
- Chudzinski, Pawel: "Mapping the Emerging Non-Fungible Token Landscape", Jun 15, 2018: https://medium.com/point-nine-news/mapping-the-emerging-non-fungible-token-landscape-ee56f0d1079f
- Conley, John P. ,'Blockchain and the Economics of Crypto-tokens and Initial Coin Offerings'', Vanderbilt University Department of Economics Working Papers, VUECON-17-00008, 2017.
- De La Rouviere, Simon, Taylor, A.: "A Token-Powered Future on Ethereum", 2015, https://medium.com/@ConsenSys/tokens-on-ethereum-e9e61dac9b4e
- Diedrich, Henning: "Ethereum: Blockchains, Digital Assets, Smart Contracts, Decentralized Autonomous Organizations", ISBN-13 978-1523930470, CreateSpace Independent Publishing Platform, 2016.
- Ehrsam, Fred: "Blockchain Tokens and the dawn of the Decentralized Business Model", 2016, https://blog.coinbase.com/app-coins-and-the-dawn-of-the-decentralized-business-model8b8c951e734f
- Ehrsam, Fred: "Value of the Token Model", 2017: https://medium.com/@FEhrsam/value-of-the-tokenmodel-6c65f09bcba8
- Euler, Thomas: "The Token Classification Framework: A multi-dimensional tool for understanding and classifying crypto tokens" January 18, 2018: http://www.untitled-inc.com/the-token-classifi-cation-framework-a-multi-dimensional-tool-for-understanding-and-classifying-crypto-tokens/
- Evans, David S., 2014, "Economic Aspects of Bitcoin and Other Decentralized Public-Ledger Currency Platforms". University of Chicago Coase-Sandor Institute for Law & Economics Research
- Flynn, Brian: "Designing Non-Fungible Tokens as Open Ecosystems Airdrops, Interoperability & Extensibility, and Royalties", Aug 7, 2018: https://tokeneconomy.co/designing-non-fungible-tokens-as-open-ecosystems-a0f28ae213ee
- Genestoux, Julien: "Non Fungible Tokens An intro to non fungible tokens", Mar 5, 2018: https://hackernoon.com/non-fungible-tokens-5ba83906b275
- Gaúcho Pereira, Felipe: "On the immaturity of tokenized value capture mechanisms Pursuing value in an age of borderless-ness, experimental monetary policies, costless forks and unlimited innovation", Apr 1, 2018: https://medium.com/paratii/on-the-immaturity-of-tokenized-value-capture-mechanisms-1fde33f2bc8e
- Glatz, Florian: "A Blockchain Token Taxonomy", 2016: https://medium.com/@heckerhut/a-blockchain-tokentaxonomy-fadf5c56139a
- Gregor, S., and Hevner, A. R. 2013. "Positioning and Presenting Design Science Research for Maximum Impact," MIS Quarterly, (37:2), pp. 337–355 (doi: 10.2753/MIS0742-1222240302).
- Hevner, A. R. 2007. "A three cycle view of design science research," Scandinavian journal of information systems, (19:2), p. 4.
- Hurwicz, Leonid; Reiter, Stanley: "Designing Economic Mechanisms", Cambridge University, 2006

- Jackson, K.: "Hackenberg, T.D.: Token reinforcement, choice, and self-control in pigeons", *Journal of the Experimental Analysis of Behavior*, 1996 July; 66(1): 29–49.
- Kazdin, A.E.: "The Token Economy. A review and evaluation", *Plenum Press*, 1977.
- Lee, J. S., Pries-Heje, J., and Baskerville, R. 2011. "Theorizing in design science research," in *International Conference on Design Science Research in Information Systems*, Springer, pp. 1–16 (available at http://link.springer.com/chapter/10.1007/978-3-642-20633-7_1) Lewis, A., 2015, "A gentle introduction to digital tokens", https://bitsonblocks.net/2015/09/28/a-gentleintroduction-to-digital-tokens/
- Lena and Oxana, 2017, "What are you token about? Blockchain token economics and rights.", https://hackernoon.com/token-economy-4a38ad02a239
- Lielacher, Alexander: "Tokenomics: What are the Classifications of ICO Tokens?" March 13, 2018: https://blog.icoalert.com/tokenomics-what-are-the-different-types-of-tokens-you-can-buy-in-icos
- Miscione, G., Ziolkowski, R., Zavolokina, L. and Schwabe, G., 2018, "Tribal Governance: The Business of Blockchain Authentication", *51st Hawaii International Conference on System Sciences (HICSS 2018)* University of Hawai'i at Manoa 2018-01-03 Hawaii, USA conference 51st Hawaii International Conference on System Sciences (HICSS 2018) ISBN: 978-0-9981331-1-9 In Proceeding
- Mougayar, William: "Tokenomics – A Business Guide to Token Usage, Utility and Value", 2017, https://medium.com/@wmougayar/tokenomics-a-business-guide-to-token-usage-utility-and-valueb19242053416
- N.N.: "What Is a Dusting Attack?", Binance Academy, Nov 28, 2018: https://binance.vision/security/what-is-a-dusting-attack
- N.N.: "Guidelines for enquiries regarding the regulatory framework for initial coin offerings (ICOs)", Paper 685 Finma, Published 16 February 2018: https://finma.ch/en/~/media/finma/dokumente/dokumentencenter/myfinma/1bewilligung/fintech/wegleitung-ico.pdf?la=en
- Nunamaker, J. F., Briggs, R. O., Derrick, D. C., and Schwabe, G. 2015. "The Last Research Mile: Achieving Both Rigor and Relevance in Information Systems Research," *Journal of Management Information Systems*, (32:3), pp. 10–47 (doi: 10.1080/07421222.2015.1094961).
- Oliveira, Luis; Zavolokina, Liudmila; Bauer,Ingrid; Schwabe,Gerhard: "To Token or not to Token: Tools for Understanding Blockchain Tokens": https://aisel.aisnet.org/icis2018/crypto/Presentations/5
- Pilkington, Marc, 2015. "Blockchain Technology: Principles and Applications", *Research Handbook on Digital Transformations*.
- Rudolf, M., 2017, "Economics of Entangled Tokens", https://blog.neufund.org/economics-of-entangledtokens-9fc5b084e2d2
- Ritchey, Tom: "General Morphological Analysis: A general method for non-quantified modeling", 1998
- Ritchey, Tom: "Modelling Complex Socio-Technical Systems Using Morphological Analysis", 2003
- Saldana, J., 2015, „The Coding Manual for Qualitative Researchers"
- Siegel, David "The Token Handbook", Sep 13, 2017: https://hackernoon.com/the-token-handbook-a80244a6aacb
- Tomuletiu, David Gabriel: "The art of tokenization", Caleum Labs, Medium, Nov 27, 2018 https://medium.com/caelumlabs/the-art-of-tokenization-2b5f76f71596
- Tomaino, Nick : "On Token Value", Aug 6, 2017: https://thecontrol.co/on-token-value-e61b10b6175e
- Voshmgir, Shermin: „Fungible Tokens vs. Non-Fungible Tokens - The rise of ERC-721"Medium, BlockchainHub, Sep 23, 2018: https://medium.com/@sherminvoshmgir/fungible-tokens-vs-non-fungible-tokens-69871b0e37a9
- Xrphodor: „Tokens – Trust on the XRP Ledger", January 11, 2018: https://xrphodor.wordpress.com/2018/01/11/tokens-trust-on-the-xrp-ledger/
- Zwicky, Fritz: "Discovery, Invention, Research - Through the Morphological Approach", 1969
- Zwicky, Fritz. & Wilson A.: "New Methods of Thought and Procedure", Contributions to the S ymposium on Methodologies, Berlin, 1967

- *Cosmos: https://cosmos.network/*
- *Polkadot: https://polkadot.network/*
- *Crypto Kitties: https://cryptokitties.co/*
- *Cryptofighters: https://cryptofighters.io/?utm_source=dappradar*
- *Decentraland: http://decentraland.org/*
- *Etherbots: https://etherbots.io/*
- *Ethermon: http://ethermon.net/*
- *Gods unchained: https://godsunchained.com/*
- *Plasmabaers: https://plasmabears.com/*
- *0x universe: https://0xuniverse.com/*
- *Hyperdragons: https://hyperdragons.alfakingdom.com/*
- *Spells of Genesis: https://spellsofgenesis.com/*
- *Crafty: https://crafty.zeppelin.solutions/*
- *Superrare: https://superrare.co/*
- *Unico: https://unico.global/*
- *Opensea: https://opensea.io/*
- *OpSkins: https://opskins.com/*
- *Rarebits: https://rarebits.io/*

PART 3

Token Economics & DeFi

This part will focus on cryptographic tokens as the atomic unit of the Web3. The first chapter will explain the properties and functions of money and outline the emerging field of decentralized finance (DeFi) that might power a potential future digital barter economy. The following chapters will focus on specific DeFi applications such as stable tokens and privacy tokens, as well as the topic of issuing, trading, and lending of tokens.

The Future of Money & Decentralized Finance (DeFi)[44]

In a market economy based on division of labor, the role of money issued by governmental bodies is to facilitate the exchange of goods and services. Money makes economic exchange much more efficient than gift economies and barter economies, avoiding the inefficiencies of such systems like the "coincidence of wants" problem.

There is a widespread misconception that Bitcoin and native blockchain tokens are currencies comparable to fiat currencies such as EUR, USD, or YEN, which are issued by central banks of nation states. Referring to tokens as "currencies" sparks a lot of controversy and is not entirely true. While native protocol tokens and some asset tokens have certain properties of money, they have more resemblance with commodity money or representative money, but not so much with modern fiat money. The biggest challenge that we face when we try to explain or talk about cryptographic tokens is that we are trying to explain new phenomena with old terminology. Using old terminology to explain new phenomena does not always do justice to the full range of possibilities this new technology has to offer. To be able to draw similarities and make accurate distinctions, it is important to understand the historic evolution of money, as well as the purpose and functionalities of money. The primary purpose of money is to facilitate an economic exchange of goods and services within and between economies. It makes economic exchange much more efficient than gift economies and barter economies, avoiding the inefficiencies of such systems like the "coincidence of wants" problem. The coincidence of wants

[44] This chapter is based on texts that have been published before, originally in: Voshmgir, Shermin: „Token Economy - The Future of Currencies?", Medium blog, Jan 31, 2018: https://medium.com/crypto3conomics/token-economy-the-future-of-currencies-d26487fd3945. Variations of this text have been published in following publication: https://www.creative.nrw.de/fileadmin/user_upload/Pdf/180423_HIDDENVALUES_148x210_DIGITAL.pdf, https://www.derstandard.at/story/2000081901719/warum-bitcoin-keine-waehrung-ist, Sinner, Martin; Harlinghausen, Curt Simon; Voshmgir, Shermin; Solmecke,Christian; Smith, Monika: "Business Purpose Design Business Purpose Design", 2018 Santiago Berlin GmbH"

problem refers to the improbability that two parties, each of which own different goods, can agree on a deal, unless each party wants the specific good the other party offers, at the same time. To mitigate this problem, one can agree on a universal asset of value as a medium of exchange. Shells, precious metals, or livestock were first used as such assets to counter the inefficiencies of a barter economy. Over time, however, more neutral artificial mediums of exchange developed, which we started to refer to as money. Money has proved to be an efficient technology for intermediating the exchange of goods and services, providing a tool to compare values of dissimilar objects. Money needs to serve as a medium of exchange, store of value, and unit of account in which debt can be denominated. It provides a basis for market prices, which are necessary for an efficient accounting system and the basis for the formulation of commercial agreements. A currency is a system of money of a closed group of people, like a nation state, often serving as legal tender within that nation. If a currency has the status of legal tender, it is a unit with which debts are denominated in a nation state by its legal system. As legal tender, it represents an accepted way to meet a financial obligation as a result of economic activities and settle a debt within the geographical boundaries of that nation state. However, the exact definition of a legal tender varies along jurisdictions.

Properties of Money

Properties of money include liquidity, fungibility, durability, portability, cognizability, and stability. Money also needs some inbuilt anti-counterfeiting measures to avoid forging.

Liquidity refers to the fact that the substrate that represents money must be easily tradable, at low transaction costs.

Divisibility and portability refer to the fact that assets must be easily transportable. While a barrel of oil is divisible and durable, oil isn't easily portable in barrels. Comparable to a barrel of oil, a bar of gold is equally durable but easier to transfer. However, divisibility of such a gold bar, the process of melting and minting it into smaller units, comes at a high cost.

Fungibility refers to the fact that units of money are equal. Every token of that currency must be treated equally, even if it has been used for illegal purposes by previous owners. This is to protect the rights of innocent recipients of those tokens, who might not have known of the illegal activities. Fungibility is not guaranteed if a token can be censored or blacklisted based on the behavior of previous token holders.

Durability refers to the ability to withstand repeated use so it can serve as a store of value. Money must have the ability to be reliably saved, stored, and retrieved, and to be predictably usable as a medium of exchange when retrieved. This means that the substrate of that currency should not easily vanish, decay, or rot. Metals or durable foods like wheat, flour, and sugar have high durability, and were therefore often used as commodity money; they were considered precious to almost all members of society, and to be a workaround to the "coincidence of wants" problem.

Stability refers to the fact that value should not fluctuate too much; otherwise, it will not be able to serve as a reliable store of value. Without a reliable store of value, economic planning of individual households and companies, but also of governments, will be difficult. High volatility is counterproductive for trust in future prices, salaries, debts, and therefore trade. Inflation reduces the value of money and, as a result, it's ability to function as a store of value. If price levels rise, each unit of currency buys fewer goods and services. Deflation, on the other hand, decreases general price levels of goods and services.

Cognizability refers to the fact that the value of a currency token must be easily identifiable.

Types of Money

Different types of money have evolved over time. In modern economies, the dominant type of money is fiat money. Prior to the existence of modern day fiat currencies, commodity money and representative money were in widespread use.

Commodity money is any object which has an intrinsic and standardized value in a local economy. The value of such commodity money derives from the commodity of which it is made: gold coins, silver coins, and other rare metal coins, salt, barley, animal pelts, cigarettes, or ramen packs. Before smoking was banned in prisons, cigarettes were used among others as an underground currency, but were then replaced by tuna cans, instant ramen packs, and similar durable and portable objects of high value for prisoners. The price is determined by comparing the perceived value of the commodity to the perceived value of other products.

Representative money, on the other hand, is a medium of exchange that represents something of value but has little or no value on its own. It's a claim on a commodity: gold or silver certificates, or paper money and coins backed by gold reserves. Asset tokens also represent a physical good and could be classified as commodity money.

Fiat money is established by government regulation, similar to any check or note of debt. Fiat money, like the coins and bills we use today, do not have an intrinsic physical value like a commodity. Their face value, which is denominated on the banknote, is greater than their material substance. "It derives its value by being declared by a government to be legal tender... It must be accepted as a form of payment within the boundaries of the country, for all debts, public and private... The money supply of a country consists of currency (banknotes and coins) and, depending on the particular definition used, one or more types of bank money (the balances held in checking accounts, savings accounts, and other types of bank accounts). Bank money, which consists only of records (mostly computerized in modern banking), forms by far the largest part of broad money in developed countries."[45] In modern economies, most money in circulation is not in the form of bills and coins anymore, but rather an entry in the digital ledgers of a bank, managing money saved in current accounts, checking accounts, and in the form of other financial instruments. The assigned value results from the fact that governments can use their power to enforce the value of a fiat currency.

Fiat currencies have evolved over time. While banknotes and coins were pegged to scarce commodities like gold and other precious metals in the past, the gold standard was abolished. Hardly any currencies today are pegged to commodities. Central banks influence the money supply with monetary policy, by issuing more or less money by issuing credit, as they see fit. However, many economists would argue that fiat currencies, in most stable economies, are backed by the collective value of the underlying economic activity of a nation, measured as its gross domestic product (GDP).

Money or Not?

While Bitcoin was originally designed with the purpose to create P2P money without banks, the underlying P2P payment network has proven to be a gateway to a new type of economic value creation. The Bitcoin protocol is designed to incentivize individual contributions to a collective good, a public and permissionless P2P payment network. Using the vocabulary of a computer scientist, the protocol hereby provides an operating system for a new type of economy. Using the vocabulary of a political scientist, the protocol represents the constitutional foundation for a distributed Internet tribe collectively maintaining that network, a group of voluntary participants that transcends the geographical boundaries of nation states. Bitcoin tokens can be considered as the legal tender of the Bitcoin network; Bitcoin tokens are the only accepted form of payment within the network. BTC is needed to pay for transaction costs in the network. They cannot be paid with fiat money like USD, EUR, or other cryptographic tokens. The price of the network token should

---

[45] *https://en.wikipedia.org/wiki/Money*

reflect the stability of the payment network, similar to how the value of fiat currencies should reflect the economic activities of a country.

Protocol tokens have certain properties of money, however, they seem to have more similarities to commodity money or representative money than to fiat money. The production process is distributed (similar to real life commodities) and the price is determined by supply and demand, thus subject to fluctuation (much like the price of tokens, which are determined by the supply and demand on exchanges). As opposed to fiat currencies, no single centralized entity like governments and central banks can influence the price or the accessibility of protocol tokens. Control is therefore distributed, much like with commodities, where no single government or other entity controls the mining of gold, silver, oil, etc. Who has how much control in the system is subject to the token creation rules defined in the protocol. The token creation and supply policy (monetary policy of the network) is the point of centralization that can only be changed by majority consensus of all network actors in the form of a software upgrade. The protocol therefore has functions of a central bank. Potential "central bank smart contracts" could account for more adaptive monetary policy than the one Bitcoin network provides. Such trends to make the monetary policy of a token more adaptive and stable are emerging (read more: Part 3 - Stable Tokens).

While distributed production and control applies to protocol tokens, it is not necessarily true for application tokens. Application tokens or sidechain tokens are often issued by one centralized entity, a private company or a foundation. Tokens that are pegged to an asset, or a security, could also have similarities to commodity money. As opposed to commodities that are already being traded on legacy systems, asset tokens might provide much higher liquidity due to the frictionless settlement infrastructure a distributed ledger provides. This could be especially true for asset tokens that represent real life assets that currently do not have high market liquidity, or goods that hardly have a market at all. Asset tokens make the underlying asset more tradable, while the asset itself is still illiquid. Tokenization of assets can convert previously "non-bankable funds" into "bankable funds." Non-bankable funds are assets that are not accepted as a method of payment in a bank. Bankable funds are forms of payment that are accepted at financial institutions and easily liquidated into local currencies such as checks and money orders. They can be converted into cash with short notice and are generally accepted by merchants as a method of payment. In light of potential widespread tokenization, any tokenized asset could receive the status of a "bankable fund." Such developments could make any tokenized asset a potential medium of exchange. However, as of today, most tokens do not fulfill some important properties of money: stability, and to some extent, also fungibility. Furthermore, usability and scalability are also entry barriers to potential mass adoption.

<u>Stability</u>: Bitcoin and similar blockchain protocols simply regulate and limit the amount of tokens minted over time. Their protocols do not provide a sophisticated economic algorithm that guarantees price stability; their exchange rate is determined by supply and demand on markets and is often highly volatile. While fiat currencies of most modern economies also have fluctuating exchange rates that are determined on foreign exchange markets, national institutions can perform currency intervention via foreign exchange markets or other currency manipulation. In such an intervention process, governments or central banks buy and sell currency in exchange for their own currency to manipulate the market price. They do that in order to avoid excessive short-term volatility, which makes economic actions hard to plan. Short-term volatility also tends to erode market confidence, generating extra costs and reducing the profits of firms, forcing investors to make investments in foreign financial assets. With the emergence of hedging options, stable tokens (read more: Part 3 - Stable Tokens), and atomic swaps (read more: Part 3 - Decentralized Exchanges & Atomic Swaps) on the rise, price volatility might be a non-issue in the future. However, it is unclear whether, how, and when these solutions will gain traction.

<u>Privacy</u>: Most tokens today have no inbuilt privacy by design. This makes them non-fungible, and therefore non-usable as a medium of exchange. For a token to potentially serve as a medium of exchange, it needs to be fully fungible. If you can taint addresses, as in the case of Bitcoin, the token will not serve as a medium of exchange in the long run. Even though Bitcoin addresses are pseudonymous, simple chain analysis of the ledger can link the data flow from a particular address with other data points outside the blockchain, and identify who is behind a Bitcoin address. While this requires time and effort, and access to other data points, it is not unfeasible. Potential traceability destroys the fungibility of a token (read more: Part 3 - Privacy Tokens).

<u>Scalability</u>: Current settlement infrastructures of public blockchain networks are secure but not very scalable. Alternative distributed ledger solutions have better scalability but tend to be more centralized. This is due to the "scalability trilemma," the trade-off between security, scalability, and decentralization. While scalability is still a big issue, many solutions are already on the horizon (read more: Annex - Scalability).

<u>Usability</u>: Wallet usability also still has a long way to go. Most current wallets support only a handful of tokens, some only one. This means that you often need a separate wallet application for each token, or type of tokens. Furthermore, key management is a nightmare: if you lose your key, you lose access to your funds. If that issue is not resolved, hosted wallets in the custody of trusted third parties, such as online exchanges, will become mainstream. This, however, would undermine the efforts of autonomous asset management in the sense of P2P electronic cash, as originally envisioned by Satoshi Nakamoto.

Decentralized Finance (DeFi): Toward a Digital Barter Economy

Cryptographic tokens represent a new heterogenous asset class that can fulfill a diverse range of economic functions. Their frictionless issuance and settlement process could potentially convert many assets or access rights of the real world into "bankable funds." Tokenizing economic activities, from real assets to digital assets and all types of access rights, could impact the role of central bank money as a geographical monopolist providing a medium of exchange, once mass adoption of the Web3 manifests and necessary network effects kick in. The speed at which these tokens are being issued is an indicator that a new tokenized economic system is emerging (read more: Part 2 - Tokens & Part 4 - Token Use Cases). Such tokenization of the real economy could gradually lead to the merging of the money system, with the financial system and the real economy.

A range of easy-to-use decentralized financial (DeFi) applications have been emerging beyond simple payments networks that facilitate frictional and P2P asset issuance, trading, lending and hedging. The term "DeFi" encompasses any decentralized and permissionless financial application that builds on top of distributed ledgers, including privacy-preserving payment systems (privacy tokens), stability preserving payment systems (stable tokens), P2P exchanges (token exchanges), P2P fundraising (token sales), and P2P credit and lending (decentralized lending), P2P insurance, and a growing list of P2P derivatives. These Web3-based DeFi applications could, potentially, open traditional financial services to the general public, mitigating current inefficiencies of financial markets.

The current financial system, even in it's electronic form, requires a range of intermediary services for (i) mitigating counterparty risk, (ii) market making, and (iii) securing funds from being stolen. This is a result of the server-centric nature of the current Internet. In a tokenized economy, however, distributed ledgers and user-centric identity solutions could increase ecosystem transparency, accountability, and market efficiency:

- Due to the public nature of distributed ledgers, DeFi applications are designed to be globally accessible by anyone around the world with an Internet connection and a Web3 wallet. Once the smart contract is deployed, DeFi applications self-execute with little institutional intervention except for code upgrades, bug fixes, and dispute resolution.

- If users choose "non-custodial" wallet solutions, they remain in possession of the private keys and in full control of the funds, potentially disintermediating many financial services that currently provide services to mitigate counterparty risk, act as market makers, or secure funds from being stolen.

- Any smart contract code can be audited by anyone and is subject to collective loophole fixing, which is the basis for the rapidly evolving DeFi ecosystem.

- All token transactions are publicly verifiable, reducing market friction and increasing the interoperability of financial services. As a result of such interoperability, DeFi applications can be built in a modular way, which is why many refer to them as "money legos."

Combining various DeFi solutions, such as "stable tokens," "decentralized exchanges," and "decentralized lending," can produce completely new products available to retail investors and the general public. Any private person could, in such a setup, tokenize their real assets and use them as collateral for P2P lending solutions without bureaucracy by using a combination of simple DeFi applications (read more: Part 3 - Decentralized Lending). Such new services could, in the long run, change the dynamics of our economic system and contribute to the merging of the real economy and the financial system, making their distinction increasingly impossible.

While such "money legos" are quickly emerging, they are still nascent and often prone to exploits and attacks as a result of unintended programming mistakes and malicious hacks. The governance/business logic of the underlying smart contracts needs extensive auditing and bug fixing, especially in light of a growing and complex network of interoperable DeFi applications (read more: Chapter 3 - Token Lending). Furthermore, most DeFi applications today are built for developers, not for users. Their current lack of usability undermines decentralization efforts. However, once the user experience improves, and user-centric identities become mainstream, any non-bankable funds could be managed by a public infrastructure and converted into a financial product that can be easily used as collateral or traded with a simple mobile wallet where you are in full control of all your assets and all your data (read more: Part 1 - User-Centric Identities).

Many economists remain skeptical that cryptographic tokens can permanently replace conventional currencies since: (i) There are strong network externalities that favor existing conventional currencies; (ii) The lack of sophisticated token supply rules leading to socially desirable stability and liquidity of tokenized economies. Furthermore, (iii) from a classic economic perspective, it seems impossible to pre-specify socially optimal "lender-of-last resort" rules in a smart contract. Lender-of-last resort refers to a safety-net institution, usually provided by central banks, to reduce the risk of a lack of liquidity of financial systems as a result of financial panics and bank runs. It represents government-guaranteed liquidity to financial institutions. The lack of such a lender-of-last resort makes financial systems susceptible to financial crises and systemic panics.

I would like to argue that we are still in the very early stages of a tokenized economy. I am confident that economic methods and practices will find their way into the smart contracts and token governance rules of future token systems. We can already see this happening in the cases of algorithmic stable tokens. Furthermore, many central banks are currently looking into or have already started to tokenize central bank currencies (Central Bank Digital Currencies) and make them distributed ledger compatible (read more: Part 3 - Stable Tokens). New legal frameworks will be needed as these new structures transition from an early innovation phase to a more mature infrastructure phase.

One important bottleneck will be the emergence of multi-token capability of wallets and better key recovery solutions (read more: Part 1 - Token Security, Wallets). Another bottleneck will be overcoming the challenge of token trading through the inefficiency of centralized exchanges. Once P2P swapping of tokens matures and is adopted by wallet software, anyone will be able to exchange any token P2P, wallet to wallet, without any intermediary (read more: Part 3 - Trading Tokens, Atomic Swaps & DEX). In such a future scenario, powered by AI and DeFi applications, atomic swaps could potentially introduce a tokenized barter economy powered by global trading platforms, without the coincidence-of-wants problem we face today.

Chapter Summary

- *In a market economy based on division of labor and money issued by governmental bodies, the role of money is to facilitate the exchange of goods and services. It makes economic exchange much more efficient than gift economies and barter economies, avoiding the inefficiencies of such systems like the "coincidence of wants" problem.*

- *Money proved to be an efficient tool for comparing values of different goods and services. It has different functions and properties. It acts as a (i) medium of exchange; (ii) measure of value and unit of account in which debt can be denominated; and as a (iii) store of value.*

- *Properties of money include (i) liquidity, (ii) fungibility, (iii) durability, (iv) portability, (v) cognizability, and (vi) stability. It also needs some (vii) inbuilt anti-counterfeiting measures to avoid forging. Different types of money have evolved over time.*

- *In modern economies, the dominant type of money is so-called (i) fiat currency. Prior to the existence of modern day fiat currencies, we had (ii) commodity money and (iii) representative money.*

- *Protocol tokens like Bitcoin or Ether are needed to pay for transactions in their respective networks. They represent the "legal tender" of the network, which is needed to pay for* network services. The Bitcoin network is a public infrastructure for "P2P remittances." Transaction fees for these remittances need to be paid with BTC tokens.

- As of today, most tokens do not fulfill one of the most important properties of money: stability of value, and to some extent, also fungibility. Usability and scalability are other entry barriers to potential mass adoption.

- Cryptographic tokens represent a new heterogenous asset class that can fulfill a diverse range of economic functions. Their frictionless issuance and settlement process could potentially convert many assets or access rights of the real world into "bankable funds."

- It is likely that tokenizing economic activities, from real assets to digital assets and all types of access rights, will impact the role of central bank money as a geographical monopolist providing a medium of exchange in the long run.

- Cryptographic tokens represent a new heterogenous asset class that can fulfill a diverse range of economic functions. Their frictionless issuance and settlement process could potentially convert many assets or access rights of the real world into "bankable funds."

- Tokenizing economic activities, from real assets to digital assets and all types of access rights, could impact the role of central bank money as a geographical monopolist providing a medium of exchange, once mass adoption of the Web3 manifests and necessary network effects kick in. Such tokenization of the real economy could also lead to the merging of the financial stems with the real economy.

- The term "DeFi" encompasses any decentralized and permissionless financial application that builds on top of distributed ledgers, including privacy-preserving payment systems (privacy tokens), stability preserving payment systems (stable tokens), P2P exchanges (token exchanges), P2P fundraising (token sales), and P2P credit and lending (decentralized lending), P2P insurance, and a growing list of P2P derivatives. These Web3-based DeFi applications could, potentially, open traditional financial services to the general public, mitigating current inefficiencies of financial markets.

- Combining various DeFi solutions, such as "stable tokens," "decentralized exchanges," and "decentralized lending," can produce completely new products available to retail investors and the general public and could, in the long run, change the dynamics of our economic system and contribute to the merging of the real economy and the financial system, making their distinction increasingly impossible.

Chapter References & Further Reading

- Atkeson, Andrew; Kehoe, Patrick J.: Deflation and Depression: Is There an Empirical Link?", Federal Reserve Bank of Minneapolis, January 2004, retrieved from: https://www.minneapolisfed.org/research/sr/sr331.pdf
- Dixon, Chris: "Crypto Tokens: A Breakthrough in Open Network Design", Jun 1, 2017, retrieved from: https://medium.com/@cdixon/crypto-tokens-a-breakthrough-in-open-network-design-e600975be2ef

- Chudzinski, Pawel: "Mapping the Emerging Non-Fungible Token Landscape", Jun 15 2018, retrieved from: https://medium.com/point-nine-news/mapping-the-emerging-non-fungible-token-landscape-ee56f0d1079f

- Flynn, Brian: "Designing Non-Fungible Tokens as Open Ecosystems", August 7, 2018, retrieved from: https://tokeneconomy.co/designing-non-fungible-tokens-as-open-ecosystems-a0f28ae213ee

- Flynn, Brian: „Designing for composability in crypto," NFTY News, Jul 29 2019, https://medium.com/nfty-news/designing-for-composability-in-crypto-6e138790a7d6

- Freixas, X.; Giannini, C.; Hoggarth, G.; Soussa, F.: „Lender of Last Resort: What Have We Learned Since Bagehot?", Journal of Financial Services Research. 18: 64, 2000

- Friedman, Milton; Schwartz, Anna J.: "Has Government Any Role in Money?", p. 289 - 314, Volume Title: published in "Money in Historical Perspective", University of Chicago Press, 1987

- Genestoux, Julien: "Non Fungible Tokens", Hackernoon, March 5, 2018, retrieved from: https://hackernoon.com/non-fungible-tokens-5ba83906b275

- Glatz, Florian: "A Blockchain Token Taxonomy", September 10, 2016, retrieved from: https://medium.com/@heckerhut/a-blockchain-token-taxonomy-fadf5c56139a

- Glazer, Phil: "An Overview of Non-fungible Tokens", Crypto Research, April 2, 2018, retrieved from: https://hackernoon.com/an-overview-of-non-fungible-tokens-5f140c32a70a

- Hayek, Friedrich: "The Denationalization of Money", 1976

- Hoffman, David: „Ethereum: The Digital Finance Stack," Jul 25 2019, https://medium.com/pov-crypto/ethereum-the-digital-finance-stack-4ba988c6c14b

- Hummel, J. R.: „Death and Taxes, Including Inflation: the Public versus Economists", Econ Journal Watch, Volume 4, Number 1, January 2007, pp 46-59, retrieved from: https://econjwatch.org/File+download/139/2007-01-hummel-com.pdf

- Krugman, Paul. „Why is Deflation Bad?". New York Times, August 2, 2010, retrieved from: https://krugman.blogs.nytimes.com/2010/08/02/why-is-deflation-bad/

- Lewis, Anthony: "A gentle introduction to digital tokens", Sept 28, 2015, retrieved from: https://bitsonblocks.net/2015/09/28/gentle-introduction-digital-tokens/

- Mankiw, N. Gregory: „Macroeconomics", 5th ed., 2002

- Menger, Carl: "On the Origin of Money", Economic Journal, Volume 2, 1892, pp. 239–55.

- N.N.: "Getting Your Instant Nexo Loan in Three Easy Steps in 200+ jurisdictions and 45+ currencies," Nexo Aug 28, 2018, https://medium.com/nexo/getting-your-nexo-loan-in-three-easy-steps-f0d4bec5c7ea

- N.N.: "ERC-721 Hitting a Home Run", 0xcert, May 31 2018, retrieved from: https://medium.com/0xcert/erc-721-hitting-a-home-run-77d6b4fca33d?source=read_next_metabar

- N.N.: "Smart Event Ticketing Protocol", GET Foundation Team, August 5, 2017, retrieved from: https://guts.tickets/files/GET-Whitepaper-GUTS-Tickets-latest.pdf

- N.N.: "ERC-721," retrieved from: http://erc721.org/

- N.N.: "Ethereum mainnet token market capitalization", retrieved from: https://etherscan.io/tokens

- N.N.: "Fungible vs non-fungible tokens on the blockchain", 0xcert, Apr 26 2018, retrieved from: https://medium.com/0xcert/fungible-vs-non-fungible-tokens-on-the-blockchain-ab4b12e0181a

- N.N.: „Treatment of Crypto Assets in Macroeconomic Statistics", IMF, retrieved from: https://www.imf.org/external/pubs/ft/bop/2019/pdf/Clarification0422.pdf

- Radocchia, Samantha: "How Non-Fungible Tokens From Physical Collectibles Are Strengthening Asset-Backed Securities", Jul 5, 2018, retrieved from: https://www.forbes.com/sites/samantharadocchia/2018/07/05/how-non-fungible-tokens-from-physical-collectibles-are-strengthening-asset-backed-securities/#575d30ca1b2e

- Srinivasan, Balaji S.: "Thoughts on Tokens Tokens are early today, but will transform technology tomorrow," May 27, 2017, retrieved from: https://docs.google.com/document/d/1SAAsC7lDF4fj9lPo0qbE6nQqyfYXvQ4vVwQbrwQ6dKw/edit

- Tomaino, Nick: "Tokens, Tokens and More Tokens Over $331M has been raised in token sales in the past 12 months. What's really going on?", May 1, 2017, retrieved from: https://thecontrol.co/tokens-tokens-and-more-tokens-d4b177fbb443

- Voshmgir, Shermin: „Token Economy — The Future of Currencies?" Jan 31, 2018, retrieved from: https://medium.com/crypto3conomics/token-economy-the-future-of-currencies-d26487fd3945

- Wikipedia contributors, „Money," Wikipedia, The Free Encyclopedia, https://en.wikipedia.org/wiki/Money (accessed February 10, 2020).

Stable Tokens

Stability of value is one of the most important functions of money so it can fulfill its purpose as a unit of account. Stable tokens are designed to represent a store of value, medium of exchange, and unit of account that has a stable value against another currency or commodity, and could resolve a major bottleneck to mass adoption of tokens as a medium of exchange.

Disclaimer: A few of the below mentioned stable-token examples like "Tether" and "DAI" are subject to frequent updates or current events. Certain details mentioned in the following chapter might therefore be out of date by the time of reading this book. The content of this chapter is structured in a way that it paints the big picture of the complexities of designing stable tokens independent of future changes.

Short-term stability of value is one of the most important functions of money so it can serve as a unit of account. Stability is a fundamental criteria for meaningful economic planning for all actors in an economy. In order for a token to serve as a means of payment, store of value, or unit of account, the token needs a relatively stable value, so that the price we pay for goods and services can be reliably planned. Otherwise, it is just an object of speculation. While the Bitcoin protocol introduced a groundbreaking consensus algorithm, it comes with a rudimentary monetary policy that simply regulates and limits the amount of tokens minted over time. The protocol does not provide a sophisticated economic algorithm that regulates price stability. As a result, Bitcoin and similar protocol tokens are subject to price volatility, which makes them an object of speculation rather than a means of day-to-day payment. From a monetary policy point of view, Bitcoin does not live up to its own value proposition stated in the white paper, as it cannot serve as electronic cash, which is why it is referred to by many as "electronic gold."

Just as developing a secure consensus algorithm required decades of research and development, an equivalent amount of academic rigor would be needed to develop a resilient "monetary policy" in P2P electronic cash protocols. Token price also needs to be stable and resilient, hence attack resistant. However, there is no need to reinvent the wheel. Governments have been using macroeconomic models to stabilize national currencies with measures like currency intervention. There is much one can learn from this, both the dos and the don'ts. However, history has shown that protecting currency stability from outside attacks is not easy to achieve. In 1992, for example, George Soros hacked the stability mechanism of the Bank of England, successfully manipulating the foreign exchange price of the British pound, in an event that is now referred to as "Black Wednesday" and ended up costing the UK more than three billion pounds at the time.

State-of-the-art protocol tokens are currently impractical for day-to-day payments (at least in countries with stable inflation rates) and only attractive to speculators or long-time investors. Token values are volatile for several reasons: (i) a static monetary policy as a result of a token supply that does not adjust to price levels, (ii) shifting public perception about the value of the token, (iii) the fact that they represent assets in an emerging market that most people don't understand, and potentially also (iv) market reaction to regulatory uncertainty. Without a stable medium of exchange, no party to a smart contract can rely on the price denominated of a certain token. This lack of price stability has led to the emergence of stable tokens over the last few years.

Stable tokens are emerging as an indispensable building block for a tokenized economy. Businesses and individuals are not likely to accept tokens as a method of payment if their value can drop within a short amount of time. Salaries, investments, and household expenses such as rent, utility payments, and groceries cannot be reliably denominated or planned for with an unstable medium of exchange. Without stability mechanisms, smart contracts and decentralized applications will stay a fringe phenomenon, as they would pose a high risk for both parties to a smart contract, the buyer and the seller. Over the years, various attempts have been made to achieve token stability: (i) fiat-collateralized or commodity-collateralized stable tokens, (ii) crypto-collateralized stable tokens, and (iii) algorithmic stable tokens, like seigniorage shares. Lately (iv) central banks have started looking into tokenizing their currencies, as these already come with inbuilt price stability mechanisms.

Asset-Collateralized Stable Tokens

A simple way to achieve a stable token is to back them with off-chain assets that have stable or relatively stable prices, such as fiat currency or a commodity like gold or diamonds. "Tether" and "TrueUSD" are tokens backed by the US Dollar. "Digix Gold" is an example of a token that is backed by gold. Alternatively, a basket

191

of commodities or fiat currencies can be used to back the token. While asset-backed stable tokens are relatively easy to achieve, they have a centralization problem. This is also why some refer to them as "centralized" stable tokens. One single company manages the assets that guarantee coverage of the tokens, usually in a bank account or secure vault. Trust is outsourced to a single entity, which guarantees that the amount of tokens issued corresponds to the amount held in a secure vault, making the system subject to counterparty risk. This might change when hardware and software oracles are programmed to feed the token contracts with data from IoT devices, like video cameras monitoring the vaults. Current solutions, however, rely on trusting a centralized service provider and a handful of auditors to guarantee that the backing of assets is not tampered with. Furthermore, costs and processes are often opaque and can involve higher fees and delays.

Tether (USDT) is one of the more senior and popular stable tokens. It has a one-to-one peg against the USD, which means that for every USDT in circulation, one USD is allegedly added to a centrally managed savings account as collateral. Supposedly, there is a bank account that holds over two billion USD, which represents the current valuation of USDT. However, Tether is managed by a private company, and has so far not seen a complete audit process. Some people doubt that Tether is fully collateralized, and US authorities are investigating the case. They changed their terms, admitting that some of their reserves might be loans to other entities, for example, token exchanges like Bitfinex. Their general counsels have furthermore admitted that only 74 percent of USDT is backed by cash and cash equivalents. This could be critical, as USDT is one of the top traded tokens. A significant amount of BTC trading results from Tether. As a result, many are worried that if allegations are true, fake Tethers could be used to buy BTC, driving up the market price and resulting in market manipulation. If there are serious doubts about the backing of Tether, the price system might collapse, and if it does, it might affect the BTC as well.

TrueUSD (TUSD) is a similar stable token to Tether, but appears much more trustworthy. So far, they have regularly published independent audits to verify their claims of the funds they hold.

Circle (USDC) is an ERC-20 token that allows one to wire transfer USD in exchange for USDC tokens. This serves as an on-ramp and off-ramp between the USD and Ethereum ecosystems.

Digix Gold Token (DGX) is a stable token pegged to gold. It has been live since 2018. The gold is secured in a vault managed by a custodian company in Singapore. DGX token holders pay a management fee to cover the costs of securely storing the gold. As opposed to Tether, DGX is subject to regular independent auditors and seems more trustworthy. In this auditing process, custodians and auditors time-stamp the reports on Ethereum's ledger to provide publicly verifiable evidence that the gold is really where it is supposed to be. First, the scans of the paperwork are uploaded to IPFS, a decentralized file storage network, and the hashes of these scans are recorded on the Ethereum network, creating an on-chain audit trail. In their white paper, Digix describes a Proof-of-Provenance protocol for the verification of real-world assets. The same protocol could be applied to other assets, such as art, silver, platinum, diamonds, real estate, etc. The governance mechanism behind Digix is organized as a DAO (decentralized autonomous organization). This DAO comes with a separate token, the DigixDAO token (DGD), which grants voting rights for the governance of Digix. Managerial questions around the governance of the DGX token are therefore decentralized and performed by DigixDAO.

Globcoin is a stable token initiative backed by currencies of the fifteen largest economies in addition to gold.

AAA Reserve is backed by a basket of national currencies, AAA-rated credit investments, and government-backed bonds.

Libra is being developed as a stable token for cross-border online payments. The Libra consortium, spearheaded by Facebook, will be operating its own distributed ledger. According to their white paper, they are planning to back the token with a basket of currencies and other assets (read more annex: Libra - Facebook's move into the Web3)

Crypto-Collateralized Stable Tokens

One way to mitigate the centralization problem is to back the stable tokens with a native blockchain token such as BTC or ETH, which is why these stable tokens are sometimes also referred to as "decentralized stable tokens." In such a setup, the stable token is collateralized with BTC or ETH. The collateral token (BTC or ETH) is managed entirely on-chain by a smart contract, instead of a third party. The public and verifiable nature of native blockchain tokens makes the system more trustworthy. The risk of under-collateralization can be mitigated. BitUSD introduced this model in 2013, and inspired many other projects, such as "MakerDAO" (DAI), "Sweetbridge," "Augmint," and "Synthetix" (formerly Havven), to use variations of this mechanism. Other variations of crypto-collateralized stable tokens are: "Reserve," "StatiCoin," "Alchemint," "Boreal," "Celo," and "Unum."

DAI is a stable token operated by MakerDAO. The price is pegged 1:1 to the USD. DAI is backed by ETH (and recently also some other tokens) that can be collateralized in a smart contract. It is considered the most promising crypto-collateralized stable token project. ETH token holders can deposit their tokens in a smart contract to generate DAI tokens. The smart contract locks the deposited ETH until the DAI tokens are paid back. The collateral token (ETH) is automatically released by the smart contract when all debts (DAI tokens) are paid back. Collateralizing ETH against DAI results in a debt position for DAI token holders, which is why the smart contract is referred to as a "collateralized debt position" (CDP).

Crypto-collateralized stable tokens are prone to the volatility of the underlying token used as collateral. This volatility makes it harder for the 1:1 peg of DAI to USD to be maintained. This is why DAI uses a 150 percent collateral-to-debt ratio. Other stable tokens might use even higher ratios. This means that if the ETH price crashes, and when the individual CDP drops below 150, the smart contract will auto-liquidate the collateral token. DAI tokens are locked by the smart contract if the value of ETH falls below this threshold, and the smart contract sells the ETH to offset the risk of non-payment. A significant price crash of the collateral token below the peg could make DAI token holders lose capital. If the value of the collateral asset (ETH) drops too quickly, the stable tokens (DAI) issued could become undercollateralized. DAI has more complex mechanisms in place to protect against price fluctuations. Details of this process are beyond the scope of this book, but can be studied reading the white paper and Web documentation of the project website.

Many economists claim that if price volatility of the underlying asset is too high, crypto-collateralized solutions are susceptible to black swan events. DAI can end up undercollateralized if a crash is rapid enough that the system is unable to close enough CDPs, and buy back their DAI, before overall system collateralization drops below 100 percent. Another challenge is the lack of oracles with reliable price-feeds about asset prices across exchanges. Currently, a patchwork of centralized solutions are used, but they are prone to manipulation and attack.

Initially, DAI only supported one type of collateral (ETH), but since 2019, it also supports any number of assets as a basket of collaterals, to mitigate the volatility risks associated with a single asset. The current list of accepted collaterals is: Augur (REP), Basic Attention Token (BAT), DigixDAO (DGD), Ether (ETH), Golem (GNT), OmiseGo (OMG), and 0x (ZRX). The project also launched the Dai Savings Rate (DSR), an additional service that makes it possible to earn savings simply by holding Dai.

Central Bank Digital Currency

While the crypto community has been experimenting with various privately initiated stable token solutions, central banks have also started to look into tokenizing their own currencies, which already come with inbuilt stability mechanisms. Such a central bank token, referred to as Central Bank Digital Currency (CBDC), acts as a tokenized representation of a country's fiat currency. The stability mechanisms are provided by established players like central banks in collaboration with the fiscal and monetary policy of a national government. The tokens would be part of the base money supply, together with other forms of money: cash and other cash equivalents (M0 & M1), short-term deposits (M2), and long-term deposits (M3). CBDCs could be used for the settlement of smart contracts, since their tokenized equivalent can be managed by an underlying distributed ledger.

Some economists believe that CBDCs compete with commercial bank deposits and reduce the cost of managing the local and international payment system. Currently, the cost of managing cash supply of a country is high, as are cross-border transactions. In the long run, CBDCs could eliminate the need for classic bank accounts, replacing them with easy to download mobile crypto wallets, and potentially increase inclusion of the underbanked. However, such disintermediation of commercial banks and of cross-border payments could also destabilize the credit systems and foreign exchange markets, at least in the short term. CBDCs could furthermore challenge the practice of fractional reserve banking[46] and eliminate the need for deposit guarantees. Issuing central bank money directly to the public could also provide a new channel for monetary policy execution. This would allow for direct control of the money supply and could complement or substitute indirect tools such as interest rates or quantitative easing.[47] Some economists even think that CBDC could be a method to achieve a full reserve banking system.[48]

According to a study conducted by the Bank of International Settlement, many governments are thinking of tokenizing their currency or have already started to do so to various degrees (around 80 percent), such as the Bank of England, Central Bank of Sweden, Central Bank of Uruguay, Marshall Islands, China, Iran, Switzerland, and the European Central Bank. It is, therefore, quite likely that within the next three to five years, many central bank–issued currencies will have a tokenized equivalent. "Synthetic CBDCs" (sCBDC) is an alternative concept whereby private institutions issue tokens fully backed with central bank reserves. The question is whether CBDCs and sCBDCs might render private stable token efforts obsolete, or if they will become just some of many other tokens in this new tokenized economy ahead of us.

---

[46] *A banking system in which only a fraction of bank deposits are backed by actual cash that is available for withdrawal is referred to as fractional reserve banking. While banks are required to keep a certain amount of the cash that depositors give them, they are not required to keep the entire amount. They are only required to keep 10% of the deposit as "reserves." This system frees capital for lending, and is used as an expansionary economic policy tool.*

[47] *Quantitative easing is a monetary policy intervention mechanism in which a central bank purchases securities from the market in order to provide banks with more liquidity, encourage investment, and increase the money supply with newly created bank reserves. This is a rather unconventional method which is used when interest rates are already near zero percent.*

[48] *Full-reserve banking is a banking system where banks have to store the full amount of each depositor's funds in cash, so it can be withdrawn by the depositor at any point in time. Funds would not be lent to someone else.*

Algorithmic Stable Tokens

Stable tokens that are pegged to assets using legacy financial services might seem simple and obvious at first sight, but could also be perceived as somewhat contrary to the spirit of the underlying decentralized technology. This is similar to how Yahoo and many other search engines of the early 1990s tried to make Internet content available by cataloging websites, just as you would catalogue books or magazines in the library. While these search engines were popular and intuitive in the early days of the Internet, they were not scalable at all, nor did they reflect the potential of the underlying technology. Eventually, algorithmic search, as offered by Google and other companies, replaced manually cataloguing content. Similarly, asset-backed stable tokens might seem tempting at first, but some interesting algorithmic solutions are on the rise that might do more justice to the nature of smart contracts.

"Seigniorage[49] Shares" is a concept for an algorithmic stable token that was first proposed by Robert Sams in 2014. In his white paper, he outlined how one can use smart contracts to fulfill the role of a central bank to formalize monetary policy mechanisms so the token trades at a stable price. Elastic supply mechanisms can be designed to either stimulate expansion or contraction of the token supply, similar to how central banks control the supply of fiat currencies. If the demand for stable tokens rises or falls, the algorithm automatically adjusts to keep a stable price. If the price is too high, the mechanism will increase the supply. If the price is too low, tokens need to be "frozen," in one way or another. The question of how to increase and decrease token supply in an attack-resistant and resilient way has not been conclusively resolved. Depending on the project, different algorithmic methods are used for expansion and contraction. Examples of algorithmic stable tokens are: Ampleforth (formerly Fragments), Carbon, Kowala, BitBay Official, SteemDollar, Corion, Topl, Stable, StableUnit, and TerraMoney.

For example, if a stable token with a 1:1 peg to the EUR is traded above 1 EUR, it would indicate that supply is higher than demand. Token supply needs to be increased to stabilize the price back to 1 EUR. The smart contract is programmed to mint new tokens (seigniorage shares) and sell them on the open market, thereby increasing the supply until the price returns to a stable level. If the value is traded below a price of 1 EUR, the token supply must be contracted. The smart contract can't just destroy circulating tokens that belong to someone. The smart contract, however, could be designed to buy tokens on the open market to reduce the circulating supply, and increase the price. While token supply can be easily expanded by

---

[49] *Seigniorage is a form of inflation tax, returning resources to the currency issuer, and can be a source of revenue for a government. It derives from the difference of the cost to produce and distribute money and the value of it.*

issuing new tokens, contracting token supply requires more sophisticated mechanisms. Why should token holders agree to sell tokens, and how can they be meaningfully incentivized to do so? If the smart contract does not have enough newly minted tokens, it could issue bonds in exchange for a stable token in proportion to the tokens that need to be destroyed. These bonds are sold at a discount and can be paid out at a future date, with the bond holders being the first to be paid out. The discount serves as an incentive for holders to remove their stable tokens from circulation.

While the idea of using smart contracts to replace certain functions of a central bank is intriguing, some mechanisms rely on partially unproven economic assumptions and untested monetary policies, especially around incentive design for contracting cycles. In some cases, stabilization is still partially maintained via centralized mechanisms. Furthermore, the challenge of decentralized and trustless price oracles[50] has to be resolved. Many economists therefore believe algorithmic stable tokens cannot work, as this method assumes unlimited growth of the system. Each contraction cycle initiates the potential for a future increase in the total supply of the stable token, which could lead to a death spiral in the price of bonds, increase the time to payout, and decrease the odds that each bond is paid. This could lead to a recursive feedback loop, which could undermine the aim of supply contraction on a large scale unless other measures are taken to prevent such a loop. As a solution to this problem, some projects allow token holders to temporarily freeze tokens; others projects issue bonds that expire after a certain time.

Challenges & Outlook

While many stable token projects attempt to achieve token stability, no clear best practices have been established yet (other than potential CBDCs). The emergence of stable tokens is a relatively new phenomenon, and many proposals outlined in white papers are not even implemented yet or are highly experimental, especially the crypto-collateralized and algorithmic methods. Only a few projects are live, most of which suffer from price volatility. For those projects that are still in the white paper stage, it is hard to tell if and when they will be successful or fully operational. Current adoption of stable tokens shows that Tether and similar fiat-collateralized or commodity-collateralized tokens are leading the field in terms of market capitalization. DAI (MakerDAO) and other crypto-collateralized projects seem to be the most promising alternatives. However, they still have many short-

---

[50] *Seigniorage is a form of inflation tax, returning resources to the currency issuer, and can be a source of revenue for a government. It derives from the difference of the cost to produce and distribute money and the value of it.*

comings, potentially more at larger scales, such as facing the robustness of their mechanisms in the case of a black swan event.

All stable tokens, even the more decentralized ones, are in some way pegged to another underlying asset in a 1:1 ratio. Depending on market dynamics, the pegging ratio could be volatile. Once economies develop around the stable token, creating certain network effects, the peg might start to matter less. This could be the case if businesses are willing to accept a stable token, which is also accepted by other businesses. Maintaining a perfect peg becomes less important as the token becomes a widely accepted medium of exchange.

Furthermore, any stable token implementation needs to address the oracle problem. If the token is pegged to the value of an asset, the system needs a decentralized way to receive data about the exchange rate between the stable token and the asset that it is pegged to. However, none of the existing solutions are fully decentralized or fully reliable yet.

Stable tokens always face "the impossible trinity" conventional currencies are also confronted with, the trade-off between (i) autonomous monetary policy, (ii) exchange rate stability, and (iii) capital mobility. As capital mobility is a given in the context of a cryptographic token, and exchange rate stability needs to be achieved, one has to give up autonomous monetary policy (see Tether). Economists argue that token systems with more autonomous token supply rules will never have stable exchange rates vis á vis conventional currencies. One may put this verdict into perspective, however, if one considers a crypto token not as a competitor to a conventional currency but rather as a new, alternative asset. Nobody would come up with the idea that conventional assets such as stock have to be stable in value, nor has this lack of stability hindered their widespread adoption.

Last but not least, it is important to point out that stable tokens may not be the only solution to token price volatility. Insurances or financial derivatives could provide alternatives or at least complementary methods to mitigating price volatility. Hedging is an investment strategy that can be used to reduce financial risk, balancing positions in the market to protect against price volatilities. A combination of DeFi applications could be used to create such P2P derivative and hedging solutions (read more: Part 3 - Decentralized Lending).

Successful stable token solutions could resolve the bottleneck of using tokens as a unit of account, and therefore as a medium of day-to-day exchange. It is a major catalyst for decentralized applications and a fluid token economy. However, stability is only one of many challenges to make tokens a medium of exchange for day-to-day payments. Without privacy, no token will be fungible, and without scalability and better wallet usability, businesses as well as consumers will not adopt this new technology.

Chapter Summary

- *Stability of value is one of the most important functions of money to serve as a unit of account. The aim of stable tokens is to provide a stable value against the price of another asset.*

- *Bitcoin's protocol introduced a groundbreaking consensus algorithm, but the protocol defines only a rudimentary monetary policy that simply regulates and limits the amount of tokens minted over time. The protocol does not provide price stability.*

- *State-of-the-art protocol tokens are impractical for day-to-day payments. Without a stable medium of exchange, no party to a smart contract can rely on the price denominated of a certain token. This lack of price stability has led to the emergence of stable tokens over the last few years.*

- *Just as developing a secure consensus algorithm required decades of research and development, an equivalent amount of academic rigor is required to develop monetary policy aspects of tokens. There is a lot one can learn from macroeconomics and decades of experience with monetary policies set by governments and central banks trying to achieve currency stability, both the dos and the don'ts.*

- *Types of stable tokens: (i) asset-backed stable tokens; (ii) collateralized stable tokens; (iii) Central Bank Digital Currencies, and (iv) algorithmic stable tokens.*

- *Stable tokens are indispensable building blocks for a thriving token economy; otherwise, smart contracts and decentralized applications will stay a fringe phenomena, as they pose a high risk for both parties to a smart contract, the buyer and the seller.*

- *Businesses are not likely to accept tokens on a large scale if their value can drastically drop within a short amount of time, or if there are no other ways to mitigate this risk.*

- *Stable tokens may not be the only solution to token price volatility. Insurances or financial derivatives could provide alternatives or at least complementary methods to mitigating price volatility. Hedging is an investment strategy that can be used to reduce financial risk, balancing positions in the market to protect against price volatilities. A combination of DeFi applications could be used to create such P2P derivative and hedging solutions.*

Chapter References & Further Reading

- *Bech, M; Garratt, R.: "Central bank cryptocurrencies", BIS Quarterly Review, September, pp 55–70, 2017*
- *Bergmann, C.: "Bitcoin Blog", January 31, 2018: https://bitcoinblog.de/2018/01/31/bitfinex-und-tether-bekommen-vorladung-von-us-regulierern/*
- *Bryne, Preston: "Stablecoins are doomed to fail, Part II: MakerDAO's "DAI" stablecoin is breaking, as predicted", January 11, 2018: https://prestonbyrne.com/2018/01/11/epicaricacy/*

- Boar, Codruta; Holden, Henry; Wadsworth, Amber: "Impending arrival – a sequel to the survey on central bank digital currency,"BIS Papers No 107, Monetary and Economic Department January 2020, rerieved from: https://www.bis.org/publ/bppdf/bispap107.pdf

- Buterin, Vitalik: "SchellingCoin: A Minimal-Trust Universal Data Feed", March 28, 2014 https://blog.ethereum.org/2014/03/28/schellingcoin-a-minimal-trust-universal-data-feed/

- Buterin, Vitalik: "The Search for a Stable Cryptocurrency", November 11, 2014: https://blog.ethereum.org/2014/11/11/search-stable-cryptocurrency/

- Chohan, Usman W.: "Are Stable Coins Stable?", UNSW Business School; Critical Blockchain Research Initiative (CBRI), Discussion Paper Discussion Paper Series: Notes on the 21st Century, January 24, 2019: https://papers.ssrn.com/sol3/papers.cfm?abstract_id=3326823

- De, Nikhilesh: "Tether Lawyer Admits Stablecoin Now 74% Backed by Cash and Equivalents", Apr 30, 2019: https://coindesk.com/tether-lawyer-confirms-stablecoin-74-percent-backed-by-cash-and-equivalents

- Hochstein, Marc: "Tether Review Claims Crypto Asset Fully Backed – But There's a Catch", June 20, 2018: https://coindesk.com/tether-review-claims-crypto-asset-fully-backed-theres-catch

- Jenkinson, Gareth: "Changes to Tether's Terms of Reserves Raises Fresh Concerns", March 24, 2019: https://cointelegraph.com/news/changes-to-tethers-terms-of-reserves-raises-fresh-concerns

- Lee, Sherman: "Explaining Stable Coins", March 12, 2018: https://www.forbes.com/sites/shermanlee/2018/03/12/explaining-stable-coins-the-holy-grail-of-crytpocurrency/#498839354fc6

- Mulder, Ronald: "Why "stablecoins" make no sense" Feb 26, 2018: https://medium.com/@ronaldmulder/why-stablecoins-make-no-sense-999490b08910

- N.N.: „Central Bank Digital Currencies", Bank for International Settlements, March 2018: https://bis.org/cpmi/publ/d174.pdf

- N.N.: "The Dai Stablecoin System Whitepaper", Maker Team, https://makerdao.com/whitepaper/DaiDec17WP.pdf

- N.N.: "blockchain.info", Retrieved, 10. Sept 2018: https://blockchain.info/block-index/14849

- N.N.: "OFFSHORE LEAKS DATABASE" The International Consortium of Investigative Journalists, https://offshoreleaks.icij.org/nodes/82024464

- N.N.: "A brief history of Stablecoins Part 1", Bitmex Research, July 8, 2018: https://blog.bitmex.com/a-brief-history-of-stablecoins-part-1/

- N.N.: „Stablecoins - everything you need to know", Cryptoinsider: https://archive.21mil.com/stablecoins-everything-need-know/

- Orcutt, Mike: "Connectivity "Stablecoins" are trending, but they may ignore basic economics Pegging cryptocurrencies to "real" money could stabilize them—or ruin them entirely", June 7, 2018: https://technologyreview.com/s/611370/stablecoins-are-trending-but-they-may-ignore-basic-economics/

- Orlicki, Jose I.: "A Stable Coin with Pro-rated Rebasement and Price Manipulation Protection", Cornell University, arXiv:1708.00157, Computer Science, Cryptography and Security, August 1 2017: https://arxiv.org/abs/1708.00157

- Peng, Ting: "Turning A Crisis Into An Opportunity, China Gets One Step Closer to CBDC", March 20, 2020, rerieved from: https://cointelegraph.com/news/turning-a-crisis-into-an-opportunity-china-getting-one-step-closer-to-cbdc

- Purdy, Jack: „Maker (MKR) - Investment Thesis Fundamental Analysis and Valuation", Coinmonks: Dec 18, 2018: https://medium.com/coinmonks/cryptoasset-research-maker-mkr-a0e89fccb985

- Qureshi, Haseeb: "Stablecoins: designing a price-stable cryptocurrency", February 19, 2018: https://hackernoon.com/stablecoins-designing-a-price-stable-cryptocurrency-6bf24e2689e5

- Ronald J. Balvers; McDonald, Bill; "Designing a Global Digital Currency", Oct 9 2017: https://papers.ssrn.com/sol3/papers.cfm?abstract_id=3049000

- Sams, Robert: "A Note on Cryptocurrency Stabilisation: Seigniorage Shares", October 24, 2014: https://github.com/rmsams/stablecoins/blob/master/paper.pdf

- Sexer, Nathan: "State of Stablecoins", Consensys, Jul 24, 2018: https://media.consensys.net/the-state-of-stablecoins-2018-79ccb9988e63
- T., Alex: "The Rise Of Stablecoins", April 8, 2018: https://coinjournal.net/the-rise-of-stablecoins/
- Snider, Myles: "An Overview of Stablecoins", January 17, 2018: https://multicoin.capital/2018/01/17/an-overview-of-stablecoins/
- Willemse, Linda: "The Future of Central Bank Digital Currency (CBDC)", Feb 27 2019: https://hackernoon.com/the-future-of-central-bank-digital-currency-cbdc-64797b645887
- Willemse, Linda: "CBDC: 19 Countries Creating or Researching the Issuance of a Digital Decentralized Currency", Feb 12 2019: https://hackernoon.com/cbcd-19-countries-creating-or-researching-the-issuance-of-a-digital-decentralized-currency-b57a609e695b
- Wikipedia contributors, „Central bank digital currency," Wikipedia, The Free Encyclopedia, https://en.wikipedia.org/wiki/Central_bank_digital_currency (accessed April 30, 2019).
- Wikipedia contributors, „Seigniorage," Wikipedia, The Free Encyclopedia, https://en.wikipedia.org/wiki/Seigniorage (accessed February 20, 2019).
- Zhang, Tao: " Central Bank Digital Currency," Keynote Address, March 19, 2020, retrieved from: https://www.imf.org/en/News/Articles/2020/03/19/sp031920-deputy-managing-director-tao-zhangs-keynote-address-on-central-bank-digital-currency
- Alchemint: https://medium.com/@AlchemintIO
- Ampleforth: https://ampleforth.org/
- Augmint: https://augmint.cc/
- BitBay Official: https://medium.com/@bitbay
- Boreal: https://auroradao.com/platform/boreal/
- Carbon: https://.carbon.money/
- Celo: https://celo.org/technology
- Circle: https://circle.com/en/usdc
- Corion: https://corion.io/
- Digix Gold Token: https://digix.global/
- Havven: https://havven.io/
- Kowala: https://kowala.tech/
- NuBits: https://nubits.com/
- Maker (DAI): https://makerdao.com/
- Reserve: https://reserve.org/
- StatiCoin: http://www.staticoin.com/
- Sweetbridge: https://sweetbridge.com/
- Stable: https://stable.foundation/
- StableUnit: https://stableunit.org/
- Stablecoins index website: https://stablecoinindex.com/
- Stablecoins index repo: https://github.com/sdtsui/awesome-stablecoins
- SteemDollar: http://steemdollar.com/
- TerraMoney: https://terra.money/
- Tether: https://tether.to/
- Topl: https://topl.co/
- TrueUSD: https://www.trusttoken.com/trueusd
- Unum: https://unum.one/

Privacy Tokens

Early blockchain networks provide a high level of transparency, which makes the history of a token visible to anyone. This compromises the privacy of token holders and also makes a token less fungible. Alternative token systems have, therefore, set out to create more privacy-preserving protocols.

Disclaimer: Most of the below mentioned privacy token examples are subject to frequent protocol changes. Certain details mentioned in the following chapter might, therefore, be out of date by the time of reading this chapter. The content of this chapter, however, is structured in a way that it paints the big picture of designing privacy tokens, independent of future protocol changes.

A payment token is only useful as a medium of exchange if it satisfies the fungibility criteria. Fungibility refers to the fact that individual units of a token are equal, and can be substituted with each other. The level of fungibility correlates with the level of privacy/anonymity a token provides. This requires both "non-individualization" (obfuscating the traceability with identifiable individuals) and in-transparency of other data related to transaction flows.

Analogue forms of money, like coins or bills, do not give any information about the transaction history, as there is no economically feasible way to track a list of the previous owners. Cash can therefore be considered as the most anonymous and most fungible form of money. In the past, some countries have provided legal precedent for the necessity of fungibility in a currency. Scotland, for example, determined the fungibility of state-issued money tokens in the form of banknotes and coins back in 1749, saying that the history of an individual coin or banknote was to be considered irrelevant. Such precedents, however, have been challenged by the growing digitalization of our global financial systems. While state-issued money, in the form of cash, allows for a high degree of privacy and therefore also fungibility, cash is being less commonly used in modern economies for payments, in some cases accounting for less than 10 percent of the financial activities of an economy.[51]

---

[51] *The use of cash for transaction purposes is only one driver of banknote demand. Cash is also still used as a "store of value."*

The rise of credit card payments, electronic banking services before the Internet, and Web2 based financial technology services have increased the possibilities of tracing money flows. Even though our personal data is scattered over banks and other institutions worldwide, each of these institutions holds partial knowledge of our digital financial footprint. Electronic records have reduced the costs of monitoring how we use our money with simple algorithms. Furthermore, increasing anti-money laundering (AML) regulation and efforts by taxation authorities have forced financial institutions worldwide to monitor, and sometimes even reveal, information about the financial activities of their clients. AML regulation in the United States dates back to the Bank Secrecy Act of 1970. The rise of international drug trafficking and money laundering concerns of governments worldwide led to the creation of the international Financial Action Task Force (FATF) by G-7 Summit countries in 1989, creating a more global regulatory base. Post 9/11 in 2001, FATF expanded its ALM regulation to combat terror financing. As a result, many countries started to impose Know Your Customer (KYC) regulations that require financial institutions and other regulated industries to establish the identity of their customers, keep records of transactions, and notify authorities of potentially suspicious activities of their customers in case of government-defined "threshold transactions." Such practices, as a result of regulatory impositions, are gradually eroding the fungibility and hence quality of money.

Privacy of Blockchain Tokens

The Bitcoin network and similar public and permissionless networks use asymmetric cryptography to create online identities in the form of blockchain addresses. This way, a user can create multiple addresses without KYC requirements while trustfully sending and receiving tokens via a public network (read more: Part 1 - Token Security). These addresses consist of an alphanumeric string that does not give any indication of the user's identity, similar to traditional swiss bank accounts, but this only provides pseudonymity. Public disclosure of one's blockchain addresses, either via social media or as a result of one's activity on a token exchange, makes users susceptible to de-anonymization efforts using data analysis. Privacy of nodes can only be guaranteed as long as the real-world identity of a wallet owner cannot be linked to a certain network address.

The publicly verifiable nature of blockchain networks makes transactions traceable. All transactions are registered in plaintext (unencrypted) to the ledger. Transaction data is visible to anyone using a block explorer and can therefore be linked to other transactions made by the same token holder. Such transaction data could potentially reveal sensitive information: the sender's address, the receiver's address, the link between these two addresses, and the amount of tokens sent. More complicated smart contract transactions involve even more data, depending on the use case. Furthermore, in the process of broadcasting transactions, nodes can reveal their IP addresses. Metadata from token transactions can be used to trace the IP address of a user, sometimes even when anonymization services such as Tor or I2P are used. With today's data analysis possibilities, such linking does not take much effort, especially by government authorities. As an example: "Researchers at MIT and the Université Catholique de Louvain, in Belgium, analyzed data on 1.5 million cellphone users in a small European country over a span of 15 months and found that just four points of reference, with fairly low spatial and temporal resolution, was enough to uniquely identify 95 percent of them. In other words, to extract the complete location information for a single person from an 'anonymized' data set of more than a million people, all you would need to do is place him or her within a couple of hundred yards of a cellphone transmitter, sometime over the course of an hour, four times in one year. A few Twitter posts would probably provide all the information you needed, if they contained specific information about the person's whereabouts."[52]

Most users today purchase tokens in exchange for fiat currency using online token exchanges that are more and more subject to KYC regulation. Even if they are not, fiat currencies that are sent to a token exchange usually require interaction with the banking system, and these banks are subject to KYC requirements. Anyone with access to an exchange's database can therefore link these pseudonymous addresses to real names. There is growing evidence such data is shared amongst exchanges and with law-enforcement agencies or chain-analysis companies. Simple "chain analysis" and correlation against the digital footprint of a user outside the blockchain network might, therefore, allow the individualization of identities and user profiling. Individual researchers, state authorities, and private blockchain forensic services such as "Chainalysis," and "Elliptic" can conduct chain-analysis to detect general transaction patterns, including potential money laundering activities, fraud, and other possible compliance violations. Depending on a token's provenance, individual tokens may not be accepted by merchants due to their tainted transaction history. This reduces the fungibility of a token.

More recent blockchain networks have set out to improve the level of privacy of token transactions. Such "privacy tokens" use various obfuscating techniques to make token history less transparent. The goal of privacy tokens is to design a protocol that reveals the minimum information needed and obfuscates all other information. Depending on the blockchain protocol, various elements of a transaction can be anonymized to different extents: (i) wallet/address anonymity, (ii) confidentiality of transaction data like payment amounts, (iii) privacy about total network state.

---

[52] *Hardesty, Larry: „How hard is it to ‚de-anonymize' cellphone data?" MIT news: https://news.mit.edu/2013/how-hard-it-de-anonymize-cellphone-data (retrieved March 26, 2020)*

- User privacy (full anonymity): the identity of the user sending or receiving a token is obfuscated in such a way that the user's actions cannot be linked to their real-world identity.

- Transaction data privacy: Obfuscating data specific to a token transaction using cryptographic tools, like the sender and recipient address or transaction amount, will make chain analysis difficult, as important data points will be missing.

- Privacy of network state: If certain transaction data can be made private, the ledger only reveals partial information on the network state. Different attributes of the state could be made private to different users. However, there is a trade-off between individual privacy and the integrity/security of the network that needs to be considered.

History of Privacy Tokens

Over the past decade, a growing list of projects have been experimenting with a range of methods, from transaction aggregation to alternative cryptographic algorithms. This chapter will provide a general overview. A technical deep dive into the full range of cryptographic tools is beyond the scope of this book and would require a separate publication.

Mixing Services: Early methods of anonymizing token transactions started out with aggregation techniques used by tumblers and mixing services. Such services generally mix inputs and outputs of different token transactions, aggregating them into one collective transaction and thereby obfuscating the connections between sender and recipient. "Bitmixer" was one of the earliest projects that tried to increase the difficulty of linking real-world identities to blockchain addresses. The service, however, was not fully decentralized. "CoinJoin" replaced the need for a trusted third party like Bitmixer with cryptographic security, leveraging security provisions of the Bitcoin network. In the early years, however, CoinJoin transactions only had a handful of users, which made the mixing service prone to chain analysis. Furthermore, CoinJoin relied on off-chain coordination, where users had to find other users to run CoinJoin with them. "TumbleBit" used a modified method, which was slightly better, but also had its limitations and never gained widespread adoption. Most privacy tokens and privacy preserving blockchain clients today, except for Zcash, use a variation of such mixing services as part of their obfuscation techniques. In most cases, they use a variation of CoinJoin.

Dash was originally released as "XCoin," then renamed to "Darkcoin" before it was rebranded as "Dash." It is a software fork of the Bitcoin codebase that went live in 2014. It is a Proof-of-Work network with different types of nodes, the "diggers" (miners) and "masternodes." New blocks are created by the miners. Masternodes perform governance and privacy functions: "PrivateSend" (financial privacy) and "InstantSend" (instant transactions). "PrivateSend" uses a variation of the token-mixing methods of CoinJoin. However, Dash resolved CoinJoin's need for off-chain coordination by incentivizing masternodes with network tokens to perform CoinJoin transactions. "InstantSend" allows for near-instant transactions where inputs are locked to specific transactions and verified by consensus of the masternode network. The block reward is split between miners and masternodes: miners (45%), masternodes (45%), governance and the budget system, which is created by so-called "superblocks" (10%).

Monero was originally based on the "Bytecoin" protocol proposed by an anonymous developer under the pseudonym Nicolas van Saberhagen. The network was forked by several developers (some of which have stayed anonymous) into "Bitmonero" due to protocol issues, and was forked to Monero in 2014 due to disagreements within the developer team over the future of the network. Monero is not only the oldest but also the most widespread privacy token network. The protocol and data structures have been modified several times over the years, including the migration to a different database structure that provides greater efficiency and flexibility. As opposed to the Bitcoin network, where tokens are sent to a public address, tokens in the Monero network are sent to a newly created anonymous address intended for one-time use (stealth addresses). A "private spent key" is needed to create the stealth address and authorize token transactions. Only the recipient of the transaction can "discover" this newly created address with their "secret view key." The discovery process is performed by the recipient's Monero wallet, scanning the network for new stealth addresses. Monero currently uses "Ring Confidential Transactions" (Ring CT), a variation of ring signatures that replaced the original ring signature protocol. Minimum ring signature sizes were modified so that all transactions are "private by mandate." Monero uses a variation of CoinJoin where nodes do not need to coordinate off-chain. Miners can asynchronously batch (and thus mix) transactions in a block. Transaction amounts are obfuscated with the use of homomorphic (Pedersen) commitments, a specific type of homomorphic "commitment schemes,"[53] in combination with "blinding." At a certain point, the Monero team was also planning to implement privacy-preserving packet routing into the protocol with the "Kovri" project, which would have allowed users to hide their IP addresses and locations.

Zcash was launched in 2016. It grew out of the "Zerocoin" and the "Zerocash" protocol, using a variation of the zero-knowledge proofs called "zk-SNARKs"

---

[53] *A commitment scheme is a cryptographic method that allows a user to commit to the value of a piece of data (so that it cannot be changed later) while keeping the data secret.*

(Zero-Knowledge Succinct Non-Interactive Argument of Knowledge), which was developed in 2015 and implemented for the first time in the Zcash protocol. Zero-knowledge proofs are a cryptographic algorithm that allow network nodes to prove possession of certain data without revealing the data itself. They can be used to obfuscate transaction data stored on the ledger (sender's address, receiver's address, amount transferred), allowing nodes to check the validity of encrypted transaction data without knowledge of the data. In such a setup, the "prover" can prove to the "verifier" that a statement is true, without revealing any information beyond the validity of the statement. The Zcash network offers "optional privacy," which means that users can choose to use "transparent addresses" or "shielded addresses." "Transparent addresses" are similar to addresses in the Bitcoin network. Shielded addresses anonymize transaction data. Token transactions can therefore be (i) transparent-to-transparent (similar to Bitcoin); (ii) transparent-to-shielded (shielding transactions that break transaction linkability), (iii) shielded-to-transparent (deshielding transactions that return previously shielded ZECs public without the returned ZECs being linked to prior transparent addresses), (iv) shielded-to-shielded (private transactions where the addresses and transaction value are anonymous); (v) hybrid (partially shielding of sending addresses and/or the receiving addresses). However, sending shielded transactions is computationally expensive, which is why many Zcash transactions were sent in the clear. The Zcash team worked on a protocol upgrade to improve the performance and functionality of shielded transactions that did not change the metrics. At the time of writing this book, most transactions are still sent in clear.[54]

Mimblewimble is a proposal for a blockchain protocol with the aim to increase privacy and network scalability. It was introduced in 2016 in a paper by pseudonymous user "Tom Elvis Jedusor." Mimblewimble uses "Confidential Transactions" and "Pedersen Commitments" to obfuscate transactions that are publicly verifiable without revealing the transaction data. Nodes only have to verify the authenticity of specific inputs rather than the entire ledger, removing the need for storing past transaction data in the ledger. The history of the ledger contains the block headers, system state, and the output signatures of so-called "dummy outputs". Combined with some other methods, the result is a more compact ledger, which means that nodes need less bandwidth and storage to synchronize the ledger. Network nodes don't need the full transaction history to check that the state is valid. Similar to Monero, the protocol proposes transaction aggregation by hiding all transaction amounts and balances, and obscuring sender and receiver addresses, but the sender and recipient must coordinate off-chain before making a transaction. While the Monero protocol uses "fake transactions" to bloat the ledger, Mimblewimble merges old transactions. The Mimblewimble proposal inspired several projects: among

---

[54] https://explorer.zcha.in/statistics/values

others, "Grin" in 2017 and the "Beam" project in 2018.

Grin was the first project to implement the Mimblewimble protocol. It was initiated on "Github" by a user with the pseudonym "Ignotus Peverell." A "Blockstream" researcher published a modified version of the protocol that gained a lot of traction in the Bitcoin developer community. Grin released various testnets before the mainnet was launched in 2019. Grin uses Cuckoo Cycle Proof-of-Work, a consensus mechanism that was designed to be ASIC-resistant, but has turned out not to be ASIC-resistant.

Beam is another implementation of Mimblewimble but uses Equihash as a consensus algorithm. Beam was launched in 2018 on a public testnet, and in 2019 on the mainnet. In addition to confidential payments, the Beam network allows for the creation of privacy-preserving asset tokens and debt instruments, supporting complex transactions such as atomic swaps, time-locked transfers, and escrow payments. Alternatively, the network also allows for on-chain auditability. In compliance with existing regulations, this could allow authorized auditors to see the full list of transactions and any relevant documentation.

Other privacy-preserving token projects are: "Aced," "Apollo," "Arqma," "Arpa chain," "Beldex," "Bulwark," "Bytecoin," "Bzedge," "Crypticcoin," "CloakCoin," "CUTcoin," "Cova," "DAPS Coin," "Deeponion," "Digitalnote," "Dusk," "Horizen," "Hush" "Innovacoin," "Komodo," "Loki," "Lobstex," "Navcoin," "Nix," "Noir," "Nonerov," "Origo," "Particl," "pEOS"" "Pivx," "Piratechain," "Phore," "Ryo," "Safex cash," "Safecoin," "Solariscoin," "Spectrecoin," "Stealthcoin," "Sumokoin," "Tarush," "Tixl," "Veil," "Verge," "zClassic," "ZCoin," "Zumcoin," and "Xuez." Depending on their evolutionary stages and the combination of methods they use, privacy token networks have varying trade-offs with different strengths and weaknesses. There is no clear case for one protocol over the other. Given the complex socio-economic implications involved with privacy tokens, protocol design questions not only involve technical questions, but also ethical and legal questions, which will be discussed later in this chapter. A full list of publicly traded privacy tokens, including the market capitalization and other data, can be found, among others, on "cryptoslate.com."[55]

Full Web3 Privacy

The projects analyzed above are, for the most part, protocol tokens of classic payment networks. Many other distributed ledgers today offer smart contracts, processed by virtual machines, which need additional processes and Web3 building

---

[55] https://cryptoslate.com/cryptos/privacy/

blocks, that also require inbuilt privacy-preserving features, so end-to-end privacy can be provided. They use similar cryptographic tools and mixing mechanisms to those mentioned above.

At the time of writing this book, everyone can monitor smart contract transactions on the Ethereum network using applications like "DappRadar," which is why the Ethereum ecosystem has started to develop privacy-preserving solutions. "Zether" is a project that researches resource-friendly private payment mechanisms for Ethereum smart contracts, including applications that build on top of Ethereum, such as payment channels. The "Keen Network" is also developing a privacy layer for the Ethereum network. Their approach is to create off-chain containers for private data to avoid data trails on the ledger. "Starkware" is implementing zk-STARKs, a protocol that focuses on moving computations and storage off-chain while also providing a certain level of privacy. Project "Nightfall" is being developed by EY with the aim to "integrate a set of smart contracts and microservices, and the ZoKrates zk-snark toolkit, to enable standard ERC-20 and ERC-721 tokens to be transacted on the Ethereum blockchain with complete privacy." The Ethereum network is planning to include Zk-Snarks on the protocol level in a future upgrade. "Parity" is also working on private transaction features that allow the storage, modification, and viewing of encrypted data on the Ethereum blockchain. Other smart contract networks like "Enigma," "Origo," and "Covalent" and Oasis Labs (Ekiden protocol) have also started to develop privacy-preserving features natively into their protocols.

Payment channels and sidechains allow users to transact off-chain and only store the summaries of state changes on the main network, which means that any transaction that is settled off-chain, never appears on the main network. However, privacy of the off-chain data depends on the privacy features provided by the respective protocols. "BOLT," for example, is a solution for a private payment channel using blind signatures and zero-knowledge proofs. It is being built on top of the Zcash network but should be able to interoperate with the Bitcoin and Ethereum network in the future. "Orchid" is an alternative to the Tor network with the aim of making it more difficult to trace Internet activity of users. Such networks need relay nodes and bridge nodes to conceal the location of a computer from network surveillance or traffic analysis. In Tor, there are only around 6000 relay nodes and less than 2000 bridge nodes.[56] Governments that want to prohibit the Tor network could blacklist all relay and bridge nodes, preventing their citizens from accessing the Tor network. This is why Orchid is developing tokenized incentives to attract more users and institutions to become "relayers" in the network, to increase the difficulty of blocking the network without blocking a big part of the Internet. The Mysterium

---

[56] *Find up to date metrics here: https://metrics.torproject.org/networksize.html*

network is building a decentralized version of Virtual Private Network. "NuCypher" is working on a decentralized key management solution (a decentralized HTTPS) to protect against imposters (so-called "man-in-the-middle" attacks) authenticating the accessed website. It uses "proxy re-encryption"[57] to protect the integrity and privacy of the exchanged data.

Legal & Political Aspects of Privacy

The Oxford dictionary defines privacy as a "state in which one is not observed or disturbed by other people" or the "state of being free from public attention." In the context of democratically governed countries, individual privacy is explicitly regulated in various contexts and to various extents, sometimes even on a constitutional level. The secrecy of correspondence act, for example, is a fundamental constitutional right dating back to the 17th and 18th century in countries such as Germany, Austria, or France. It guarantees the right that letters in transit will not be opened by governmental or private institutions. This right has been adopted to later communication technologies like the telephone and the Internet. While the United States does not grant the right to secrecy of correspondence explicitly on a constitutional level, such rights have been argued through case law based on the Fourth Amendment to the Constitution of the United States of America. The Fourth Amendment also regulates the privacy rights related to the privacy of the home and private property. One might be able to reinterpret the secrecy of communication and the sanctity of the private property and the home as the "right to cryptographic encryption." However, national jurisdictions vary on the "right to use encryption." In some countries, such as France, the right to cryptographic encryption has been included into the national law.[58] UNESCO has also published documents with recommendations on the human right to encryption. Other democratic countries such as Germany, the USA, and the UK have no such laws.

While the Internet era has boosted entrepreneurship, revolutionized communication, empowered citizen journalism, and enabled platforms such as Wikileaks, it has also triggered a discussion about how to deal with an increasing digital footprint that Internet applications are generating. In the context of Internet applications in general and e-commerce in particular, regulatory authorities have started to pass increasing privacy-preserving regulation. Adopted in 2016, the General Data Protection Regulation (GDPR) of the European Union has inspired other

---

[57] *Proxy re-encryption allows someone to transform ciphertexts from one public key to another without learning anything about the underlying message.*

[58] *"Article 30(I) of Law No. 2004-575 of 21 June 2004 on confidence in the digital economy provides that the use of means of cryptology are free" [2].*

countries outside the EU to adopt similar regulations. According to that regulation, privacy is about "empowering users to make their own decisions about who can process their data and for what purpose." However, this regulation is deeply rooted in the client-server-centered Web2, in which much of our private data is managed by trusted institutions that are the custodians of our data.

In the context of the Web3, The Czech Republic and Finland have regulations in place that require citizens to hand over their private keys to their wallets in case the law enforcement authority obliges them to do so. Other countries, such as South Korea and Japan, have banned privacy-tokens altogether. In 2018, the German Federal Ministry of Finance expressed concerns about the increased use of privacy tokens such as Monero in the context of criminal activities and Darknet transactions. Recent FATF regulation, passed in 2019, requires all so-called "Virtual Asset Service Providers" to reveal the identity of the transaction parties, making them subject to KYC requirements. Some token exchanges have already started to delist privacy tokens, except for Zcash, which does not provide privacy by default. Monero still seems to be listed on many token exchanges, but it remains to be seen for how long this will last.

Even when privacy, and the right to encryption, are explicitly regulated, the trade-off between individual privacy and public interest is subject to political viewpoints. It is often a matter of human discretion decided by judges, and regulated and enforced with great variation depending on the governance philosophy of a country or a community of nation states. The trade-offs between public and private interests are subject to ongoing public discussions and treated differently by governments worldwide. Legislation can range from granting the right to encryption to all citizens, to requiring de-encryption of personal data on request of government authorities. The General Data Protection Regulation (GDPR) of the European Union and similar privacy preserving regulations contradict the growing reach of anti-money-laundering (AML) and subsequent know-your-customer (KYC) regulation worldwide. It is unclear whether the two contradicting regulatory efforts will coordinate nationally or internationally, in order to find a balance between public and private interests. The issue of our growing digital footprint and subsequent surveillance possibilities have been discussed by activists and authors like Evgeny Morozov (who warned of mass surveillance, political repression, and fake news, calling for a more socio-economic perspective on technology)[59], Edward Snowden

---

[59] *Morozov has been skeptical of the Internet's ability to make the world more "democratic," referring to it as "cyber-utopianism." Instead, it can be used for information control and social engineering. He claims that the Internet provides powerful tools for "mass surveillance, political repression, and spreading nationalist and extremist propaganda." He calls for a more socio-economic perspective on technology and criticizes "internet libertarians" for their often unreflected claims about the nature of the Internet and describes it as pseudo-open, pseudo-disruptive, and pseudo-innovative.*

(who disclosed a series of international surveillance programs)[60], or more lately by authors like Shoshana Zuboff (who wrote about "surveillance capitalism" and the commodification of personal information).[61]

A similar trade-off between transparency and privacy exists in the Web3 and needs more widespread discussions. The question of "enforced privacy" vs. "public-by-default" for example, is a tricky one. The Monero network uses "enforced privacy" by default for all transactions. As a result, regulatory bodies will have a hard time to coerce users to deliberately reveal their data. In such a setup, users are also protected from accidentally revealing their data. Zcash, on the other hand, uses a "public-by-default" mechanism. Users can voluntarily choose to be transparent or not, which in theory makes this technology more flexible for use cases in regulated industries where certain transparency and auditability is required. However, in such a setup, users can also be penalized by regulators if they make use of private transactions, leading to non-use of privacy features altogether. This might be one of the reasons why most Zcash transactions are still conducted in the open, even though in theory they do provide "shielded transactions."

The promise of the Web3 is a more empowered and decentralized (inclusive) Internet. But how we design the protocols of these Web3 networks is not set in stone yet, and will need a broad socio-economic discussion. Depending on the level of obfuscation techniques implemented, or lack thereof, blockchain networks can either become liberation machines (more privacy by design), or effective surveillance and execution machines (no privacy by design). In a 100 percent obfuscated network, it would not be possible to, for example, track the provenance of goods or services, and national governments would have difficulties determining and enforcing tax payments, unless there was a more sophisticated "privacy by design" that revealed only selected socio-economic data to relevant entities, while respecting data protection regulation. This, however, is a political discussion that needs to be resolved based on consensus of the members of various internet communities, nation states, and on the level of international institutions.

---

[60] *Edward Joseph Snowden copied and leaked highly classified information from the National Security Agency (NSA) in 2013 during his time as a CIA subcontractor, disclosing a series of surveillance programs run by various institutions of different countries. Over time, he revealed thousands of classified NSA documents, which sparked a global discussion about national security and individual privacy. He now lives in Russian exile.*

[61] *Zuboff describes the commodification of personal information. She describes the tendency of accumulation of data, criticizing that many companies and institutions harvest and capitalize personal data without mechanisms of consent. She compares "industrial capitalism" and "surveillance capitalism," explaining "industrial capitalism" as exploitation of nature, and "surveillance capitalism" as exploitation of human nature.*

Chapter Summary

- *A payment token is only useful as a medium of exchange if it satisfies the fungibility criteria. Fungibility refers to the fact that individual units of a token are equal, and can be substituted with each other. The level of fungibility correlates with the level of privacy/ anonymity a token provides. This requires both "non-individualization" (obfuscating the traceability with identifiable individuals) and intransparency of other data related to transaction flows.*

- *Analogue forms of money, like coins or bills, do not give any information about the transaction history, as there is no economically feasible way to track a list of the previous owners. Cash can be considered as the most anonymous and most fungible form of money. While state-issued money, in the form of cash, allows for a high degree of privacy and therefore also fungibility, cash is being less commonly used in modern economies for daily payments and has been replaced with electronic forms of money.*

- *Electronic records have reduced the costs of monitoring how we use our money with simple algorithms. Furthermore, increasing anti-money laundering (AML) regulation and efforts by taxation authorities have forced financial institutions worldwide to monitor, and sometimes even reveal, information about the financial activities of their clients. Such practices, as a result of regulatory impositions, are gradually eroding the fungibility and hence quality of money.*

- *The Bitcoin network and similar public and permissionless networks use asymmetric cryptography to create online identities in the form of blockchain addresses. This way, a user can create multiple addresses without KYC requirements while trustfully sending and receiving tokens via a public network.*

- *Privacy of nodes can only be guaranteed as long as the real-world identity of a wallet owner cannot be linked to a certain network address. The publicly verifiable nature of blockchain networks makes transactions traceable, since all transactions are registered in plaintext (unencrypted) to the ledger, and transaction data is visible to anyone using a block explorer and can therefore be linked to other transactions made by the same token holder.*

- *Public disclosure of one's blockchain addresses, either via social media or as a result of one's activity on a token exchange, makes users susceptible to de-anonymization efforts using data analysis. Metadata from token transactions can be used to trace the IP address of a user, sometimes even when anonymization services such as Tor or I2P are used.*

- *Depending on a token's provenance, individual tokens may not be accepted by merchants due to their tainted transaction history. This reduces the fungibility of a token.*

- More recent blockchain networks have set out to improve the level of privacy of token transactions. Such "privacy tokens" use various obfuscating techniques to make token history less transparent. The goal of privacy tokens is to design a protocol that reveals the minimum information needed and obfuscates all other information.

- Depending on the blockchain protocol, various elements of a transaction can be anonymized to different extents: (i) wallet/address anonymity, (ii) confidentiality of transaction data like payment amounts, (iii) privacy about total network state. User privacy (full anonymity): the identity of the user sending or receiving a token is obfuscated in such a way that the user's actions cannot be linked to their real-world identity.

- Over the past decade, a growing list of projects have been experimenting with a range of methods, from transaction aggregation to alternative cryptographic algorithms.

- Depending on the level of obfuscation techniques implemented, or lack thereof, blockchain networks can either become liberation machines (more privacy by design), or effective surveillance and execution machines (no privacy by design).

- Even when privacy, and the right to encryption, are explicitly regulated, the trade-off between individual privacy and public interest is subject to political viewpoints. It is often a matter of human discretion decided by judges, and regulated and enforced with great variation depending on the governance philosophy of a country or a community of nation states. The trade-offs between public and private interests are subject to ongoing public discussions and treated differently by governments worldwide.

Chapter References & Further Reading

- Abramova, Svetlana; Böhme, Rainer: "Your Money or Your Privacy: A Systematic Approach to Coin Selection" Cryptoeconomics Systems Journal: https://assets.pubpub.org/dwq1f9g6/71581340076503.pdf

- Adrian, Richard M.: "Explaining Ripple's Most Recent Law- suit with SEC", 2019, available at: https://www.publish0x.com/crypto-info/explaining-ripples-most-recent-lawsuit-sec-xnnejn,.

- Alexandre, Ana: "Germany Warns of Privacy Token Usage in Money Laundering and Terrorism", Cointelegraph, Oct 22, 2019, available at: https://cointelegraph.com/news/germany-warns-of-privacy-token-usage-in-money-laundering-and-terrorism

- Alonso, Kurt M.: "Zero to Monero: First Editional technical guide to a private digital currency; for beginners, amateurs, and experts," Monero website, 2018, https://www.getmonero.org/library/zero-to-monero-1-0-0.pdf

- Androulaki, Elli; Karame, Ghassan O.; Roeschlin, Marc; Scherer, Tobias; Capkun, Srdjan: "Evaluating User Privacy in Bitcoin" In Ahmad-Reza Sadeghi (Editor): "Financial Cryptography and Data Security", Ahmad-Reza Sadeghi (Ed.) Financial Cryptography and Data Security 17th International Conference, FC 2013 Okinawa, Japan, April 1-5, 2013 Revised Selected Papers, pages 34–51. Springer, 2013

- Ashish: "Introduction to Zero Knowledge Proof: The protocol of next generation Blockchain", Medium, Oct 8, 2018, available at: https://medium.com/@kotsbtechcdac/introduction-to-zero-knowledge-proof-the-protocol-of-next-generation-blockchain-305b2fc7f8e5

- Beam, Linda: "The Privacy Focused Cryptocurrency Built on The Mimblewimble Protocol," Hackernoon, 2019, https://hackernoon.com/beam-the-privacy-focused-cryptocurrency-built-on-the-mimblewimble-protocol-7540b289a45

- Behera, Chandan K.; Bhaskari, Lalitha D.: " Procedia Computer Science," 70:757 – 763, 2015

- Berg, A: "The Identity, Fungibility, and Anonymity of Money", SSRN Electronic Journal. 10.2139/ssrn.3211011, 2018: https://www.researchgate.net/profile/Alastair_Berg/publication/326438277_The_Identity_Fungibility_and_Anonymity_of_Money/links/5dc3a1a84585151435e-f6eb7/The-Identity-Fungibility-and-Anonymity-of-Money.pdf

- Berg, A.: "Identity in Economics: A Review", RMIT University Working Paper, 2019, available at: https://papers.ssrn.com/sol3/cf_dev/AbsByAuth.cfm?per_id=2802158,

- Berg, A., Berg, C., Davidson, S. and Potts, J.: 'The Institutional Economics of Identity," RMIT University working paper, 2017, available at: https://papers.ssrn.com/sol3/papers.cfm?abstract_id=3072823

- Berg, C.: "The Classical Liberal Case for Privacy in a World of Surveillance and Technological Change," Palgrave Macmillan, London, 2018.

- Berg, C. and Davidson, S.: "Selling Your Data Without Selling Your Soul," Competitive Enterprise Institute Issue Analysis 4, 1-32. 14, 2019

- Birch, Joseph:"FATF AML Regulation: Can the Crypto Industry Adapt to the Travel Rule?," Cointelegraph, 2019, available at: https://cointelegraph.com/news/fatf-aml-regulation-can-the-crypto-industry-adapt-to-the-travel-rule

- Chaum, David: "Achieving Electronic Privacy," Scientific American, pages 96–101, 1992.

- Chen, Richard: "An Overview of Privacy in Cryptocurrencies" Aug 9, 2018, available at: https://thecontrol.co/an-overview-of-privacy-in-cryptocurrencies-893dc078d0d7

- Coase, R.H.: 'The problem of social cost," The Journal of Law and Economics, 56, 837-77,1960

- Coase, R.H.: "'The nature of the firm', Economica, 4, 386-405, 1937

- Curran, Brian: "What is the BEAM Coin? Mimblewimble & Grin vs Beam, " Blockonomi website, 2019, https://blockonomi.com/beam-coin-guide

- @Dennis_Z: "Comparative Review of Privacy Token and Token Economics", Medium, Feb. 15th 2019, available at: https://hackernoon.com/2019-privacy-token-review-c28b6ceef637

- Goldfeder, Steven; Kalodner, Harry; Reisman, Dillon; Narayanan, Arvind: "When the cookie meets the blockchain: Privacy risks of web payments via cryptocurrencies," 2017, retrieved February 4, 2020 from https://arxiv.org/abs/1708.04748.

- Kappos, George; Yousaf, Haaroon; Maller, Mary; Meiklejohn, Sarah: "An Empirical Analysis of Anonymity in Zcash, " published in 27th USENIX Security Symposium (USENIX Security 18), Baltimore, MD, 2018. Retrieved February, 4 2020 from https://www.usenix.org/conference/usenixsecurity18/presentation/kappos

- Jedusor, Tom Elvis: "Mimblewimble Proposal, " 19 July, 2016, available at: https://download.wpsoftware.net/bitcoin/wizardry/mimblewimble.txt

- Kahn, Charles M; McAndrews, James; Roberds, William: „Money Is Privacy." International Economic Review 46, no. 2, 2005, 377-99. Accessed March 2, 2020. www.jstor.org/stable/3663561.

- Kumar, Amrit; Fischer, Clément; Tople, Shruti; Saxena, Prateek: "A Traceability Analysis of Monero's Blockchain, " published in Foley, Simon N.; Gollmann, Dieter; Snekkenes, Einar (Editors) Computer Security – ESORICS 2017, pages 153–173, Cham, 2017. Springer International Publishing

- Lalouette, Laure; Esselink, Henk: "Trends and developments in the use of euro cash over the past ten years," published as part of the ECB Economic Bulletin, Issue 6/2018, available at: https://www.ecb.europa.eu/pub/economic-bulletin/articles/2018/html/ecb.ebart201806_03.en.html#toc1

- N.N.: Market Capitalization of Privacy Tokens on Cryptoslate.com: https://cryptoslate.com/cryptos/privacy/

- Patel, Nik: "Coin Report 36,": Piratechain.

215

- N.N.: *"Challenges and issues in cryptocurrency trading: beyond the controversies, "* Medium, Cassiopeia Services, 2019, available at: https://medium.com/@cassiopeiaservicesltd/challenges-and-issues-in-cryptocurrency-trading-beyond-the-controversies-12bebb7c3849

- N.N.: *"What is monero? everything you need to know,* "skalex GmbH website, 2017, available at: https://www.skalex.io/what-is-monero/

- N.N. *"Zero Knowledge Smart Contracts on Dusk Network Today",* Medium, Dusk Network, Jul 1, 2019, available at: https://medium.com/dusk-network/zero-knowledge-smart-contracts-on-dusk-network-85f95644d673

- N.N.: *"What are zk-SNARKs?",* Zcash website, retrieved Nov20, 2019: https://z.cash/technology/zksnarks

- N.N.: *"German Officials Claim Monero is Untraceable, "* Darknetlive, 2019, available at: https://darknetlive.com/post/german-officials-claim-monero-poses-a-money-laundering-threat

- N.N.:*"About monero, a brief history, "* Monero website, 2014, available at: https://web.getmonero.org/resources/about/

- N.N.: *"Beam,"* Beam website, Beampedia, 2019, available at: https://beam.mw/beampedia-item/beam

- N.N.: *"EY Scaling Ethereum with ZK-Snarks, 20 Transactions For the Cost of One,"* December 5, 2019, https://www.trustnodes.com/2019/12/05/ey-scaling-ethereum-with-zk-snarks-20-transactions-for-the-cost-of-one

- Quesnelle, Jeffrey: *"On the linkability of Zcash transactions,"* arXiv preprint:1712.01210, 2017, Retrieved February, 4 2020 from https://arxiv.org/abs/1712.01210

- Meiklejohn, Sarah; Pomarole, Marjori; Jordan, Grant; Levchenko, Kirill; McCoy, Damon; Voelker, Geoffrey M.;Savage, Stefan: *"A Fistful of Bitcoins: Characterizing Payments Among Men with No Names,"* published in ACM *"Proceedings of the 2013 Conference on Internet Measurement Conference",* pages 127–140, New York, NY, USA, 2013.

- Möser, Malte; Soska, Kyle; Heilman, Ethan, Kevin; Lee, Henry Heffan, Srivastava, Shashvat; Hogan, Kyle; Hennessey, Jason; Miller, Andrew; Narayanan, Arvind; Christin, Nicolas: *"An Empirical Analysis of Traceability in the Monero Blockchain, "* published in *"Proceedings on Privacy Enhancing Technologies",* volume 3, pages 143–163, 2018

- Reid, Fergal; Harrigan, Martin: *"An Analysis of Anonymity in the Bitcoin System, "* in Altshuler, Yaniv; Elovici B., Yuval; , Cremers, Armin; Aharony, Nadav; Pentland, Alex (Editors) *"Security and Privacy in Social Networks",* pages 197–223. Springer, New York, 2013

- Riggins, Jennifer: *"Are Programmers Ethically (and Legally) Responsible for Their Code?",* Thenewstack, 2018, available at: https://thenewstack.io/are-programmers-ethically-and-legally-responsible-for-their-code/

- Reid, K.: *"Banknotes and their vindication in eighteenth-century Scotland,".* University of Edinburgh, School of Law, Research Paper Series No 2013/19, 2013

- Ron, Dorit; Shamir, Adi: *"Quantitative Analysis of the Full Bitcoin Transaction Graph, "* in Ahmad-Reza Sadeghi (Editor) Financial Cryptography and Data Security, volume 7859 of Lecture Notes in Computer Science, pages 6–24. Springer, Heidelberg, 2013.

- Schulz, Wolfgang; Hoboken, Joris.: *"Human rights and encryption,"* UNESCO, Assistant Director-General for Communication and Information, 2016-2018 (La Rue, F.). ISBN:978-92-3-100185-7 Collation: 83 p.2016, retrieved from: https://unesdoc.unesco.org/ark:/48223/pf0000246527

- Stanley, R.L.; Buckley, R.P.: *"Protecting the west, excluding the rest: The impact of the AML/CTF regime on financial inclusion in the pacific and potential responses,"* Melbourne Journal of International Law, 17 (1), 83-106, 2016

- Sun, Yi; Zhang, Yan: *"Privacy in Cryptocurrencies: An Overview,"* Medium, Oct 25, 2018, available at: https://medium.com/@yi.sun/privacy-in-cryptocurrencies-d4b268157f6c

- Sun, Yi; Zhang, Yan: *"Privacy in Cryptocurrencies: Zero-Knowledge and zk-SNARKs (1/2)",* Medium, Jan 25, 2019, available at: https://medium.com/@krzhang/privacy-in-cryptocurrencies-zero-knowledge-and-zk-snarks-1-2-68ce1838fd9c

- Sun, Yi; Zhang, Yan: *"Privacy in Cryptocurrencies: Mixing-based Approaches,"* Medium, Dec 4, 2018, available at:
  https://medium.com/@yi.sun/privacy-in-cryptocurrencies-mixing-based-approaches-ce08d0040c88
- Vikati, Alex: *"How Private Are Privacy Coins: Closer Look at Zcash and Zclassic's Blockchains, "* Hackernoon, 2018, available at: https://hackernoon.com/how-private-are-privacy-coins-a-closer-look-at-zcash-and-zclassics-blockchains-32dae60d5b9f
- Walters, Steve: *" BEAM Review: Mimblewimble Based Scalable Privacy Coin,"* Coinbuerau, 2019, available at: https://www.coinbureau.com/review/beam-coin/
- Young, Joseph: *"Privacy-Focused Cryptos Hunted Down by Forensics and Exchanges, "* Cointelegraph, 2019 available at: https://cointelegraph.com/news/privacy-focused-cryptos-hunted-down-by-forensics-and-exchanges
- Yousaf, Haaroon; Kappos, George; Meiklejohn, Sarah: *"Tracing Transactions across Cryptocurrency Ledgers, "* in *"Proceedings of the 28th USENIX Conference on Security Symposium,"* SEC'19, pages 837–850, USA, 2019. USENIX Association.
- Williamson, O.E.: *"Transaction-cost economics: the governance of contractual relations, "* The Journal of Law and Economics, 22 (2), 233-61. 1979
- Williamson, O.E.: *"The Economic Institutions of Capitalism,"* Free Press, New York, 1985
- Zhang, Rui, Xue, Rui; Liu, Ling: *"Cryptography and Security Security and Privacy on Blockchain",* Computer Science, Submitted on 18 Mar 2019 (v1), last revised 16 Aug 2019 (this version, v2), available at: https://arxiv.org/pdf/1903.07602.pdf
- Aced: *https://www.acedcoin.com/*
- Anoncoin - *https://anoncrypto.io/*
- Apollo: *https://apollocurrency.com/*
- Arqma: *https://arqma.com/*
- Arpa chain:*https://arpachain.io/*
- Beam: *https://beam.mw/*
- Beldex:*https://www.beldex.io/coin*
- Bulwark: *https://bulwarkcrypto.com/*
- Bytecoin: *https://bytecoin.org/*
- Bzedge - *https://getbze.com/*
- Crypticcoin: *https://crypticcoin.io/*
- CloakCoin: *https://www.cloakcoin.com/*
- CUTcoin: *http://cutcoin.org/*
- Cova: *https://covalent.ai/*
- Cuckoo: *https://github.com/tromp/cuckoo*
- DAPS Coin: *https://officialdapscoin.com/*
- Dash: *https://www.dash.org/*
- Deeponion: *https://deeponion.org/*
- Digitalnote xdn: *https://www.digitalnote.biz/*
- Dusk network: *https://dusk.network/*
- Grin: *https://grin-tech.org/*
- Horizen: *https://horizen.global/*
- Hush: *https://myhush.org/*
- Innovacoin: *https://innovacoin.io/*

- *Komodo: https://komodoplatform.com/*
- *Loki : https://loki.network/*
- *Lobstex: http://lobstex.com*
- *Navcoin: https://navcoin.org/en*
- *Nightfall: https://github.com/EYBlockchain/nightfall*
- *Nix: https://nixplatform.io/*
- *Noir - https://noirofficial.org/*
- *Nonerov: https://monerov.org/*
- *Monero: https://www.getmonero.org/*
- *Origo: https://origo.network/*
- *Parity Tech, Private Transactions: https://wiki.parity.io/Private-Transactions*
- *Particl: https://particl.io/*
- *pEOS: https://peos.one/*
- *Pivx: https://pivx.org/*
- *Piratechain: https://pirate.black/*
- *Phore - https://phore.io/*
- *Ryo: https://ryo-currency.com/*
- *Safex cash: https://safex.io/*
- *Safecoin: https://safecoin.org/*
- *Solariscoin: https://solariscoin.com/*
- *Spectrecoin: https://spectreproject.io/*
- *Stealthcoin: https://stealth.org/*
- *Sumokoin: https://www.sumokoin.org/*
- *Tarush: https://tarush.tech/*
- *Tixl - https://tixl.me/*
- *Veil - https://veil-project.com*
- *Verge: https://www.theverge.com/*
- *Zcash: https://z.cash/*
- *zClassic - https://zclassic.org/*
- *ZCoin: https://zcoin.io/*
- *Zumcoin - https://zumcoin.org/*
- *Xuez: https://xuezcoin.com/*

Trading Tokens, Atomic Swaps & DEX

Online exchanges offer services to those who want to buy and sell tokens. They act as trusted intermediaries and market makers. While they are an important player in this new token economy, they are still predominantly centralized, which makes them vulnerable to hacks, mismanagement, volume volatility, or censorship. Atomic swaps and decentralized exchanges try to mitigate these risks.

While blockchain networks and other distributed ledgers allow the transfer of tokens without intermediaries, they only allow sending tokens from one wallet in the network to another wallet in the network. A token can only be managed by one type of network and cannot natively move between networks for interoperability reasons. As a result, the buying and selling of tokens still requires the services of token exchanges. Various online exchanges offer such services and act as trusted intermediaries. They resemble online banks that take the tokens of their clients into their custody and manage the trading of tokens between users of their platforms.

For users, trading one token for another can be difficult and time consuming, depending on the popularity and legal status of a particular token. Less popular or highly controversial tokens might only be listed on smaller exchanges with limited token pairings, which means that users would need to (i) register for all of these exchanges and (ii) swap tokens several times, before being able to buy the token of interest. Even if many tokens are listed on the same exchange, token pairings, or token/fiat pairings, are often limited. As a result of this, trading tokens might often be time consuming and expensive. Sometimes, even reputable tokens are listed on one exchange only, forcing users to trade on an exchange that they would otherwise not use. Potential buyers of a token might, therefore, decide not to buy a certain token if it is too complicated or too risky to do so. Exchanges that list many tokens have become more popular, as they offer token holders a one-stop shop to buy and sell between multiple token types, without the need to register on another exchange.

Token exchanges get to decide whether they include a token or not. They have become the market makers and new gatekeepers in this emerging tokenized economy. In August 2016, for example, when the Ethereum network performed the controversial hard fork as a result of TheDAO exploit,[62] the shorter Ethereum chain ("Ethereum Classic") did not have any market value. However, when "Poloniex," an online exchange, decided to list the "Ethereum Classic" token, the market dynamics changed and other exchanges started listing the token too. While it was not the first time that there was a fork in a blockchain network, it was the first time the token of a minority chain was listed on an exchange, giving the network an economic value.

Challenges of Centralized Exchanges

Most exchanges today are centralized exchanges (CEX) performing intermediary services between buyers and sellers of tokens. They allow simple buying and selling of tokens, also against fiat currencies, and provide easy wallet creation and token management, including the safeguarding of private keys. As opposed to many early crypto enthusiasts, who still manage their tokens with their own wallets (hardware wallet, software wallet, or paper wallet), newcomers often prefer to outsource wallet management to online exchanges, which act as the custodian of their tokens. Centralized exchanges operate on classic client-server technology and are not subject to the same security mechanisms of blockchain networks. While they offer important services, they are vulnerable to hacks, mismanagement, volume volatility, or censorship. Hacks and mismanagement have been the biggest issues in the past, especially in the early years, when the market was less mature and unregulated. "Mt. Gox," which was the largest Bitcoin exchange at the time, suspended trading and filed for bankruptcy in 2014. Due to mismanagement, approximately 850,000 BTC went missing, most likely stolen. Many other cases followed, such as "Bitfinex" or "Coincheck." These incidents have led to the misconception in the general public that blockchain networks are not safe.

Centralized exchanges very often don't give their customers full control over their private keys, as they trade on their own books, a.k.a. off-chain. They often don't have dedicated user wallets for their clients, making a private key useless. Customers surrender full control over their tokens. Smaller exchanges that have less liquidity can experience price volatilities such as flash crashes and price spikes,

---

[62] *A vulnerability in one of the smart contract functions, designed to represent minority rights, was exploited and used to drain 3.6m Ether from TheDAO balance (roughly 150 million USD at the time).*

if there is a sudden shift in the supply and demand of tokens. This makes smaller exchanges subject to market manipulation and less attractive for users. Centralized exchanges are also subject to government regulation and must therefore meet the countries' KYC (know your customer) requirements, which means that customers have to fully identify themselves when registering on an exchange; this could raise privacy and censorship issues.

General blockchain interoperability is a solution to the centralization problem, which is currently being addressed by projects such as "Cosmos," "Polkadot," "Wanchain," "Chainlink," "Arc," "Aion," and "AVA." Atomic swaps are another solution, with more immediate feasibility.

Atomic Swaps

Atomic swaps allow for P2P cross-chain trading and can be directly executed between separate blockchain networks, wallet to wallet, without a trusted intermediary like an exchange. They use a type of smart contract called a hash time-locked contract (HTLC) to secure the token transaction, making sure that both parties to the token trade fulfill the requirements. HTLCs are similar to state channels that deal with off-chain payment settlement via smart contract (read more: Annex - Scalability Solutions). Users remain in full control of their private keys, and their tokens, when conducting such a trade.

Let's assume that Alice and Bob want to swap tokens from different blockchain networks P2P without an intermediary like an exchange. Bob wants to sell his Bitcoin (BTC) for Litecoin (LTC), and Alice wants to sell her Litecoin (LTC) for Bitcoin (BTC). Since the two networks cannot communicate directly, Alice and Bob use a hash time-locked contract to lock up their tokens for a predefined amount of time. Both recipients, Bob and Alice, need to create a cryptographic proof of payment before the time expires. The tokens are locked via multi-signature in a smart contract. This state lock is registered on both networks. Tokens are only swapped if their secret keys match. To deposit her tokens, Alice first has to create an HTLC. She creates a secret key and generates a hash, from which the smart contract address is derived and to which she can now send her tokens. She also sends this hash to Bob, who can use the hash to replicate the address of the smart contract and deposit his tokens in that smart contract. Alice can unlock the tokens Bob deposited using her secret key, which triggers an event where Bob receives the secret key to unlock Alice's tokens. In a closing transaction, the last commitment is sent to be added to the blockchain.

Atomic Swaps

 Alice and Bob want to swap the tokens from different blockchains P2P without an intermediary like an exchange. Bob wants to sell his Bitcoin (BTC) for Litecoin (LTC), and Alice wants to sell her Litecoin (LTC) for Bitcoin (BTC). The two blockchain networks cannot communicate directly. Atomic swaps resolve the issue.

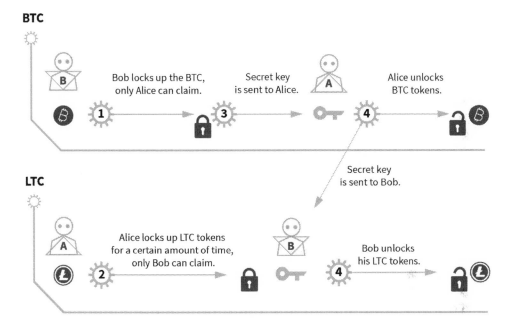

Atomic swaps require that (i) both parties to the swap need to download the ledgers of both networks; (ii) both networks managing the swapped tokens must support hash time-locked contracts and use the same cryptographic hash function. Furthermore, in order to conduct wallet-to-wallet transactions, (iii) the wallet used must also have atomic swap capabilities. While atomic swaps enable P2P swapping of tokens, they do not resolve the coincidence-of-wants problem. They will only be useful to people who know other people willing to buy the exact amount of tokens one wants to sell at exactly the same time one wants to sell them. The likeliness of this happening for retail investors is quite low. Decentralized exchanges using atomic swaps, however, could resolve both problems.

Decentralized Exchanges

Decentralized exchanges (DEX) are decentralized applications running on a distributed ledger to allow users to trade tokens without the need for an institution clearing the settlements. The trade is settled directly by the ledgers (on-chain) and could potentially mitigate many challenges of centralized exchanges. A fully decentralized exchange would make use of atomic swaps, or similar methods, with an added discovery layer that enables trading between two random token owners who do not know each other, might live in different countries, and would not otherwise know how to find each other. Existing decentralized exchanges provide various levels of decentralization, often running on a partially centralized infrastructure, and not offering wallet-to-wallet swaps. Current examples are "Komodo," "WavesDex," "OasisDex," "Radar Relay," "BarterDex," "Bisq," "StellarDex," and "EtherDelta."

Most self-proclaimed decentralized exchanges are not fully decentralized (yet) and are subject to many challenges. Due to on-chain order books, they are also slow and expensive, at least as long as the scalability issues of public blockchain networks are unresolved. Each time an order is posted or modified, this generates high overhead in network transaction costs and bloats the ledger. Currently, decentralized exchanges mainly benefit traders who are already positioned in token markets. DEX are not necessarily suitable for newcomers to the market, as they don't resolve the question of trading national fiat currencies for tokens. Newcomers to the crypto token market will probably still use centralized exchanges, which allow them to easily buy tokens with fiat. The current usability issues of decentralized exchanges further contribute to low liquidity of tokens and low trading volumes, which makes them prone to market manipulation. However, once those challenges are resolved, DEX could allow for a more liquid and less manipulation-susceptible market, where demand and supply could exist without arbitrary middlemen.

For decentralized exchanges to reach mainstream adoption, we still lack necessary network effects. These network effects rely on when and how general ledger interoperability will be resolved, including resilient cross-chain atomic swaps, interoperability standards, or piggyback solutions like the "Pantos" token. Furthermore, current assets, including fiat currencies, need to be tokenized to catalyze necessary network effects. Decentralized exchanges will likely come to fruition if and when everyday transactions are predominantly settled using cryptographic tokens and distributed ledgers. We will probably need a mesh of interconnected exchanges to have enough market depth for global and widespread use of P2P token exchanges.

Chapter Summary

- *A token can only be managed by one type of network and cannot natively move between networks for interoperability reasons. The buying and selling of tokens therefore requires the services of token exchanges. They resemble online banks that take the tokens of their clients into their custody and manage the trading of tokens between users of their platforms.*

- *Most exchanges today are centralized exchanges (CEX) performing intermediary services between buyers and sellers of tokens. They allow simple buying and selling of tokens, also against fiat currencies, and provide easy wallet creation and token management, including the safeguarding of private keys.*

- *Token exchanges get to decide whether they include a token or not. They act as trusted intermediaries and market makers have become the new gatekeepers in this emerging tokenized economy. While they are an important player in this new token economy, they are still predominantly centralized, which makes them vulnerable to hacks, mismanagement, volume volatility, or censorship. Atomic swaps and decentralized exchanges try to mitigate these risks.*

- *Atomic swaps allow for P2P cross-chain trading and can be directly executed between separate blockchains, wallet to wallet, without a trusted intermediary like exchanges. They use a type of smart contract called a hash time-locked contract (HTLC) to secure the transaction, making sure that both parties to the trade fulfill the requirements.*

- *Atomic swaps do not resolve the "coincidence of wants" problem. They only benefit people who know another person who is willing to buy the exact amount of tokens at exactly the same time.*

- *Decentralized exchanges (DEX) are decentralized applications running on a distributed ledger to allow users to trade tokens without the need for an institution clearing the settlements. The trade is settled directly by the ledgers (on-chain). They combine atomic swaps with matching algorithms to mitigate the coincidence-of-wants problem.*

- *A fully decentralized exchange would make use of atomic swaps, or similar methods, with an added discovery layer that enables trading between two random token owners who do not know each other, might live in different countries, and would not otherwise know how to find each other.*

Chapter References & Further Reading

- Borkowski, Michael; McDonald, Daniel; Ritzer, Christoph; Schulte, Stefan: "Towards Atomic Cross-Chain Token Transfers: State of the Art and Open Questions within TAST", Pantos GmbH Vienna, May 2018, revised version 1.2, August 2018, retrieved from: https://www.dsg.tuwien.ac.at/projects/tast/pub/tast-white-paper-1.pdf

- Gazi Güçlütürk, Osman: "TheDAO Hack explained: Unfortunate take off of smart contracts", Aug 1, 2018: https://medium.com/@ogucluturk/the-dao-hack-explained-unfortunate-take-off-of-smart-contracts-2bd8c8db3562

- Herlihy, Maurice: "Atomic Cross-Chain Swaps", May 18, 2018: https://arxiv.org/pdf/1801.09515.pdf

- Higgins, Stan: „The Bitfinex Bitcoin Hack: What We Know (And Don't Know)," Aug 3, 2016, updated Jun 20, 2018, retrieved from: https://www.coindesk.com/bitfinex-bitcoin-hack-know-dont-know

- Madeira, Antonio: "What Are Atomic Swaps?", 28 Sep 2017: https://www.cryptocompare.com/coins/guides/what-are-atomic-swaps/

- N.N.: "How to Steal $500 Million in Cryptocurrency," Fortune Magazine, January 31, 2018, retrieved from: EST https://fortune.com/2018/01/31/coincheck-hack-how/

- N.N.: "What Are Atomic Swaps?", https://blockgeeks.com/guides/atomic-swaps/

- N.N".: Komodo White Paper", https://komodoplatform.com/wp-content/uploads/2018/04/2018-04-04-Komodo-White-Paper-Full.pdf

- N.N.: „5 Predictions for Our Security Token Futur" Coin Crunch, Jun 16, 2018: https://medium.com/hackernoon/5-predictions-for-our-security-token-futur-57ce9cf01256

- Noashh: "With Atomic Swaps, Komodo Supports 95% Of All Coins In Existence!", March 16, 2018: https://komodoplatform.com/komodo-now-covers-atomic-swaps-between-95-of-all-coins-in-existence/

- Binance: https://www.binance.com/en

- Bisq: https://bisq.network/

- EtherDelta: https://etherdelta.com/

- Komodo: https://komodoplatform.com/

- Mt. Gox Hack: https://en.wikipedia.org/wiki/Mt._Gox

- OasisDex: https://developer.makerdao.com/oasis/

- Pantos: https://pantos.io/

- Poloniex: https://poloniex.com/

- Radar Relay: https://radarrelay.com/

- WavesDex: https://wavesplatform.com/products-exchange

Lending Tokens - Decentralized Credit Systems

Decentralized lending services use smart contracts to create two-sided markets for a P2P credit and lending system. Any non-bankable asset such as commodities, securities, real estate, artworks, or SME shares could, in the future, be tokenized and collateralized, which could lead to a convergence of financial markets and the real economy.

Smart contract–based execution of credit and lending services have lower operational costs than legacy financial services, as compliance verification could be executed on the fly. In a fully decentralized setup, P2P financial services only require a crypto-wallet, without complex identification systems. They allow for more control, security, and inclusion. Security and control refers to the fact that you can choose non-custodial services where you are in control of your private keys.[63] Inclusion refers to the fact that these services, which are currently complementary to our current financial systems, could grant access to individuals who have been excluded from financial services before.

Fully decentralized lending services enable a two-sided market, using smart contracts for P2P credit and P2P lending of tokens. Any non-bankable asset such as commodities, securities, real estate, art, SME shares, etc. could, in the future, be represented by a token. Commodities, national currencies, and securities are already being tokenized and can be traded on markets today, while tokenized real estate, art, and SME shares are still in their early stages of conceptualization. Any transferable tokens representing an asset could be used as collateral for open decentralized lending solutions, which could change the dynamics of our global economic system. The integrations of such tokenized non-bankable assets with lending and

---

[63] *The reality in the near future, however, could be more complex due to regulatory requirements, which will, very likely, oversee this still nascent scene.*

borrowing schemes would allow for instant transactions, which surpasses the possibilities of the legacy systems we have today.

P2P Lending

Most investors today buy tokens for long-term investment only. The tokens usually stay dormant, in a hardware wallet, software wallet, or paper wallet, as token holders expect their value to grow over time and don't use them for daily payments. P2P lending protocols allow token holders to convert their "dormant capital" into "working capital" by using smart contracts that earn periodic interest rates. P2P lending could easily be brokered by a smart contract. Dormant and previously non-bankable assets from around the world can now be tokenized to create a liquid P2P lending market. Anyone can earn passive income relatively risk free on their token holdings through interest paid by the borrowers. On the other hand, lower operational costs could also make loans more affordable for a wider array of people and institutions.

P2P Borrowing

P2P borrowing allows for the borrowing of funds against a collateral of tokens you own, potentially paying lower interest rates than in the current financial system. Previously non-bankable assets, such as commodities, securities, art, or real estate, can be tokenized and leveraged against (i) fiat money or other (ii) transferable crypto-tokens. Borrowers can lock up tokens they own as collateral in a smart contract. This collateral serves as a guarantee that the lenders will be repaid. Since most tokens have volatile prices, decentralized lending applications only let you borrow a certain percentage of the value of your collateral. If the market price of the collateral begins to drop, the smart contract is programmed to sell collateral tokens at a pre-defined spot price or a market auction to mitigate counterparty risk of the lender. Collateralized borrowing is currently the only option, as decentralized systems have no KYC process to secure funds based on identification and reputation. That, however, might change as more sophisticated identification and reputation solutions evolve. At the time of writing this book, the main use case for P2P borrowing is for the sake of margin trading (the practice of borrowing funds to make an investment where one anticipates to make a higher profit off the investment than the interest one has to pay. Borrowed funds are used for leverage, which means that both profits and losses will be big).

Flash Loans

Flash loans are a specific type of P2P loan that is valid within one network transaction and must be repaid by the end of that transaction. The lender can offer loans at zero-risk and the borrower can get any amount of tokens, without a collateral, provided the borrower can return all tokens borrowed within the same transaction. The default and illiquidity risk that a lender usually bears is reduced to zero due to the fact that the borrower has to repay the borrowed tokens within the same transaction, otherwise the smart contract won't execute the deal. A series of smart contract operations can be programmed in a way that either all occur, or nothing occurs. Due to the atomic nature[64] of blockchain networks, smart contract-based transactions can be reverted during execution, if the condition of a repayment is not satisfied. The concept was first introduced in 2018 by the "Marble Protocol." Flash loan transactions will fail in the case of (i) insufficient transaction fees, (ii) conflicting transactions, or (iii) if another condition within the transaction cannot be met. The loans are taken from a public smart contract–governed liquidity pool, which means that anyone could borrow the entire amount of tokens available in the pool at any point in time. DeFi services relevant in the context of a flash loan are decentralized exchanges, decentralized margin trading, or credit/lending services.

P2P Lending Protocols

MakerDAO is one of the more seasoned projects, that was launched in 2017 to create a stable token system. The stable token DAI comes with inbuilt decentralized lending aspects. DAI is issued against a collateral token (ETH). Borrowers receive newly created DAI tokens by locking up their ETH tokens as collateral, using a smart contract–based collateralized debt position (CDP). The current collateralization ratio is 150 percent. The interest rate is volatile and around 2.5 percent to 19.5 percent each month. A range of tokens are supported as collateral (read more: Part 3 - Stable Tokens).

Uniswap: Uniswap is a decentralized token exchange that runs without an order book. Instead of order books they use "liquidity pools" to facilitate the exchange of tokens. Each token has a global borrow and lend pool that represents a market for that token's borrow and lend positions. In such a setup, any token holder can contribute their tokens to the liquidity pool and earn interest on their token

---

[64] *Atomicity of atomic transactions" is a computer science term that refers to database systems where a series of database operations can be programmed in a way that either all occur, or nothing occurs. Either all transactions (in this case, within the smart contract) execute or none of them execute. This prevents partial updates to the database system.*

holdings. The 2020 upgrade of the Uniswap protocol allows direct token-to-token swaps, instead of relying on asset pairs with ETH as a fixed base token. The protocol upgrade also introduced "flash swaps," a flash loan function that allows users to withdraw tokens for instant on-chain trades and return them by the end of the transaction. The upgrade was furthrmore designed to be more resistant against potential attacks and manipulation such as the "flash attacks" of February 2020 which will be described later in this chapter.

Compound was launched in 2018 as a decentralized lending protocol with liquidity pools. Lenders can deposit their tokens into lending pools to earn interest. Loans are tokenized. The interest rate of each token lent is algorithmically defined based on supply and demand of tokens in each pool and thus variable. One can receive one type of token in exchange for depositing another type of token (e.g. cDAI for DAI.) The loans have no fixed durations, which means that lenders can withdraw their funds at any time. Loans also have an unlimited duration. The current collateralization ratio is 150 percent. Tokens supported as collateral are currently: ETH, DAI, BAT, REP, USDC, WBTC, and ZRX.

Dharma was launched in 2019 and was initially not fully decentralized, offering lending and borrowing at fixed interest rates and fixed durations of up to 90 days. Borrowers collateralized their smart contract account with 150 percent of the value of the funds being borrowed, and the interest rate was determined by Dharma's management, instead of a market algorithm. They later pivoted and are now using Compound's liquidity pools, which determine the interest rates algorithmically based on supply and demand in these pools. Tokens supported as collateral are currently: DAI.

dYdX is a decentralized lending platform and an exchange. Supporting trading in addition to borrowing and lending allows for more functionalities than other lending platforms, which is why many margin traders seem to prefer the service. Similar to "Compound," it uses a pool-based approach with algorithmically determined variable interest rates. It has lower collateral requirements (125% initial, 115% minimum) and borrowing is limited to 28 days. Tokens supported as collateral are currently: DAI, ETH, and USDC.

Nexo is a smart contract–based lending platform that offers instant loans in over 45 fiat currencies. Anyone can collatoralize their existing tokens (asset tokens, payment tokens) in a smart contract and immediately borrow. It comes with an off-ramping service that delivers the money to your bank account at a fixed interest rate. The loan can be paid back any time against release of the tokens.

Other examples for decentralized lending systems are "Aave," "Bloqboard," "BlockFi," "Cred," "Colendi," "Curve," "ETHLend," "EOS REX, "Lendoit," "NUO," "SALT," "Iearn," "InstaDapp," "Uniswap," "Crypto.com," "Nexo," "INLOCK," "ICO-

NOMI," "CoinLoan," "Nuo Network," "LendaBit," "Bitbond," "BTCpop," "Helio Lending," "Lendingblock," "xCoins," and "Genesis Capital," who all offer various degrees of decentralization and functionalities.

Flash Attacks

Flash attacks refer to capital-intensive attack vectors on decentralized financial services enabled by flash loans. The first flash attacks occurred in 2020 on "bZx," a decentralized lending service. An anonymous person or group of people without any funds instantaneously borrowed hundreds of thousands of USD with ETH, exploiting a series of vulnerable on-chain protocols that had not been stress tested before within a single ethereum transaction. This happened in spite of prior warnings from different people within the crypto community. Months before, an anonymous hacker, SamCZSun,[65] exposed the possibility that flash loans could be used to manipulate data feeds about asset prices (oracles). Taylor Monahan, the founder of Mycrypto.com, had also pointed out vulnerabilities in public tweets.[66] Even though bZx claimed to have fixed the problem, flash loans were used to drain around 954,000 USD total in two attacks within four days: once on February 14, 2020 (350,000 USD), and the second time during a copycat attack with a few modifications on February 18, 2020 (600,000 USD). The attacker(s) took advantage of these oracle vulnerabilities and a bug within the bZx protocol's code to secure the payout.

In a DeFi setup, smart contracts must have information about the value of the collateral token at all times. This data is collected from the outside oracles provided by, for example, token exchanges. However, as opposed to traditional financial markets, where stock prices are traded on one particular stock exchange only, and a stock's price has one reliable source, tokens can be traded on various exchanges, and very often have highly volatile price spreads across and within exchanges. This spread across different token exchanges creates arbitrage opportunities. One could, therefore, profit by borrowing tokens at a low price, then selling at a higher price before repaying the loan. This whole process can be performed within the same transaction, on-chain, since most DeFi services, including many decentralized exchanges, run on the Ethereum network.

Flash loan borrowers can leverage almost unlimited amounts of funds to profit from arbitrage possibilities by coding all the steps into the same smart contract, which is how the flash attacks on "bZx" were conducted. The attacker(s) used

[65] https://samczsun.com/taking-undercollateralized-loans-for-fun-and-for-profit/
[66] https://twitter.com/tayvano_/status/1229708599867232256

the borrowed tokens of the flash loan to manipulate the market price of an ERC-20 token backed by BTC on a decentralized exchange with little market depth, pumping the price to 109.8 from the original 38, using a chain of transactions and also exploiting other loopholes in the code, and repaying the flash loan with a 350,000 USD and later 600,000 USD profit. In the current financial industry, such market manipulation can only be conducted by individuals or institutions with many assets. In a way, flash loans democratize market manipulation. However, while you don't need any assets, you do need a market know-how. The recent exploits showed how markets with low liquidity and smart contracts are prone to attacks, and that flash loans in combination with smart contracts that have unintentional loopholes and/or unreliable data feeds can be exploited.

There is a discussion regarding whether to refer to these incidents as "attacks," "hacks," or "exploits" and is reminiscent of the discussions back in 2016 around TheDAO incident. The attacks demonstrate that the DeFi community has not yet developed attack-resistant mechanisms for a sustainable DeFi architecture. Smart contract code needs to be audited, including attack surfaces that can result from oracles. Reliable data feeds are well known architectural issues in smart contracts, so the bZx flash attack was evitable. Furthermore, liquidity of token markets is essential for efficient pricing mechanisms.

While P2P lending protocols create exciting new possibilities, the scene is still nascent. At the time of writing this book, decentralized lending services cannot compete with legacy financial systems: (i) many services are not fully decentralized yet, (ii) missing regulation, and (iii) not stress tested processes, which make smart contract exploits possible, and have (iv) limited usability and unintuitive user experience (control of their own private key), (v) low liquidity of decentralized exchanges, and (vi) many DeFi products are still over-collateralized as a result of missing credit scoring or shared collateral. These are just some of the many challenges ahead.

Chapter Summary

- *Smart contract–based execution of credit and lending services have lower operational costs than legacy financial services, as compliance verification could be executed on the fly. In a fully decentralized setup, P2P financial services only require a crypto-wallet, without complex identification systems. They allow for more control, security, and inclusion.*

- *Decentralized lending services use smart contracts to create two-sided markets for a P2P credit and lending system. Any non-bankable asset such as commodities, securities, real estate, artworks, or SME shares could, in theory, be tokenized and collateralized, which could lead to a convergence of financial markets and the real economy. Commodities, national currencies, and securities are already being tokenized and can be traded on markets today, while tokenized real estate, art, and SME shares are still in their early stages of conceptualization.*

- *The integrations of such tokenized non-bankable assets with lending and borrowing schemes would allow for instant transactions, which surpasses the possibilities of the legacy systems we have today. Any transferable tokens representing an asset could be used as collateral for open decentralized lending solutions, which could change the dynamics of our global economic system.*

- *P2P lending could easily be brokered by a smart contract. Dormant and previously non-bankable assets from around the world can now be tokenized to create a liquid P2P lending market. Anyone can earn passive income relatively risk free on their token holdings through interest paid by the borrowers. On the other hand, lower operational costs could also make loans more affordable for a wider array of people and institutions.*

- *P2P borrowing allows for the borrowing of funds against a collateral of tokens you own, potentially paying lower interest rates than in the current financial system. Previously non-bankable assets, such as commodities, securities, art, or real estate, can be tokenized and leveraged against (i) fiat money or other (ii) transferable crypto-tokens. Borrowers can lock up tokens they own as collateral in a smart contract. This collateral serves as a guarantee that the lenders will be repaid.*

- *Since most tokens have volatile prices, decentralized lending applications only let you borrow a certain percentage of the value of your collateral. If the market price of the collateral begins to drop, the smart contract is programmed to sell collateral tokens at a pre-defined spot price or a market auction to mitigate counterparty risk of the lender.*

- *Flash Loans Flash loans are a specific type of P2P loan that is valid within one transaction and must be repaid by the end of that transaction. The lender can offer loans at zero-risk and the borrower can get any amount of tokens, without a collateral, provided the borrower can return all tokens borrowed within the same transaction. A series of smart contract operations can be programmed in a way that either all occur, or nothing occurs.*

- *Flash Attacks Flash attacks refer to capital-intensive attack vectors on decentralized financial services enabled by flash loans. Flash loan borrowers can leverage almost unlimited amounts of funds to profit from arbitrage possibilities by coding all the steps into the same smart contract, and profit by borrowing tokens at a low price, then selling at a higher price before repaying the loan. This whole process can be performed within the same transaction, on-chain.*

- In the current financial industry, such market manipulation can only be conducted by individuals or institutions with many assets. In a way, flash loans democratize market manipulation.

Chapter References & Further Reading

- Asolo, Bisade: „What is Uniswap? A Detailed Beginner's Guide," MyCryptopedia, March 28 2019, https://www.mycryptopedia.com/what-is-uniswap-a-detailed-beginners-guide/

- Chandler, Simon: "DeFi and Credit on the Blockchain: Why Loans Are Better When They're Decentralized," May 25, 2019, retrieved from: https://cointelegraph.com/news/defi-and-credit-on-the-blockchain-why-loans-are-better-when-theyre-decentralized

- Curran, Brian: "What is DeFi? Understanding The Decentralized Finance Landscape," Oct 24, 2019, retrieved from: https://blockonomi.com/what-is-decentralized-finance-defi/

- Juliano, Antonio: "Decentralized Lending: An Overview," May 21, 2019, retrieved from: https://medium.com/dydxderivatives/decentralized-lending-an-overview-1e00fdc2d3ee

- Foxley, William: "Everything You Ever Wanted to Know About the DeFi 'Flash Loan' Attack," Feb 19, 2020, https://www.coindesk.com/everything-you-ever-wanted-to-know-about-the-defi-flash-loan-attack

- Kistner, Kyle J.: "Post-Mortem," Feb 17 2020, retrieved from: https://bzx.network/blog/postmortem-ethdenver

- Kohli, Kerman: "How Decentralised is bZx? Some alarming conclusions about a protocol that has over $15m USD locked up,", Defi weekly, retrieved from: https://defiweekly.substack.com/p/how-decentralised-is-bzx

- Kohli, Kerman: "Announcing DeFi Audits & The Holistic bZx Post-Mortem)," Feb 20, 2020, retrieved from: https://defiweekly.substack.com/p/announcing-defi-audits-and-the-holistic

- Koksal, Ilker: "The Shift Toward Decentralized Finance: Why Are Financial Firms Turning To Crypto?" Enterprise Tech, Sep 29, 2019, retrieved from: https://www.forbes.com/sites/ilkerkoksal/2019/09/29/the-shift-toward-decentralized-finance-why-are-financial-firms-turning-to-crypto/#56da02636392

- Lau, Darren; Lau, Daryl, Teh Sze Jin, Kho, Kristian; Azmi, Erina; Lee, TM; Ong, Bobby: "How to DeFi," 1st Edition, March 2020, CoinGecko.

- Monahan, Taylor: Twitter feed, @tayvano, Feb 18. 2020, retrieved from: https://twitter.com/tayvano_/status/1229708599867232256

- N.N.: „A Beginner's Guide to Decentralized Finance (DeFi)," Coinbase Blog, Jan 6 2020, https://blog.coinbase.com/a-beginners-guide-to-decentralized-finance-defi-574c68ff43c4

- Qin, Kaihua; Zhou, Liyi;Livshits, Benjamin; Gervais, Arthur: "Attacking the DeFi Ecosystem with Flash Loans for Fun and Profit," submitted on 8 Mar 2020 (v1), last revised 11 Mar 2020 (this version, v2), retrieved from: https://arxiv.org/abs/2003.03810

- Qureshi, Haseeb: "The DeFi 'Flash Loan' Attack That Changed Everything," Feb 27, 2020, retrieved from: https://www.coindesk.com/the-defi-flash-loan-attack-that-changed-everything

- Redman,Jamie:"Understanding Defi Flash Loans: Complex Attacks, Inflation and Composable Systems," Feb 22, 2020, https://news.bitcoin.com/defi-flash-loans/

- Sandner, Philipp "Decentralized Finance (DeFi): What Do You Need To Know?", Dec 9, 2019, retrieved from: https://medium.com/@philippsandner/decentralized-finance-defi-what-do-you-need-to-know-9cd5e8c2a48

- samczsun: „ Taking undercollateralized loans for fun and for profit", Sept 30 2019, retrieved from: https://samczsun.com/taking-undercollateralized-loans-for-fun-and-for-profit/

- Wolff, Max: "Introducing Marble, A Smart Contract Bank" Jul 16, 2018, retrieved from: https://medium.com/marbleorg/introducing-marble-a-smart-contract-bank-c9c438a12890

- Zafar, Taha: „Uniswap v2 Launch Targeted For Q2 2020, Team Announces" On April 5 2020, https://cryptoticker.io/en/uniswap-v2-launch/

- Blockboard: https://github.com/bloqboard/bloqboard-lending-wallet

- *BlockFi: https://blockfi.com/*
- *bZx:https://bzx.network/*
- *Cred: https://mycred.io/*
- *Colendi: https://www.colendi.com/*
- *Compound: https://compound.finance/*
- *Curve: https://www.curve.fi/*
- *Dharma: https://www.dharma.io/*
- *Dydx: https://dydx.exchange/*
- *ETHLend: https://ethlend.io/*
- *EOS REX: https://eosrex.io/*
- *Iearn: https://iearn.finance/*
- *InstaDapp: https://instadapp.io/*
- *Lendoit: https://lendoit.com/*
- *MakerDAO: https://makerdao.com/*
- *Nexo: https://nexo.io*
- *Nuo: https://www.nuo.network/*
- *Salt: https://saltlending.com/*
- *Uniswap: https://uniswap.io/*

Token Sales - ICOs, ITOs, IEOs, STOs

In a token sale, smart contracts are used to issue cryptographic tokens in exchange for existing tokens entirely P2P. As opposed to native blockchain tokens that are minted upon successful mining of a block (Proof-of-Work), for individual contributions to the network to keep it safe, token sales introduced a static mechanism for issuing tokens against a direct financial fee, often even before the project is operational.

Token sales allow the issuance of cryptographic tokens in exchange for existing tokens, entirely P2P. They became popular with the advent of the Ethereum network. Anyone can issue and sell tokens with a smart contract. These first token sales were referred to as Initial Coin Offerings (ICOs), but as the term "token" became more mainstream, token offerings or ITOs (Initial Token Offerings), and in the specific cases of securities, STOs (Security Token Offering), became the term of the hour. The main idea of those token sales was to fund new projects by pre-selling tokens to supporters. These tokens would typically be exchanged for BTC and ETH, as both tokens offer high market liquidity and are easier to exchange for fiat currencies. Unlike highly regulated Initial Public Offerings (IPOs), many of the early ICOs were conducted without lawyers, financial intermediaries, or regulatory approval, and therefore seemed more similar to crowdfunding. Early supporters were often crypto enthusiasts rather than professional investors. Over time, professional investors became interested in these token sales for the high returns on investments that were possible in the bull markets of 2015 to 2017.

Before launching a token sale, developers would present a so-called white paper describing the technical specifications of a project. However, as opposed to the Bitcoin white paper, which described a technological solution, many white papers of recent token sales would often resemble business plans and often lack technical or economic specification. Early token sales were often unclear about the type and role of the token, which often made it hard for an investor or contributor to identify whether they resembled crowdfunding or crowd-investing vehicles. As opposed to crowdfunding, where the investment is considered to be a donation, or a pre-buy of a product, early token sales gave supporters the possibility of a return on their investment. Early token sales often seemed to be a mix between a donation, investment, or risk capital. As regulators became more aware of token sales, the definitions also became more stringent. Offering a possible return on an investment, especially if the token could resemble a security, would be an indicator that the token might fall under the regulatory authority of securities commissions (security tokens). Network tokens that allow for use of service within a network mostly do not. Legislators worldwide are still catching up to understand the different types of tokens, and derive necessary regulations.

It is important to point out that the Bitcoin blockchain never had a token sale, and that Bitcoin tokens are continuously minted each time a block of transactions is created (read more: Part 1 - Bitcoin, Blockchain, & other DLTs, Part 4 - Purpose-Driven Tokens). As opposed to native blockchain tokens that are issued upon Proof-of-Work, and incentivize individual contributions to the network to keep it safe, token sales introduced a static mechanism for issuing tokens against a direct financial fee, before the project becomes operational. Tokens would be created only once, before the launch of the project, and issued to investors. In such a setup, a certain portion of the token supply, or the entire token supply, is released before the launch of a project, in many cases even before any code is written.

History of Token Sales

The first token sale was conducted in 2013, when the "Mastercoin" project issued newly minted Mastercoin tokens against the payment of Bitcoin tokens. The sale happened entirely P2P, raising around 500,000 USD worth of BTC for the Mastercoin project. The success of this fundraising campaign inspired other projects that followed to use the Bitcoin blockchain for P2P crowdfunding purposes. In 2014, the Ethereum project conducted a token sale that lasted forty-two days and raised around 18 million USD worth of BTC, breaking all crowdfunding records at the time. This initial crowdfunding money was used to develop the Ethereum white paper into an operational blockchain network. Once operational, the Ethereum network allowed the creation of a decentralized application for any type of P2P value exchange, using a smart contract with just a few lines of code. This smart contract functionality later became popular among other developers and entrepreneurs looking to fundraise money for their projects. Ethereum smart contracts simplified the process of issuing and trading newly issued tokens for other tokens, thereby sparking a series of record-breaking token sales conducted in 2016 and 2017.

"TheDAO" was an example of one of the earliest token sales conducted on the Ethereum blockchain. Resulting in the biggest token sale at its time, TheDAO collected an equivalent of 150 million USD in Ether within a four-week time period. Everybody willing to invest was guaranteed a proportional share of the future revenues of that decentralized investment fund. However, TheDAO experiment ended prematurely with a spectacular and highly controversial draining of funds, and a subsequent hard fork of the Ethereum network (read more: Part 2 - Institutional Economics of DAOs). The scope of the fundraising success, paired with the dramatic events and controversial hard fork, brought a lot of attention to this new type of fundraising vehicle in international mainstream media and inspired many other projects to raise funds with a token sale. In the ICO boom of 2016 to 2017, more than 800 token sales were conducted, raising a total of about 20 billion in USD. Many of them were oversubscribed, which means that it's likely much more money could have been raised.

Most of the earlier token sales had experienced engineers fundraising for research and development of alternative blockchain protocols. As token sales became known to a wider public, they also became a fundraising vehicle for any type of project, many of which are not even related to blockchains or the Web3. Many of these newer token sales launched without any serious business plan, merely marketing a simple idea without any proof of expertise or development. Often, the role and function of the token was unclear, giving the impression that a token was merely issued for fundraising purposes on a simple marketing promise. Especially in the bull market of 2016 and 2017, white papers would throw around marketing buzzwords, lacking technical and economic specifications of how a goal should be achieved, and what the exact function of the token would be. At best, they would lay out project specifics like a timeline for the project, budget, specified token distribution, token supply, and a promise to deliver a piece of software at a future date.

After a two-year rally and token-sale boom, the market sentiment started to change in 2018. Most tokens ended up having a much lower valuation than the total money raised, often just a few weeks or months after successful fundraising. At some point, many tokens only had value if investors could get in early and buy at a discount, just to sell right after the public token sale ended and at a higher price, hoping that someone else would buy their tokens for more than they paid, which often was the case. In finance and economics, this phenomenon is referred to as "greater fool theory." So-called pump-and-dump tactics proliferated, where coordinated groups manipulated prices on mostly illiquid tokens. Applying coordinated buying action, artificial demand for the token drives prices up quickly, to make it appear as the new rising star to outsiders. As they were trying to profit from this sudden price hike, the insiders of the group would quickly sell their tokens before prices fell. While such schemes are illegal in most jurisdictions, persecution was difficult as identities were easier to obfuscate, at least back then.

P2P Token Sales

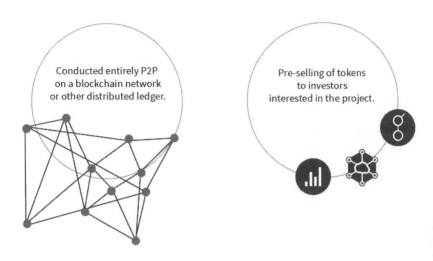

Conducted entirely P2P on a blockchain network or other distributed ledger.

Pre-selling of tokens to investors interested in the project.

ICO, ITO , STO and IEOs have become the state-of-the-art crowd-funding / crowd-investing method for blockchain ventures.

Comparison of Fundraising Methods

	Web 2	Web 3
Idea	Business Plan	Whitepaper
Communication	Elevator Pitch & Personal Intro	Website, Slack, Reddit, Twitter, etc.
Investors	Institutions (Banks & VCs)	Everyone (ICO, ITO, IEO, STO)

Only a third of tokens released in 2017 were listed on any exchange. Unless a token gets listed on an exchange, it will hardly have any market value, as the investment in the token will be hard to liquidate. Listing tokens on an exchange thus became a bottleneck for many projects conducting token sales, since exchanges had a hard time keeping up with running due diligence on applications of potential new tokens that wanted to be listed. As a result, the listing fees became competitively high. Since exchanges don't tend to disclose their fees, one can only rely on the information given out by individuals, which disclosed that listing fees range from 6000 EUR to 2.5 million EUR.

The overwhelming number of token sales combined with the rise of failed projects and intentional scams made individual investors more critical. The level of scrutiny rose with time, especially as institutional investors entered the crypto-market. Token sales subsequently shifted from public token sales to a pre-sale of tokens that was limited to a small number of wealthy investors before the launch of a public sale. Over time, the increase of private pre-sales outgrew the public token sale process.

As investors became more critical and regulators started to be more vigilant, token prices declined. According to some statistics, more than 70 percent of projects turned out to be intentional or unintentional scams that could not or would not allocate their received funds as promised. A total of 7 percent failed or got abandoned before trading. Only 15 percent of the projects were publicly listed at all. In 2017, out of over seven hundred token sales, over 15 percent of them failed at funding, 40 percent got funding but then failed, and another 14 percent got funding but slowly faded into obscurity. In spite of successful fundraising, many projects are not generating any economic results, with negative ROIs for the token investors. While by the end of 2017 many tokens were overpriced, the market seems to have flushed out many non-viable projects.

Regardless of current market sentiments, token sales have become a popular fundraising and investment vehicle. It is estimated that in 2016, token sales raised over 600 million USD. Numbers from 2017 are estimated around 7 billion USD. For 2018, estimates range from 13 billion to 25 billion, with some spectacular token sales raising over a billion alone, like Telegram (1.7 billion USD)[67] or EOS (4.1 billion USD),[68] mostly based on a simple promise and often no product at all.[69] Comparing

---

[67] *Telegram canceled the public sale of its token after raising over 1.7 billion USD in a private pre-sale, which usually allows VCs and larger investors to buy tokens at lower prices. It is unclear whether they raised enough already or whether regulatory issues forced them to abandon a public sale. Reports claim that fewer than 200 investors funded the whole sum.*

[68] *The EOS token sale lasted a whole year (June 2017 to June 2018). Their subsequent mainnet on launch had some issues, and couldn't go live for at least two weeks, with issues recurring again later.*

[69] *The statistics vary due to a lack of reporting standards, and the fact that a growing portion of tokens are offered in a pre-sale to a select number of often undisclosed investors.*

History of Token Sales

Mastercoin
$500,000 - July 2013

Maidsafe
$7,000,000 - April 2014

Ethereum
$18,000,000 - July 2014

TheDAO
$150,000,000 - April 2016

Waves
$16,000,000 - June 2016

Qtum
$15,500,000 - March 2017

Gnosis
$13,000,000 - April 2017
(total market cap: 312 million, only 4.17% of total tokens sold)

Status
$100,000,000 - June 2017

Bancor
$156,000,000 - June 2017

Tezos
$232,000,000 - July 2017

EOS
$4.2 billion - July 2017

Telegram
$1.7 billion - 2018
(private sale only, canceled their public sale)

this data with traditional forms of fundraising, we can see that global crowdfunding volume in 2015 was around 34 billion USD and is projected to grow to 100 billion USD by 2025. Global VC funding is also on the rise, with currently over 250 billion per year.

As the markets consolidated and regulators caught up, token sales started differentiating between the types of tokens they issued. Security token offerings (STOs) are token offerings that issue tokens that are classified as securities. Security tokens are an exciting new token class that offer embedded business logic that is compliant with regulatory requirements such as Know Your Customer (KYC) and Anti-Money Laundering (AML). The ability to easily fractionalize the ownership of a security token allows for new levels of fractional security investments, which will allow novel and more personalized asset types and derivatives. Any retail investors could hold a portfolio of quality investments, which until now have only been accessible to private equity firms. Regulatory bodies of many countries have already made statements or passed regulations, and many more countries are following. Furthermore, a range of service providers specialized in security tokens is emerging, from lawyers to investment advisers, insurers, and custodians. Explicit regulation of security tokens can provide more certainty not only for investors (investor protection) but also for entrepreneurs, who for a long time had to deal with frozen bank accounts and fear of litigation, due to the uncertainty of whether or not their project or token violated some kind of regulation (read more: Part 4 - Asset Tokens & Fractional Ownership).

Types of Token Sales

In the early days of token sales, due to lack of explicit regulation, many developers assumed that they had total freedom on how to conduct those token sales. Different approaches were experimented with. The most distinguishing factor of which was the price curve of the token throughout the different stages of the sale: (i) price increase; (ii) price decrease; (iii) fixed price; and (iv) undetermined price. Token sales can be issued at a fixed price throughout the duration of the sale. The exchange rate could also increase over the duration of the sale, so early stage investors get a better price (risk discount) than later stage investors. Other options include Dutch auctions, where the token sale starts at the highest price per token, and decreases with time. Furthermore, a token sale can issue a fixed amount of tokens, or an unlimited amount of tokens. A token sale might be conducted in a way where tokens are distributed as a percentage of total funds raised. The EOS project, for example, sold equal portions of their total token supply per day, and the total money invested per day decided the investors' allocation of that day's token portion. EOS was also one of the few projects that withdrew invested funds before the token sale was over, which raised concerns of whether they reinvested previously withdrawn funds to minimize tokens sold to outsiders.

After the end of a token sale, exchanges can start listing the tokens, thus allowing other people to trade them at a market price. To prevent market manipulation, projects might choose to set up freezing or cool-off periods. In some cases, it might be a cool-off period where tokens are frozen, or vested, which means that investors are not allowed to transfer their tokens for a certain amount of time. Cool-off periods are usually applied to big token holders (whales) who bought in at a discount to prevent them dumping their tokens; otherwise, the market price would crash.

Challenges of Token Sales

Many of the early founders of the projects that managed to raise funds through token sales were engineers, not entrepreneurs or asset managers. This lack of managerial scrutiny resulted in a high burn rate of the funds raised in a token sale. Many of the funds were raised in Bitcoin or Ether, which are subject to price fluctuation. Securing the value of these raised funds through adequate portfolio management is the job of an asset manager, not of a blockchain engineer, and many projects failed, or almost went into bankruptcy, just because of that. The Ethereum project, for example, successfully raised 18 million USD. However, as a result of a price drop in BTC in the weeks following their token sale (from 600 USD to 200 USD), the 18 million USD dropped to 6 million. Ethereum Classic development project (ETCDEV) had similar problems when their token price plummeted and left them with no funding. Steemit is another project that had to cut their team due to value loss of tokens.

On the investors' side, token holders of these newly issued tokens were very often not able to trade their tokens because of lack of liquidity and market depth. Relatively small amounts of tokens traded could lead to considerable price volatilities. Many token holders therefore had no other choice than to hold on to their tokens, sometimes for a very long period of time, as any minor sale could cause prices to fall.

For a more mature and transparent token sales market and to provide investor protection, the market will need more standardized procedures and better accountability. Furthermore, continuous token models and liquid pledging are being proposed as more innovative approaches. "Continuous token models" attempt to generate longer term funding by issuing and selling tokens continuously. Instead of having a one-time, often arbitrarily high funding round, where tokens are minted only once and never again, continuous token sales allow for continuous cash flow, reducing the risk for both entrepreneurs and investors. "Liquid Pledging" was introduced by the "Giveth" project and addresses the transparency problems of traditional fundraising and charity work. It allows both oversight and often even a say in how funds are used, enabled by real-time blockchain data.

Initial Exchange Offerings

As new token sale mechanisms and third-party service providers are entering the market, token exchanges have started to offer their platforms for fundraising purposes. Initial Exchange Offerings (IEO) are intermediary services where token issuers can raise funds by offering their token on a token exchange, instead of offering the tokens directly on their website. The token exchange provides the infrastructure, including the KYC process, and supervises the token sale. Token issuers send the tokens to the exchange, which then sells the tokens to investors in exchange for other tokens or fiat money. Issuers of tokens can reduce the organizational overheads and bureaucracy related to registering for a token sale with regulatory authorities and leverage the existing user base of the token exchange, reducing marketing efforts. Similar to ICOs or IEOs, sale parameters of the token sale can vary (pricing, distribution type, amount of tokens issued). IEOs offer a convenient way to conduct a token sale, while automatically listing the token for future trading on that exchange. This reduces the risk of never getting one's tokens listed.

Initial Exchange Offerings also provide more flexibility for investors, since they are not forced to pay with one particular token, but could potentially pay with any of the tokens they have already deposited on that exchange. IEOs mitigate the risk for investors to enter into a "gas war" and worry about transaction fees.[70] Investors also avoid going through a separate identification process, if they are already registered on the exchange. Since exchanges have a reputation to lose, they can be expected to audit the issuer, perform technical analysis, and assess the potential of a token, reducing the possibility for scammers to sell their tokens, thereby providing a certain level of investor protection. Exchanges could hereby introduce necessary standardization of the industry. Exchanges, on the other hand, benefit from conducting IEOs as an additional source of revenue. They might attract new

---

[70] *In Ethereum, transactions can range from simple „send money" to complex smart contract interactions. To reflect the difference, transactions consume Gas - a measure of computational steps. Users can't change how many computational steps are needed for an action, but they are able to decide how much they are willing to spend for these computational steps. By paying a higher or lower price per computational step, they can help miners make a decision on including the transaction in the next block. In a Gas War, several users are competing for a spot in the next block. Especially during ICOs, being included in the next block or not can make a difference in being successful in an auction. During peak times, users have paid many multiples of average transaction fees, effectively outbidding each other for miners to include their transaction as soon as possible.*

users, who sign up for the exchange in order to participate in a particular token, to become long-term users of the exchange. However, as long as token exchanges are not decentralized, IEOs also eradicate the P2P nature of early token sales.

Chapter Summary

- *Token sales allow the issuance of cryptographic tokens in exchange for existing tokens, entirely P2P. They became popular with the advent of the Ethereum network. Anyone can issue and sell tokens with a smart contract.*

- *These first token sales were referred to as Initial Coin Offerings (ICOs), but as the term "token" became more mainstream, token offerings or ITOs (Initial Token Offerings), and in the specific cases of securities, STOs (Security Token Offering), became the term of the hour.*

- *Token sales introduced a static mechanism for issuing tokens against a direct financial fee, before the project becomes operational. Tokens would be created only once, before the launch of the project, and issued to investors. In such a setup, a certain portion of the token supply, or the entire token supply, is released before the launch of a project, in many cases even before any code is written.*

- *In the early days of token sales, due to lack of explicit regulation, many developers assumed that they had total freedom on how to conduct those token sales. Different approaches were experimented with. The most distinguishing factor of which was the price curve of the token throughout the different stages of the sale: (i) price increase; (ii) price decrease; (iii) fixed price; and (iv) undetermined price.*

- *Token sales can be issued at a fixed price throughout the duration of the sale. The exchange rate could also increase over the duration of the sale, so early stage investors get a better price (risk discount) than later stage investors. Other options include Dutch auctions, where the token sale starts at the highest price per token, and decreases with time. Furthermore, a token sale can issue a fixed amount of tokens, or an unlimited amount of tokens. A token sale might be conducted in a way where tokens are distributed as a percentage of total funds raised.*

- *As new token sale mechanisms and third-party service providers are entering the market, token exchanges have started to offer their platforms for fundraising purposes. Initial Exchange Offerings (IEO) are intermediary services where token issuers can raise funds by offering their token on a token exchange, instead of offering the tokens directly on their website.*

- *In an IEO, the token exchange provides the infrastructure, including the KYC process, and supervises the token sale. Token issuers send the tokens to the exchange, which then sells the tokens to investors in exchange for other tokens or fiat money. Issuers of tokens can reduce the organizational overheads and bureaucracy related to registering for a token sale with regulatory authorities and leverage the existing user base of the token exchange, reducing marketing efforts.*

- *IEOs offer a convenient way to conduct a token sale, while automatically listing the token for future trading on that exchange. This reduces the risk of never getting one's tokens listed. Initial Exchange Offerings also provide more flexibility for investors, since they are not forced to pay with one particular token, but could potentially pay with any of the tokens they have already deposited on that exchange.*

Chapter References & Further Reading

- *Alethio: "A Retrospective of the EOS Token Sale", Oct 25, 2018:*
  https://media.consensys.net/a-retrospective-of-the-eos-token-sale-172d3437932b
- *Baker, Paddy: "ETCDev Shuts Down As Crash Destroys Company Finances The market downturn meant it could no longer remain in operation", Dec 3, 2018: https://cryptobriefing.com/etcdev-ethereum-classic/*
- *Bansal, Lalit: "Initial Exchange Offering (IEO) is the new ICO", ICO Bench, 29 Mar 2019:*
  https://icobench.com/thebench-post/260-initial-exchange-offering-ieo-is-the-new-ico
- *Biggs, John: "Steemit, a decentralized sharing system, lays off 70% of staff", Nov 28, 2018: https:// techcrunch.com/2018/11/28/Steemit-a-decentralized-sharing-system-lays-of-70-of-staff/?guccounter=2*
- *Castor, Amy: "The Ethereum ICO: Where did all the tokens go?" Dec 2018:*
  https://theblockcrypto.com/2018/12/18/the-ethereum-ico-where-did-all-the-tokens-go
- *Cremades, Alejandro: "Venture Capital Investors That Every Entrepreneur Should Be Pitching Right Now", Jul 18, 2018, https://forbes.com/sites/alejandrocremades/2018/07/18/top-10-venture-capital-investors-that-every-entrepreneur-should-be-pitching-right-now/#784eb7d1ceda*
- *Curran, Brian: "What Is an IEO? Complete Guide to Initial Exchange Offerings", April 5, 2019:*
  https://blockonomi.com/what-is-an-ieo/
- *De la Rouviere Simon: "Exploring Continuous Token Models: Towards a Million Networks of Value", Feb 9, 2017: https://media.consensys.net/exploring-continuous-token-models-towards-a-million-networks-of-value-fff153175776*
- *DeSue, Tedra: "Going Dutch Leaves Gnosis ICO Investors Unhappy", August 23, 2017:*
  https://cryptovest.com/reviews/gnosis-leaves-investors-unhappy/
- *Huang, Zheping: "How China's crackdown helped Binance become the world's largest cryptocurrency exchange", 3 Oct, 2018: https://www.scmp.com/tech/start-ups/article/2166704/how-chinas-crackdown-helped-binance-become-worlds-largest*
- *Lee, Justina: "How Much Have ICOs Raised in 2018? Depends on Who You Ask", November 5, 2018:*
  https://www.bloomberg.com/news/articles/2018-11-05/how-much-have-token-sales-raised-in-2018-depends-on-who-you-ask
- *N.N.: „Guidance on Cryptoassets" Financial Conduct Authority, UK, CP 19/3 January 2019:*
  https://www.fca.org.uk/publication/consultation/cp19-03.pdf
- *Kauflin, Jeff: "Where did the Money go?", Forbes, https://www.forbes.com/sites/jeffkauflin/2018/10/29/ where-did-the-money-go-inside-the-big-crypto-icos-of-2017/*
- *Lielacher, Alex: "The Cost to Get Listed on a Crypto Exchange", September 18, 2018:*
  https://www.bitcoinmarketjournal.com/crypto-exchange/
- *Little, W., 2017, "A Primer on Blockchains, Protocols, and Token Sales",*
  https://hackernoon.com/aprimer-on-blockchains-protocols-and-token-sales-9ebe117b5759

- *Marinoff, Nick: "Binance Says All Listing Fees Will be Disclosed and Donated to Charity", October 9, 2018: https://blockonomi.com/binance-listing-fees-charity/*

- *McIntosh, Rachel: "Pay for Play: Why Exchange's Token Listing Fees are Bad for the Industry", September 20, 2018: https://www.financemagnates.com/cryptocurrency/news/pay-for-play-why-exchanges-token-listing-fees-are-bad-for-the-industry/*

- *N.N.: UNITED STATES SECURITIES AND EXCHANGE COMMISSION Washington, D.C. 20549 FORM D Notice of Exempt Offering of Securities: https://www.sec.gov/Archi-ves/edgar/data/1729650/000095017218000060/xslFormDX01/primary_doc.xml*

- *N.N.: "Crowdfunding Statistics", www.sdfinance.undp.org/content/sdfinance/en/home/solutions/template-fiche12.html#mst-803174702-1*

- *N.N.: "Initial Coin Offerings", PWC Report, June 2018, https://cryptovalley.swiss/wp-content/uploads/20180628_PwC-S-CVA-ICO-Report_EN.pdf*

- *N.N.: "Initial coin offerings (ICOs)", EY research, December 2017, https://www.ey.com/Publication/vwLUAssets/ey-research-initial-coin-offerings-icos/$File/ey-research-initial-coin-offerings-icos.pdf*

- *N.N.: "Cryptoasset Market Coverage Initiation: Network Creation", July 11, 2018: https://research.bloomberg.com/pub/res/d28giW28tf6G7T_Wr77aU0gDgFQ*

- *N.N.: "Token Sales", Data Set, https://www.tokendata.io*

- *N.N.: "Initial Coin Offerings - ICOs", BlockchainHub, September 2017: https://blockchainhub.net/ico-initial-coin-offerings/*

- *N.N.: "ICO portfolio is down by 66% in the first half of 2018, according to EY study", Press release, 19 Oct 2018: https://www.ey.com/en_gl/news/2018/10/i-c-o-portfolio-is-down-by-sixty-six-percent-in-the-first-half-according-to-ey-study*

- *N.N.: "Security Token Offerings in Singapore", January 22, 2019: https://www.cnplaw.com/security-token-offerings-in-singapore/*

- *N.N.: "Biggest ICO Exit scam to date in Vietnam – $660 million raised and disappeared", April 12, 2018: https://decentralpost.com/2018/04/12/biggest-ico-exit-scam-to-date-in-vietnam-660-millionraised-and-disappeared/*

- *Sedgwick, Kai: "46% of Last Year's ICOs Have Failed Already", Feb 23, 2018: https://news.bitcoin.com/46-last-years-icos-failed-already/*

- *Shen, Lucinda: "The Price of Bitcoin Cratered in 2018. But Here's Why ICOs and VC Funding to Crypto Is Breaking Records", June 1, 2018: http://fortune.com/2018/06/01/bitcoin-price-ico-2018-record-billions/)*

- *Tucker, Jeffrey: "Despite What You Hear, The ICO Is Not Over", Aug 18, 2018: https://www.forbes.com/sites/jeffreytucker/2018/08/18/despite-what-you-hear-the-ico-is-not-rip/#796c27f53192*

- *Woodford, Isabel: "Surviving the crypto price-plunge: the ICO projects weathering the storm", Dec 11, 2018: https://theblockcrypto.com/2018/12/11/surviving-the-crypto-price-plunge-the-ico-projects-weathering-the-storm/*

- *Varshney, Neer "The EOS mainnet nightmare: How not to launch a blockchain network", June 8, 2018: https://thenextweb.com/hardfork/2018/06/08/eos-mainnet-nightmare/*

- *Vigna, Paul: "Telegram Messaging App Scraps Plans for Public Coin Offering", May 2, 2018: https://www.wsj.com/articles/telegram-messaging-app-scraps-plans-for-public-coin-offering-1525281933*

- *FINMA, Switzerland: https://www.finma.ch/en/*

- *SEC, USA: https://www.sec.gov/ICO*

- *MAS, Singapore: http://www.mas.gov.sg/*

PART 4

Token Use Cases

This part will deep-dive into a selection of token use cases and industries that might be disrupted as a result of tokenization. While some of the outlined use cases are already operational, many are still in a conceptual phase. To cover a range of topics, each chapter has been kept compact, describing the issues at hand on a high level. For a deep-dive, the references at the end of each chapter might be useful for further reading on each topic. The last chapter will give a practical guideline on how to design your own token system.

Asset Tokens & Fractional Ownership

Asset tokens allow the creation of a digital representative for physical assets or securities and could introduce a range of new use cases that might not have been feasible before. They are the next step in the automation of the securities and asset markets, replacing entire back offices with smart contracts.

The tokenization of an existing asset refers to the process of creating a tokenized digital twin for any physical object or financial asset. The token hereby represents the physical counterpart, collectively managed by a distributed ledger. "Asset token" is a general term that can include any assets, such as commodities, artwork, real estate, or securities. "Security tokens" are a specific type of asset tokens that are classified as securities under financial market regulations. The interpretation of what constitutes a security, however, is subject to local legislation.

From a legal perspective, tokenization of (rights to) a physical asset and other (virtual) rights seems important. Tools that aim to represent virtual assets (such as paper certificates and other digital certificates) are likely to be substituted by tokens soon; for physical assets, possession seems likely to remain the most important link. Depending on the regulatory environment and how the smart contract is set up, asset tokens may be eligible for global trading. An investor in France could easily buy equity tokens in a restaurant in Canada with a few clicks. An investor in Mexico could fund an apartment building in India. Opening up global markets adds even more liquidity and provides new opportunities for entrepreneurs and investors alike. This trend might make it feasible to buy shares of assets in foreign countries that were previously much more difficult to obtain.

Any physical good or share in a small- or medium-sized enterprise can be tokenized at a fraction of what it would cost in the client-server world and divided into representative tokens, which could be traded on an open market. In order to tokenize a real asset like an apartment, one generates a token with a smart contract, and associates a value of the real asset with that token. The ownership right in such an asset and its corresponding digital representation can be divided into parts and sold to several (co-)owners. Even if a token represents a physical asset that is not divisible, like a piece of art or real estate, the token itself is divisible. Asset markets, such as fine art or real estate, that usually have high economic buy-ins can be tokenized and fractionalized, potentially generating new use cases that were not feasible before. Instead of investing millions of Euros for an art piece, one can now buy a fraction of a painting. This allows for increased market depth and liquidity.

Tokenizing real-world assets could lead to a market capitalization of trillions of EUR, but it needs a few prerequisites: (i) online exchanges specialized in asset tokens, (ii) trusted custodians of wallets that can manage multiple assets and ideally also grant self-custodianship to the token holders, and (iii) a well-defined regulatory environment for different types of asset tokens.

The risks and ramifications of asset tokens are harder to predict than those of security tokens, and pose a challenge for investors, entrepreneurs, and regulators alike. Security tokens can be compared to the early days of the Web, when publishers started to post their content online as if it were a printed paper. At first, the Internet only provided a new distribution channel but did not change the type and format of content. It took years until the first comment sections were added to websites, where readers could interactively discuss the topics. It also took a while until publishers understood that they could add new types of content that would normally not make it into the paper or the magazine. It wasn't until the emergence of social media that the publishing industry was truly disrupted, by the introduction of more fragmented and dynamic distribution channels, when any individual could become an "influencer." Asset tokens are to financial markets what social media was to the publishing industry. They are much more likely to revolutionize our economy, and security tokens are the gateway drug to get there.

Use Case 1: Security Tokens

Security tokens provide a new form of representation, management, and distribution of existing securities. Paying out dividends could be conducted with a smart contract and on the fly, which is an upgrade for state-of-the-art financial settlement systems. From a regulator's point of view, these tokens are traditional securities that are simply represented and managed by a new technology. They are not a new product, and therefore are fairly easy to regulate. Financial conduct authorities and similar regulatory bodies worldwide have concluded that any token that might be considered a security token is subject to regulatory bodies worldwide, like the Securities and Exchange Commision (USA), FMA (Austria), Monetary Authority of Singapore (MAS), BaFin (Germany), and FCA - Financial Conduct Authority (UK), just to name a few examples.

There is no common global understanding of what constitutes a security token; regulation differs from country to country. In some jurisdictions, the term "security token" applies to any token that represents a recognized asset or investment concept, and other jurisdictions have a more narrow definition of what constitutes a security. The Securities and Exchange Commission (SEC) in the US, for example, defines a token as a security if one invests money with the idea to profit from the efforts of someone else. More specifically, a token would be considered a security if there is: (i) an investment of money; (ii) an expectation of profits; (iii) that money is held by a common enterprise; and (iv) profits are a result of third-party efforts. In contrast, the European definition of securities includes standardized assets that are transferable and negotiable on capital markets, have no instrument of payment, and are comparable to equity or debt instruments.

In the current financial system, securities and other financial products take a long time to settle. In spite of the fact that the processes have improved with the advent of computers and then the Internet, the settlement is still far from real time. Transactions can take a minimum of two work days to settle. While operational twenty-four-hour markets exist already today, they are rarely P2P. Security tokens can facilitate frictionless settlement processes, without sacrificing legal protection.[71] The smart contract replaces the intermediary and executes the settlement process between sellers and buyers, minimizing brokerage fees. Fully operational 24/7 markets could reduce settlement time to a few minutes or less.

Compliance comes inbuilt with the smart contract. The self-enforcing code is an efficient answer to a complex aspect of trading securities, where regulation can vary depending on asset type or investor type, taking into account that all stakeholders—the buyer, the seller, and the issuer—might be subject to varying jurisdiction. Today, a complex document-handling process is performed by a series of separate ledgers, where data is managed behind the walled gardens of the servers of each stakeholder involved. This document-management nightmare creates many inefficiencies and time lags. The programmable nature of tokens also makes it cheaper and easier to formalize special conditions, which could introduce more personalized asset types that were not feasible before. However, any system for

---

[71] *While there seems to be at least broad consensus on the applicability of regulatory regimes among the regulators, the situation is different with regard to many countries' civil law and thus the token holders "protection." The qualification in regulatory law seems easier, because it aims to address certain risks (protection of markets and investors) and therefore allows for a "substance over form" approach. In civil law, legal protection of securities (such as bona fide acquisition) is typically connected to either paper certificates or book entries by regulated intermediaries. Legislative amendments will be necessary to achieve legal certainty (see consultations in Liechtenstein, Switzerland, Germany).*

trading security tokens needs to incorporate a myriad of legal contracts. The implementation of security tokens is a complex techno-legal question and depends on network effects. Third-party service providers have started to provide token standards designed to allow transparent issuance of asset tokens and security tokens, including processes for KYC and AML requirements.

More and more market players are announcing services around security tokens. Some established companies have announced specialized trading platforms, including NYSE founders who are investing in relevant startups. The Swiss Exchange is also planning to build a regulated exchange for security tokens. Other players active in this field: "Bakkt," "Securitize," "OTCXN," "tZERO," "Polymath," "Neufund," "Binance" partnering with Malta Stock Exchange, "Cezex," Gibraltar Blockchain Exchange, "Templum," "Coinbase," and London Stock Exchange (Bancor).

Use Case 2: Tokenizing Real Estate

Real estate is one of the largest asset classes worldwide in terms of market capitalization, however, real estate ownership is not open to all members of society. Many low-income households can never afford to buy real estate. To receive a loan, buyers must have a positive credit score, a steady and well-paid job, or a collateral of other assets. Furthermore, the real estate market is highly fragmented and centralized. Data is managed by a series of third parties like banks, attorneys, notaries, and land registries who all use their own proprietary and costly software that, for the most part, is not interoperable. Smart contracts have the potential to facilitate rights management in the real estate industry, including the whole settlement process. Once real estate ownership is tokenized, it can be easily registered and managed on a public infrastructure and traded P2P, if it complies with regulation. The hashed data of each property could be recorded on a distributed ledger to provide a universally shared data set on all real estate–related activities, such as previous owner, repairs conducted, and amenities.

Real estate is an illiquid asset, which means that buying and selling the asset is a lengthy and bureaucratic process; ownership does not swap hands quickly. Research shows that using Web3-based land registries could minimize bureaucracy and reduce market friction and the considerable costs involved in the transfer of ownership. The tokens could be easily fractionalized, which means that real estate owners could sell off fractional shares of their apartments. While selling shares of a property is not a new concept, tokenizing real estate would be the next step in the automation process, making it more efficient to issue and sell these assets at a fraction of the costs that were needed before.

Tokens could either be issued for existing real estate or for a real estate project under development. Private homeowners could issue fractional tokens of an apartment they want to buy, which would allow them to raise funds without needing to go through a bank or take out a private loan. The token holders would be co-investors and could collect fractional rent in proportion to the amount of shares they hold. People who were previously excluded from such investments for economic reasons could now invest in only a fraction of a whole unit, which would make the market more inclusive to those who have less economic means. Rent collection is administered by the smart contract and ownership is more easily transferred. If, for example, another person buys 5 percent of the tokenized value of your apartment, proportional rent could be paid out on a monthly basis automatically by the smart contract. In the case of a sale of the apartment at a future date, fractional token holders of that apartment could get their money back, which might also be automatically managed and enforced by the smart contract.

With fractional tokens, it is important to distinguish the type of rights that are granted with the token acquired: ownership (as an investment, I can sell and monetize any time) and access right (I can access that property). Ownership rights also need to be detached from the management of that real good. The governance rules of the token will need to regulate who gets to decide on selling the apartment. In most cases, it would only be feasible to grant profit sharing rights, but not voting rights. However, there would need to be a regulation in place to specify the rights of token holders, in the case that the issuer of the tokens fails to pay rent to the fractional token holder. Details of such business cases would need to comply with regulatory standards and have a meaningful way to be executed. There is a variety of established legal options for conflict solutions in fractional ownership situations, like so-called "drag along" and "tag along" rights[72] or "Dutch auctions,"[73] which could all be modeled in a smart contract to arrive at a solution fit for the purpose of a given situation.

The current process of taking out a loan for home ownership comes with a lot of regulatory oversight and due diligence from the bank side to make sure that the person taking out the loan will also be able to pay the loan, including interest, back. If they can't, the bank is co-registered in the land titles. If the homeowner fails to pay back the loan, the bank can claim the property, sell it, and liquidate the apartment on the market to get back the credit they gave out. In the case of fractional ownership, how will such a case be managed? By trusted third parties and liquidators? Maintenance processes also need to be covered by the smart contract;

---

[72] *In a shareholders' agreement, a"drag along" clause requires minority shareholders to sell their shares, while the "tag along" clause requires majority shareholders to allow the minority to join in on a sale.*
[73] *In a Dutch auction, investors bid for the amount they are willing to buy a token. The token price is determined after all bids have been conducted, to determine the highest price at which the total offering can be sold.*

otherwise, it would be a regulatory nightmare to try and force litigation against hundreds, if not thousands, of owners of an office building who don't take care of maintenance.

While tokenizing real estate has a lot of potential, this use case comes with many practical challenges, most of which concern legal and regulatory questions, which vary from country to country, or state to state. One prerequisite for tokenizing real estate would be that the legal process of the real estate market is made Web3 compatible, from the land registry process to the general regulatory environment accepting smart contract processes. In some countries, land ownership is barely tracked at all; in most countries, the process is still predominantly paper-based, requiring a myriad of intermediaries. All involved stakeholders of the real estate market, from developers and brokers to banks, real estate funds, and facility managers, also need to be distributed-ledger compatible before such a use case can become feasible.

Tokenizing and fractionalizing real estate could also have potentially negative ramifications that would require regulatory oversight. There is much learning to incorporate from the housing market collapse in the United States that led to the financial crisis of 2008.[74] When many people do not understand what they're buying into, fractional ownership of real estate can become a dangerous investment game and result in the same "magical thinking" by uninformed investors who have little understanding of the big picture of the market dynamics when making investment decisions.

Many countries are already looking into registering land titles on some kind of distributed ledger, and many more are following. A fast-growing ecosystem of service providers offering fractional ownership solutions and other tokenized real estate services is evolving, such as "Atlant," "IHT Real Estate Protocol," "LATOKEN," "Max Property Group," "Meridio," "BitRent," "Etherty," "Caviar," "Propy," "PropertyShare," "Rentberry," "Treehouse," or "Trust."

Use Case 3: Tokenizing Art

From an investment perspective, fine art is an asset class that makes up an integral part of the investment portfolios of many high–net worth individuals.

---

[74] *The housing bubble preceding the crisis was financed with mortgage-backed securities (MBSes) and collateralized debt obligations (CDOs), which initially offered higher interest rates (i.e. better returns) than government securities, along with attractive risk ratings from rating agencies." The collapse of the housing bubble led to the devaluation of housing-related securities which were mostly unregulated. https://en.wikipedia.org/wiki/Subprime_mortgage_crisis*

However, investors with less economic means have no access to this type of asset class, as the most attractive investment objects are very expensive and the prices are dictated by auction houses and galleries that usually have very limited market participants, which all results in low market liquidity. To complicate matters further, the maintenance of fine art is expensive and conducted in bunkers, not in the living rooms of people who have invested in them. Furthermore, the buying and selling of fine art is currently accompanied by a heavy documentation process, to guarantee the authenticity and provenance of an art piece, which is a prerequisite of guaranteeing value. The current system relies on trusted third parties managing a patchwork of databases across the art supply chain, managing those digital certificates that guarantee value. The same is true for the music industry, film industry, and publishing industry when it comes to settlement of royalties for artists by publishers, music labels, film studios, or online streaming services. Royalty settlement happens with a considerable time lag of several months to sometimes years. The process is inefficient and highly intransparent. Tokenizing the art and entertainment market could, potentially, resolve many of the inefficiencies of the current systems, from fractional ownership, provenance, digital rights management, and settlement to crowdfunding. Tokens could also enable new derivative artworks. Selected examples of projects that are already involved in the tokenization of art are: "Artex," "Artory," "Ara," "ArtWook," "Audius," "BitSong," "Blockchain Art Collective," "Blockgraph," "Braid," "Custos," "Comcast," "Curio," "Cards," "Dada.nyc," "Feedbands," "Filmchain," "Livepeer," "Looklateral," "Maecenas," "Musicoin," "Plantoid," "re8tor," "RNDR," "Snark.art," "SOUNDACC," "Tatatu," "The Art Token," "Ujo," "Verisart," "VooGlue," "Vezt," "Viberate," "Vevue," and "White Rabbit."

Fractional Ownership: Low–net worth individuals, who would usually be excluded from this investment opportunity, would be able to buy a fraction of an expensive work of art. This could lead to an increased demand for art investments, potentially increasing overall art prices and the production of new types of art, democratizing and diversifying the market. The main question that arises in this context is how collective ownership of a piece of art can be managed. The artwork itself could, for example, be maintained by a custodian who has the experience to maintain an art collection, the cost of which would be borne by all of the piece's token holders. The payments would be managed and enforced by the smart contract. An early example is Andy Warhol's painting, "14 Small Electric Chairs," which was tokenized and sold on "Maecenas" in 2018. The painting was tokenized and fractionalized on the Ethereum network, the ownership certificates were managed by a smart contract and became publicly verifiable, and could thus be traded on the Maecenas platform.

Provenance: Tokenizing art could pave the way for a more transparent market, where potential investors have access to verified artworks. Assigning provenance using tokens managed by a public infrastructure could resolve the challenges of conventional systems, like corruption, counterfeiting, and hacking. The current system relies on trusted third parties managing a fragmented patchwork of databases, where these digital certificates are stored. Conversely, tokenized systems would use hashes and cryptography to publicly verify the provenance of artworks. Management of ownership transfers would be conducted by smart contracts, at drastically lower costs, allowing for real-time settlement.

Rights management: Smart contracts are rights management tools. Tokenization allows for more transparent and disintermediated management of intellectual property rights and subsequent real-time settlement of royalties. Artworks could easily be rented out to a gallery, musicians could collect their royalties faster, and general revenue sharing between platform providers and artists could be managed by the smart contract on the fly as a song/movie/book was streamed or downloaded. The royalty fees could be settled directly, without publishers, film studios, or streaming services acting as intermediaries, which often compensate the artists and contributors with a significant time lag. Royalties could be settled in the form of tokens that are sent to the artist in real time, based on the number of people who viewed their art, streamed their movie or audiotrack, or read their post.

Crowdfunding/investing: Tokens can also be used to crowdfund future art projects, which their investors could own as a fraction or as a whole. Anyone who contributes to the funding of an art project could receive a proportional share of the tokenized value of that project, accepting the terms laid out in a smart contract. The artist could define the smart contract in such a way that the artist maintains a share of the artwork produced, while other token holders are free to sell their tokens on the open market, or alternatively cash out, should the piece be collectively sold. In such a setup, an artist can receive funding before production, while maintaining partial ownership of the art. Tokens could also enable galleries to pre-fund purchases of artworks.

Derivative artworks: The emergence of new derivative artworks could be another application of tokenized art. One could create convoluted smart contracts that give access rights to derivative artworks with the purchase of a real painting. One could add extra features, such as linking a digital file into the physical artwork, like integrating augmented reality features into the token. For example, a video documenting the process of producing the art piece. Tokens can permanently connect physical artwork to its digital file, such that the digital file becomes part of the physical artwork and increases its value. Art tokens also open up new forms of artistic expression and value creation, like gamification, and could lead to the fusion of art, virtual reality, and gaming.

Use Case 4:
Collective Fractional Ownership

The exact business logic of a smart contract that manages fractional collective ownership depends on the use case. An office building, for example, could be collectively bought by members of a co-working space, in which case the decision making could also be collectively managed. The tokens would grant voting rights. The co-working space could be tokenized based on usage rights, where members would have a right to use a certain share of the space. Collective ownership could also be useful for many NGOs or grassroots efforts. A community of neighbors could buy and collectively operate a renewable energy–powered micro-grid, as it is more feasible for a collective of neighbors to cover the cost than for an individual. The smart contract would send monthly revenues from the excess energy produced and sold to all members of the collective, in proportion to the shares they owned (read more: Part 2 - Institutional Economics of DAOs).

Such a setup could also be attractive for taxi drivers. Many drivers lack the money to invest in their own car, and thus work for a company to provide the infrastructure, sharing their revenues or paying a fixed rent to the vehicle's owner. Fractional collective ownership tokens would allow several taxi drivers to collectively purchase a car, instead of renting it from someone, and split up the shifts as well as the costs and revenues involved with buying and maintaining the car for their rides. A smart contract could collect a portion of everyone's revenues, allocated for the expenses involved.

Collective fractional ownership tokens could furthermore manage the commons of a larger community, and settle the right of an individual to the benefits from community-owned assets. The state of Alaska in the United States and Norway have already passed their residents a share of their oil sales, either directly or in the form of wealth funds. Such a process could be tokenized to reduce settlement costs, while increasing transparency and accountability.

Chapter Summary

- Asset tokens allow the creation of a digital representative for physical assets or securities. They are the next step in the automation of the securities and asset markets, replacing entire back offices with smart contracts.

- The tokenization of an existing asset refers to the process of creating a tokenized digital twin for any physical object or financial asset. The token hereby represents the physical counterpart, collectively managed by a distributed ledger.

- "Asset token" is a general term that can include any assets, such as commodities, artwork, real estate, or securities. "Security tokens" are a specific type of asset tokens that are classified as securities under financial market regulations. The interpretation of what constitutes a security, however, is subject to local legislation.

- Security tokens provide a new form of representation, management, and distribution of existing securities. Paying out dividends could be conducted with a smart contract and on the fly, which is an upgrade for state-of-the-art financial settlement systems. From a regulator's point of view, these tokens are traditional securities that are simply represented and managed by a new technology. They are not a new product, and therefore are fairly easy to regulate.

- Asset tokens are to financial markets what social media was to the publishing industry. They are much more likely to revolutionize our economy, and security tokens are the gateway drug to get there.

- From a legal perspective, tokenization of (rights to) a physical asset and other (virtual) rights seems important. Tools that aim to represent virtual assets (such as paper certificates and other digital certificates) are likely to be substituted by tokens soon; for physical assets, possession seems likely to remain the most important link.

- Depending on the regulatory environment and how the smart contract is set up, asset tokens may be eligible for global trading. Opening up global markets adds even more liquidity and provides new opportunities for entrepreneurs and investors alike. This trend might make it feasible to buy shares of assets in foreign countries that were previously much more difficult to obtain.

- Smart contracts have the potential to facilitate rights management in the real estate industry, including the whole settlement process. Once real estate ownership is tokenized, it can be easily registered and managed on a public infrastructure and traded P2P, if it complies with regulation. The hashed data of each property could be recorded on a distributed ledger to provide a universally shared data set on all real estate–related activities, such as previous owner, repairs conducted, and amenities. Tokens could either be issued for existing real estate or for a real estate project under development.

- In order to tokenize a real asset like an apartment, one generates a token with a smart contract, and associates a value of the real asset with that token. The ownership right in such an asset and its corresponding digital representation can be divided into parts and sold to several (co-)owners. Even if a token represents a physical asset that is not divisible, like a piece of art or real estate, the token itself is divisible.

- One prerequisite for tokenizing real estate would be that the legal process of the real estate market is made Web3 compatible, from the land registry process to the general regulatory environment accepting smart contract processes.

- Tokenizing the art and entertainment market could, potentially, resolve many of the inefficiencies of the current systems, from fractional ownership, provenance, digital rights management, and settlement to crowdfunding. Tokens could also enable new derivative artworks.

- Asset markets, such as fine art or real estate, that usually have high economic buy-ins can be tokenized and fractionalized, potentially generating new use cases that were not feasible before. Instead of investing millions of Euros for an art piece, one can now buy a fraction of a painting. This allows for increased market depth and liquidity.

- Any physical good or share in a small- or medium-sized enterprise can also be tokenized at a fraction of what it would cost in the client-server world and divided into representative tokens, which could be traded on an open market.

Chapter References & Further Reading

- Acheson, Noelle: "Security Tokens vs. Tokenized Securities: It's More Than Semantics", Feb 2, 2019: https://www.coindesk.com/security-tokens-vs-tokenized-securities-its-more-than-semantics

- Aki, Jimmy: "Snark.art Launches Blockchain Laboratory for Tokenizing Artworks", Nov 22, 2018: https://bitcoinmagazine.com/articles/snarkart-launches-blockchain-laboratory-tokenizing-artworks/

- Anand, Shefali: "A Pioneer in Real Estate Blockchain Emerges in Europe Sweden's Lantmäteriet will test using blockchain technology for property sales", March 6, 2018: https://www.wsj.com/articles/a-pio-neer-in-real-estate-blockchain-emerges-in-europe-1520337601?mod=searchresults&page=1&pos=3Dubai

- Ben David, Ami: "Long the Bankers! Why Security Tokens Need Trusted Middlemen", Mar 2, 2019: https://www.coindesk.com/long-the-bankers-why-security-tokens-need-trusted-middlemen

- Campbell, Rebecca: "Andy Warhol Painting Tokenised and Sold on the Blockchain Opens Access to Art", September 6, 2018: https://coinjournal.net/andy-warhol-painting-tokenised-and-sold-on-the-blockchain-opens-access-to-art

- Dale, Brady: "Real Estate ICOs Are Moving In, But Investors Aren't Floored", Feb 13, 2018: https://www.coindesk.com/real-estate-icos-moving-investors-arent-floored

- Don, Bastiaan: "Blockchain and the Future of Real Estate", Mar 24, 2018: https://medium.com/blockimmo/blockchain-and-the-future-of-real-estate-6b1fdfb06f56

- Hamilton, David: "Blockchain Land Registry: The New Kid on the Block", January 11 2019: https://coincentral.com/blockchain-land-registry

- Khatri, Yogita: "Polymath Tests Show Security Tokens Can Be Compliant on a DEX", Feb 27, 2019: https://www.coindesk.com/polymath-tests-show-security-tokens-can-be-compliant-on-a-dex

- Lifthrasir, Ragnar: "Best Principles and Practices for Using Blockchain for Real Estate", May 4, 2017: https://medium.com/@RagnarLifthrasir/best-principles-and-practices-for-using-blockchain-for-real-estate-title-e6d9be1d481a

- Murphy, Matthew: "Three Ways Blockchain Could Transform Real Estate In 2018", Jan 12, 2018: https://www.forbes.com/sites/forbesrealestatecouncil/2018/01/12/three-ways-blockchain-could-transform- real-estate-in-2018/#1b40e5623638

- De, Nikhilesh: "2 Crypto Startups Unveil Security Token Issuance and Trading Service", Feb 19, 2019: https://www.coindesk.com/2-crypto-startups-unveil-security-token-issuance-and-trading-service

- Iakovou, Pascal: "Putting Real Estate on the blockchain Could Asia be the gateway to global acceptance?", January 14, 2019: https://www.globalrealestateexperts.com/2019/01/putting-real-estate-on-the-blockchain/

- N.N.: "HM Land Registry to explore the benefits of blockchain", Press Release, October 1 2018, https://www.gov.uk/government/news/hm-land-registry-to-explore-the-benefits-of-blockchain

- N.N.: "ICON adds a token specification to support the development of tokenized securities" ICON Foundation, Mar 8, 2019: https://medium.com/helloiconworld/icon-adds-a-token-specification-to-support-the-development-of-tokenized-securities-58b773607c13

- N.N.: "The Tokenist, Security Tokens Explained for Beginners", https://thetokenist.io/security-tokens-explained/

- N.N.: „How the Decentralization Movement Will Change the Art World" VooGlue, Feb 8, 2018 : https://medium.com/vooluenews/how-the-decentralization-movement-will-change-the-art-world-7fe79b984596

- Garriga, Marc: "Maecenas successfully tokenises first multi-million dollar artwork on the blockchain", September 6 2018: https://blog.maecenas.co/blockchain-art-auction-andy-warhol

- N.N.: "How the Decentralization Movement Will Change the Art World", VooGlue, Jan 31, 2018: https://medium.com/@vooglue/how-the-decentralization-movement-will-change-the-art-world-a1309b620a7f

- N.N.: "Global Real Estate - Trends in the world's largest asset class", HSBC Report, July 2017: https://internationalservices.hsbc.com/content/dam/hsbcis/pdf/HSBC_Global_Real_Estate_Report_July2017.pdf

- Reese, Adam: "Collective Fractional Ownership: A Proposed Blockchain Use Case", June 2, 2018: https://www.ethnews.com/collective-fractional-ownership-a-proposed-blockchain-use-case

- Sheth, Alpen: "Blockchain Ownership & Crypto Anticommons Patents, open source and beyond", Nov 12, 2018: https://blog.goodaudience.com/blockchain-ownership-e46a5cc7d921

- Voshmgir, Shermin: "Tokenizing Art & Fractional Ownership," published in "Art and Finance Report 2019," ArtTactic, Deloitte, retrieved from: https://www2.deloitte.com/content/dam/Deloitte/ch/Documents/privatemarket/deloitte-ch-private-art-and-finance-report-2019.pdf

- Zhao, Helen: "Soon you could own shares of this Brooklyn apartment building with tokens costing just a few dollars", 19 March 2018: https://www.cnbc.com/2018/03/19/own-shares-of-brooklyn-building-with-tokens-blockchain-real-estate.html

- Artex: https://artex.global/

- Artory: http://artory.com

- BitRent: https://bitrent.io/

- Etherty: http://www.etherty.com/

- Looklateral: https://www.looklateral.com/

- Maecenas: https://www.maecenas.co/

- Meridio: https://www.meridio.co/

- Trust: https://trustx.io/

- Verisart: https://verisart.com/

- VooGlue: https://vooglue.com/

Purpose-Driven Tokens

Purpose-driven tokens incentivize individual behavior to contribute to a collective goal. This collective goal might be a public good or the reduction of negative externalities to a common good. Purpose-driven tokens introduce a new form of collective value creation without traditional intermediaries. They provide an alternative to the conventional economic system, which predominantly incentivizes individual value creation in the form of private goods.

Public blockchain networks can be described with many metaphors: (i) distributed ledger, (ii) universal state machine, (iii) governance machine, (iv) accounting machine, and (v) decentralized autonomous organization. However, all these characteristics are derived from the fact that the Bitcoin network and similar distributed ledgers are first and foremost (vi) incentive machines. Proof-of-Work revolutionized collective value creation in the absence of intermediaries. It introduced a consensus mechanism to get network actors to collectively manage a distributed ledger in a truthful manner, by rewarding them with tokens. The idea of aligning incentives among a tribe of anonymous actors introduced a new type of public infrastructure that is autonomous, self-sustaining, and attack resistant (read more: Part 1 - Bitcoin, Blockchain, & other DLTs). This has since inspired many projects to build on this principle of incentivizing behavior with what I call a "purpose-driven token." With purpose, I refer to the idea of a collective goal, in addition to maximizing one's personal profit. The collective goal might be a public good (for example, a P2P payment network) or the reduction of negative externalities of a common good (for example, the reduction of CO_2 emissions).

Bitcoin's Proof-of-Work introduced a novel approach that transcends classic economic value creation. The protocol provides an operating system for a new type of economy that can transcend nation states and individual organizations. The open-source nature of the Bitcoin protocol allowed anyone to take the code, copy and modify it, and issue their own purpose-driven network. Networks like Ethereum took the idea of collective value creation to the next level by providing a public infrastructure for creating an application token with only a few lines of code. With these application tokens, we can now create completely new types of economies with a simple smart contract that runs on a public and verifiable infrastructure. These tokens are an easily programmable vehicle to model individual decision-making processes into a smart contract. Any purpose can be incentivized. Any behavior can be modeled. Examples of different types of purpose-driven tokens are:

Incentivizing consensus on the state of a network: In a Proof-of-Work network, consensus among the nodes is reached by incentivizing miners with native network tokens to use their computing power to secure the network. The aim is to reach distributed consensus among untrusted network actors on the state of the network. The reward mechanism is based on the assumption that all network actors are potentially corrupt, and therefore the process of writing transactions to the blockchain is intentionally made difficult and inefficient, making it costly for malicious actors to attack the network. Bitcoin, Ethereum, and similar networks provide a public good similar to the ones governments usually provide to their citizens: public utility networks like railroads, waterworks, or electricity grids. However, as opposed to state-controlled public goods, blockchain networks have distributed upkeep, development, and control, which are all aligned and incentivized by the native token. In the case of Bitcoin, the public good represents a P2P payment infrastructure. In the case of Ethereum, the public good represents a P2P computing infrastructure. However, Proof-of-Work is not the only incentive mechanism to achieve a universal state. Alternative consensus protocols that might be faster or more resource efficient are being researched and developed (read more: Part 1 - Bitcoin, Blockchain, & other Distributed Ledgers).

Incentivizing social media contributions: Steemit is a blockchain-based social network designed to incentivize content creation and content curation. Any user can join and contribute for free, and as such, contribute to the public good. The aim of this P2P social network is to reward those who contribute to the growth and resilience of the social media network. Steemit is an application similar to "Facebook" or "Reddit," but as opposed to Facebook or Reddit, the network is collectively governed and maintained. Contributors to the network get rewarded for contributing to the underlying blockchain infrastructure (Steem blockchain), or for uploading or curating content on the Steemit Website. How much you get paid is a function of the number of contributions, and the popularity of your contributions. Examples for other networks incentivizing contributions are "E-chat," "Akasha," "Minds," or "Golos" (read more: Part 4 - Steemit).

Incentivizing contributions to a listing: Token Curated Registries (TCRs) are a cryptoeconomic mechanism designed to incentivize the collective curation of public lists or content feeds in a social network. The collective goal is a useful and high-quality list. Tokens are used to provide an economic incentive to curate the ranking of information in such a list. The mechanism of a TCR aims to align token holder incentives in order to produce lists that are valuable to consumers and provide a reliable signal of quality on something a user cannot directly observe. Each list has its own native token (read more: Part 4 - TCRs).

Incentivizing CO_2 emission reduction: Cryptographic tokens issued by a smart contract can also be used to incentivize individuals and corporations to act in a sustainable manner. In such a setup, individuals and organizations who can prove that they reduced CO_2 emissions can be rewarded with a token that is created (minted) upon such proof. Depending on the design of the token, the CO_2 rewards could be exchanged for some other services provided by the organization issuing these tokens, and can vary greatly from project to project. Tokens might be tied to the identity of a user (non-fungible), or they might be designed to be tradable (transferable). They might be designed to expire after a while, or have unlimited durability. "Vienna Kultur-Token," "Sweatcoin," or "Changers" incentivize riding a bike, walking, or using public transportation instead of using a car. Other projects incentivize the production or consumption of renewable energies such as "Solar Coin," "Electric Chain," and "Sun Exchange." Alternatively, people could be incentivized with a token every time they prove that they have used less energy by using energy-efficient devices, or turning the lights off, as in the case of "Energi Mine" or "Electron." One could also be incentivized for planting trees (Proof-of-Tree-Planted), or cleaning a beach (Proof-of-Bottles-Recycled), reduction of food waste, and many more. Some examples of which are: "Plastic Bank," "Earth Dollar," "Bit Seeds," "Eco Coin," "Earth Token," and "Recycle To Coi."

Purpose-driven tokens provide an alternative to conventional economic systems, which predominantly incentivize individual value creation: private actors to extract rent from nature or from the workforce, and transform this into products, often externalizing costs to society, while internalizing (and maximizing) private profits. However, this new and collective value creation phenomena that Bitcoin introduced will likely need much more research and development, and a long phase of trial and error, before we can better understand the potential of incentivizing contributions to a public good. Operational use cases are still limited.

The "monetary policy" of purpose-driven tokens can be regulated by a smart contract governing the issuance and rights management of these tokens. These tokens can be fungible (tradable for other tokens of the same kind) or non-fungible (identity-based reputation tokens). CO_2 tokens, for example, could be designed to incentivize only the person who earned the tokens (non-transferable). Tokens could also come with an inbuilt expiry date. Bitcoin and other blockchain protocol tokens have been designed to be transferable and thus tradable. Tokens can be programmed to have limited transferability so they can only be exchanged for products and services within the community, therefore never leaving the internal system and being exchanged for fiat money, but still useful in the internal economy of a network (community currency).

The study of economics, public choice theory, theory of public goods, and behavioral sciences will be essential for a better understanding, and as a result, also a better design and engineering process of purpose-driven tokens (read more: Part 4 - How to Design a Token System).

Public Goods & the Tragedy of the Commons

In economics, the term "public goods" refers to goods that any individual can use without paying for them (non-excludable, or permissionless), and where use by one individual does not reduce availability to others (non-rivalrous, or un-limited). Public goods that satisfy both conditions only to a certain extent are referred to as impure public goods. Public goods can be provided by a government, or be available in nature. Global public goods have no geographical restrictions, and are globally available. Examples thereof are: knowledge, the Internet, and certain natural resources. The Bitcoin payment network could be seen as a new form of tech-driven public good, albeit an impure one. Upkeep and maintenance of the network are collective and permissionless. Usage of the network is permissionless and non-rivalrous, but only as long as capacity limits are not reached. In their current form, public blockchain networks don't scale well and can be considered as rival-rous when the network becomes clogged. P2P social networks and Token Curated Registries are also tech-driven public goods.

Public goods tend to be subject to free-rider problems, where some individuals consume a public good without (sufficiently) contributing to its creation or maintenance. If a certain threshold of people and institutions decide to free-ride, the market will fail to provide a good or service for which there is a need. Open-source software is a public good that is typically subject to the free-rider problem. The Bitcoin protocol is also a good example for this free-rider problem, as only a few contribute to the code, with little or no direct incentive to do so, but many people use it. Tokenized social media networks or token curated registries also face many free-rider problems that need to be anticipated when designing the token governance mechanisms (read more: Part 4 - Steemit & Token Curated Registries).

If public goods become subject to restrictions, they become club goods or private goods. Exclusion mechanisms might be in the form of memberships, co-pyrights, patents, or paywalls. Club goods represent artificially scarce goods. Per-missioned ledgers could be seen as such club goods, where only members of the federation (club) have access to the distributed ledger and can write transactions to it (read more: Part 1 - Bitcoin, Blockchain, & other Distributed Ledgers).

Common goods are similar to public goods, as they are non-excludable (permissionless), but they are rivalrous, which means that the consumption of a good by one person excludes others from consuming it. Examples of common goods are water and air, forests, and natural resources in general. They are public but scarce, often to varying extents. If natural resources are exploited or polluted beyond their sustainable capacity, it prevents others from consuming them. "Tragedy of the commons" occurs when individuals withdraw resources for their own short-term profit, disregarding collective dynamics of individual behavior and long-term consequences to the common good. Tragedy of the commons might be avoided with regulations to limit the extraction of goods beyond a sustainable level.

While the world's fish stocks can be seen as a non-excludable resource, they are finite and diminishing because of continuous deep-sea fishing by different private actors worldwide. State-of-the-art public ledgers are on some level always rivalrous, but have more public good character, at least currently. This might change as the technology evolves. Purpose-driven tokens can be programmed to maintain or restore a common good, and could possibly resolve many tragedy-of-the-commons problems society faces today. CO_2 tokens, as previously described, could provide a mechanism for "nudging" individuals to collectively contribute to the reduction of negative externalities of a common good.

Positive & Negative Externalities

Our current economic system predominantly incentivizes individual value creation in the form of private goods. Private goods come with private property rights attached that prevent others from using the good or consuming its benefits, unless they pay for it (excludable). With physical goods, consumption by one person prevents that of another (rivalrous). The case is different for digital goods, but artificial scarcity can be created with digital rights management tools (copyright protection). A private good can be rented out to another person, granting temporary access rights. Patents also create artificial scarcity by providing temporary monopolies. They are legal mechanisms to enforce excludability of anyone else seeking to use the patented technology.

The creation of private goods often leads to "negative externalities" to common goods, like the environment. Such negative externalities are regulated by local, national, and international organizations, with laws (mostly negative incentives), taxation (negative incentives except tax break legislation), nudging (positive incentives), and privatization (market mechanisms). Externalities in economics refers to the costs or benefits that affect a person or community, who did not choose to incur that cost or benefit. "Negative externalities" are a result of activities of people and institutions that cause an indirect cost (negative effect) on other people or institutions. Pollution is an example thereof. Consuming goods with a negative CO_2 footprint is another. Manufacturing can cause air pollution, imposing health and clean-up costs on the whole society. If those costs are not internalized through government regulation, those who create the externalities will continue to do so. "Positive externalities" can arise if, for example, two neighboring farmers have positive ecological effects on each other. Incentivizing CO_2 emission reduction with a token could be another example of a positive externality. that could contribute to the wellbeing of a common good, like contributing to a better air quality of a city. Even though the collective production of public goods can result in positive externalities, it does not necessarily exclude other negative externalities. If not well designed, purpose-driven tokens can have positive and negative externalities: while Proof-of-Work is an essential mechanism for the maintenance of a public good, the act of Bitcoin mining itself is energy intense, producing negative externalities to society.

Behavioral Economics & Nudging

The current design of tokenized networks is faced with many "free-rider" and "tragedy of the commons" problems that need to be anticipated when designing the token governance mechanisms of these tokenized networks. Furthermore, most approaches of modeling of tokens are based on the assumption of rationality: all agents act egotistically and logically consistent with their preferences and beliefs, and base their decisions on full use of information. Current consensus mechanisms are based on the idea of a neoclassical economic theory and the concept of a rational economic actor—"homo economicus"—who reduces economic decision making to simple profit maximization based on an individual profit maximization and the idea of "perfect selfishness." While the idea of "perfect selfishness" and rationality assumptions might make sense in the context of blockchain protocols, as "consensus" isn't actually directly managed by humans and is almost exclusively bot activity, such rationality assumptions might not make sense for the mechanism design of human behavior toward CO_2 emission reduction, contributions to a social network, or contributions to a token-curated list.

Alternative economic theories, such as behavioral economics, are based on the assumption that individual action is more complex. Behavioral economics is a field of economics that studies the economic decision process of individuals and

271

institutions that are impacted by other factors than economic rationality. Psychological, emotional, cultural, cognitive, and social factors are also taken into account, with the conclusion that people make over 90 percent of their decisions based on mental shortcuts or "rules of thumb." Especially under pressure and in situations of high uncertainty, humans tend to rely on anecdotal evidence and stereotypes to help them understand and respond to events more quickly. It is assumed that the rationality of individuals and institutions is "bounded" by time and cognitive limitations, and that good enough solutions are preferred over perfect solutions. Behavioral economics builds on the learnings of cognitive psychology, a field of psychology that studies mental processes.

Nudging suggests building on the assumption of "bounded rationality" and suggests that individuals can be supported in their decision-making process by, for example, placing healthier food at sight-level in supermarkets to increase the chance of selection by buyers. Nudging is a concept that was developed in the 1990s and was adopted by some politicians in select countries. Behavioral economics has been applied in the context of policy making, business environments, and for modeling machine learning algorithms. Critics, however, argue that nudging equals psychological manipulation and social engineering. Purpose-driven tokens can also be used to "nudge" or "steer" individuals toward certain actions, like reducing CO_2 emissions. However, any type of governance system is steering collective action and per definition aims at social engineering. Behavioral economics and methods like nudging can therefore provide important tools when designing the token governance rules of purpose-driven tokens as a means to provide public goods.

Cognitive Psychology & Behavioral Analysis

Tokenized incentives are not a new thing and have been experimented with in psychology to condition behavior. In psychology, the term "token economy" refers to a type of behavior modification program using operant conditioning, which was described by A.E. Kazdin in 1977. In behavioral analysis, the term "operant conditioning" refers to a learning process through which behavior is modified by reinforcement or punishment. It studies the relationship between behavior and external stimulus, or events that influence behavior. Nudging can be seen as a collective behavioral conditioning tool that was derived from disciplines like behavioral analysis and operant conditioning. Kazdin was also critical of controlling human behavior, attitude, and thought, and pointed out the ethical implications that could lead to totalitarian control. While he describes "behavioral technology" as ethically neutral, he states that the governance process, deciding the purposes and how much control will interfere with individual freedoms, determines whether this system will be used or abused. Various authors before him discussed the use of behavioral principles to design society, and these concerns are similar to the concerns related to nudging theory.

In the mechanism design of purpose-driven tokens, such ethical considerations need to be made. There is much we can learn, and not only from the ethics of behavioral economics. Related disciplines like engineering and cybernetics have also developed ethical principles that can be relevant to token engineering. Business ethics as part of the philosophy of economics also deals with the philosophical, political, and ethical underpinnings of business and economics. Engineering ethics, for example, require that anything you design, especially public infrastructure, be rigorously and carefully tested to minimize risk of harm; engineering in infrastructure fields has licensing and liability for engineers who fail to practice due diligence or respect best practices. The cybernetics discipline has the concept of "second-order cybernetics," where you are aware of your interventions, which makes you part of the system you are designing or attempting to influence.

Over the past several years, the data science and AI communities have, for the most part, disregarded these principles, probably as a result of profit maximization over ethics. Ethical discourse in the business context was very often sacrificed over short-term efficiency thinking. This was a systematic problem that started with universities, like my own alma mater, eradicating business ethics from the general curriculum of studies back in the 1990s. Integrating ethical principles from engineering, cybernetics, and economics with modern AI expertise is the closest thing available to a reference case for cryptoeconomic design of purpose-driven tokens.

Behavioral Finance & Behavioral Game Theory

Behavioral finance studies why market actors are economically "irrational" and the resulting market inefficiencies of such irrational behavior, as well as how others can profit from such (predictable) irrationality. Among others, behavioral finance explains how reactions to new information affect market movements such as bubbles and crashes. Findings from behavioral finance are important aspects to consider when modeling purpose-driven tokens and DeFi market mechanisms, some of which are discussed in Part 4 - Token Curated Registries.

Behavioral game theory is a subfield of behavioral economics that analyzes the interaction of strategic decisions made by different market participants. It required the understanding of what motivates people toward their actions. Applied methods are game theory, experimental economics, and experimental psychology, which all study the paradoxes in decision making by participants in a game. It provides alternatives for traditional decision-making models, such as "regret theory," "hyperbolic discounting," and "prospect theory." For example, people might want to minimize the feeling of regret after having made a decision, and therefore might assess their options based on how much regret they might suffer due to the outcome of their strategies.

The design of purpose-driven tokens uses game theory to model human reasoning into an automated steering mechanism formalized by the protocol or smart contract, and should account for the behavioral complexities. There is, furthermore, an entire class of games in the network science literature called "network formation games," that covers everything from how academic citation and collaboration networks emerge, to Twitter graphs, etc.

As the field of cryptoeconomics and purpose-driven tokens matures, it is likely that behavioral finance and behavioral game theory will find its way into the cryptoeconomic modeling of such purpose-driven tokens. Many tokenized use cases like consensus protocols, token-curated registries (TCRs), token bonding curves, and algorithmic stable tokens were built on assumptions of rationality: all agents act egotistically, profit-maximizing, and logically consistent with their preferences and beliefs, and base their decisions on full use of information. However, as we have learned from the research in behavioral disciplines, this assumption needs to be complemented by other forms of behavior. It is, therefore, necessary to enlarge the assumptions of current cryptoeconomic primitives by taking concepts from behavioral economics, behavioral finance, behavioral game theory, and cognitive psychology, which could help develop more sophisticated cryptoeconomic mechanisms.

Mechanism Design & Token Engineering

The design of consensus protocols is related to a sub-field of economics called "mechanism design," which deals with the question of how to design a game that incentivizes everyone to contribute to a collective goal. Mechanism design theory uses economic incentives in combination with cryptography. The aim is to achieve a desired goal in a strategic setting where it is assumed that all players act rationally. It is also referred to as "reverse game theory," since it starts at the end of the game, then goes backward when designing the mechanism. Hurwicz, Maskin, and Myerson were awarded the 2007 Nobel Prize in economics for their research on Mechanism Design.

Not every token needs to be a product of cryptoeconomic mechanisms. Asset tokens such as security tokens can simply represent property rights or access rights utilizing simple smart contracts. Purpose-driven tokens, on the other hand, need purpose-oriented mechanisms. Token mechanism design, also referred to as "token engineering" is an emerging field. However, best practices beyond Proof-of-Work and Proof-of-Stake are scarce, and many of the existing use cases have considerable design flaws. Incentivizing CO_2 emission reduction with a token, for example, is not trivial and probably requires at least as much rigorous research as was needed to develop Proof-of-Work. The use case is more complex and requires data feeds from the outside world, such as hardware oracles and software oracles. The mechanism designs of most existing purpose-driven tokens fail to integrate more complex behavioral dynamics into their protocols. In order to be able to adequately address issues like the "tragedy of the commons" and "free-rider" problems, we need a much more nuanced mechanism design of these tokens.

"Token engineering" is an emerging term with a more interdisciplinary approach that was coined by Trent McConaghy in his article, "Towards a Practice of Token Engineering." He defines token engineering as the theory, practice, and tools to analyze, design, and verify tokenized ecosystems. He draws similarities between creating token mechanisms and electrical engineering, swarm robotics, operations research, software engineering, civil engineering, aerospace engineering, complex systems design, public policy design, specific economics, robotics, machine learning, and AI. All these disciplines share a heavy dependence on the mathematics of optimization and decision making (read more: Part 4 - How to Design a Token System.)

However, due to the social nature of tokenized networks, mechanism design and market design as subfields of economics and public policy need to be included in the list of relevant fields. The protocols that govern an autonomous network of actors, including their rules, agents, nodes, tokens, and governance structures, resemble nation states, not companies. One therefore needs to analyze tools that nation states use to model their agents' behavior: macroeconomics, microeconomics, and specifically behavioral economics, behavioral finance, behavioral game theory, and some heterodox schools, like institutional economics, ecological economics, and complexity economics. It will be necessary to identify existing models, approaches, and solutions, and evaluate if and how they can be adapted for the creation of useful mechanisms in the context of tokenized networks with the aim to achieve a collective goal.

Economics and mathematics, and even engineering disciplines, have already developed various models and approaches to formalize economic motives and mannerisms of rational agents, which have been and still are being used by national governments, regulators, and institutions. The question to resolve is whether and to what extent these economic models can be applied in the context of token-driven ecosystems. This can be done by (i) identifying similarities between token economics and existing scientific fields of economics, but also robotics, automation, and control engineering, which also provide methods to work despite uncertainty. There is also much to learn from Cyber Physical Systems (CPS), which control power grids that represent decentralized physical infrastructure with varying environmental conditions and decentralized strategic agent behavior on the part of the power consumers. Furthermore, by (ii) formalizing network-design and network-evaluation models for tokenized ecosystems based on existing economic and mathematical models, and by (iii) designing a bottom-up token engineering framework to enable future state-of-the-art design of ecosystems.

Creating a mechanism is an optimization problem that aims to maximize an objective function for individual actors (such as their revenue or reputation), under a set of constraints. While Ethereum and similar protocols have made it possible to create any type of token with a few lines of code, using a simple smart contract that runs on a public infrastructure, we still (i) lack archetypical building blocks and standards, also referred to as "cryptoeconomic primitives"[75]; (ii) We also lack the necessary modeling and forecasting tools to design the governance functionalities of those tokens, especially for more complex types of purpose-driven tokens that intend to auto-incentivize some kind of behavior in a network of autonomous agents; (iii) Furthermore, there are few best practices for token design. While a lot of tokens have been issued through token sales over the last few years—mostly for fundraising purposes—most of these issued tokens lack proper functionality and mechanism design. So far, there has been little overlap with the academic community studying this field and the developers of many "purpose-driven tokens." The community of token issuers will be advised to use methods and findings from mechanism design when designing purpose-driven token protocols.

---

[75] *Cryptoeconomic primitives can be defined as cryptographic tools, standards, and building blocks that allow us to build decentralized economic applications. Simpler primitives are cryptographic tokens. Higher-level primitives have a regulatory nature and include consensus mechanisms, token-curated registries, stable tokens, or prediction markets.*

Chapter Summary

- *Purpose-driven tokens incentivize individual behavior to contribute to a collective goal. This collective goal might be a public good or the reduction of negative externalities to a common good.*

- *Purpose, refers to the idea of a collective goal, in addition to maximizing one's personal profit.*

- *Web3 tokens are an easily programmable vehicle to model individual decision-making processes into a smart contract. Any purpose can be incentivized. Any behavior can be modeled. Examples of different types of purpose-driven tokens are: (i) incentivizing consensus on the state of a network; (ii) incentivizing social media contributions; (iii) incentivizing contributions to a listing; (iv) incentivize the collective curation of public lists or content feeds in a social network; or (v) incentivizing CO_2 emission reduction.*

- *Purpose-driven tokens provide an alternative to conventional economic systems, which predominantly incentivize individual value creation: private actors to extract rent from nature or from the workforce, and transform this into products, often externalizing costs to society, while internalizing (and maximizing) private profits.*

- *The study of economics, public choice theory, theory of public goods, and behavioral sciences will be essential for a better understanding, and as a result, also a better design and engineering process of purpose-driven tokens.*

- *The term "public good" refers to goods that any individual can use without paying for them (non-excludable, or permissionless), and where use by one individual does not reduce availability to others (non-rivalrous, or unlimited). Public goods that satisfy both conditions only to a certain extent are referred to as impure public goods.*

- *The Bitcoin payment network could be seen as a new form of tech-driven public good, albeit an impure one. Upkeep and maintenance of the network is collective and permissionless. Usage of the network is permissionless and non-rivalrous, but only as long as capacity limits are not reached. In their current form, public blockchain networks don't scale well and can be considered as rivalrous when the network becomes clogged.*

- *Public goods tend to be subject to free-rider problems, where some individuals consume a public good without (sufficiently) contributing to their creation or maintenance. Open-source software is a public good that is typically subject to the free-rider problems. The Bitcoin protocol is also a good example for this free-rider problem, as only a few contribute to the code, with little or no direct incentive to do so, but many people use it. Tokenized social media networks or token curated registries also face many free-rider problems that need to be anticipated when designing the token governance mechanisms.*

- *If public goods become subject to restrictions, they become club goods or private goods. Exclusion mechanisms might be in the form of memberships, copyright, patents, or pay-*

walls. Club goods represent artificially scarce goods. Permissioned ledgers could be seen as such club goods, where only members of the federation (club) have access to the distributed ledger and can write transactions to it.

- *The creation of private goods often leads to "negative externalities" to common goods, like the environment. Externalities in economics refers to the costs or benefits that affect a person or community, who did not choose to incur that cost or benefit. "Negative externalities" are a result of activities of people and institutions that cause an indirect cost (negative effect) on other people or institutions. "Positive externalities" can arise if, for example, two neighboring farmers have positive ecological effects on each other.*

- *Incentivizing CO_2 emission reduction with a token is an example of a positive externality that could contribute to the wellbeing of a common good, like the air quality of a city.*

- *Even though the collective production of public goods can result in positive externalities, it does not necessarily exclude other negative externalities. If not well designed, purpose-driven tokens can have positive and negative externalities: while Proof-of-Work is an essential mechanism for the maintenance of a public good, the act of Bitcoin mining itself is energy intense, producing negative externalities to society.*

- *The current design of tokenized networks is faced with many „free-rider" and „tragedy of the commons problems" that need to be anticipated when designing the token governance mechanisms of these tokenized networks.*

- *Current consensus mechanisms are based on the idea of a neoclassical economic theory and the concept of a rational economic actor-„homo economicus"-who reduces economic decision making to simple profit maximization based on an individual profit maximization and the idea of „perfect selfishness." While the idea of „perfect selfishness" and rationality assumptions might make sense in the context of blockchain protocols, as "consensus" isn't actually directly managed by humans and almost exclusively bot activity, such rationality assumptions might not make sense for the mechanism design of human behavior towards CO_2 emission reductions, contributions to a social network, or contributions to a token curated list.*

- *Alternative economic theories, such as behavioral economics, are based on the assumption that individual action is more complex. Behavioral economics is a field of economics that studies the economic decision process of individuals and institutions are impacted by other factors than economic rationality.*

- *Tokenized incentives are not a new thing and have been experimented with in psychology to condition behavior. In psychology the term „token economy" refers to a type of behavior modification program using „operant conditioning," a learning process through which behavior is modified by reinforcement or punishment. It studies the relationship between behavior and external stimulus or events that influence behavior.*

- *Behavioral finance studies why market actors are economically „irrational" and resulting market inefficiencies such irrational behaviour and how others can profit from such (predictable) irrationality. Findings from behavioral finance are important aspects to consider when modelling purpose-driven tokens and DeFi market mechanisms, some of which are discussed*

- *The design of purpose-driven tokens uses game theory to model human reasoning into an automated steering mechanism formalized by the protocol or smart contract and should account for the behavioural complexities. There is, furthermore, an entire class of games in the network science literature, called "network formation games" that cover everything from how academic citation and collaboration networks emerge, to Twitter graphs, etc.*

- *The design of consensus protocols is related to a sub-field of economics called „mechanism design" which deals with the question of how to design a game that incentivizes everyone to contribute to a collective goal. It is also referred to as „reverse game theory" since it starts at the end of the game, then goes backward when designing the mechanism.*

- *Not every token needs to be a product of cryptoeconomic mechanisms. Asset tokens such as security tokens can simply represent property rights or access rights utilizing simple smart contracts. Purpose-driven tokens, on the other hand, need purpose-oriented mechanisms. Token mechanisms design, also referred to as „token engineering," an emerging field.*

- *The protocols that govern an autonomous network of actors, including their rules, agents, nodes, tokens, and governance structures, resemble nation states, not companies. One therefore needs to analyze tools that nation states use to model their agents' behavior: macroeconomics, microeconomics, and specifically behavioral economics, behavioral finance, behavioral game theory, and some heterodox schools, like institutional economics, ecological economics, and complexity economics.*

Chapter References & Further Reading

- *Aggarwal, Raj: „Animal Spirits in Financial Economics: A Review of Deviations from Economic Rationality". International Review of Financial Analysis, 32 (1): 179–87, 2014*
- *Camerer, Colin: „Progress in behavioral game theory". Journal of Economic Perspectives. 11 (4): 172, 1997: http://authors.library.caltech.edu/22122/1/2138470%5B1%5D.pdf*
- *Camerer, Colin; Ho, Teck-Hua: „Violations of the betweenness axiom and nonlinearity in probability". Journal of Risk and Uncertainty. 8 (2): 167–96, 1994.*
- *Cass R. Sunstein. „NUDGING AND CHOICE ARCHITECTURE: ETHICAL CONSIDERATIONS", Law.harvard.edu, Discussion Paper No. 809, Harvard Law School Cambridge, MA 02138, 01/2015: http://www.law.harvard.edu/programs/olin_center/papers/pdf/Sunstein_809.pdf*

- Filcheck, H.A.; McNeil, C.B.: "The use of token economies in preschool classrooms: practical and philosophical concerns", Journal of Early and Intensive Behavior Intervention, 2004, 1, 94-104.7ZSo50JxWtIYGKsIHt4Jj7tA/edit#

- Finestone, Matthew: „Game Theory and Blockchain", Medium, Jan 5, 2018: https://medium.com/@matthewfinestone/game-theory-and-blockchain-db46e67933d7

- Grafstein, R.: „Rationality as Conditional Expected Utility Maximization", Political Psychology, 16 (1): 63–80, 1995

- Gigerenzer, Gerd; Selten, Reinhard: "Bounded Rationality: The Adaptive Toolbox", MIT Press, 2002

- Hallgren, M.M.; McAdams, A.K.: „A model for efficient aggregation of resources for economic public goods on the internet". The Journal of Electronic Publishing, 1, 1995

- Hess, Charlotte; Ostrom, Elinor: "Understanding Knowledge as a Commons: From Theory to Practice", Cambridge: Massachusetts Institute of Technology. pp. 12–13, 2007

- Kazdin, Alan. E.: „Behavior Modification in Applied Settings f Behavior Modification in Applied Settings", Digitized by the Internet Archive in 2018: https://archive.org/details/, originally in: The Dorsey Press Homewood, 1975

- Kazdin, Alan. E.: "The Token Economy. A review and evaluation", Plenum Press, 1977.

- Kazdin, Alan. E.: "The token economy: a decade later", Journal of Applied Behavior Analysis, 1982, 15, 431-445.

- Malkin, J.; Wildavasky, A.: „Why the traditional distinction between public and private goods should be abandoned". Journal of Theoretical Politics, 3: 355–378, 1991

- McConaghy, Trent: "Nature 2.0 The Cradle of Civilization Gets an Upgrade", Jun 6, 2018: https://blog.oceanprotocol.com/nature-2-0-27bdf8238071

- McConaghy, Trent: "Can Blockchains Go Rogue? AI Whack-A-Mole, Incentive Machines, and Life. TE Series Part I", Feb 27, 2018: https://blog.oceanprotocol.com/can-blockchains-go-rogue-5134300ce790

- McConaghy, Trent: "Towards a Practice of Token Engineering Methodology, Patterns & Tools. TE Series Part II", Mar 1, 2018: https://blog.oceanprotocol.com/towards-a-practice-of-token-engineering-b02feeeff7ca

- McFadden, Daniel: "The human side of mechanism design: a tribute to Leo Hurwicz and Jean-Jacque Laffont", Review of Economic Design, April 2009, Volume 13, Issue 1–2, pp 77–100

- Nicholson, Walter: "Intermediate Microeconomics And Its Application", 2004

- Ostrom, Elinor: "Understanding Institutional Diversity", Princeton, NJ: Princeton University Press, 2005

- Ostrom, Elinor; Walker, James; Gardner, Roy: „Covenants With and without a Sword: Self-Governance Is Possible". American Political Science Review. 86 (2): 404–17, June 1992

- Paruch, Krzysztof: "Token Engineering from an Economic Perspective", Medium, Crypto3conomics, Nov 6, 2018: https://medium.com/crypto3conomics/token-engineering-from-an-economic-perspective-b6c464f20241

- Powell, Ray:"10: Private goods, public goods and externalities", AQA AS Economics, 2013

- Shafir, E., Tversky, A.: „Thinking through uncertainty: nonconsequential reasoning and choice", Cognitive Psychology, 24 (4): 449–74, 1992

- Rice, Charles; Zargham, Michael: "On the Practice of Token Engineering, Part I: Enter the Token Engineer", BlockScience, Feb 11 2019: https://medium.com/block-science/on-the-practice-of-token-engineering-part-i-c2cc2434e727

- Sugden, Robert: „Do people really want to be nudged towards healthy lifestyles?". International Review of Economics. 64 (2): 113–123, 2017

- Thaler, Richard H., Sunstein, Cass R.: "Nudge: Improving Decisions about Health, Wealth, and Happiness", Yale University Press, 2008

- Tapson, Mark: „The Soft Totalitarianism of Nudging: The Left's new social engineering tool to steer Americans toward making the "correct" choices", August 13, 2013: https://www.frontpagemag.com/fpm/200533/soft-totalitarianism-nudging-mark-tapson

- *Thaler, Richard H., Sunstein, Cass R. and Balz, John P.: "Choice Architecture", 2010: https://papers.ssrn.com/sol3/papers.cfm?abstract_id=1583509*
- *Token Engineering Wiki: http://tokenengineering.net/*
- *Verbin, Elad: Comment on: "Towards a Practice of Token Engineering Methodology, Patterns & Tools. TE Series Part II" by McConaghy, Trent: Mar 5, 2018: https://medium.com/@elad.verbin/i-feel-the-right-kind-of-engineering-expertise-that-youre-looking-for-is-actually-public-policy-78fb28a698bb*
- *Voshmgir, Shermin: "Token Engineering Research", Medium, Crypto3conomics, Nov 6, 2018: https://medium.com/crypto3conomics/token-engineering-research-b6627add09ee*
- *Voshmgir, Shermin: "Purpose-Driven Tokens", Medium, Crypto3conomics, Apr 11, 2019: https://medium.com/crypto3conomics/purpose-driven-tokens-51334d278c32*
- *Voshmgir, Shermin: "Blockchain & Sustainability", Medium, Crypto3conomics, Aug 11, 2018: https://medium.com/crypto3conomics/blockchain-sustainability-7d1dd90e9db6*
- *Voshmgir, S.; Zargham, M.: "Foundations of Cryptoeconomic Systems," Cryptoeconomic Systems Journal, March 2020, retreived from: https://assets.pubpub.org/sy02t720/31581340240758.pdf*
- *Wei, Bai: "Mechanism Design in Cryptoeconomics", May 31, 2018: https://medium.com/secbit-media/mechanism-design-in-cryptoeconomics-6630673b79af*
- *Wikipedia contributors, „Behavioral economics," Wikipedia, The Free Encyclopedia, https://en.wikipedia.org/w/index.php?title=Behavioral_economics&oldid=939800984 (accessed Dec 1, 2018).*
- *Wikipedia contributors, „Behavioral game theory," Wikipedia, The Free Encyclopedia, https://en.wikipedia.org/w/index.php?title=Behavioral_game_theory&oldid=935922120 (accessed Dec 2, 2018).*
- *Wikipedia contributors, „Nudge theory," Wikipedia, The Free Encyclopedia, https://en.wikipedia.org/w/index.php?title=Nudge_theory&oldid=935454086 (accessed January 18, 2019).*
- *Wikipedia contributors, „Externality," Wikipedia, The Free Encyclopedia, https://en.wikipedia.org/w/index.php?title=Externality&oldid=939366287 (accessed January 18, 2019).*
- *Wikipedia contributors, „Private good," Wikipedia, The Free Encyclopedia, https://en.wikipedia.org/w/index.php?title=Private_good&oldid=937503748 (accessed January 18, 2019).*
- *Wilk, J.: „Mind, nature and the emerging science of change: An introduction to metamorphology.",in G. Cornelis; S. Smets; J. Van Bendegem, in "Einstein meets Magritte: An Interdisciplinary Reflection on Science, Nature, Art, Human Action and Society", Metadebates on science, 6, Springer Netherlands, pp. 71–87, 1999.*
- *Zlomke, K.; Zlomke, L.: "Token economy plus self-monitoring to reduce disruptive classroom behaviors", The Behavior Analyst Today, 2003, 4, 177-182. G. LeBlanc: Enhancing intrinsic motivation through the use of a token economy. Essays in Education, 2004, 11.*
- *Zargham, Michael; Zhang, Zixuan; Preciado, Victor: "A State-Space Modeling Framework for Engineering Blockchain-Enabled Economic Systems," 2018: https://static1.squarespace.com/static/5b68a4e4a-2772c2a206180a1/t/5cd470fdc830253030167665/1557426435054/book_final_1.pdf#page=5*
- *Zargham, Michael; Bulkin, Aleksandr, Nelson, J. Scott: "Raising Social Capital: Tokenizing a Customer-Driven Business An Introduction to Discount Token Economics Publication", Version 1.0, Sweetbridge: https://images.sweetbridge.org/main/WP-Sweetbridge-Discount-Tokens.pdf*
- *Zargham, Michael: "Token Engineering 101: Why Engineering is Necessary", Jul 1, 2018: https://medium.com/@michaelzargham/token-engineering-101-why-engineering-is-necessary-3bac27ccb8b7*
- *Akasha: https://akasha.world*
- *Bit Seeds: http://bitseeds.org/*
- *Changers: http://changers.com*
- *Earth Token: https://earth-token.com/*
- *Eco Coin: https://www.ecocoin.com/*
- *E-chat: https://investors.echat.io/*
- *Electric Chain: http://www.electricchain.org/*

- *Energi Mine: https://energimine.com/*
- *Electron: http://www.electron.org.uk/*
- *Earth Dollar: https://earthdollar.org/home/*
- *Golos: https://golos.io/*
- *Minds: https://www.minds.com/*
- *Plastic Bank: https://www.plasticbank.org/*
- *Recycle To Coin: https://iywto.com/things/recycle-cans/recycle-to-coin*
- *Sweatcoin: https://sweatco.in/*
- *Solar Coin: https://solarcoin.org/*
- *Sun Exchange: http://www.thesunexchange.com/*

Steemit, Hive & Reddit: Tokenized Social Networks

Steemit is a decentralized social network where contributions to the network get rewarded with network tokens. It runs on the Steem blockchain, a special-purpose blockchain that provides a public infrastructure for the decentralized social network.

Disclaimer: The governance rules of Steemit and the underlying Steem blockchain are subject to frequent protocol changes. Documentation is patchy and some facts are hard to research. In order to fully grasp the current governance rules, one has to read the current code. Some facts mentioned in the following chapters might, therefore, be out of date or inconsistent. They should nevertheless help paint a picture of the complexities of the system. At the time of writing the book, the Steemit network split in a new continuation (Hive) driven by the core community and is subject to current events. Even though the network seems to be on the decline, it nevertheless serves as a tangible use case for the exploration of best practices and worst practices for tokenizing social networks

Steemit is a decentralized application that runs on the Steem blockchain. As opposed to Web2-based social media applications, Steemit has (i) no advertisements; (ii) all data is public on the ledger, which means that no single institution owns your transaction data; and (iii) contributors to the network are rewarded with network tokens. How much you get paid is a function of the number of your contributions, and the popularity of your contributions. Steemit is permissionless, allowing any user to join for free. Sign up is either by email or phone number and manually verified by an administrator. Alternatively, one can pay a fee to create the account. Both procedures intend to create an effort/cost for account creation, in order to combat spam, bots, and name squatters.

Steemit is probably the first and longest-running decentralized application. It was conceptualized in 2015 and has been operational since 2016. At the time of writing this book, the network has over one million registered users, 25,000 posts, and

100,000 comments, and 1.4 million transactions on the Steem blockchain per day. It is therefore one of the more seasoned projects in the crypto community. Steemit went online about the same time that the Ethereum network emerged, which was before it was possible to create a decentralized application without having to create your own distributed infrastructure. From today's point of view, the Steemit protocol seems too complex and outdated. Back then, however, it was a visionary project that was ahead of its time. The project founders created their own special-purpose infrastructure (the Steem blockchain with the native token, STEEM) and their own stable token (STEEM dollar). Today, this level of complexity would not be necessary, given that anyone could build a decentralized social network on a smart contract network such as Ethereum, and use one of many publicly available stable tokens. The founder, Dan Larimer, also created "BitShares" and the "EOS" blockchain network, which both use "Graphene" as a consensus mechanism. The Steem blockchain also uses Graphene and provides an infrastructure for the Steemit social media network, as well as for other decentralized applications such as (i) "d.tube," a decentralized video platform similar to YouTube, and (ii) "d.sound," a decentralized audio streaming service similar to Spotify or Soundcloud. Both d.tube and d.sound use the Steem blockchain to enforce their smart contracts, but have less users and traffic than Steemit. Video and sound files are stored on "IPFS," a decentralized file storage protocol. While Steemit has many design flaws, it provides an insightful use case for understanding tokenized and decentralized social media applications.

Problems in Social Media Today

Over the last decade, social media has become an important part of how people communicate with their peers and consume information. With the emergence of social media, traditional media has become de-professionalized. Everyone can contribute and curate content to influence public opinion, simply by creating a social media account. Facebook, Twitter, and Reddit replaced newspapers, YouTube replaced television, and swiping and scrolling has become the new channel hopping. As these social media platforms gained traction, they transformed from an open space for free expression into an oligopoly of a few big players.

In the early years, the curation process on social media sites such as Facebook and Twitter used to be in the autonomy of the user. This autonomy was replaced by data feeds based on algorithms developed by the platform providers, and the feeds are now being injected with an increasing number of ads. Social media platforms have become the curators of our content and are in full control of our data feed. Very often, these socially engineered data feeds are programmed to retain the user on the platform as long as possible, make them addicted, and optimize advertising revenue, often giving priority to posts with more popular content and repressing fringe posts that don't get as many likes (read more: Basic Attention Token & Token Curated Registries).

While users contribute with valuable content and curation services, they have no way to directly monetize their contributions to the network. Furthermore, content that is posted on those platforms is subject to potential censorship and control by the companies that operate them, and in some countries, even by government authorities. Users can be prohibited from posting specific types of content, and user accounts can be deactivated any time. Data privacy and control is another issue of these Web2-based social media platforms. Personal information and user behavior, such as content preferences, buying patterns, sexual orientation, race, gender, or political views, are tracked and stored on the servers of the companies that provide those social media services. That data can also be passed on to other companies and institutions. While such data collection mostly serves as the basis for generating advertising revenue from targeted advertising, it has also been used for political manipulation, and could serve as a basis for character assessments and social profiling. Incidents such as the Cambridge Analytica scandal, where personal data was passed on to other institutions who subsequently used the data to manipulate voters in the 2016 US presidential election or before Brexit referendum, have eroded the trust of the general public in the social media networks.

Token Economics of Steemit

Decentralized social networks such as Steemit have (i) no data monopoly, meaning everyone has access to all transaction data, which is publicly visible on the Steem block explorer, and (ii) no advertising revenues are necessary, as the network is collectively managed by (iii) contributors who get rewarded with tokens for their contributions to the network. To find or tag content, one can use "tags and topics" that help sort content into individualized streams. As such, Steemit is much more similar to Reddit than Facebook. Users are rewarded for contributions to the network with three different types of network tokens: "Steem," "Steem Dollar," and "Steem Power."

Steem (STEEM) is the native token of the Steem blockchain. As with any native blockchain tokens, the tokens are transferable and new tokens are created every day.

Steem Power (SP) is a reputation token designed to reflect one's influence in the social network. Anyone who opens a new account receives an initial amount of SP tokes. After that, one can be rewarded for contribution to the network in SP. Alternatively, SP can be bought with Steem at a 1:1 ratio. This process is referred to as "powering up." The more SP one has, the more one's contributions to the network are rewarded. If someone with a lot of SP upvotes a post of another user, that user will get rewarded with more tokens than they would receive if another user with less SP upvoted their content. SP can be converted back into Steem, which is referred to as powering down, but the process is intentionally slowed down to thirteen weeks to keep users from selling their tokens all at once to prevent price crashes and market manipulations.

Steem Dollar (SBD) is designed as a stable token that is pegged to the US dollar in a 1:1 ratio. It can be bought on the open market or earned (fifty percent of the reward for contributions to the social media network are paid out in SBD). Once earned, these SBD tokens can be: (i) cashed out; (ii) held; or (iii) converted into Steem and then sold on the open market after a 3.5-day conversion process to avoid "arbitrage attacks." Since SBD is designed to have a stable price, SBD token holders miss out on Steem price increases. To incentivize SBD token holders to hold onto their SBD, they receive 10 percent interest per year. This interest rate is variable and can be changed in a protocol upgrade.

The Steemit network has three different types of users: (i) content creators: publish content; (ii) active users: curate content by upvoting (liking) the content, and (iii) passive users: consume content. A content creator can publish a post but will only get rewarded with tokens if and when the post is upvoted by other users (content curators). If a post performs well, a curator who upvoted this post will earn more SP than for upvoting a less popular post. Rewards are paid out from two reward pools and distributed in a mix of the different tokens, Steem Power and Steem Dollar, and this distribution is determined individually by the content creator. Rewards are only paid in the first seven days after content is posted. After that period, the post will still be online, but one will not be able to earn rewards with the post anymore. Anyone can post and upvote content, therefore contributing to the collective curation of content.

The exact amount of tokens earned is a function of the number of upvotes a post receives, and also a function of the amount of Steem Power the curators making the upvotes have. If a curator has 2,000 Steem Power and another has 20,000 Steem Power, the effects of those two upvotes will be different. To incentivize quality content, the number of upvotes a user can perform within a certain period of time is limited. To add to the complexity, if the same user decides to upvote several posts, the weight of each vote will diminish, depending on how much time passes between votes. The network recharges voting power by 20 percent a day. The idea of both mechanisms is to prevent vote spamming and incentivize quality decisions. In reality, however, in order to earn more tokens, people vote for content they expect to be popular, such as memes, and not necessarily what they would regard as quality content.

The Steemit application runs on the Steem blockchain network that uses "Delegated Proof-of-Stake" (DPoS)" as a consensus algorithm. DPoS is a variation of Proof-of-Stake where the community of token holders on the underlying blockchain network votes for 21 so-called "witnesses" to which they delegate their STEEM tokens. The witnesses verify transactions and create blocks on behalf of the token holders who delegated their tokens to them. When it comes to network performance, DPoS is much more scalable than Proof-of-Work, which is a prerequisite for a social network with thousands of transactions per second.

The Steem blockchain consistently creates new STEEM tokens, which are added to a "rewards pool" from which token holders will be rewarded according to the governance rules defined in the protocol. According to the current governance rules, 15 percent of the newly minted STEEM tokens are awarded to the people who hold SP, 75 percent go to content creators and curators, and 10 percent of the new STEEM tokens are paid to witnesses. The initial monetary policy of the STEEM token was highly inflationary in supply, almost doubling every year. Due to community pressure, the inflation rate of STEEM was adjusted to 9.5 percent per year. At the time of writing the book the inflation rate of STEEM is 9 percent, and it will decrease by 0.5 percent every year.

Criticism of Steemit

While Steemit and the underlying Steem blockchain infrastructure are a great use case for how we can redefine social networks, the economics behind the token design have a few fundamental design flaws. Furthermore, since all data on the Steem blockchain is public, anyone can create decentralized applications with this data to create useful tools for the Steemit community, such as "Catch a Whale"[76] or "Steem Market."[77]

Open Data: As opposed to Web2 social media platforms, all transaction data on the Steemit blockchain is public and transparent to everyone with simple chain-analysis. This means that anyone can inspect what happened when or who did what in the Steemit ecosystem. As such, Steemit is less like Facebook (where only your friends can see what you publish), but more like Twitter, Medium, or YouTube, where everyone can see what you did. Alternative cryptographic algorithms like

---

[76] *"Catch a Whale" is an application that tracks what large token holders (whales) have voted for.*
[77] *"Steem Market" lets users buy, sell, and rent goods with Steem.*

multiparty computation[78] or zero-knowledge proofs[79] and additional obfuscation techniques need to be implemented in the protocol to provide more privacy by design[80]. The current trend in the Web3 community to build more privacy-preserving blockchain networks seems to have inspired Steemit to develop a roadmap for obfuscating at least some of the public data.

Reputation can be bought with money: Steemit originally intended to design a social media network for quality content. However, due to the design flaws of the reputation token, there are currently many issues with incentivizing and providing quality content. While Steem Power (SP) was supposed to be a reputation token, it is based on oversimplified assumptions of how network actors behave. The token mechanisms don't take into account tragedy-of-the-commons or short-term economic thinking. Reputation tokens, in the form of Steem Power, can be bought with fiat money. Users who are willing to invest a considerable amount of money in Steem Power can, therefore, bootstrap their network power and earn more money more quickly than users who try to organically build up reputation. This rather simplistic token design is based on the assumption that those who have more tokens, a.k.a. stake in the network, are automatically incentivized to contribute to the network with the best quality content or curation activity. Furthermore, the design of the reputation token does not take into account that different users have different interests, and that individual tastes are relative. Any meaningful reputation token design probably needs to be subjectified, instead of being a universal metric for all users in the network. Over the years, these design flaws have led to a monopolization of power by a few wealthy token holders, creating large power asymmetries in the network. Whether or not it pays off economically to contribute to the network depends on current exchange rates of all tokens, and is also a function of your own SP. Recent network analysis shows that only 2 percent of posts get noteworthy returns, most of which probably do not offset the costs of production, which is largely also a result of the power asymmetries.

Power Asymmetries: There seems to be a lot of intransparency around the state of token distribution, which is odd for a blockchain-based application. Steemwhales.com and steemd.com have published distribution charts at some point in the past, but stopped operations. The current level of intransparency around this

---

[78] *Multiparty computation is a cryptographic effort that allows several servers to jointly compute an output without any single server knowing all the inputs, and can help anonymous aggregated advertising.*

[79] *Zero-knowledge proofs are cryptographic schemes that allow a party to verify a solution with as little to no information conveyed as possible. Usually, applications here are confidential transactions, and allow proving authenticity without giving up personal details. Another possible use case could be in proving applicability of ads to publishers without giving up personal data.*

[80] *Privacy by design refers to efforts undertaken when designing a system to protect privacy in all possible steps, rather than neglecting privacy and trying to find ways to implement it later.*

topic is striking, as exact numbers are hard to research, mainly as Steem Power and Steem Dollar are convertible, and lists thereof are weirdly ranked or have been abandoned. Any online request concerning this topic is answered by bots providing non-answers (check sources at the end of the chapter). The only reliable numbers are from several years ago, when the top ten token holders controlled 79.3 percent of SP, 85 percent of Steem, and 45 percent of SBD. Based on the available numbers, the median users hold an average of roughly 2,000 SP or less, while high–net worth token holders, also referred to as whales, hold 2,000,000 SP. Please note that it is unclear if rich-lists published are up to date, and that there is no distribution graph to be found. The available lists (see links in references) have little documentation. It is safe to assume that this power divide has widened in the last two years, based on the current incentive design that favors large token holders to make proportionally more tokens in one contribution.

Bots & Vote Selling: In theory, the incentive mechanism was designed to encourage users to create and curate relevant and quality content. The reality of the network activity has shown that the reward model very often encourages the creation of clickbait-style content driven by bots. While there is some bot prevention, related to the process of account creation, Steem Power is a transferable token, which means that it can be delegated from one user to another. This has led to the emergence of bots programmed to upvote posts based on their potential profitability. Bots can split the reward with the token holders that delegated their SP to them. As a result, curation of content on Steemit is often not based on quality but optimized for maximizing profits. Content is produced to be potentially profitable, and creators can take into account which content will likely be noticed by high-reputation curators and bots. Bots can upvote other bots to create circular feedback on profit expectations, taking into account that a vote is more profitable if it's cast relatively early, and in a case that more votes will follow. Other challenges of Steemit's governance design are vote-selling and bullying by wealthier members, as well as the monopolization of influence to set policy, overt control by large token holders, and forced censorship.

Self-upvoting: Steemit allows users to self-upvote one's own posts, and this has been subject to many discussions in the network. Opponents criticize the bias in the act of self-upvoting, as it reduces the quality of the curation process. Proponents say that not upvoting your own content means diluting your own stake, and giving your power only to other users. Furthermore, they argue that if users want to self-upvote and are no longer able to, they will simply create a second account.

Governance of content: Content on Steemit is not being moderated or censored. Some see this as a lack of governance. While some members of the community favor "censorship-resistant decentralized applications," others criticize the lack of moderation of content, especially when it comes to child pornography. On the other hand, it seems that some users have been banned from Steemit for "Terms of Service" violations.

Key Management: Usability of wallet software and key recovery is important. Blockchain-based systems don't allow for centralized password recovery. Steemit users who lose their passwords, and don't have a backup, lose access to their funds. As long as social key recovery solutions are not in place, secure key management will be a bottleneck to user adoption.

User attraction & retention: While many early Steemit users joined the network for ideological reasons, a large majority of users are one-time users only, or make a few posts and never came back for several reasons: It takes time to build a following before you can start earning money with your contributions. Furthermore, the current distribution inequalities in the network, which are a result of the token incentive mechanisms that favor first movers and large token holders who have a disproportionate number of network tokens, don't make it attractive for users to remain on the network.

Steemit Hard Fork & Hive Network

In February 2020, Steemit Inc. was acquired by the Tron foundation, which manages the Tron blockchain. Community members of the Steem ecosystem expressed concerns about this takeover and the new leadership, in particular about the CEO Justin Sun who, among other things, proposed a plan to migrate STEEM tokens to the Tron network. The biggest concern, however, was that with this takeover, the Tron Foundation also gained control over an estimated twenty percent of the total supply of STEEM tokens that the community colloquially refers to as the "Steemit Inc ninja-mined stake." These ninja tokens were pre-mined years ago and distributed to the founders of STEEM, who now sold Steemit Inc. to the Tron foundation. While the ninja tokens had always posed a threat, they had never been actively used (such as for voting on Steemit upgrades). In the past, the STEEM community was confident that the network founders would not misuse the tokens to take control of the network. However, due to mistrust of the new owners and fear over a potential power grab, STEEM witnesses almost immediately executed a soft fork of the Steem blockchain using votes of network users that had been delegated to them.

With this soft fork, ninja token addresses were blocked from future activities to seize control over the network. The community voted for this soft fork to prevent the new owners (the Tron Foundation) from using the ninja tokens. The witnesses justified the soft fork as a "temporary protective protocol to maintain the status quo currently established in regards to Steemit Inc's stake and its intended usage [...] and its continued use of the assets it controls." Early in March 2020, a community-led fork failed because the Tron foundation coordinated with a handful of token exchanges to retroactively undo the soft fork with the STEEM tokens of users tokens hosted on those exchanges. This misuse of user token by the exchanges was highly disputed.

Instead of fighting over power within the Steem network, a secession was conducted by the core community via a hard fork. Mid-March 2020 saw the fork of the Steem blockchain protocol and the Steemit app into a new network called "Hive." All ninja tokens controlled by Steemit Inc. were censored and will not be reflected on the Hive network. All other network tokens are being ported to Hive. All the blogging data from the Steemit application has also been ported to the Hive network. It will depend on each single blogger to decide which applications to use in the future, Steemit or Hive. If bloggers continue to post on Steemit, their new posts will still be managed by the Steem blockchain; if they choose otherwise, their new posts will get posted on the HIVE network. In theory, all other applications running on the Steem blockchain, such as "Splinterlands," "Steemian," "d-tube," and "d.sound" could, in theory, also migrate to the Hive network.

The takeover and subsequent soft-fork and hard-fork demonstrated the decentralized nature of blockchain networks and also showcased potential attack vectors with Delegated-Proof-of-Stake (DPoS) consensus mechanism. What was originally intended as a decentralized social network proved to be prone to centralization efforts, both on the side of Tron foundation's takeover and their collusion with the exchanges who used the tokens of their users to conduct votes (without prior consent of their users). It also showed the power of witnesses, who acted as the ring leaders of these forks.

The Tron foundation CEO perceived the forks to be an act of "malicious hackers" violating the "sanctity of private property" and censored around 4500 posts and comments related to the Hive hard-fork. However, given the diaspora of bloggers to Hive, the Tron foundation and the exchanges involved in blocking community activities later backtracked their decisions and moderated their tone. The new Steemit Inc. owners admitted that they had censored Steemit-based posts that discussed the Hive hard-fork and justified it with preserving private interests. The diaspora of users forced the new owners to put out a blog post in an attempt to regain trust, saying that they wanted to "put governance back in the hands of the community as soon as possible [...] and to convince users to come back to the Steemit project." The whole conflict reflects the cultural change between the Web2 and the Web3, and shows that some individuals and institutions are still struggling to understand the decentralized nature of the Web3 and the paradigm change regarding centralized control.

While Steemit has paved the way for a new era of social media networks, demonstrating how we can rethink social networks in a tokenized economy, the design flaws are considerable. If Steemit or Hive want to survive, they will need to change the token economics and eradicate the inequalities in power structures and design a reputation token that is tied to a user's identity. Otherwise, new content creators will have a hard time getting noticed in the system. While the Steem blockchain and the Steemit application have continuously adapted the governance rules, taking some of the community's feedback seriously, the token design flaws might be too fundamental. New competitors, such as "Akasha," "all.me," "Belacam," "DLive," "E-chat," "Golos" "Minds," "Mithril," "5media," "Social X," or "UUNIO," might provide more resilient token economics in the years to come.

Reddit - Tokenizing Web2 Platforms

"Reddit" is a Web2 social media platform for topic oriented discussions - subreddits - and comes with a contribution rating system. The subreddits represent user-created boards that help to channel discussions around a variety of topics. Users can submit their comments which can be upvoted, downvoted or commented upon by other users. The ranking of a post's visibility is determined by the number of up-and downvotes. „Karma" points determine the user's reputation in the network. Reddit was originally founded in 2005 and has over 2 million subreddit communities[81] and is ranked in the top 20 most visited websites worldwide.[82] In May 2020 two subreddits - r/Cryptocurrency and r/FortNiteBR - with over 2.4 million users announced the launch of their own subreddit tokens - MOON and BRICK - that will each be managed by the Ethereum network. Both tokens could be seen as a test use case for tokenizing all subreddits with their special purpose community tokens. The tokens will be initially managed by the Ethereum testnet "Rinkeby" for a few months before migrating to Ethereum's mainnet. "Reddit Vault" is an Ethereum wallet integrated into Reddit's mobile apps and communications with the Ethereum network. Both tokens are designed to be transferable, and users can send their MOON and Brick tokens to any other ERC-20 compatible wallets. The tokens also come with special voting rights within the community, however, it is still unclear how such a voting process will look like. In this initial design, the tokens can be used to animated emojis, exclusive badges and to reply to Reddit comments using gifs. The monetary policy of the tokens varies and can be determined by the community of each subreddit, at least to some extent. This means that each sub-

---

[81] https://redditmetrics.com/history
[82] https://www.alexa.com/siteinfo/reddit.com

reddit community will have certain control over the properties and function of the token (issuance rate, minting process, voting rights, transferability, utility properties.) "r/Cryptocurrency" announced that MOON tokens have a fixed issuance rate per month, 5 million MOONs, which will decrease by 2.5% every month until a total of 250 million is reached. "r/FortNiteBR" has not specified an issuance rate for their BRICKS tokens. At the time of writing this book it is still unclear if or when exchanges will list the token. With this move, Reddit is the first Web2 based social media network that has officially announced to tokenize their social media activities. It is likely that other existing social media networks will follow soon. The greatest challenge will be to design the token so the desired purpose of the economic system created by the token cannot be gamed.

Chapter Summary

- *Steemit is a decentralized social network where contributions to the network get rewarded with network tokens. It is a decentralized application that runs on the Steem blockchain. As opposed to Web2-based social media applications.*

- *Decentralized social networks such as Steemit have no data monopoly, meaning everyone has access to all transaction data, which is publicly visible on the Steem block explorer, and no advertising revenues are necessary, as the network is collectively managed by contributors who get rewarded with tokens for their contributions to the network. How much you get paid is a function of the number of your contributions, and the popularity of your contributions.*

- *Steemit has three different types of users: (a) content creators: publish content; (b) active users: curate content by upvoting (liking) the content, and (c) passive users: consume content. Users are rewarded for contributions to the network with three different types of network tokens: "Steem," "Steem Dollar," and "Steem Power."*

- *While Steemit and the underlying Steem blockchain infrastructure are a great use case for how we can redefine social networks, the economics behind the token design have a few fundamental design flaws.*

- *Due to the design flaws of the reputation token, there are currently many issues with incentivizing and providing quality content. While Steem Power (SP) was supposed to be a reputation token, it is based on oversimplified assumptions of how network actors behave.*

- *The token mechanisms don't take into account tragedy-of-the-commons or short-term economic thinking. Reputation tokens, in the form of Steem Power, can be bought with fiat money. Users who are willing to invest a considerable amount of money in Steem Power can, therefore, bootstrap their network power and earn more money more qui-*

ckly than users who try to organically build up reputation. Furthermore, the design of the reputation token does not take into account that different users have different interests, and that individual tastes are relative.

- *The reality of the network activity has shown that the reward model very often encourages the creation of clickbait-style content driven by bots. While there is some bot prevention, related to the process of account creation, Steem Power is a transferable token, which means that it can be delegated from one user to another. This has led to the emergence of bots programmed to upvote posts based on their potential profitability. Bots can split the reward with the token holders that delegated their SP to them. Bots can upvote other bots to create circular feedback on profit expectations, taking into account that a vote is more profitable if it's cast relatively early, and in a case that more votes will follow.*

- *Steemit allows users to self-upvote one's own posts, and this has been subject to many discussions in the network. Opponents criticize the bias in the act of self-upvoting, as it reduces the quality of the curation process. Proponents say that not upvoting your own content means diluting your own stake, and giving your power only to other users. Furthermore, they argue that if users want to self-upvote and are no longer able to, they will simply create a second account.*

- *As opposed to Web2 social media platforms, all transaction data on the Steemit blockchain is public and transparent to everyone with simple chain-analysis. This means that anyone can inspect what happened when or who did what in the Steemit ecosystem. Alternative cryptographic algorithms like multiparty computation or zero-knowledge proofs and additional obfuscation techniques need to be implemented in the protocol to provide more privacy by design.*

- *In March 2020 there was a hostile takeover and a contentious hard fork where the community forked into a new network called "Hive."*

- *New competitors, such as "Akasha," "all.me," "Belacam," "DLive," "E-chat," "Golos" "Minds," "Mithril," "5media," "Social X," or "UUNIO," might provide more resilient token economics in the years to come.*

Chapter References & Further Reading

- *Adams, Colin: „Steemit Review: How Does It Work And Can You Really Earn From It?", Invest in Blockchain, March 20, 2018: https://www.investinblockchain.com/steemit-review/*
- *Barbaras, C.; Narula, N; Zuckerman E.: "Decentralized Social Networks sound great. Too bad they will never work", https://www.wired.com/story/decentralized-social-networks-sound-great-too-bad-theyll-never-work*
- *Cadwalladr, Carole; Graham-Harrison, Emma: "How Cambridge Analytica turned Facebook 'likes' into a lucrative political tool" 17 Mar 2018: https://www.theguardian.com/technology/2018/mar/17/facebook-cambridge-analytica-kogan-data-algorith*

- Cadwalladr, Carole; Graham-Harrison, Emma: "Revealed: 50 million Facebook profiles harvested for Cambridge Analytica in major data breach", 17 Mar 2018: https://www.theguardian.com/news/2018/mar/17/cambridge-analytica-facebook-influence-us-election
- De, Nikhilesh: "Steemit Sets Up Shop on Tron Network, " Feb 14, 2020, retrieved from: https://www.coindesk.com/steemit-sets-up-shop-on-tron-network
- Dale, Brad: „Steem Community Plans Hostile Hard Fork to Flee Justin Sun's Steemit" Mar 17, 2020, retrieved from: https://www.coindesk.com/steem-community-plans-hostile-hard-fork-to-flee-justin-suns-steemit
- Dale, Brad: "Justin Sun Bought Steemit. Steem Moved to Limit His Power," Feb 24, 2020, retrieved from:https://www.coindesk.com/justin-sun-bought-steemit-steem-moved-to-limit-his-power
- Donnelly, Jacob: "Steemit Bridges Blockchain and Social Media, But How Does It Work?", Aug 26, 2016: https://www.coindesk.com/security-token-trades-on-regulated-platform-in-market-first
- Frost, Liam: "Community-led fork of Steemit is outperforming its predecessor Hive, a hard fork of decentralized social network Steem, is already outperforming its parent blockchain." Mar 28, 2020, retrieved from:https://decrypt.co/23854/hive-decentralized-fork-outperforms-steemit
- Harper, Colin: "Reddit Is Launching Ethereum Tokens For Its Subreddits,"Forbes, Crypto & Blockchain, May 14 2020: https://www.forbes.com/sites/colinharper/2020/05/14/reddit-launches-ethereum-tokens-for-subbredits-in-new-community-points-campaign/
- Kharif, Olga: "Reddit Launching a Cryptocurrency to Reward Users for Engagement," Bloomberg, Cryptocurrencies, 15 May 2020, retrieved from: https://www.bloomberg.com/news/articles/2020-05-15/reddit-launching-a-cryptocurrency-to-reward-users-for-engagement
- N.N.: „Steem An incentivized, blockchain-based, public content platform" June 2018: https://steem.com/steem-whitepaper.pdf
- N.N.: "Steemitboard.com", Ranking: https://steemitboard.com/ranking/index.php?p=0&s=vests
- N.N.: "Steemit FAQ", https://steemit.com/faq.html#What_is_Steemit_com
- N.N.: "Steem Upvote Bot Tracker": https://steembottracker.com/
- Redman, James: „Free from Tron: Steemit's Blockchain Fork Hive Outperforms Steem Token Value, MArch 30 2020, retrieved from: https://news.bitcoin.com/tron-steemits-fork-hive-outperforms-steem/
- Thelwall, M. "Can social news websites pay for content and curation? The Steemit cryptocurrency model", Journal of Information Science, 2017
- Usman W. Chohan: "The Concept and Criticisms of Steemit", Feb 23 2018, Electronic copy: https://papers.ssrn.com/sol3/papers.cfm?abstract_id=3129410
- @arcange: "Steemit Statistics – 2018.07.30": https://steemit.com/statistics/@arcange/steemit-statistics-20180730-en
- @blocktrades: "Why I won't be compromising with Justin Sun by blocktrades," steempeak.com steem, retrieved from: https://steemd.com/steem/@blocktrades/why-i-won-t-be-compromising-with-justin-sun
- @chasad75: "2018 Best and Most Profitable Bots on Steemit": https://steemit.com/steem/@chasad75/2018-best-and-most-profitable-bots-on-steemit
- @capgains: "Major Problems With STEEMIT That Sadly go Ignored": https://steemit.com/steemit/@capgains/major-problems-with-steemit-that-sadly-go-ignored
- Chohan, U. "The Concept and Criticisms of Steemit", 2018
- @hisnameisolllie: "STEEMIT Statistics, WEEK 3": https://steemit.com/steem-stats/@hisnameisolllie/steemit-statistics-week-3
- @ibrahimmurtaza: "Top 50 steemit user who has highest steem power": https://steemit.com/cryptocurrency/@ibrahimmurtaza/top-50-steemit-user-who-has-highest-steem-power
- @Initforthemoney: "Steemit's Three Major Problems": https://steemit.com/steemit/@initforthemoney/steemit-s-three-major-problems
- @liberosist: "Steem Power distribution trends - Steemit is becoming more democratic, diver-

se and equal! A detailed analysis," : https://steemit.com/steemit/@liberosist/steem-power-distri-bution-trends- steemit-is-becoming-more-democratic-diverse-and-equal-a-detailed-analysis

- @ned; @theoretical: "Smart Media Tokens A new way for publishers to monetize their online content and community, based on battle-tested blockchain technology", https://smt.steem.com/smt-whitepaper.pdf
- @nickypapers: „Basic Attention Token: Everything You Need To Know" Steemit, Category: bitcoin: https://steemit.com/bitcoin/@nickypapers/basic-attention-token-everything-you-need-to-know
- u/jarins: "Introducing r/CryptoCurrency Moons," r/CryptoCurrency, May 2020, retreived from: https://www.reddit.com/r/CryptoCurrency/comments/gj96lb/introducing_rcryptocurrency_moons/
- u/jarins: „Introducing r/FortNiteBR Bricks," r/FortNiteBR, May 2020, retreived from: https://www.reddit.com/r/FortNiteBR/comments/gj8tm1/introducing_rfortnitebr_bricks/
- Akasha: https://akasha.world/
- DLive: https://dlive.tv/
- E-chat: https://investors.echat.io
- Golos: https://golos.io/
- Hive: https://hive.io
- Minds: https://www.minds.com/
- UUNIO: https://uun.io/
- d.tube: https://dsound.audio/#!/feed
- d.sound: https://d.tube/

Basic Attention Token:
Advertising Reinvented

The idea of the Basic Attention Token project is to tokenize users' attention and to create a more transparent and efficient advertising market. The Basic Attention Token reverses the roles of the players in the advertising industry, and redefines the question of who owns your attention and your web browsing experience, and who gets paid for what from whom.

Historically, economic transactions were, for the most part, based on exchanging products against money, debt, or other products. Choice was limited and customers' expectations relatively low. Due to the scarcity of goods, producers did not need to personalize their product or differentiate from other products. The industrial revolution (1860-1920) reduced production costs, changing the dynamics between supply and demand of goods. As production started to surpass demand, markets became increasingly competitive, products commoditized, and sales and marketing became a way for companies to differentiate their products from the competition. What followed was a sales revolution (1920-1940). A marketing revolution followed (1940-1990), which then led into the finer-grained marketing revolutions of the late twentieth and early twenty-first century, focusing on relationship marketing and social media marketing. Free trade agreements and the emergence of the Internet allowed companies to increasingly outsource production and services to other countries and focus on product design, branding, and advertising.

For the first time since the agricultural revolution, humans are approaching a stage where there is an abundance of resources like food, money, and knowledge. Most modern-day shortages are due to allocation inefficiencies, and are rarely a product of real shortages. In the age of information overflow, supply chain optimization, and algorithmic market mechanisms, this inefficiency can be further reduced. While the invention of the printing press in the 15th century can be seen as the first information revolution, the emergence of the Internet brought the second information revolution, and with that, the abundance of information. Data has become the fuel of this information economy, and attention is the scarce resource. As we are approaching a "zero marginal cost society,"[83] time and attention are becoming two of the most scarce resources. The amount of time a person has to pay attention to advertising is limited.

Attention Economy, Data Markets & Privacy

Web2 platforms, in particular social media platforms and search engines, did not have a direct business model to generate income from the services they provided. The only thing they had was user data, which served as a basis for targeted advertising based on user behavior. This revolutionized the advertising industry forever. The current ad-tech ecosystem has been developed and is predominantly controlled by two companies: Alphabet (Google) and Facebook. Anything from web-browsing history to location-based data, our everyday movement is being tracked by the companies whose services we use, and then resold to the data brokers of the marketing industry. The data brokers analyze and resell this data to advertisers. Algorithmic methods extract information from this raw data to evaluate which customers are the most relevant for which advertiser. Users today have little or no direct control over what happens with their personal data behind the walled gardens of the servers of the Web2 service providers.

Collecting lists of people that group consumers by specific characteristics and selling these lists to marketing companies and advertisers was not a new thing. The Internet, however, has radically reduced the costs of collecting and processing such lists, and allowes to do so on a much more personalized level. Paired with machine-learning applications, we can now personalize advertising at an unprecedented level that was not feasible before. In the early years of targeted advertising, marketers who used Facebook, Google, and similar advertising networks could only target individuals based on the data collected by one single service provider. In 2012, however, Facebook started to allow companies to upload their own lists, correlating their data against Facebook data. This allowed companies to link datasets from different sources and target people based on their email addresses

---

[83] "Zero Marginal Cost Society" is the title of a book by Jeremy Rifkin, describing how emerging technologies are speeding us to an era of nearly free goods and services, precipitating the meteoric rise of a global so-called "Collaborative Commons." The book describes the paradox that capitalism has become so efficient that it is abolishing itself. While economists have always promoted a reduction in marginal cost, they probably did not anticipate the possibility of a technological revolution that might bring marginal costs near zero, nearly free, and abundant, and no longer subject to market forces.

or phone numbers. Other companies, such as Google and Twitter, soon launched similar features. Sophisticated methods have been developed to profile the behavior of Internet users by linking data sets collected by different companies across different user accounts, devices, and sometimes even offline data. These data sets can easily be linked using pseudonymous identifiers that refer to individuals, like email addresses, phone numbers, and cookies. Cookies are a powerful tool that publishers use to track and link the preferences and behavior of individuals across Internet services.

Furthermore, in the current client-server–based Internet, both users and advertisers have little direct control over what happens with their data. Big data companies are a honeypot for data breaches and privacy violations, as has become publicly evident with the "Cambridge Analytica Files" of how Facebook data was used to manipulate the British and US elections.[84] Targeted advertisements combined with personalized data feeds is seen by many as a tool to undermine the autonomy of users and has also catalyzed echo chambers of one's own opinion. Millions of users have installed ad-blockers on their devices to counteract this surveillance trend. Publishers reacted by bombarding users with pop-ups and messages asking them to whitelist a website or disable their ad-blocker completely. Over 600 million devices seem to be using ad-blocking software.

The advertising industry is also prone to intransparencies along the supply chain of these data brokers and service providers. Unscrupulous and sometimes fraudulent ad-tech providers pretend to deliver targeted advertising, when in fact, users might get delivered an ad of products they have recently bought. Advertisers buying such "custom audiences" have no direct insight into what really happens behind the walled gardens of ad-tech providers. They have to trust the third-party providers that ads are properly delivered. It is estimated that more than 7 billion USD in online ad fraud was committed in 2016, from misplaced to outright malicious ads.

Basic Attention Token (BAT)

Digital advertising today involves two main stakeholders, the advertisers and publishers, and many intermediary services that have been established to serve the needs of advertisers and publishers. Users have almost no active role in the system,

---

[84] *Due to the General Data Protection Regulation (GDPR) that was passed by the European Union, previous practices are becoming problematic in certain jurisdictions. A recent treatment on the consequences of the GDPR on data analytics one can find in: Wieringa, J., Kannan, P.K., Ma, X., Reutterer, T., Risselada, H., and B. Skiera (2019): Data Analytics in a Privacy-Concerned World. Journal of Business Research (forthcoming).*

except for maybe limited opt-out possibilities. The Basic Attention Token project reverses the roles of the players in the advertising industry and redefines the question of who owns your attention and your web browsing experience, and who gets paid for what from whom. The Basic Attention Token provides tokenized solutions to current challenges of the industry. The idea is to use cryptographic tokens and a privacy-preserving browser to create a decentralized advertising system. Advertising is performed P2P, directly in the "Brave" browser, a decentralized application that communicates with the Ethereum network and manages two tokens: BAT (Basic Attention Token) and BAM (Basic Attention Metrics).

The BAT token can be used as a transfer of value between publishers, advertisers, and users in a way that (i) users are compensated for viewing ads in a privacy-preserving manner, (ii) publishers receive a bigger stake of the ad revenue than they would today, and (iii) advertisers could gain a better return on investment, as well as more accurate data. Users can opt to see certain ads from companies they are genuinely interested in, or pay a fee to not see any advertisements at all.

Basic Attention Metrics (BAM) allows for the accurate tracking and reporting of user attention directly in the browser. In spite of the fact that the browser constantly tracks one's attention, this data is anonymized, as it never leaves the browser software locally running on one's device. In-device machine-learning algorithms determine relevant content for personalized advertising. The "attention value" for each ad depends on how long the ad is viewed and other metrics such as the number of ad pixels that are visible in proportion to relevant content, etc. Data analysis is performed directly on the browser for the sake of serving targeted advertising without revealing the base data to the company that delivers the ad (advertiser). Advertisers have direct access to trustful metrics without the need for third-party tracking and without compromising the privacy of the user. Such a level of disintermediation can improve the effectiveness of targeted advertising.

At the time of writing the book, the Brave browser has over 13 million monthly active users who use Brave to browse the web to manage their tokens and perform other operations. As opposed to current web browsers, ad blocking is built into the Brave browser using the Tor network. Such ad-blocking also makes the browser faster. Furthermore, the Brave browser provides more inbuilt security, as it upgrades websites that don't have HTTPS to use the HTTPS protocol. Privacy is not an optional browser extension that needs to be manually installed. The browser also provides an analytics dashboard to monitor and manage features such as incentive programs, ad matching algorithms, and attention measurement systems.

Some argue that cloud-based services like personal data micro-servers, such as "Hub of All Things," already offer the opportunity to shift control over one's personal data back to individual customers, where users can configure their own personal data storage infrastructure. However, they have remained a fringe phenomena. While such services do offer more control over where your data is stored, one still has to rely on third parties for identity management and hosting services, which does not provide the same level of autonomy and security as blockchain solutions such as BAT.

How BAT works in detail: Anyone who downloads the app receives an initial amount of BAT tokens. Advertisers pay publishers BAT tokens to display personalized ads, which are filtered by the algorithm in the Brave browser, based on locally collected data only. This means that users maintain ownership and control over their data. When delivering an ad, the advertisers send BAT tokens in a locked state using a smart contract. If and when users view the ads, the smart contract unlocks the BAT tokens, which compensate the user with up to 70 percent of the advertising revenue. The publisher hosting the advertisement receives the rest, which could incentivize them to deliver relevant quality content instead of random spamming with irrelevant ads. Users can get compensated for their time and attention, and in turn, spend these tokens for other online activities, such as tipping artists and content creators for their free online content.

This tipping option works in a similar way to services such as "Patreon," but eliminates the need for third-party services such as Patreon. One could also use BAT tokens to pay for subscriptions, digital goods, and other services in the future. At the time of writing the book, BAT tokens can be used for charity donations to over 1000 organizations, such as the Red Cross or the World WildLife Fund. BAT has partnered with the TAP Network, a rewards-as-a-service tech company, which has more than 250,000 commercial partners such as Amazon, Apple, Walmart, American Airlines, Starbucks, and HBO. Users will also be able to redeem their BAT tokens for rewards from any of those companies, which could be a further incentive for users to adopt Brave and BAT. Furthermore, there are over 28,000 Brave-verified publishers where BAT tokens are also accepted, such as Vimeo, Vice, Washington Post, The Guardian, and MarketWatch.

Outlook & Challenges

Web3-based advertising solutions provide more transparency for the publishers without compromising the privacy of the user. Due to the open-source nature of this solution, the browser software can be audited, and all transactions are publicly verifiable. The open-source nature could make the systems more resilient and reduce fraud. However, there are also some challenges that need to be resolved before BAT can reach mass market adoption.

As opposed to Steemit, BAT is a centralized solution, at least when it comes to their token economics and token governance. While STEEM and Steem Power are purpose-driven tokens that are minted upon proof-of-contribution to the Steem ecosystem, the BAT token is pegged to fiat currencies. BAT tokens are not minted upon proof of certain behavior, but were initially funded with fiat money in a token sale. The token flow and value creation in the BAT model seem to be reflecting old-school value creation models, and are based on a pool of pre-mined BAT tokens. The Brave founders and managers decide how many tokens are issued and how the token flow works: After a private capital injection from VCs, the BAT project conducted a token sale in 2017, which ended within 30 seconds, raising around 35 million USD (156,250 ETH). In total, 1.5 billion tokens were created, with 1 billion sold in the token sale, and the remaining tokens retained. The Brave team was allocated 200 million for funding of future development (BAT development pool), and 300 million will be given away for free in multiple batches on a first-come/first-served basis when users download the browser (user growth pool). The first payouts started in December 2017. The user growth pool still holds around 250 million BAT. As for token distribution, the top one hundred own 72 percent of all token supply.

The BAT project is still in the early stages of roll out and many features are under development. Anti-fraud mechanisms need to be developed to limit the amount of ads served per user. This is a challenge, as anyone could open any number of wallets on different devices. Furthermore, for token withdrawals to be compliant with regulatory authorities, certain KYC (Know Your Customer) mechanisms will probably be necessary, especially in light of anti-money laundering legislation. The wallet is currently one-directional; tokens cannot be withdrawn. Users need to use third-party services to convert fiat money to BAT and vice versa. This is probably a short-term restriction and will eventually be resolved as the system matures.

It might be difficult to motivate users to switch to a new web browser like Brave, since browser market shares have historically been quite stable. However, as opposed to traditional browsers, Brave offers privacy features and revenue possibilities. The opportunity to make money by watching ads, while promising an unprecedented level of privacy, might change the dynamic in the browser market. Once all of Brave's functionalities are fully rolled out and operational, it might be attractive enough for users to go through the effort of installing a new piece of software on their devices.

However, advertisers might be the biggest bottleneck to BAT adoption. Google and Facebook currently dominate the ad-tech industry, with an estimated market share of roughly 70 percent. Their large user base makes them popular among advertisers and publishers. While they offer advertisement options in-line with their newsfeed or search results, BAT currently only offers display ads, which is not as attractive to advertisers. The BAT project has it on their roadmap to implement BAT usage beyond advertising use cases, for any in-browser value transfer. Whether they will be able to succeed at implementing this plan remains unclear.

In the long run, it is likely that the BAT ecosystem or a similar attention token could become a mainstream method for micro-payments on social media, not only for advertising payments but also for rewarding content creation and content curation. Apart from BAT, other projects are developing similar solutions, such as AdEx, a project that focuses on video ads.

Chapter Summary

- *The Basic Attention Token provides tokenized solutions to current challenges of the advertising industry, reinventing the way users, publishers, and advertisers interact. It redefines the question of who owns your attention and your web browsing experience, and who gets paid for what from whom. They use tokenized incentives and a privacy-preserving browser application to create a decentralized ad exchange.*

- *The "Brave" browser is a decentralized application that communicates with the Ethereum network, which manages two tokens: BAT (Basic Attention Token) and BAM (Basic Attention Metrics).*

- *The BAT token can be used as a transfer of value between publishers, advertisers, and users in a way that (i) users are compensated for viewing ads in a privacy-preserving manner, (ii) publishers receive a bigger stake of the ad revenue than they would today, and (iii) advertisers could gain a better return on investment, as well as more accurate data. Users can opt to see certain ads from companies they are genuinely interested in, or pay a fee to not see any advertisements at all. Advertising is performed P2P, directly in the users in the wallet & browser.*

- *Basic Attention Metrics (BAM) allows for the accurate tracking and reporting of user attention directly in the browser. In-device machine-learning algorithms determine relevant content for personalized advertising. Data analysis is performed directly on the browser for the sake of serving targeted advertising without revealing the base data to the company that delivers the ad (advertiser). Advertisers have direct access to trustful metrics without the need for third-party tracking and without compromising the privacy of the user.*

- *In spite of the fact that the browser constantly tracks one's attention, this data is anonymized, as it never leaves the browser software locally running on one's device. Users maintain ownership and control over their data.*

- *Web3-based advertising solutions provide more transparency for the publishers without compromising the privacy of the user. Due to the open-source nature of this solution, the* browser software can be audited, and all transactions are publicly verifiable. The open-source nature could make the systems more resilient and reduce fraud.

- When delivering an ad, the advertisers send BAT tokens in a locked state using a smart contract. If and when users view the ads, the smart contract unlocks the BAT tokens, which compensate the user with up to 70 percent of the advertising revenue. The publisher hosting the advertisement receives the rest, which could incentivize them to deliver relevant quality content instead of random spamming with irrelevant ads.

- Users can get compensated for their time and attention, and in turn, spend these tokens for other online activities, such as tipping artists and content creators for their free online content. BAT tokens can also be used for charity donations to thrid-party organizations.

Chapter References & Further Reading

- Agarwal, Ajay; Gans, Joshua; Goldfab, Avi: "Prediction Machines The Simple Economics of Artificial Intelligence" Harvard Business Review Press Boston, Massachusetts, 2018
- Berry, Leonard L.: "Relationship marketing", In: Berry, L.L./Shostack, G.L./ Upah, G.D. (Hrsg.): Emerging perspectives in services marketing. Chicago, Illinois: American Marketing Association, 25-28, 1983
- Buchko, Steven: „What Is the Basic Attention Token (BAT)? The All-Encompassing Guide", Coincetral, Nov 7 2018: https://coincentral.com/what-is-bat/
- Christl, Wolfie: "Corporate surveillance in everyday life", Cracked Labs Report, Cracked Labs, June 2017: https://crackedlabs.org/en/corporate-surveillance
- Dall, Carlos Eduardo; Freitas, Acqua: "Basic Attention Token (BAT) has a visionary purpose, but powerful nemeses", March 27, 2018: http://globalcoinreport.com/basic-attention-token-bat-has-a-visionary-purpose-but-powerful-nemeses/
- Deighton, John; Peter A. Johnson: "The Value of Data: Consequences for Insight, Innovation & Efficiency in the U.S. Economy", October 8, 2013. Available at: https://www.ipc.be/~/media/documents/public/markets/the-value-of-data-consequences-for-insight-innovation-and-efficiency-in-the-us-economy.pdf
- Fader, Peter; Toms , Sarah E.: "The Customer Centricity Playbook: Implement a Winning Strategy Driven by Customer Lifetime", 2018
- Fullerton, Ronald: "How Modern Is Modern Marketing? Marketing's Evolution and the Myth of the Production Era", Journal of Marketing, Jan. 1988 (Vol. 52, No. 1)
- Fullerton, Ronald, Jagdish, Sheth: "Research in Marketing" Jai Press Ltd., Supplement 6, 1994
- Ghose, A.: "What blockchain could mean for marketing", Harvard Business Review. No. 5, 2-5, 2018
- Grant, Leboff: "Sticky Marketing", Kogan Page, 2011
- Greenfield, Patrick: "The Cambridge Analytica files: the story so far What is the company accused of, how is Facebook involved and what is the Brexit link?", 26 March, 2018: https://www.theguardian.com/news/2018/mar/26/the-cambridge-analytica-files-the-story-so-far
- Grönroos, Christian: "In Search of a New Logic for Marketing. Foundations of Contemporary Theory", Chichester: John Wiley & Sons, Ltd, 2007
- Hammer Cornelia et. al: "Big Data: Potential, Challenges, and Statistical Implications", International Monetary Fund, 2006
- Hub of All Things: https://hubofallthings.com

- Kimmel, Alan: "Marketing Communication", Oxford, 2005
- Kotler, Philip: "Marketing Management: Analysis, Planning and Control. Englewood Cliffs, N.J.: Prentice-Hall", 1967
- Kotler, Philip, Zaltman, Gerald: „Social Marketing: An Approach to Planned Social Change". Journal of Marketing. 35 (3). pp. 3–12, July 1971
- Kotler, Philip; Levy, Sidney J.: „Demarketing, Yes, Demarketing". Harvard Business Review. 49 (6). pp. 74–80, November – December 1971
- Little, John D. C.;Blattberg, Robert C.; Glazer, Rashi: "The Marketing Information Revolution", 1994
- Narayanan, Arvind; Dillon Reisman: "The Princeton Web Transparency and Accountability Project", 2017: http://randomwalker.info/publications/webtap-chapter.pdf
- Nguyen, Winnie: "Basic Attention Token (BAT) Pros & Cons – Blockchain Digital Ad Exchange!" Aug 15, 2018, Cryptocurrency Reviews: https://www.bitcoinforbeginners.io/cryptocurrency-reviews/basic-attention-token-bat/
- N.N.:"Basic Attention Token (BAT) Blockchain Based Digital Advertising", Brave Software, March 13, 2018: https://basicattentiontoken.org/BasicAttentionTokenWhitePaper-4.pdf
- N.N.: "BAT Publishers List": https://batgrowth.com/publishers
- N.N.: "BAT user statistics": https://brave.com/2018-highlights
- N.N.: Brave Browser Website: https://brave.com/
- Parvatiyar, Atul; Sisodia, Rajendra: "Handbook of Advances in Marketing in an Era of Disruptions: Essays in Honour of Jagdish N. Sheth", SAGE Publications India, 2019
- Platzer, Michael; Reutterer, Thomas: "Ticking Away the Moments: Timing Regularity Helps to Better Predict Customer Activity" This article was downloaded by: [137.208.149.244] On: 22 September 2016, At: 14:22 Publisher: Institute for Operations Research and the Management Sciences (INFORMS) www.reutterer.com/papers/platzer&reutterer_pareto-ggg_2016.pdf
- Rifkin, Jeremy: "Zero Marginal Cost Society", 2014
- Schröder, N.; Falke, A.; Hruschka, H., Reutterer, T.: "Analyzing the Browsing Basket: A Latent Interests-Based Segmentation Tool", Journal of Interactive Marketing (forthcoming), 2019
- Tompkins, Jonathan: "Crypto Review — Basic Attention Token (BAT)" Medium, Jul 3, 2017: https://medium.com/@jon.tomp/crypto-review-basic-attention-token-bat-79f16bc3dd66
- Trusov, Michael; Ma, Liye; Jamal, Zainab:"Crumbs of the Cookie: User Profiling in Customer-Base Analysis and Behavioral Targeting", Marketing Science, Vol. 35, No. 3, Published Online: 28 Apr 2016: https://doi.org/10.1287/mksc.2015.0956
- Valendin, J., T. Reutterer, C. Kalcher, and M. Platzer: From RFM to LSTM: How Machines Learn to Understand Customer History. WU Vienna Working Paper.
- Walker, Saint John: "Big Data: A Revolution That Will Transform How We Live, Work, and Think", International Journal of Advertising, 2014
- Yan, Jun; Ning Liu, Gang Wang, Wen Zhang, Yun Jiang, and Zheng Chen: "How much can behavioral targeting help online advertising?" Proceedings of the 18th international conference on the World Wide Web (WWW ,09). ACM, 261-270. Available at: http://dl.acm.org/citation.cfm?id=1526745
- Basic Attention Token: https://basicattentiontoken.org/
- Brave Browser: https://brave.com/

Token Curated Registries - The New Search?

Token Curated Registries provide a market mechanism for content curation that could complement centralized curation services. Tokens are hereby used as economic incentives to curate lists, or rank information in such a list, including content feeds in a social network or recommendation algorithms for e-commerce platforms.

Listings and registries have proven to be a useful tool to organize, rank, and share information. We use lists for our daily decision-making processes, such as "best books," "best restaurants," "top universities," "tokens to invest in," "best movies," "best classic movies," "best horror movies," "best rated products of a certain category of an e-commerce platform," "best budget or luxury hotel in a region." These lists or registries can be private or public and are usually centrally managed. One can use whitelists or blacklists to filter relevant information. Any newspaper and magazine is also a curated list of relevant information. Whether daily news or a fashion magazine, the content in these publications is carefully selected and sorted, highlighting more important information on the cover and the first pages, rather than in the middle or the end. Such filtering is a result of a third-party curation process, which is useful as the readers save much time researching and filtering information themselves. The curation process is outsourced to the editors who are trusted to curate with diligence.

Ever since the emergence of the Internet, such listings, rankings or recommendation services have become more important. The Internet has radically reduced the costs of publishing and sharing information. As a result, it has become difficult to filter meaningful information from all the online noise. The first online lists were websites that collected and sorted information from other websites to help users search for relevant information on the web. Early "search engines" were manually created by people who were paid for categorizing online content like books in library shelves, but this process was not scalable. The sheer information load triggered a new form of creating public lists by applying (i) machine learning algorithms and (ii) wisdom of the crowd mechanisms to derive meaningful lists and rankings. Google was one of the first search engines to introduce algorithmic search, and Tripadvisor introduced "wisdom of the crowd" solutions to produce a listing for "best hotel in the region," aggregating a collection of personal recommendations. Such third-party curation, whether public or private, algorithmic or wisdom-of-the-crowd based, is prone to censorship and manipulation, as they are centrally managed.

Users of online services have to trust that the internet platform providing such curation services act honestly, and hope that their taste for restaurants or hotels aligns well with their own tastes. In privately managed lists, the owner of that list can arbitrarily add or remove list members or require payments from people who want to be listed. Their ranking methods are often undisclosed, can be gamed, or might not coincide with the taste or judgement of their users. Public lists such as Tripadvisor can also be manipulated by a load of pseudonymous users who spam the list, perform fake ratings, or socially engineer the list. To mitigate these problems of collectively curated lists, semi-centralized list moderators are often appointed to manually intervene, which is a point of centralization and does not scale well. Facebook, for example, outsources most of its manual content curation moderation to low-income countries like the Philippines to save costs.

The methods of third party curation and recommendation service providers are, for the most part, undisclosed, resulting in intransparent filtering algorithms. The curation tasks involve maintaining whitelists or blacklists, managing data feeds, filtering comments, or providing context-specific recommendations. Machine-learning algorithms derive their suggestions by correlating personalized user data with statistical data of the behavior of all other users. E-commerce platforms such as eBay or Amazon use machine learning to rank the search results, and once you select an item of your choice, suggest other products that might be relevant for you. Video streaming services such as Netflix use machine learning to suggest movies that might be relevant for you, while music platforms like Soundcloud or Spotify suggest music playlists that you might like. Social media platforms such as Twitter, Facebook, or Instagram use machine learning to rank the posts and ads in your data feed. However, only a handful of companies control the curation process of the search engines, social media networks and other digital services we use today.

How TCRs Work

Token Curated Registries (TCRs) are a market mechanism introduced by Mike Goldin for collectively curating lists in the absence of third-party coordination. Tokens provide an economic incentive to curate lists that are valuable to consumers. Transactions are settled and cleared autonomously by a distributed ledger. TCRs are designed to represent a public good. Anyone can participate.

Prerequisites: In order to set up a TCR, one needs to (i) define a purpose for the list, (ii) a native token, and (iii) a governance mechanism that makes sure that all token holders are incentivized to maintain a high-quality list.

Stakeholders: (i) candidates provide content for the list, (ii) consumers use the list, and (iii) curators collectively manage the quality of the list (token holders).

Process: Candidates have to deposit a certain amount of tokens to apply for the list. Any token holder can participate in the curation process, and has a certain time to cast a vote on whether or not the candidate's application should be included in the list. If they think that the application should be excluded, they can challenge the listing. To do so, they must make a deposit of a certain amount of tokens into a smart contract, locking a part of their network stake. Once a challenge has been initiated, all other token holders can vote by also staking their tokens. If at the end of the voting period, the application is rejected by the majority of token holders, the applicant's deposit is split between the challenger and all other token holders who voted to reject the application. Otherwise the listing of the candidate is added to the registry, and the smart contract distributes the challenger's deposit between the applicant and all token holders who voted for accepting the listing. It is advised that TCRs divide the voting process into two phases, the commit phase and the reveal phase. Results are only openly broadcasted after the commit phase is completed to avoid "coordination attacks," where one curator could have influence over the voting process of other curators. Tokens are locked in the commit phase and unlocked during the reveal phase.

Token: Tokens are designed to be transferable and fungible (all tokens are designed to be equal). It is assumed that each list needs their own token to give a reliable signal of the quality of the list and the value of the network. The price of a token is a result of supply and demand, and as such, assumed to be a performance indicator for the collective actions of all token holders. If a TCR would accept a non-native token as a means of payment, such as BTC or ETH, the collective performance of the token holders would not reflect performance of the list and the economic incentive mechanisms would therefore not work.

Mechanism Design: The incentive mechanism needs to align incentives in a way to make sure that it pays off for token holders to vote truthfully, and that it does not pay to cheat the system. Candidates who believe they will be rejected are not likely to apply; otherwise, they would lose their tokens. Token holders, on the other hand, could theoretically reject every candidate, but that would collide with their interest to increase the value of their tokens. An empty list is not interesting for anyone. Profitability and quality of all stakeholders need to be well-aligned, so that objective and high-quality lists can be produced.

Design assumptions: The concept of a TCR is based on the assumption that a free market for listings could potentially provide a better mechanism for quality curation of lists than centrally managed lists and data feeds. It is also assumed that economic actors want to maximize their profits and act rationally at all times. Candidates are assumed to have an interest to be included on the list for advertising purposes, and be willing to pay a listing fee, as placement on such a list serves as validation of quality of their services. Curators, who also have a stake in the network in the form of network tokens, would make more money from well-maintained lists with a lot of traction, which means that they have an incentive to curate the list truthfully. The vote of token holders is proportional to the number of tokens they own, or stake. Proportional voting rights are based on the idea that those who have the most at stake are most incentivized to act in the network's best interest. Consumers, on the other hand, seek high-quality information and use lists to make decisions. If the quality of the listing is good, consumers will be interested in consulting the listing, which will make it more attractive for candidates to apply to be listed and strengthens the overall economy of that list.

Attack Vectors

The economics behind the registry needs to be designed in a way that it accounts for all possible attack vectors. A number of attack vectors have been identified, such as "trolling," "madman attacks," "registry poisoning," or "coin flipping." A solution to each of these potential attacks needs to be reflected in the governance rules of the TCR to guarantee high-quality listings.

Trolls might try to add content to the list that does not satisfy the list's criteria. Such trolling also happens on current Web2 platforms, such as Amazon, where adding reviews does not cost anything, except for the costs of writing the review. As a solution, the mechanism needs to be designed in a way to make it expensive for a troll to add low-quality listings. Losing one's deposited listing fee is such a mechanism. But even if the listing fee is high enough for most users, an attacker with non-economic reasons, or an attacker with many funds at their disposal, might still be able to flood the system with non-relevant listings. One could raise the minimum deposit, which might exclude eligible applicants with little funds at their disposal to apply for a listing, thus creating an economic barrier of entry into the system.

Registry poisoning refers to the problem of what happens to a listing that was once accepted for good reasons, but the quality of its services has since declined so they do not meet the listing requirements anymore. The mechanism needs to be designed in a way to incentivize token holders to find and challenge listings that "poison" the registry.

Free riding: Token holders could decide to free-ride the system, and not actively participate in any of the voting processes, hoping that other token holders will maintain the quality of the list and therefore also the value of their token holdings.

Coin flipping: There are no direct penalties for making bad decisions, only indirect long-term ones that might reflect in the token price once the quality of the list does down. A profit-maximizing token holder might find it more rational in the short term to cast a random vote (coin flipping) instead of investing the time in making rational assessments over a potential listing. It is assumed that a certain distribution of votes between "coin flippers" and "truthful token holders" can maintain the integrity of the list in spite of such coin flipping behavior, but if too many curators decide to free-ride the system by coin flipping, the quality of the list could be jeopardized.

Madman Attack: This refers to a potential manipulation attempt of someone who might have an economic reason to undermine the quality of the list, in which they spend a large amount of funds to flood the registry with low-quality listings (51-percent attack). The mechanism needs to be designed in a way to make a 51-percent attack expensive. However, given potential "free-rider" problems, only a minority of token holders are likely to actively participate in voting for and against proposals, which means that, in reality, madman attacks may not be as expensive as a theoretical 51-percent attack of all token holders.

Vote memeing refers to the fact that some token holders might copy group behavior in the interest of always being in the majority voting block, thus being on the winning side and always earning tokens. To avoid this, commit-reveal schemes have been introduced to make sure that votes of others will only be revealed after the voting period ends.

Criticism of TCRs

Token Curated Registries could be a game changer if they manage to provide a manipulation-resistant alternative to centralized curation services. However, critics argue that TCRs that use token-weighted votes (i) cannot provide nuanced curation, (ii) cannot replace subjective reputation systems, and (iii) have a problem with "minimum economy" size. They claim that having a stake in a system alone cannot build quality curation, as token holders are more likely to maximize short-term profits, since they can sell their tokens any time and exit the system, which is harmful to the collective quality of the list in the long run. Furthermore, any TCR will need a minimum market size to resist manipulation attempts, which means that new lists have a chicken-and-egg problem. Also, consumers will not be interested in a small or half-empty registry, and candidates won't be interested to apply to a registry that is not visited by anyone. Another issue is that TCRs are not useful for all types of registries. Bulkin, for example, is an outspoken critic and distinguishes between "subjective TCRs" and "objective TCRs." In his opinion, a TCR can only be successful if (i) an objective answer to the listing question exists and if (ii) the answer is publicly observable, such as air temperature in a certain geographic area.

Bulkin criticizes that token-based voting does not necessarily result in higher quality curation for subjective lists, and is furthermore tainted by power asymmetries between small and big token holders, especially if registry tokens can be acquired with money, not reputation. To end up on the winning side, token holders will likely be incentivized to vote for the choices they believe the majority of token holders, or the big token holder, will vote for. Bulkin states that subjective questions cannot be accurately answered by an objective mechanism as proposed by Goldin. Lists that are prone to subjective tastes or opinions need a stronger coordination signal, which would require a well-defined set of curators with well-aligned values. In such a setup, trusting the people curating information and understanding their motives is important. For quality subjective lists, Bulkin suggests combining TCRs with social reputation systems could add necessary context to a TCR. As different people have different social values, adding the context of social value is important in curating certain types of lists. He also argues that reputation scores are more likely to be uniformly distributed than wealth, and that TCRs are easier to bootstrap when they include a subjective reputation system, which would resolve the "minimum economy" problem to make a list attractive enough for early adopters. Adding social reputation could also resolve the problem of vote-memeing, if bad actors could lose their reputation or if accounts could get blacklisted. Such a setup could also mitigate voting rings and some cases of vote-buying attacks.

Furthermore, Mike Goldin's approach does not account for possible "free-rider" problems, where some token holders might choose to stay passive, simply investing in a token for speculative reasons. Such "free-riders" would hope that other curators will vote in a trustful manner, thus keeping the quality of the network high. "Free-riding" is a typical problem for public goods (read more: Part 4 - Purpose-Driven Tokens). To resolve this, the governance rules could be designed in a way where token holders are forced to vote. This, however, will very likely result in so-called "vote memeing" (copying someone else's voting behavior) or "coin flipping" (making a random vote to save time in research and decision making), which could also reduce the registry's quality over time. While the concept of TCRs could be used to make a decentralized list manipulation resistant, it will not work without a reputation system.

Since TCRs haven't been tested publicly yet, it is unclear which governance rules will work in the long run, and how to optimally set the variables that govern the internal economy of a list. These variables may vary, depending on the type and purpose of the list, such as: (i) the amount of time token holders have to commit votes to a challenge; (ii) the amount of time token holders have to reveal their votes to a challenge; and (iii) the percentage of votes necessary for a certain outcome to take effect. One challenge in defining these variables could be the amount of time token holders have to challenge an application. If it is set for too long, token holders might forget to cast their votes. Changes to the parameters of the token governance rules could be voted for in a similar fashion to how new applications to the registry are voted for. To propose a new governance mechanism, token holders could stake tokens and submit the application to all other token holders to vote on. Applications of a new governance mechanism could be evaluated the same way that applications to the registry are voted upon, which means that they would be subject to the same attack vectors.

Other Types of TCRs

Alternative proposals have been made as to how to modify the initial concept introduced by Mike Goldin, to mitigate some of the attack vectors described above, or to add quality of information to the listing. The token governance rules of the TCR variations mentioned below cannot be explained in detail in this chapter, but can be researched online (check references at the end of the chapter).

Ordered TCRs: Simple TCRs are unordered, which means that they are just a list of entries that have made it into the list. Curators vote to include or exclude and decide on the ranking to each entry in the list. Each listing has an exclusive rank, which means that two listings cannot have the same rank. The number of entries can be limited or unlimited.

Graded TCRs are a simple variation of an ordered TCR where two listings can have the same amount of reputation points. Listings can have the same rank and don't occupy a unique index. They give a better signal about the qualitative range of a listing.

Layered TCRs are more complete, as they introduce different layers of acceptance. In a first qualification round, a listing could qualify via some predefined rules, and would have to meet some additional criteria to qualify for the next layer, which could be helpful for building a more sophisticated hierarchy, allowing for more diversity or subjectiveness. Such an approach could increase the overall quality of a list.

Nested TCRs are lists where the entries of a listing have pointers to other lists. Nested TCRs can be used to reflect relationships between attributes rated in one list and attributes of the same listing that are rated in another list.

Combinatorial TCRs allow us to visualize an array of items in one list. Token holders can collectively define acceptable sets, ranges, and parameters.

Continuous Token-Curated Registries combine continuous token models with TCRs to create a liquid market for curation. Instead of generating and pre-selling tokens at one specific point in time, tokens are minted according to a predetermined algorithmic curve. The value of the registry is a function of the usefulness of the list and whether it can act as a natural "Schelling point." A Schelling point, in this context, refers to a list that most users would agree on in the absence of communication. Continuous TCRs are useful to reflect the long tail of categorization that wasn't possible or feasible before.

While the classic proposal of TCRs might have limited use cases, the emergence of more complex and sophisticated proposals is an interesting phenomenon to follow. More and more projects are starting to implement aspects of various TCR proposals in their token design. "Relevant" is building a reputation protocol that combines subjective criteria with TCRs. They want to use this to build a fake news–resistant social news reader, using token-backed qualitative metrics, valuing quality over clicks. Other examples of projects that use TCRs in their token design are "AdChain," "Distric0x," and "Messari."

Chapter Summary

- *Online lists and recommendation engines use (i) machine learning algorithms and (ii) wisdom of the crowd mechanisms to derive meaningful lists, rankings and recommendations. Such lists or registries can be private or public and are usually centrally managed. Whitelists or blacklists are used to filter relevant information and saves the users time researching and filtering information themselves. Third-party curation, however, is prone to censorship and manipulation, as they are centrally managed.*

- *The curation tasks involve managing and maintaining data feeds, filtering comments, or providing context-specific recommendations. Machine-learning algorithms derive their suggestions by correlating personalized user data with statistical data of the behavior of all other users. Their methods are, for the most part, undisclosed, resulting in intransparent filtering algorithms.*

- *Token Curated Registries provide a tokenized market mechanism for collectively curating lists in the absence of third-party coordination and centralized list management. Tokens are used as economic incentives to perform curation tasks. Transactions are settled and cleared autonomously by a distributed ledger.*

- *TCRs are designed to represent a public good. Anyone can participate. In order to set up a TCR, one needs to (i) define a purpose for the list, (ii) a native token, and (iii) a governance mechanism that makes sure that all token holders are incentivized to maintain a high-quality list.*

- *The stakeholders are (i) candidates provide content for the list, (ii) consumers use the list, and (iii) curators collectively manage the quality of the list (token holders).*

- *Candidates have to deposit a certain amount of tokens to apply for the list. Any token holder can participate in the curation process, and has a certain time to cast a vote on whether or not the candidate's application should be included in the list. To do so, they must make a deposit of a certain amount of tokens into a smart contract, locking a part of their network stake.*

- *If at the end of the voting period, the application is rejected by the majority of token holders, the applicant's deposit is split between the challenger and all other token holders who voted to reject the application. Otherwise the listing of the candidate is added to the registry, and the smart contract distributes the challenger's deposit between the applicant and all token holders who voted for accepting the listing.*

- *Candidates who believe they will be rejected are not likely to apply; otherwise, they would lose their tokens. Token holders, on the other hand, could theoretically reject every candidate, but that would collide with their interest to increase the value of their tokens. An empty list is not interesting for anyone. Profitability and quality of all stakeholders need to be well-aligned, so that objective and high-quality lists can be produced.*

- *The price of a token is a result of supply and demand, and as such, assumed to be a performance indicator for the collective actions of all token holders. If a TCR would accept a non-native token as a means of payment, the collective performance of the token holders would not reflect performance of the list and the economic incentive mechanisms would therefore not work.*

- *The vote of token holders is proportional to the number of tokens they own, or stake. Proportional voting rights are based on the idea that those who have the most at stake are most incentivized to act in the network's best interest.*

- *A number of attack vectors have been identified, such as "trolling," "madman attacks," "registry poisoning," or "coin flipping." A solution to each of these potential attacks needs to be reflected in the governance rules of the TCR to guarantee high-quality curation.*

- *TCR can only be successful if (i) an objective answer to the listing question exists and if (ii) the answer is publicly observable. Subjective questions cannot be accurately answered by an objective mechanism. Lists that are prone to subjective tastes or opinions need a stronger coordination signal, which would require a well-defined set of curators with well-aligned values. Combining TCRs with social reputation systems could add necessary context to a TCR might resolve this problem, and mitigate some attack vectors of classic TCRs.*

- *Alternative proposals to objective and subjective TCRs are: (i) Ordered TCRs, (ii) Graded TCRs, (iii) Layered TCRs, (iv) Nested TCRs, (v) Combinatorial TCRs, or (vi) Continuous Token-Curated Registries. They mitigate some of the attack vectors described above, or to add quality of information to the listing. Their token governance rules vary.*

Chapter References & Further Reading

- *Balasanov, Slava: "TCR Design Flaws: Why Blockchain Needs Reputation", Jul 12, 2018: https://blog.relevant.community/tcr-design-flaws-why-blockchain-needs-reputation-c5771d97b210*

- *Bulkin, Aleksandr: "Curate This: Token Curated Registries That Don't Work", Apr 12, 2018: https://blog.coinfund.io/curate-this-token-curated-registries-that-dont-work-d76370b77150*

- *De la Rouviere, Simon: "Continuous Token-Curated Registries: The Infinity of Lists", Oct 21, 2017: https://medium.com/@simondlr/continuous-token-curated-registries-the-infinity-of-lists-69024c9eb70d*

- *De la Rouviere, Simon: "City Walls & Bo-Taoshi: Exploring the Power of Token-Curated Registries", Oct 9, 2017: https://medium.com/@simondlr/city-walls-bo-taoshi-exploring-the-power-of-token- curated-registries-588f208c17d5*

- *De Jonghe, Dimitri: "Curated Governance with Stake Machines", Dec 4, 2017: https://medium.com/@DimitriDeJonghe/curated-governance-with-stake-machines-8ae290a709b4*

- *Gajek, Sebastian: "Graded Token-Curated Decisions with Up-/Downvoting — Designing Cryptoeconomic Ranking and Reputation Systems", Apr 30, 2018: https://medium.com/coinmonks/graded-token-curated-decisions-with-up-downvoting-designing-cryptoeconomic-ranking-and-2ce7c000bb51*

- *Goldin, Mike: "Token-Curated Registries 1.0", ConsenSys: https://docs.google.com/document/d/1BWWC -Kmso9b7yCI_R7ysoGFIT9D_sfjH3axQsmB6E/edit*

- *Goldin, Mike: "Token Curated Registries 1.1, 2.0 TCRs, new theory, and dev updates", Dec 4, 2017: https://medium.com/@ilovebagels/token-curated-registries-1-1-2-0-tcrs-new-theory-and-dev-updates-34c9f079f33d*

- *Goldin, Mike: "Token-Curated Registries 1.0", Sep 14, 2017: https://medium.com/@ilovebagels/token-curated-registries-1-0-61a232f8dac7 https://medium.com/@tokencuratedregistry/the-token-curated-registry-whitepaper-bd2fb29299d*

- *Goldin, Mike: "Mike's Cryptosystems Manifesto #4", https://github.com/kleros/kleros-papers/issues/4*

- *Gibson, Kyle: "3 Questions About Community Building for TCRs", Mar 16, 2018: https://medium.com/tokenreport/questions-about-community-building-for-tcrs-d666b70ad3a7*

- *Lockyer, Matt: "Token Curated Registry (TCR) Design Patterns", May 21, 2018: https://hackernoon.com/token-curated-registry-tcr-design-patterns-4de6d18efa15*

- *N.N.: "LTCR (Layered TCR)": http://tokenengineering.net/ltcr*

- *McConaghy, Trent: "The Layered TCR", May 1, 2018: https://blog.oceanprotocol.com/the-layered-tcr-56cc5b4cdc45*

- *Praver, Moshe: "Subjective vs. Objective TCRs", Jun 27, 2018: https://medium.com/coinmonks/subjective-vs-objective-tcrs-a21f5d848553*

- *https://adchain.com/*

- *https://district0x.io/*

- *https://messari.io/*

- *https://relevant.community/*

How to Design a Token System

If you would like to tokenize your business or community and make it Web3 ready, how do you need to approach your token design? Which questions do you have to ask yourself? What know-how do you need in your team to be able to properly "design" or "engineer" these tokens? The aim of this chapter is to understand what questions are relevant in the design and engineering process of a new token system, depending on what type of token you want to create.

Design thinking approaches found widespread adoption in the product design practices of startups and scaleups of the Web2, with a particular focus on user-centered design or human-centered design. The term "design thinking" dates back to the 1950s and found widespread adoption in the business community over the 1990s. The aim was to apply creativity techniques for novel problem-solving techniques that were solution oriented, yet holistic in their approach. Design thinking approaches help to strategically plan concepts for any new technology, product, or service. The process ranges from problem definition, ideation, solution-focused strategies, modeling, prototyping, testing, and evaluating, including iterative feedback loops thereof.

With the emerging Web3, the term "engineering" is being used in the context of designing token systems by a growing "token engineering" community.[85] The motivation behind using the word engineering (instead of design) is to do justice to the infrastructural and mission-critical nature of Web3 networks and many of their potential applications. Trent McConaghy states that, "Engineering is about rigorous analysis, design, and verification of systems; all assisted by tools that reconcile theory with practice. Engineering is also a discipline of responsibility: being ethically and professionally accountable to the machines that you build, as illustrated by the Tacoma Narrows Bridge viewings and iron rings." He was probably the first person to coin the term "token engineering," hoping that "token ecosystem

---

[85] *http://tokenengineering.wikidot.com/.*

318

design would also become a field of rigorous analysis, design, and verification. It would have tools that reconcile theory with practice. It would be guided by a sense of responsibility."

The terms "design" and "engineering" are closely related but not the same. Rather, they complement each other. While the term "design" might be a more known and intuitive term, carrying a more subjective, creative, and even artistic meaning, the term "engineering" tends to bring to the forefront the technical aspects, the composition of inert parts to create a predictable and robust whole. "A design is a plan or specification for the construction of an object or system or for the implementation of an activity or process, or the result of that plan or specification in the form of a prototype, product or process."[86] Engineering refers to "the use of scientific principles to design and build machines, structures, and other items, including bridges, tunnels, roads, vehicles, and buildings."[87] Design is, therefore, a part of an engineering process. The term "engineering design" is used to describe the part of the engineering process which is open ended and ultimately more subjective.

Similar to electrical engineering and public policy design, token engineering is about rigorous analysis, design, and verification of systems and their assumptions. Their assumptions need to be assisted by tools that reconcile theory with practice. However, as opposed to electrical engineering, designing human behavior is much more similar to steering national economies, and public policy design, as it requires much more "fuzzy" modeling techniques. With the emergence of AI and better simulation tools, we might be able to design and deploy more effective purpose-driven tokens that also factor in unknown probability distributions, unknown or adversarial behaviors of agents, potential network externalities, and "tragedy of the commons" incurred to other parts of society.

While the "token engineering" community points out the necessity for rigorous software engineering practices, it often seems to me that in the theories outlined and practices lived, it mostly focuses on what I would call the "technical engineering" aspects of a token system. A look at the composition of team members of most blockchain/web3/token startups reflects this techno-centricity quite well. Engineering, however, is the practice of creating a technology that ultimately always has a social goal. Looking at engineering though a purely technological lens perpetuates a reductionist mindset on why and how we build technology.

There seems to be a growing understanding for the need of using the term "engineering" in the broader sense when designing a token system. The Web3 with its distributed ledgers and smart contracts provides a governance layer and an eco-

---

[86] *https://en.wikipedia.org/w/index.php?title=Design&oldid=943088539*
[87] *https://en.wikipedia.org/w/index.php?title=Engineering&oldid=943637749*

Token Engineering

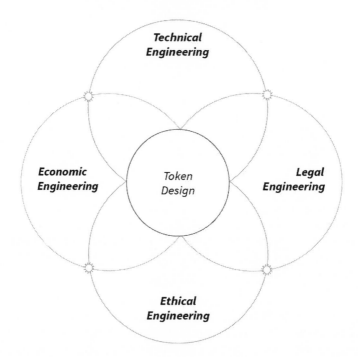

nomic layer for the Internet. If something goes wrong, the collateral damage is high, as we have seen with "TheDAO" exploits of 2016 or the "Parity" multisignature contract exploit of 2017 that resulted in millions of Euros drained from one or more smart contracts, or the more recent DeFi Hacks of 2020. I therefore suggest that we explicitly distinguish between the "technical engineering," "legal engineering," "economic engineering," and "ethical engineering" aspects of a token.

Technical Engineering

When creating a token system, one needs to decide whether to create an infrastructure token or an application token, and how to technically implement the token system. "Infrastructure tokens" are tokens that either steer public blockchain networks (1st layer) or second-layer protocols such as state channels, or other Web3 protocols such as distributed file storage networks (more: Part 1 - Web3, the Stateful Web). These infrastructure tokens are purpose driven, incentivizing collective maintenance of said networks. The most important design questions in the engineering process are related to questions of security, scalability, and privacy.

- <u>Security aspects</u> address the design of the cryptoeconomic mechanisms to provide the level of security needed (more: Part 1 - Token Security & Blockchain and other Distributed Ledgers).

- <u>Scalability aspects</u> address the trade off between security, decentralization, and scalability. Maintaining security and a high level of decentralization while enabling scalability is an engineering question with a variety of trade-offs. Different scalability techniques, such as sharding, interoperability, state channels, and alternative cryptographic tools that reduce bolting of transactions, are currently being tested to address these issues (more: Annex - Scalability).

- <u>Privacy aspects</u> address the questions of what type of cryptography should be used to allow for the right "privacy by design." In early blockchain networks, the data that is included in a token and its exchanges is public to anyone. Via additional cryptographic mechanisms, access grants can be managed in a more privacy-preserving manner (more: Part 3 - Privacy Tokens). However, that does not come for free, as every additional encryption is a cost to add up on the contract invocation.

"Application tokens" are managed by an underlying distributed ledger and other Web3 networks. The technical engineering process will need to consider which infrastructure and token standards to use. It furthermore needs to consider potential interoperability needs of the token system.

- <u>Infrastructure used</u>: Since application tokens are managed by a distributed ledger, all privacy, scalability, decentralization, and security needs of the token will have to be met by the underlying infrastructure. Infrastructural constraints, therefore, need to be considered when choosing between the trade-offs of one solution and another.

- <u>Interoperability</u>: In spite of the fact that distributed ledgers currently have limited interoperability, there are solutions on the horizon that might favor one system over the other. Depending on how much interoperability your token system requires in the long run, infrastructure questions need to be considered.

- <u>Standards</u>: The technical engineering process can choose from a growing list of standardized token contracts. The token standards used depend on the properties a token should have (privacy, fungibility, transferability, expiry date), and the properties depend on the purpose of the token, taking into account all economic, legal, or ethical constraints.

Legal Engineering

Legal Engineering of tokens is the predominant task when we deal with "simple token systems." The term "simple" is commonly used in the complex systems[88] domain. In the context of token engineering, the term "simple" refers to the fact that the dynamics of the business or governance models of a potential token are well known, as in the case of (i) central bank money, (ii) securities and other assets, (iii) identification and certification processes, (iv) voting rights, (v) vouchers and coupons, or (vi) entry tickets and other access rights. The respective business or governance processes of these use cases have been stress tested over decades, sometimes centuries. Potential loopholes have been closed over the years in a process of trial and error, and there is regulation in place. Tokenization of such business/governance processes requires predominantly legal engineering, which refers to making the tokenization of existing assets, access rights, and voting rights legally compliant with local legislation. Legal engineering, therefore, refers to the tokenization of traditional governance models where smart contracts replace many of the existing human/paper/client-server-based operations. Relevant questions in the legal engineering process of credential tokens, currency tokens, asset tokens, or voting-rights tokens are:

- Which transnational/national/local jurisdiction(s) need to be considered?

- Which regulatory bodies might be concerned?

- How do we design smart contracts so that they are legally compliant?

- Does the jurisdiction need to be changed to cater to the new possibilities/ dynamics of tokenization and the Web3?

Economic Engineering

Economic engineering is predominantly required when designing "complex token systems." The incentives and governance rules of the community are tied to "purpose-driven tokens" that steer collective action of the community through automated mechanisms (more: Part 4 - Purpose-Driven Tokens). The governance

---

[88] *Complex systems theory investigates the relationships between system parts with the system's collective behaviors and the system's environment. Complex systems differ from other systems, in that the system behavior cannot be easily inferred from the state changes induced by network actors. Properties such as emergence, nonlinearity, adaptation, spontaneous order, and feedback loops are typical to complex systems. Modeling approaches that ignore such difficulties will produce models that are not useful for modeling and steering those systems." Voshmgir, S.; Zargham, M.: "Foundations of Cryptoeconomic Systems" (see references)*

models are mostly unknown and a result of the myriad of new possibilities to regulate collective action over the Web3 in the absence of intermediaries by using smart contracts and distributed ledgers. Many refer to these tokens as "utility tokens," "work tokens," or "consensus tokens." What all these tokens have in common is that they steer collective action toward a common purpose. Such common purposes could be consensus, resource sharing, reputation and curation, reduction of CO_2 emissions, etc. The tools that are necessary to design such systems can be found in economics, network science, cyber-physical systems, and sociotechnical systems.

- Economics deals with the studies of economic institutions, policies, and ethics, including questions of resource allocation, wealth disparities, and market dynamics in the context of the production, distribution, and consumption of goods and services.

- Network science studies complex networks, from biological networks to classic telecommunication networks, computer networks to social networks. Methods used include mathematics, physics, computer science, and sociology.

- Cyber-physical systems are mechanisms that are controlled or monitored by computer-based algorithms, tightly integrated with the Internet and its users. Examples include power grids and large-scale transportation systems, which both share the property that behavior of uncontrolled human actors can create undesirable or even unsafe conditions in entirely counter-intuitive ways.

- Sociotechnical systems was first coined in the 1940s and refers to the interaction of social and technical aspects of private and public organizations and communities, online and in the real world. It refers to the studies of the complex infrastructures a society uses, such as the Internet and other communication networks, supply chains, and legal systems, and human behavior. The relation can be either simple (linear cause-and-effect relationships) or complex (non-linear and hard to steer and predict).

The main questions that need to be answered in such design processes are:

- Goal of your token system: What kind of system do you want to create?

- How many different token types do you need? Some token systems have multiple token types to steer collective action within the network. Examples that were explained in previous chapters of this book are the decentralized social media network Steemit (STEEM, SP, SBD) or the stable token MakerDAO (DAI, WETH, PETH, SIN, MKR). Other token systems only have one token, like the Bitcoin network. It can be generally assumed that the more token types, the more complex the network dynamics of steering that network.

- Purpose: The definition of a clear purpose of the token is necessary for the further design process. Having analyzed over 100 token systems, it seems that clearer the purpose, the more resilient the network. My personal opinion is that a token should only have one purpose. If you have multiple purposes, you probably need more token types. Otherwise, the mechanism design of your token system can become too complex.

- Properties: Once the purpose is defined, one can derive the properties of the token, taking into account all economic, legal, or ethical constraints that could influence the dynamics of a token system. Examples for property choice and potential dynamics are: (i) Transferability: Are the tokens tied to a unique identity (person or institution) or do they have limited transferability? Depending on the use case, the answer would be different. Limited transferability automatically reduces the liquidity of a token, making it infeasible as a medium of exchange. Reputation tokens, for example, need to be tied to the identity of a person or organization in the network and should have no transferability at all. Transferable reputation tokens could be traded on the free market, making them non-indicative for personal behavior in the network, as in the case of "Steem Power" tokens in the Steemit ecosystem. (ii) Fungibility: If tokens are identical and not tied to an identity, the monetary policy of a token system, including the inflation rate, needs to be determined because the tokens can act as a medium of exchange (payment token). (iii) Expiry Date: If a token has an expiry date, this will reduce inflation of the token. An expiry date might also be desirable in the case of coupons or entry tickets and other access rights.

- Proof-of...: The properties of a token are the basis for modeling a fault-tolerant mechanism to steer the network toward a collective goal. The aim of such a fault-tolerant mechanism is to define upon which behavior the tokens are minted, so it is resilient against corruption, attacks, or mistakes. Proof-of-Work has proven to be resilient to achieve the purpose (P2P transactions). The reputation token of the Steemit network (Steem Power), on the other hand, doesn't have a resilient token design to fit its purpose (to serve as a fault-tolerant reputation token that is indicative of quality content).

Ethical Engineering

The design of token systems also requires ethical and political thinking. What type of system we want to create is not a technological question but a socio-economic and political question. Questions of politics, morals, and ethics will need to be answered, ideally before the design of such systems. If we fail to incorporate ethical questions in the design thinking process of such systems, we will create "protocol bias." History has shown that, eventually, all these questions will need to be resolved. However, if that is done after the fact, after a system has been created, these biases are hard to reverse due to system inertia (see Cambridge Analytica scandal and the discussions on privacy, control, and social media governance that followed in the wake of the scandal, and the challenges the Facebook network is facing right now). However, we do not have to reinvent the wheel. We can apply engineering ethics[89] to the creation of Internet-based systems, something that the Silicon Valley and other big players of the Internet era have failed to do. In terms of token design, two of the most important ethical and political questions are:

- Transparency vs. Privacy: The trade-off between public and private interests is an age-old political discussion that has been studied by political science and sociology. While the privacy of the individual is important, it might undermine the public interest. Let's take the case of supply chain transparency: while most consumers probably agree that more information about what happens along the supply chain of goods and services is what they would wish for, the act of providing such a level of transparency could infringe individual rights (i.e. a camera in a factory to monitor workers' rights also violates the privacy of the workers, depending on how that data is revealed). It is therefore crucial that we hire social scientists with the right know-how when answering such questions.

- Power Structures: Trade-off between decentralization, security, and scalability is a much discussed topic in blockchain networks. The trilemma of decentralization raises the political question of how much decentralization is needed/wanted depending on the use case and the values of a community. The more decentralized, the slower the network is, and vice versa. Otherwise, one has to sacrifice security of the network. Power structures are also important when designing reputation tokens on a social media network like Steemit.com. In its current design, most reputation tokens (Steem Power) are owned by a handful of big players in the network, and only those decide on which story is relevant or not.

---

[89] *"engineering ethics identify a specific precedence with respect to the engineer's consideration for the public, clients, employers, and the profession. Many engineering professional societies have prepared codes of ethics. Some date to the early decades of the twentieth century (which) have been incorporated to a greater or lesser degree into the regulatory laws of several jurisdictions." (https://en.wikipedia.org/wiki/Engineering_ethics#General_principles) Or, as the American Society of Civil Engineers states: "Engineers shall hold paramount the safety, health and welfare of the public and shall strive to comply with the principles of sustainable development in the performance of their professional duties."*

Token Engineering Aspects

Technical Engineering

Programming of token requires a set of technical design questions to be resolved:

Infrastructure Tokens:
Security?
Scalability?
Privacy?

Application Tokens:
On which Infrastructure (distr. ledger)?
Token Standards?
Interoperability?

Computer Science

Legal Engineering

Tokenizing existing assets, access rights & voting rights in a legally compliant way. Especially relevant in "simple token systems" where the dynamics of business/governance models are well known such as identity tokens, payment tokens, asset tokens.

Questions: Relevant jurisdiction(s)? Relevant regulation? How to design legally compliant smart contracts or change existing regulation to make it Web3 ready?

Legal Studies

Economic Engineering

Especially relevant for "complex token systems" where rules of the community are tied to "purpose-driven tokens" that steer collective action with automated mechanisms.

Purpose: consensus, reputation, curation, reduction of CO_2 emissions
Questions: How many token types? Single or multi-token econ? Purpose? Proof-of... ?
Properties: Transferable? Identical? Expiry Date? Inflation? etc.

Economics, Network Science Cyber Physical Systems

Ethical Engineering

Questions of politics, morals & ethics will need to be answered, ideally before the design of such systems, otherwise "protocol bias."

Transparency & Privacy: Tradeoff between public & private interests is an age-old political discussion.
Power Structures: Tradeoff: decentralization, security & scalability? Distribution of reputation tokens in social media networks like Steemit? Who gets to vote in the network?

Political Science, Ethics, Sociology, Engineering Ethics

To cover all aspects mentioned above, one needs an interdisciplinary team with the necessary expertise in all four fields of the engineering process who work hand in hand. Having lawyers, economists, and social scientists as part of the team in addition to the technical engineers, on executive level and below, will be paramount to developing resilient token systems. However, interdisciplinary work takes time and effort, as all four categories overlap and communication between the disciplines requires some ramp-up efforts. The quick and dirty approach of the Web1 and Web2, where the development process was rather "hack now and pivot later" oriented, does not play out well in the Web3. Once the bias is in the protocol, it is hard to revert the changes without consensus of all network actors. We, therefore, need to move away from Silicon Valley "meme-based development" to an "engineering-based development" that includes all aspects of the engineering process. "Simple token systems" will probably require predominantly legal and technological engineering, while "complex token systems" will need a good balance of all four areas.

Chapter Summary

- *The terms "design" and "engineering" are closely related but not the same. Rather, they complement each other. While the term "design" might be a more known and intuitive term, carrying a more subjective, creative, and even artistic meaning, the term "engineering" tends to bring to the forefront the technical aspects, the composition of inert parts to create a predictable and robust whole.*

- *Design is a part of an engineering process. The term "engineering design" is used to describe the part of the engineering process which is open ended and ultimately more subjective. Similar to electrical engineering and public policy design, token engineering is about rigorous analysis, design, and verification of systems and their assumptions. Their assumptions need to be assisted by tools that reconcile theory with practice. As opposed to electrical engineering, designing human behavior is much more similar to steering national economies, and public policy design, as it requires much more "fuzzy" modeling techniques.*

- *With the emergence of AI and better simulation tools, we might be able to design and deploy more effective purpose-driven tokens that also factor in unknown probability distributions, unknown or adversarial behaviors of agents, potential network externalities, and "tragedy of the commons" incurred to other parts of society.*

- *Engineering is the practice of creating a technology that ultimately always has a social goal. Looking at engineering though a purely technological lens perpetuates a reductionist mindset on why and how we build technology. There seems to be a growing understanding for the need of using the term "engineering" in the broader sense when designing a token system.*

- *The Web3 with its distributed ledgers and smart contracts provides a governance layer and an economic layer for the Internet. If something goes wrong, the collateral damage is high.*

- *Technical engineering relates to the technical questions of creating an infrastructure token or an application token, and how to technically implement the token system: Infrastructure tokens or application tokens? Security aspects address the design of the cryptoeconomic mechanisms to provide the level of security needed. Scalability aspects address the trade off between security, decentralization, and scalability. Privacy aspects address the questions of what type of cryptography should be used to allow for the right "privacy by design."*

- *Legal Engineering of tokens is the predominant task when we deal with "simple token systems." The term "simple" is commonly used in the complex systems domain. In the context of token engineering, the term "simple" refers to the fact that the dynamics of the business or governance models of a potential token are well known, as in the case of (i) central bank money, (ii) securities and other assets, (iii) identification and certifi-*

cation processes, (iv) voting rights, (v) vouchers and coupons, or (vi) entry tickets and other access rights. Tokenizing known business/governance processes requires making the tokenization of existing assets, access rights, and voting rights legally compliant with local legislation.

- Economic engineering is predominantly required when designing "complex token systems." The incentives and governance rules of the community are tied to "purpose-driven tokens" that steer collective action of the community through automated mechanisms. The tools that are necessary to design such systems can be found in economics, network science, cyber-physical systems, and sociotechnical systems. The main questions that need to be answered in such design processes deal with the following questions: What kind of system do you want to create? How many different token types do you need? Purpose? Properties: Transferability, fungibility, expiry date?

- The design of token systems also requires ethical and political thinking. What type of system we want to create is not a technological question but a socio-economic and political question. Questions of politics, morals, and ethics will need to be answered, ideally before the design of such systems, the most important of which revolve around the questions of "transparency vs. privacy" and "power structures." If we fail to incorporate ethical questions in the design thinking process of such systems, we will create "protocol bias"

- Having lawyers, economists, and social scientists as part of the team in addition to the technical engineers, on executive level and below, will be paramount to developing resilient token systems. However, interdisciplinary work takes time and effort, as all four categories overlap and communication between the disciplines requires some ramp-up efforts.

Chapter References & Further Reading

- Archer, L. Bruce: "Systematic Method for Designers. Council of Industrial Design," H.M.S.O., 1965.
- Archer, L. Bruce. „Design Management," Management Decision 1.4, 47–51, 1967
- Arnold, J.E.: "Creative Engineering: Promoting Innovation by Thinking Differently, " Edited With an Introduction and Biographical Essay by William J. Clancey. Stanford Digital Repository. Retrieved September 23, 2018.
- Cooper, R.; Foster, M.:"Sociotechnical systems," American Psychologist, 26, 467-474, 1971
- Cross, N., Dorst, K.;Roozenburg, N.: " Research in Design Thinking," Delft University Press, 1992
- Cross, N.: "A Brief History of the Design Thinking," Research Symposium Series, Design Studies vol 57, 160–164, 2018
- Esener, Esen: "An Essay on Legal Engineering: From Confusion to Clarity," Sep 11, 2019: https://medium.com/@esenesener/an-essay-on-legal-engineering-from-confusion-to-clarity-908c8e731df7
- Faste, Rolf, Roth, Bernard, Wilde, Douglass J.: „Integrating Creativity into the Mechanical Engineering Curriculum," Cary A. Fisher (Editor), ASME Resource Guide to Innovation in Engineering Design, American Society of Mechanical Engineers, New York, 1993

- *Lawson, Bryan: "How Designers Think: The Design Process Demystified," London, Architectural, 1980*
- *Long, Susan: "Socioanalytic Methods: Discovering the Hidden in Organisations and Social Systems," 2018*
- *Merriam-Webster: https://www.merriam-webster.com/dictionary/design*
- *McConaghy, Trent: "Towards a Practice of Token Engineering Methodology, Patterns & Tools," TE Series Part II, Mar 1, 2018: https://blog.oceanprotocol.com/towards-a-practice-of-token-engineering-b02feeeff7ca*
- *McKim, Robert: "Experiences in Visual Thinking," Brooks/Cole Publishing Co, 1973*
- *Paruch, Krzysztof: "Token Engineering from an Economic Perspective," Nov 6, 2018: https://medium.com/crypto3conomics/token-engineering-from-an-economic-perspective-b6c464f20241*
- *Rowe, G. Peter: "Design Thinking," Cambridge, The MIT Press, 1987*
- *Simon, Herbert: "The Sciences of the Artificial, " Cambridge, MIT Press, 1969*
- *Wikipedia contributors, „Engineering," Wikipedia, The Free Encyclopedia, https://en.wikipedia.org/w/index.php?title=Engineering&oldid=943637749 (accessed March 16, 2020).*
- *Wikipedia contributors, „Design," Wikipedia, The Free Encyclopedia, https://en.wikipedia.org/w/index.php?title=Design&oldid=943088539 (accessed March 16, 2020).*
- *Voshmgir, Shermin: "Token Engineering Research," Nov 6, 2018, https://medium.com/crypto3conomics/token-engineering-research-b6627add09ee*
- *Voshmgir, Shermin: "Purpose-Driven Tokens," Apr 11, 2019: https://medium.com/crypto3conomics/purpose-driven-tokens-51334d278c32*
- *Zargham, Michael: "Token Engineering 101: Why Engineering is Necessary," Jul 1, 2018: https://medium.com/@michaelzargham/token-engineering-101-why-engineering-is-necessary-3bac27ccb8b7*
- *Token Engineering Wiki: https://twitter.com/tokengineering*
- *Token Engineering Slides: https://www.slideshare.net/tokenengineering*

Outlook

Blockchains networks and similar distributed ledgers are essentially token-management machines and the backbone of the Web3. Due to the open source nature of the Bitcoin protocol, the idea of P2P value transfer was copied and forked by many other projects, which spurred a lot of innovation around the topic. Through the backdoor of the token sales hysteria in 2016 and 2017, cryptographic tokens have emerged to be the killer application of the Web3. Just as the WWW made it easy to publish a webpage with a few lines of code, the Web3 made it just as easy to issue your own token in a few lines of code. However, it took us over a decade to figure out what we can really do with websites, and when we did, the Web2 took off. The crypto community, together with researchers, still needs to develop methods suitable for the formalization of classification, design, architecture, parameters, and behavior of agents in a tokenized network. It might, therefore, take a while before the power of this new token economy ahead of us can be unleashed.

No meaningful token application will run on distributed ledgers alone. Many use cases that are attributed to blockchain networks or other distributed ledgers only, such as transparency along the supply chain of goods and services, will only be possible in interaction with machine-learning algorithms, Big Data, and the Internet of Things. The convergence of all these emergent technologies will be more powerful than the effect of any of those technological innovations alone. However, most of these emerging technologies have not reached their inflection point yet, but when they do, network effects and exponential development will kick in. While it is hard to foresee when this could happen, it is likely that it will take less than ten years.

When talking about distributed ledgers, tokens, and the Web3, most people seem to focus on the positive potentials. But any technology is always just a tool. How we use that tool is almost never a technological question, but a governance question. The question of how we design these Web3 protocols and their tokenized applications is much more of a socio-political-economic issue than a technological one. Discussing potential negative aspects at such an early stage is therefore crucial. One of the most important aspects will revolve around developing and deploying privacy by design and power structures; otherwise, what was designed to be a free P2P value exchange can soon become an effective control machine and a perfect tool for totalitarian regimes.

Annex

Origins of Bitcoin & the Web3

The Bitcoin white paper didn't come out of thin air and P2P networks are not a new phenomenon. They are rooted in the early history of the computer and the Internet, building on decades of research of computer networks, cryptography, and game theory.

The first computer networks were invented in the 1960s. ARPANET was a private network of American university computers introduced in 1969, which was initially funded by the Advanced Research Projects Agency of the United States Department of Defense. It went global in 1973, when the computers of research institutions in England and Norway were connected to the network. In 1974, it turned commercial with the integration of the first Internet service provider—Telnet. That same year, a paper was published describing a working protocol for sharing resources using packet switching among the nodes. A central control component of this protocol was the Transmission Control Program (TCP). In 1982, TCP's monolithic architecture was divided into a modular architecture that consisted of a transport layer (TCP) and the Internet layer, also known as "Internet Protocol" (IP). Another breakthrough was achieved in 1983 with the introduction of DNS, which made the addressing of nodes within the network more readable.

In these first-generation computer networks, the main focus was on connecting a public network of computers with each other, and resolving the question of addressing computers and transmitting data. The network architecture was still based on client-server logic, and secure communication was never a mainstream focus in the early days of the Internet, but selected researchers were intrigued by exactly this question. Ralph Merkle's cryptographic research in the early 1970s laid the foundation of secure communication over P2P networks. His work conceptualized how to resolve "secure communication over insecure channels" like a computer network, and laid the foundation for modern public-key cryptography. In his dissertation, he furthermore described a method of building collision-resistant cryptographic hash functions. He also filed a patent for a special type of hash table called a Merkle tree that allowed more efficient and secure verification of the contents of large data structures.

In 1976, Whitfield Diffie and Martin Hellman built on some of his ideas and created a mechanism for securely exchanging cryptographic keys over a public network. It was one of the earliest implemented examples of public key exchange, and also introduced the concept of digital signatures. Before public key methods were invented, cryptographic keys had to be transmitted in physical form, so secure digital key exchange over public networks was groundbreaking work, without which Bitcoin and subsequent technologies would not work. In 1978, Ron Rivest, Adi Shamir, and Leonard Adleman found a way to create a one-way cryptographic function that was hard to invert. Their algorithm—now known as RSA—introduced the era of asymmetric cryptography, which then evolved into the use of elliptic curves in cryptography—suggested independently by Neal Koblitz and Victor S. Miller in 1985, also a key technology in Bitcoin.

In public computer networks, the structure of the system—network topology, network latency, and number of computers—is not known in advance. The computer network can therefore consist of unknown and untrusted computers and network links. The size and composition of the network can also change at any time during the execution of a distributed program. The ability to provide and maintain an acceptable level of service in the face of faulty processes is thus essential to the resilience of a network. The focus back in the day was on data transmission in a public network, which was already a hard problem to solve. Neither TCP or IP resolved the question of where to store and how to manage the data. For economic reasons, centralized data storage and management became mainstream. The problem with client-server networks is that the system administrators, or institutions controlling the servers, have sole control over the data, which makes those systems prone to censorship, corruption, and attack.

In the meantime, with the rise of the personal computer and the introduction of the Internet Protocol Suite, the Internet became more widespread. However, usability was still a problem. You had to navigate the Internet using command lines, a.k.a. computer language. Tim Berners-Lee resolved this problem with his vision for the World Wide Web. He introduced a standard for creating visual websites with a relatively simple markup language, and navigating the Web with links, which point to other websites with a simple click. From a publishing point of view, the WWW allowed everyone to easily be an equal contributor to information available on the Internet. However, data was still stored and managed behind the walled garden of servers.

In 1982, David Chaum introduced the concept of Blind signatures, which guaranteed the privacy of the sender of information. It was conceptualized for use in voting systems and digital cash systems. Chaum introduced the idea of "Ecash" as an anonymous cryptographic electronic money or electronic cash system, which was commercialized through his company "Digicash" and used as a micropayment

337

system at one US bank from 1995 to 1998. The system was dissolved in 1998, possibly because he was ahead of his time, as e-commerce applications were not that widespread yet.

In 1991, Stuart Haber and W. Scott Stornetta introduced a system where document timestamps could not be tampered with, introducing the earliest academic works on a cryptographically secured chain of blocks. Their aim was to certify when a document was created or modified "in a world in which all text, audio, pictures, and video documents are in digital form and in easily modifiable media." In their initial proposals, they used centralized timestamping services. They then tried to distribute trust by requiring several users—that were selected through pseudo-random number generators—to timestamp the hash, instead of a centralized institution. A year later, in 1992, Bayer, Haber, and Stornetta wrote another paper where they included Merkle trees in the mechanism. This improved the system efficiency by allowing several document certificates to be collected into one block.

In 1997, Adam Back introduced "Hashcash," the first Proof-of-Work function, to limit email spam and denial of service attacks by forcing computers to invest with computational work. The original idea was proposed by Cynthia Dwork and Moni Naor in their 1992 paper, "Pricing via Processing or Combatting Junk Mail."

In 2004, the concept introduced by Hashcash was also used as a mining mechanism in "B-money," a proposal by Wei Dai for an "anonymous, distributed electronic cash system." It was proposed on the "cypherpunk mailing list," which represented a group of activists advocating use of strong cryptography and privacy-enhancing technologies over the Internet. Many of the above mentioned individuals who contributed key technologies that were later used in Bitcoin were active "cypherpunks."

In 1998, Nick Szabo designed a mechanism for a decentralized digital currency—"BitGold"—where he implemented many of his prior ideas around smart contracts and added a PoW-based consensus algorithm where computing power would be spent to solve cryptographic puzzles (read more: Part 1 - Smart Contracts). BitGold was never deployed, possibly because it could not resolve the problem of double-spending in a fully decentralized, sybil attack–resistant way. Szabo was speculated by many to be Satoshi Nakamoto, Bitcoin's anonymous creator, but it is a rumor he has always denied.

In 1999, "Napster," a music-sharing application, introduced the concept of P2P networks that changed the way data was stored and distributed over the Internet. Napster created a virtual overlay network for decentralized file sharing applications, which was independent from the physical network of the Internet, removing the "single point of failure" of centralized data systems. However, Napster relied on the operation of central indexing servers, and was thus susceptible to shutdown, after copyright infringement claims and a legal battle.

A new family of file sharing protocols spearheaded by Gnutella in 2000 eliminated such central points of failure. It allowed users to find each other and connect remotely, searching every node on the network, and therefore was more decentralized and censorship resistant. While Gnutella resolved the decentralization problem, they did not resolve the privacy problem. Third-generation file sharing networks like BitTorrent used distributed hash tables to store resource locations throughout the entire network, in a cryptographically secure way. Distributed hash tables not only replaced indexing servers but also guaranteed anonymity of its network actors and all data being shared over the network. These distributed hash tables are now also used by blockchain networks and other Web3 protocols like IPFS and Ethereum. While P2P networks, since the emergence of Napster, have resolved the problem of efficiently distributing data within a network, they did not resolve decentralized validation or verification of data. Neither did they solve the free-rider problem, the fact that large numbers of users would use resources shared by other users while not contributing with files themselves. Users did not have a short-term economic incentive to upload files and instead consumed resources while degrading their own performance.

In 2004, Hal Finney introduced a reusable PoW system (RPoW), a concept where the value of a token is guaranteed by the value of the real-world resources required to "mint" a PoW token. The fact that Finney received the first Bitcoin transaction from Satoshi Nakamoto in 2009, and that he apparently lived in the same town as a person called "Dorian Satoshi Nakamoto," led to speculation that he may have been Satoshi, a rumor that he always denied.

Modern P2P networks such as Napster suffered from a missing incentive mechanism for network contributions, and early e-cash ideas were not able to defend against sybil attacks. The Bitcoin white paper, published in 2008 under the pseudonym Satoshi Nakamoto, resolved these issues by proposing a sybil attack–resistant incentive mechanism for collective validation of data. Proof-of-Work resolved the free-rider problem of previous P2P networks by introducing tokenized incentives to motivate all actors to contribute to the system in a truthful manner. Bitcoin was proposed in the aftermath of the financial crisis of 2008 and the collapse of major banks like Lehman Brothers. The aim was to provide a system for P2P electronic cash without banks. While the first specifications were implemented by Satoshi, a group of dedicated individuals gradually took over to implement further development of the code, which was finalized and deployed in early 2009. Interestingly, the Bitcoin white paper only mentioned a "chain of blocks." The term "blockchain" became widespread years later, when people started to replicate the Bitcoin codebase for developing similar blockchain-based protocols.

Even though Bitcoin was never designed with file sharing in mind, it eventually inspired a new class of P2P storage frameworks, a crucial building block for the Web3. Such decentralized storage networks can now use the power of tokens to build on the legacy of previous file-sharing protocols, using a blockchain as a universal state layer. Bitcoin also spurred a lot of research around sybil attack–resistant consensus mechanisms. Sibyl attack resistance, however, also depends on the resilience of the assumptions made on how network actors will react to economic incentives. How people react to incentives has long been a field of study in economics. In 2007, Hurwicz, Maskin, and Myerson won the Nobel Prize in economics for their research on Mechanism Design, an emerging field of research (read more: Part 4 - Purpose-Driven Tokens).

Chapter References & Further Reading

• *Andersen, D.; Balakrishnan, H.; Kaashoek, M.; Morris, R.: "Resilient Overlay Networks, Association for Computing Machinery", October 2001: http://nms.lcs.mit.edu/papers/ron-sosp2001.pdf*

• *Bayer, Dave; Stuart A., Haber; Wakefield Scott, Stornetta; „Improving the Efficiency And Reliability of Digital Time-Stamping". Sequences II: Methods in Communication, Security and Computer Science. Springer-Verlag: 329–334, 1992*

• *Bertsekas, D.; Gallager, R.: „Data Networks," Prentice Hall, 1992*

• *Chaum, David, „Blind signatures for untraceable payments", Advances in Cryptology Proceedings. 82 (3): 199–203, 1983: http://www.hit.bme.hu/~buttyan/courses/BMEVIHIM219/2009/Chaum.BlindSigForPayment.1982.PDF*

• *Chaum, D.; Fiat, A.; Naor, M.; „Untraceable electronic cash", Advances in Cryptology - CRYPTO, 88 Proceedings. New York: Springer-Verlag. pp. 319–327, 1990: http://blog.koehntopp.de/uploads/chaum_fiat_naor_ecash.pdf*

• *Coulouris, George; Jean Dollimore; Tim Kindberg; Gordon Blair: "Distributed Systems: Concepts and Design", 5th Edition, Addison-Wesley, 2011 Kademlia: A Peer-to-peer information system based on the XOR Metric http://www.scs.stanford.edu/~dm/home/papers/*

• *Diffie, W.; Hellman, M.E.; "New Directions in Cryptography" IEEE Transactions on Information Theory, VOL. IT-22, NO. 6, Nov. 1976: https://ee.stanford.edu/~hellman/publications/24.pdf*

• *Haber, S.; Stornetta, W. S.; „How to time-stamp a digital document", Journal of Cryptology. 3 (2), 1991*

• *Hughes, Eric; "A Cypherpunk's Manifesto", 1993: https://www.activism.net/cypherpunk/manifesto.html*

• *Hurwicz, Leonid; Reiter, Stanley: "Designing Economic Mechanisms", Cambridge University, 200*

• *Nisan, Noam; Ronen, Amir; „Algorithmic mechanism design", Proceedings of the 31st ACM Symposium on Theory of Computing (STOC ,99), pp. 129–140, 1999*

• *McFadden, Daniel: "The human side of mechanism design: a tribute to Leo Hurwicz and Jean-Jacque Laffont", Review of Economic Design, April 2009, Volume 13, Issue 1–2, pp 77–100*

• *Mansfield-Devine, Steve (December 2009). „Darknets". Computer Fraud & Security. 2009 (12): 4–6. doi:10.1016/S1361-3723(09)70150-2.*

• *Merkle, R.C.; "Secrecy, authentication, and public key systems", Stanford Ph.D. thesis 1979: http://www.merkle.com/papers/Thesis1979.pdf*

• *Merkle, R.C.; "Method of providing digital signatures", United States Patent, 4,309,569, 1979: https://patentimages.storage.googleapis.com/69/ab/d9/2ff9f94fada6ea/US4309569.pdf*

- Merkle, R.C.; *"Secure Communications Over Insecure Channels"*, Department of Electrical Engineering and Computer Sciences University of California, Berkeley, Programming Techniques s.
- L. Graham, R. L. Rivest Editors, 1974: *http://www.merkle.com/1974/PuzzlesAsPublished.pdf http://www.merkle.com/1974/Puzzles1975.12.07.pdf*
- Metcalfe, Robert M.; Boggs, David R.: „Ethernet: Distributed Packet Switching for Local Computer Networks". *Communications of the ACM. 19 (5): 395–404. July 1976: https://web.archive.org/web/20070807213308/http://www.acm.org/classics/apr96/*
- Nakamoto, Satoshi; „Bitcoin: A Peer-to-Peer Electronic Cash System". *Bitcoin.org, 2008, Archived from the original on 20 March 2014: https://bitcoin.org/bitcoin.pdf*
- Rivest, R.; Shamir, A.; Adleman, L.; „A Method for Obtaining Digital Signatures and Public-Key Cryptosystems", February 1978: *http://people.csail.mit.edu/rivest/Rsapaper.pdf*
- Saroiu, S., P., Gummadi, K., Gribble, S. D.: *"A Measurement Study of Peer-to-Peer File Sharing Systems", Technical Report UW-CSE-01-06-02, University of Washington, Department of Computer Science and Engineering, July 2001.*
- Simmonds, A; Sandilands, P; van Ekert, L.:*"An Ontology for Network Security Attack". Lecture Notes in Computer Science. 3285: 317–323.*
- Szabo, Nick; *"Bit gold"*, December 27, 2008: *http://unenumerated.blogspot.com/2005/12/bit-gold.html*
- Wei Dai, b-money, an anonymous, distributed electronic cash system: *http://www.weidai.com/bmoney.tx*
- Wood, Jessica: „The Darknet: A Digital Copyright Revolution", *Richmond Journal of Law and Technology. 16 (4), 2010: http://jolt.richmond.edu/v16i4/article14.pdf*
- IPFS: *https://ipfs.io/*
- SIA: *https://sia.tech/*
- Storj: *https://storj.io*
- Swarm: *https://swarm-guide.readthedocs.io/en/latest/*
- Wikipedia contributors: „Peer-to-peer," *Wikipedia, The Free Encyclopedia, https://en.wikipedia.org/wiki/Peer-to-peer (accessed January 9, 2019).*
- Bitcoin Wiki contributors: *"B-Money," Bitcoin Wiki: https://en.bitcoinwiki.org/wiki/B-money (accessed January 9, 2019).*

Blockchain Scalability Solutions

One of the greatest challenges of a distributed consensus like Proof-of-Work is that, while it makes the network safe, it does not scale well. This is due to the trade-off between decentralization, security, and scalability.

Disclaimer: Research and development around scalability solutions is subject to current events. This chapter will give a general overview, but is by far not complete in outlining all possible solutions and/or their tradeoffs.

The "scalability trilemma" describes the trade-off in distributed consensus between decentralization, security, and scalability. Decentralization is the premise of a distributed network, security is the most important aspect when the network involves a set of untrusted actors, and scalability refers to the number of transactions a system can process per second. In order to allow for a high degree of inclusion of computationally weaker nodes, the block size in a Proof-of-Work network is limited and blocks are created with a delay. Otherwise, since larger blocks are harder to process, network latency would prevent weaker nodes from participating in the block creation process. Such limitations, however, reduce the amount of transactions that can be validated in a given timeframe, and as a result, Proof-of-Work mechanisms are safe but don't scale well. In the early days of blockchain networks, scalability was hardly addressed by the developer community, as the traffic in those networks was still low. Today, scalability of public blockchain networks is one of the major bottlenecks of mass adoption and also one of the most worked on R&D questions.

Blockchain scalability is comparable to the early days of the Internet, where we used to pull phone cables through our apartments in order to connect our computers with the Internet. As for the connection, bandwidth was low and communication was slow; one had to wait for pages to build up pixel by pixel. The introduction of 56k modems was considered a major improvement to the 28k modem, but video streaming was considered a distant dream. While data throughput was an issue, these issues were eventually resolved, and it certainly did not stop the Internet from evolving into what it is today. In the context of blockchain networks, many solutions have been proposed to make transactions faster and cheaper, while maintaining security and a certain level of decentralization. Scalability solutions can address these issues on (i) protocol level, or on (ii) second-layer level.

When they are addressed on protocol level, it often leads to centralization. More transaction volume per second often requires granting more powers to certain nodes, thus increasing the level of centralization. Alternative consensus mechanisms try to resolve the scalability issue by introducing some kind of permission layer to guarantee trust. The chapter "Bitcoin, Blockchain & Other Distributed Ledgers" that is featured in the first part of this book, has a whole subchapter dedicated to a list of alternative distributed ledger solutions and consensus protocols that try - among others - resolve the questions of throughput. Most popular solutions for achieving higher levels of throughput are alternative consensus protocols such as delegated Proof of Stake (dPoS), practical Byzantine fault tolerance (pBFT), or permissioned networks. Sharding of the ledger or alternative cryptographic algorithms are other means to address the scalability problem on the protocol level and will be described in this chapter.

As an alternative, various efforts have been made to move scalability solutions to a second layer, such as "side chains" or "state channels." In both cases, user interactions are shifted from the blockchain layer onto a second layer, while guaranteeing risk-free P2P transactions between participants.

State Channels

State channels offer a second layer on top of a blockchain network, allowing transactions that could occur on-chain to get settled off-chain, while maintaining the security of all network participants. In this process, transaction settlements are outsourced to a private state channel, which could be described as a two-way pathway between two users. These state channels are formalized and processed by a smart contract. "State channels" allow for the transfer of any state for any type of decentralized application. "Payment channels" only allow for the transfer of payments. They are useful if two parties, Alice and Bob, have an ongoing business relationship with continuous back-and-forth payments.

Tokens are temporarily locked as a security mechanism in case of disputes: (i) Tokens can be sent from Alice to Bob and vice versa using state channels where they are locked up via a multi-signature scheme or a smart contract for a pre-defined period of time. (ii) Both Alice and Bob sign each transaction with their private key, but the transactions are kept private and are not broadcasted to the blockchain network. (iii) After the period has passed, the balance of all bilateral transactions is broadcasted to the blockchain network, which closes the state channel.

State Channels

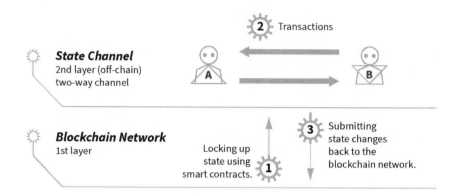

Let's assume that Alice has 200 ETH and Bob has 100 ETH. Within a certain period of time, Alice sends ten payments of 10 ETH and Bob sends Alice two payments of 25 ETH. If all transactions would be settled on the Ethereum network directly, twelve individual transactions would be registered by all nodes in the network. Not only would this bloat the number of transactions and slow the network, it would also be more expensive for both Alice and Bob, since each single transaction would incur a transaction fee. Using a state channel to settle such bilateral transactions, only the balance of all transactions needs to be settled on the blockchain directly once the pre-defined time has passed. This means that only two transactions will be registered by the network: the opening and closing transactions of the channel.

Keeping transactions off-chain and exclusively between both parties is not only cheaper and faster, but also more privacy preserving. Everything happens within a channel, rather than being publicly broadcasted over the whole network. The only transactions that are registered on-chain and visible to the public are the opening and closing transactions. The downside of this process: state channels need full availability of all participants involved. Otherwise, if the final closing of the channel, and therefore the final submission of state, were to be submitted by a bad actor, tokens could be at risk. To dispute malicious attacks, the locked tokens can be withheld by the smart contract to penalize the malicious actor. This requires monitoring and could be outsourced to service providers, so-called judge contracts, in exchange for a fee. State channels are therefore only useful in cases where participants exchange many state updates over a long period of time, to mitigate the initial cost of creating a channel and deploying a judge contract.

Sidechains

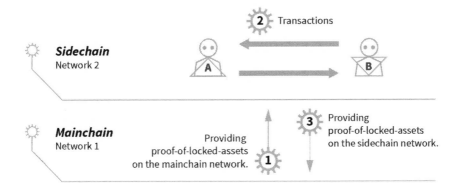

The smart contract used to lock the state must know the participants of a given channel in advance. State channels work well with a defined set of participants, but adding and removing participants requires a change in the smart contract, or the creation of a new channel. Projects such as Lightning Network (Bitcoin) or Raiden Network (Ethereum) have come up with solutions based on a mesh of participants, creating a network out of all the channels such that one doesn't have to create a new channel for every new participant. Transactions can now be routed over other people's channels, but only as long as there is some direct channel connection over the network. Here is a selected list of state channel solutions for various blockchain networks with different degrees of maturity and success: "Celer," "Counterfactual," "Fun Fair," "Liquidity," "Lightning" "Machinomy," "Perun," "Raiden," "Spankchain," or "Trinity." Most solutions are specialized on one blockchain network - such as Bitcoin, Ethereum or Neo - others are network agnostic.

Sidechains

Sidechains are separate blockchain networks, compatible with the mainchain. Sidechains have their own consensus mechanism, their own level of security, and their own tokens. The sidechain doesn't necessarily need to be public and can also be a privately managed ledger. If the security of a sidechain network is compromised, the damage will not affect the mainchain or other sidechains. Both networks are linked to each other via a "two-way peg" and can transfer any state. This way, tokens can be exchanged at a predetermined rate between the mainchain and the sidechain. The mainchain guarantees overall security and dispute resolution, and the transactions that are outsourced to the sidechain can sacrifice decentralization in return for scalability.

As opposed to state channels, transactions that occur on a sidechain are not private between the participants of a transaction. They are published on the sidechain network and thus visible to anyone who has access to the ledger. Alice and Bob don't have to be available all the time, and there are no extra administrative costs in adding or removing participants. Setting up a sidechain, however, is a big effort, as it means building a whole infrastructure from scratch.

The sidechain interacts with the computation layer on the mainchain and requires tokens to be locked to facilitate disputes. A group of servers (federation) mediates between a mainchain and its sidechains and determines when the tokens a user has used are locked up and released. This adds another security layer between the mainchain and the sidechain. The federation is selected by the sidechain developers. However, such a federation adds another layer between the mainchain and the sidechain and could introduce more attack vectors. Here is a selected list of sidechain solutions for various blockchain networks with different degrees of maturity and success: "Bitcoin Codex," "Bitcoin Extended," "Elements Projects," "Hivemind," "Loom," "Liquid," "Mimblewimble," "Plasma," "Poa Network," or "Rootstock."

Blockchain Interoperability

The number of blockchain networks and other distributed ledgers is growing. However, all these distributed ledger systems are, for the most part, isolated systems and work as a silo. Networks have no knowledge of the state of tokens managed in other networks. They also have no idea about whether other networks have idle capacities to settle transactions. Sidechains could be seen as a first step toward full blockchain interoperability and scalability. A more effective and global solution could be provided by interoperability networks, such as "Cosmos," "Polkadot," or "Wanchain," that could resolve the scalability problem for multiple networks simultaneously.

Interoperability, in the context of distributed ledgers, refers to the ability to freely share tokens and related data across different networks. In a fully interoperable environment, a user from network A could send tokens to another user on network B without the need for an intermediary, like a centralized exchange. Blockchain interoperability is a contrary idea to what some propose might happen: a winner-takes-all situation where, due to network effects, only one blockchain network will survive in the long run. The idea of "one chain to rule them all" is contrary to the core idea of decentralization. The future of the Web3 might, therefore, depend on the ability of blockchain networks to interact with one another.

Sharding

Some developers propose that sharding the network state could be a solution to the scalability problem of blockchain networks. Sharding is a concept adopted from distributed databases, which has not been tested on a global scale in the context of blockchain networks yet. Sharding could address the scalability constraints of current consensus protocols, where each node has to update their ledger regularly and maintain the full history, from the genesis block until the present day. It is suggested that the ledger history could be split into separate pieces, each of which would have their own "shard" of the network state. Multiple shards maintained by different network nodes parallel to each other, thus improving overall network scalability. Shards would be "sub-states" as part of the whole network state. The network as a whole should still operate under one single state, but each shard would have to be consistent in itself. Cross-shard communication would be handled through protocol rules. In such a process, blockchain addresses, balances, and general state would be contained on shards. Shards provide proofs to the mainchain and can communicate with other shards over the sharding protocol. Sample projects working on sharding solutions: "Prysmatic Labs," "Drops of Diamond," "Status," and "PegaSys."

Alternative Cryptographic Algorithms

One of the biggest challenges of the Bitcoin network and similar networks is the management of unspent transactions. These unspent transactions contribute to the exponential growth of the ledger. In Bitcoin, for example, they are referred to as UTXOs, and contribute to a higher payload, more expensive transactions, and less throughput per second. When a new raw transaction gets created and is later validated, before signing, the inputs can only come from unspent outputs of former transactions. Therefore, for transaction creation validating and signing, unspent transactions are more important than spent transactions (outputs). For the consistency of the ledger, unspent transactions are of importance for things like timestamping, proof of existence, data storage, and also block creation and mining. Transaction-oriented blockchain networks are all about the unspent transactions. This is why bloat of the ledger is so heavily related to them. Managing the payload-size of the UTXO, the amount of UTXOs on the ledger, and the degree up to which it becomes possible to keep them off-the-chain remedies the bloat of the chain as such. In fact, everything that keeps the payload smaller tackles bloat.

Alternative cryptographic algorithms used in collective signatures, like multi-signatures[90], ring signatures, threshold signatures,[91] or Schnorr signatures,[92] could resolve certain scalability problems, for example, by reducing information added to the ledger, or eliminating that information with multi-signatures, and redeem scripts. With multi-signature transactions, for example, receiver addresses are aggregated into one multisig receiver address and cause the accompanying redeem script to be stored offline. It also reduces the number of outputs and script size inside the transaction. The same is true for ring signatures, threshold signatures, and collective signatures.

Multi-signatures are divided into a funding transaction, which turns into a UTXO and a spending transaction, and results in a spent transaction. For the UTXO-relevant funding transactions, the aggregation of several receivers into one receiving address and the usage of less outputs, plus off-chaining the redeem-script, normally results in a smaller payload. Alternative signature schemes belong to the anti-bloat toolset, but compared to the average non-multisig transaction, payload reduction is not always the case and depends on the specific use case. "Mimblewimble," for example, is a proposal for Bitcoin to use a different approach to transaction construction. It removes most historic blockchain data, including spent transaction outputs, while still allowing users to fully verify the chain. It also allows for more privacy than current Bitcoin implementations. "Dfinity" and "Hyperledger Fabric" use threshold signatures to achieve the same goal.

---

[90] *Multi-signatures allow the creation of a vault with multiple locks and keys and assigns the keys to multiple parties. They also allow the creation of a vault mechanism that requires only some portion of these keys to open the vault. Even if one of the keys is duplicated, the attackers are not able to open the vault.*

[91] *Threshold signatures allow an arbitrary group of signers to construct one signature, as long as there are sufficiently many of them. They are more efficient, because almost all the calculation can be done by the signers before submitting it to a blockchain network.*

[92] *Schnorr signatures are based on the Schnorr signature algorithm, which is known for its simplicity, is efficient, and generates short signatures.*

Chapter References & Further Reading

- Madeira, Antonio: „What are State Channels", CryptoCompare. 7 Apr 2017: https://www.cryptocompare.com/coins/guides/what-are-state-channels/
- Ray, Shaan: „What are Sidechains?", Hackernoon: https://hackernoon.com/what-are-sidechains-1c45ea2daf3
- Stathakopoulou, C.; Cachin, C.: "Threshold Signatures for Blockchain Systems ", IBM Research, Published in: RZ3910 in 2017: https://domino.research.ibm.com/library/cyberdig.nsf/papers/CA80E201DE9C8A0A852580FA004D412F/$File/rz3910.pdf
- Saini, Vaibhav: "Difference Between SideChains and State Channels", Hackernoon, June 26 2018: https://hackernoon.com/difference-between-sidechains-and-state-channels-2f5dfbd10707
- Saini, Vaibhav: "10 State Channel Projects Every Blockchain Developer Should Know About", Hackernoon, Jun 25, 2018: https://hackernoon.com/10-state-channel-projects-every-blockchain-developer-should-know-about-293514a516fd
- Saini, Vaibhav. "11 sidechain projects every blockchain developer should know about," April 26th 2018: https://hackernoon.com/13-sidechain-projects-every-blockchain-developer-should-know-about-804b65364107
- Tual, Stephan: "What are State Channels?", Jan 4, 2017: https://blog.stephantual.com/what-are-state-channels-32a81f7accab
- Alpha Elements: https://elementsproject.org/
- Counterfactual: http://counterfactual.com/
- Celer Network: http://celer.network/
- Drops of Diamond: https://github.com/Drops-of-Diamond/diamond_drops
- FunFair: https://funfair.io/
- Hivemind: http://bitcoinhivemind.com/
- Loom: https://loomx.io/
- Liquid: https://blockstream.com/liquid/
- Liquidity Network: https://liquidity.network/
- Machinomy: https://machinomy.com/
- Lightning Network: https://lightning.network/
- PegaSys: https://medium.com/@pegasyseng
- Perun Network: https://perun.network/
- Plasma: https://plasma.io/
- POA Network: https://poa.network/
- Prysmatic Labs: https://prysmaticlabs.com/
- Raiden Network: https://raiden.network/
- Rootstock RSK: https://rsk.co/
- SpankChain: https://spankchain.com/
- Status: https://medium.com/@status.im
- Trinity Network: https://trinity.tech/

Libra & Celo

In June 2019, Facebook, a Web2-based social network with over 2 billion active users, announced a move into Web3. The media referred to this move as "Facebook launching a cryptocurrency." The reality, however, is more complex, since Facebook is not only planning to launch a token but also a whole network, thereby creating their own infrastructure to manage that token. The white paper states that the Libra consortium will launch its own distributed ledger, which will manage a native token—Libra. The Calibra wallet (renamed to „Novi" in May 2020) will be the software with which users will be able to manage their Libra tokens, and potentially also other future tokens that the network or smart contracts in that network might issue. According to the white paper, Facebook users will be able to use Libra tokens for online payments using the wallet for "low to no" fees. The white paper indicates that Libra will be a stable token, which will be backed by a basket of various fiat currencies. Key elements of the Libra network, as announced in the 2019 white paper are:

Infrastructure, Consensus & Smart Contracts: Libra will run on a permissioned/federated distributed ledger that does not use a "chain of blocks" as a security mechanism. Only the members of the network can validate transactions. Security is provided by the fact that all members of the network are known and have entered legally binding contracts where bad actors can be prosecuted by law. The network can, therefore, use a more efficient consensus algorithm, LibraBFT, a fork of the "HotStuff" consensus protocol, which is a modified version of Practical Byzantine Fault Tolerance (BFT). The protocol offers smart contract capabilities. "Move" is the programming language that has been invented for the protocol. Similar to Ethereum, Libra smart contracts will require network payments (gas) for executing code. This means that all operations require payments of Libra tokens for network transaction fees, which will also be a source of income for validating nodes.

Governance of the Network: Initially the Libra Association, headquartered in Switzerland, had around 30 founding members, all established institutions ranging from traditional payment networks (Mastercard, Visa, Paypal) to Internet companies (Uber, Lyft, eBay) to blockchain companies (Xapo), VCs (Thrive Capital, Andreessen Horowitz), and NPO's, such as Women's World Banking and Mercy

Corps. A supermajority of 2/3 would be required for protocol changes. The initial plan was to transition from a federated network (association) to a Proof-of-Stake–based public network within the first five years. Whether or not this roadmap is feasible remains to be seen.

On-chain Governance: Similar to Tezos, the protocol is subject to revision. Founding members of the Libra network will hold a second set of tokens, the Libra investment token, which grants voting rights in the network. Libra investment tokens are required to vote on governance changes of the protocol. Such governance changes, in the form of protocol updates, will be essential for (i) adding new members and (ii) transitioning from LibraBFT to a public Proof-of-Stake protocol.

Disposable Ledger: Similar to "Coda," the ledger is disposable. Nodes only need to provide a proof of the last block to make sure they are interacting with a valid ledger. This is an important feature from a usability point of view, since historical data may, over time, grow beyond the amount that can be handled, in particular by small devices.

Collateralized Stable Token: The Libra token is not a "purpose-driven token" minted upon proof-of-contribution to the network. It is a simple asset-collateralized stable token. Similar to other asset-collateralized stable tokens like Tether, tokens will be issued and burned on a regular basis, to respond to demand shifts for its reserve and keep the exchange rate stable. This is a prerequisite for any token to be useful as a medium of exchange, and a big upside to other tokens like Bitcoin, that do not have inbuilt price-stability mechanisms (read more: Part 3 - Token Economics). Interestingly, Libra is one of the very few stable token projects that has already announced what the reserve will do: invest into low-risk bonds to generate interest for costs and returns. The original "Calibra Wallet FAQ" announced low transaction fees, but did not explain the economics of it. The question is whether they will be able to hold the promise at times of high load.

Privacy: In the white paper, it is stated that, "The Libra protocol does not link accounts to a real-world identity. A user is free to create multiple accounts by generating multiple key-pairs. Accounts controlled by the same user have no inherent link to each other." This pseudonymity for users is similar to how Bitcoin and Ethereum work. The wallet, however, requires that all users will be verified via government-issued ID. It is unclear if one can run other wallet applications on the Libra network that don't abide by the same AML/KYC requirements.

The Libra token cannot be compared to Bitcoin or other native protocol tokens of permissionless blockchain networks, as it (i) builds on a federated solution, which means that it is not permissionless, and the fact that (ii) it will most likely have rigorous KYC/AML requirements. On the upside, the permissioned infrastructure allows for higher (i) scalability, and (ii) Facebook already has a user base of over 2 billion people, which will make tokens mass market compatible with what will likely be a user-friendly wallet, as Facebook has enough developer power to make much-needed wallet usability happen. If implemented, the Libra network could become a fin-tech provider, and as such, a serious competitor for current financial service providers, which charge merchants and customers considerable remittance fees, as much as 2.5 percent or more on one transaction. Libra could furthermore threaten the existence of current money-transfer companies that charge even higher settlement fees, and which many immigrants all over the world use on a daily basis in order to send money to family members back in their home countries. For better or worse, Libra has the potential to become a shadow bank, at least to the 2 billion unbanked worldwide.

The problem is that the network might not become as sovereign and decentralized as the Libra association claims that it will become in the long run. The Libra network is more likely an attempt of Facebook and the other federated members of the network to move into two new industries through the backdoor of Web3 wallets: digital identities and banking. Given the fact that Facebook, next to Google, is the biggest ad-tech provider, the Libra token could furthermore be used to incentivize future advertising consumption, similar to what the Basic Attention Token (BAT) is trying to do, reversing the roles in a highly intermediated advertising industry (read more: Part 4 - Basic Attention Token) or how Steemit is trying to incentivize contributions to the network (read more: Part 4 - Steemit).

The Libra announcements created a big media hype in 2019, but were not welcomed by most regulators worldwide and spurred considerable regulatory push back. In October 2019, PayPal, Visa, MasterCard, and Stripe dropped their support for the project, at least temporarily. Even Facebook announced that they would drop the development of the project if it failed to "make sufficient headway" with regulators, who seem to fear that the Libra token could be used for (i) illegal activities, (ii) become a shadow bank, (iii) privatize money, and also (iv) undermine user privacy.

In spite of this push back, the crypto space moved away from buzzwords like "blockchain" and "smart contracts" to the topic of tokens. The playground for super nerds, crypto-anarchists, and speculators officially took a big step toward tokenizing the economy. A study conducted by the Bank for International Settlements concluded that ever since the announcements of the Libra project, many central banks that were reluctant toward the issue of Central Bank Digital Currencies before are now investigating options of tokenizing their currencies, since Libra's instant settlement would have been a considerable threat to the current global banking system. At the time of writing the second edition of this book, a few of the remaining members of the Libra federation, such as Anchorage, Bison Trails, Coinbase Ventures, Andreessen Horowitz, and Mercy Corps, announced that they would be part of "Celo Alliance." With 50 founding members, Celo is a similar coalition to the Libra consortium, with the purpose to "deliver humanitarian aid, facilitate payments and enable microlending" with a token called "Celo Dollar" that is scheduled to launch in April 2020. Roughly around the same time, in March 2020, Libra announced that the wallet would, at least temporarily, move away from the original idea of backing the Libra token with a basket of fiat currencies. Instead, the Libra federation announced that it is planning to launch different tokenized fiat currencies that can be managed with the wallet.

Chapter References & Further Reading

- Castro, Miguel; Liskov, Barbara: "Practical Byzantine Fault Tolerance", Proceedings of the Third Symposium on Operating Systems Design and Implementation, New Orleans, USA, February 1999: http://pmg.csail.mit.edu/papers/osdi99.pdf
- Dale, Brady: "This Blockchain Tosses Blocks: Naval, MetaStable Back Twist on Crypto 'Cash'" May 9, 2018: https://www.coindesk.com/blockchain-tosses-blocks-naval-metastable-back-twist-crypto-cash
- Dale, Brady: "Libra White Paper Shows How Facebook Borrowed From Bitcoin and Ethereum", Jun 18, 2019: https://www.coindesk.com/libra-white-paper-shows-how-facebook-borrowed-from-bitcoin-and-ethereum
- Kharif, Olga: "Members of Facebook's Libra Are Making Contingency Plans," Bloomberg, March, 11 2020, retrieved from: https://www.bloomberg.com/news/articles/2020-03-11/members-of-facebook-s-libra-are-making-contingency-plans
- Lopp, Jameson: "How Will Facebook's Libra "Blockchain" Really Work? An expert guide to the social media company's foray into cryptocurrency", Jun 18, 2019: https://onezero.medium.com/thoughts-on-libra-blockchain-49b8f6c26372
- McConaghy, Trent: "Tokenize the Enterprise …And Melt It Into the Community. Rinse, Repeat", Jun 6, 2017: https://medium.com/@trentmc0/tokenize-the-enterprise-23d51bafb536
- N.N.: "Ethereum Experts Share Their Facebook Libra Insights Developers on Facebook's Libra blockchain, the white paper, and how to get testnet Libra coins"ConsenSys Jun 28 2019: https://media.consensys.net/ kauri-ethereum-experts-share-their-facebook-libra-experiences-8594b3d1239c
- N.N.: "Facebook's Libra Token: What Blockchain Insiders are Saying Industry experts weigh in after Facebook announces entrance to blockchain space", Cred, Jun 19, 2018: https://medium.com/ @ihaveCred/facebooks-libra-token-what-blockchain-insiders-are-saying-f58e42fae412
- N.N.: "First Look: Libra An in-depth review of Facebook's long-anticipated entry into cryptocurrency", Binance Research, June, 2019: https://info.binance.com/en/research/marketresearch/libra.html
- N.N.: „Calibra: Customer Commitment" https://scontent-ort2-1.xx.fbcdn.net/v/t39.2365-6/ 65083631_355528488499253_8415273665234468864_n.pdf?_nc_cat=106&_nc_ht=scontent-ort2-1.xx&oh=7385d8b3c1126ec3b5f76344a411a37f&oe=5D982AC3
- Spencer, Michael K.: , "Facebook Libra Backlash on Many Fronts", Jun 19, 2019: https://medium.com/futuresin/facebook-libra-backlash-on-many-fronts-28fb75bf79e7
- Voshmgir, Shermin: "Libra and Calibra How Facebook is going Token Economy", Medium, Crypto3conomics, Jun 20, 2019: https://medium.com/crypto3conomics/libra-and-calibra-how-facebook-is-going-token-economy-b546133927
- Yin; Maofan; Malkhi, Dahlia; Reiter, Michael K.; Golan Gueta, Guy; Abraham, Ittai: "HotStuff: BFT Consensus in the Lens of Blockchain", Submitted on 13 Mar 2018 (v1), last revised 5 Jun 2019: https://arxiv.org/abs/1803.05069
- Libra White Paper: https://developers.libra.org/docs/assets/papers/the-libra-blockchain.pdf

- *Libra Code repository: https://github.com/libra/libra*
- *Celo: https://celo.org/alliance*
- *Coda: https://codaprotocol.com/*

Tables & Figures

Made in United States
Orlando, FL
06 May 2022

17580117R00217